THE OFFICIAL ILLUSTRATED HISTORY

THE FOOTBALL LEAGUE

THE FIRST 100 YEARS

THE OFFICIAL ILLUSTRATED HISTORY

THE FOOTBALL LEAGUE

THE FIRST 100 YEARS

BYRON BUTLER

Foreword by Tom Finney

COLOUR LIBRARY BOOKS

CLB 2003
This edition published 1988 by Colour Library Books Ltd.
Guildford, Surrey GU1 2BX

ISBN 0 86283 583 6

Printed and bound in Barcelona, Spain by Cronion, S.A.

Contents

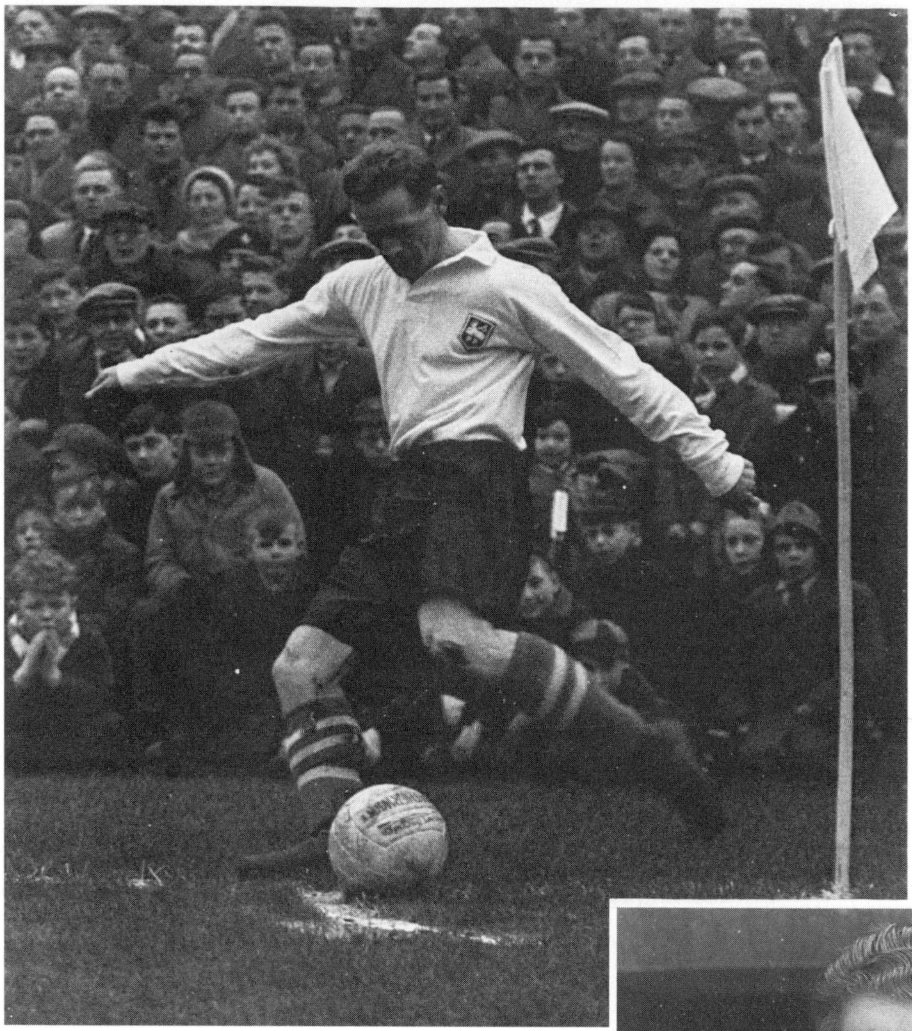

Foreword
by Tom Finney

As a Preston man I take special pride in the centenary of the Football League. Preston North End linked the golden age of the amateur and the new world of the professional a hundred years ago – and the club's famous Old Invincibles became the first champions of the League.

Preston was also the home of the Football League for more than 50 years – with its headquarters in an old vicarage, complete with nineteenth-century powder room, in Starkie Street. Preston was a cradle of the League that was eventually copied all over the world.

I was only seven when I first saw Preston play at Deepdale in 1929, and I signed for them as a part-time professional for 20 shillings a week in 1940 – a year or so after the League celebrated its fiftieth birthday. My last game for Preston was in 1960, just before the maximum wage was removed, and during all the years that I had the good fortune to play football for a living, I came to realize what a wonderful legacy the old-timers left us.

The pictures in this book splendidly illustrate why the game has given so much pleasure and excitement to countless millions, to generation after generation of people in all corners of the country, and I am just grateful that I was part of it for so long.

Of course, times are changing but nothing stands still in this life and I am sure the Football League will find the shape, strength and support to take it happily through the next hundred years.

TOM FINNEY – affectionately known as the 'Preston Plumber' – scored 187 goals in 433 League games for Preston. He also scored 30 goals in 76 internationals for England and was the first man to be twice voted Footballer of the Year.

Introduction
by Philip Carter

President of the Football League

When the Football League was founded a hundred years ago by William McGregor with only twelve clubs, no one could have imagined how it would grow and develop to span the world with its ability to entertain and enthrall countless millions.

Football provides all the emotions that are essential for superb entertainment: spectacle, competition, drama, agony, ecstasy and fulfilment. No other sport has captured the imagination of the world's people with such force and intensity of feeling.

Those of us now involved with the management of the League are proud to be its guardian during this Centenary Year.

From its small beginnings in 1888, the League structure had by 1958 developed to 44 Full and 48 Associate Members over four divisions, and has remained so to this day. For more than 30 years the League's strength has been represented by 92 clubs; and despite the rapidly changing economic circumstances of many professional sports, we have fought hard to retain clubs in all the cities and towns which value and support the presence of a League club.

In spite of the numerous rival attractions that are available to our fans, football continues to attract higher attendances than any other sport. We must, however, give greater consideration to the accommodation and service that we offer the public. Spectators are rightly demanding higher standards in all facilities; and I would like to thank, in particular, the Football Trust and the Football Grounds Improvement Trust for providing regular and substantial funds for this purpose.

As chairman of one of the founder members of the League – Everton – it gives me particular pleasure to have the honour of being League president in Centenary Year.

My colleagues and I on the management committee are confident that our clubs will continue to uphold the marvellous traditions of the past, whilst laying new foundations for improved standards of play and sportsmanship for the future.

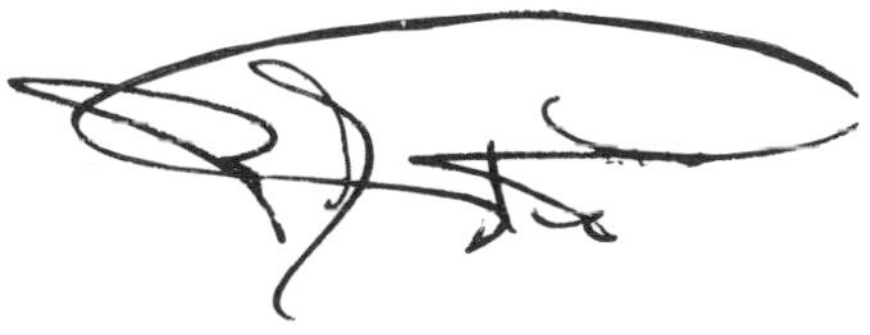

ONE
'I beg to tender . . .'
1888–1900

'I really believe that the game would have received a very severe check, and its popularity would have been paralysed once and for all, if the League had not been founded. I am not saying that football would have died, because football will never die. Even if the time should come when it ceases to be the highly organized sport it is today, it will still be the pastime of the juveniles, because it is not easy to conceive the introduction of a game which will prove its superior.'

William McGregor *(1847–1911)*
founder of the Football League.

Eighteen-eighty-eight: Queen Victoria was Queen of Great Britain and Empress of an India on which the sun was still rising. It was a year, too, in which W.G. Grace captained England's cricketers for the first time at the age of 40, John L. Sullivan was the last bare-knuckle heavyweight champion of the world and Winston Churchill was an unhappy schoolboy at Harrow. Vincent Van Gogh was still painting, Wyatt Earp still shooting and Florence Nightingale still caring. The pneumatic tyre was invented and, more prettily, less usefully, the first beauty contest was held.

It was also the year in which the Football League was founded, the first competition of its kind, a prototype for the mushrooming world of football. The idea was simple and revolutionary, and its champion was a Scot who ran a drapery shop in Birmingham and who later confessed: 'I've never taken part in active football. I tried it once when I was very young and had to take to bed for a week.'

William McGregor – the father of League football – was a portly, full-bearded Perthshire man of stirling principles, undentable optimism and gentle humour. He moved to Birmingham to improve his lot and it was football's luck that the shop he bought was near Villa Park. McGregor joined Aston Villa – and the shape of football began to change.

McGregor's timing was inspired because football was in a mess. The game had been adopted and refined by the universities, schools and officers' messes of the country, international football was well established, the FA Cup was already a big favourite and professionalism had been legalized. But friendly fixtures were cancelled at will if the weather was poor or if transport presented a problem or if key players were injured. Games were often called off on Saturday mornings. Spectators would turn up at deserted grounds. Clubs with hefty wage bills sometimes found themselves without a game, and without income, for two or three weeks. Fixture cards were meaningless.

So McGregor wrote a now famous letter to Bolton Wanderers, Blackburn Rovers, Preston North End, West Bromwich Albion and, not surprisingly, his own club Aston Villa. 'I beg to tender,' he wrote, 'the following suggestion . . . that ten or twelve of the most prominent clubs in England combine to arrange home-and-away fixtures each season . . . I would take it as a favour if you would kindly think the matter over . . . and should like to hear what other clubs you would suggest.'

A meeting took place at Anderton's Hotel in Fleet Street, London, on 22 March 1888, and by the end of a fruitful second conference, at the Royal Hotel, Manchester, on 17 April, the battle lines were agreed.

Twelve clubs were formally invited to become League members: six from Lancashire – Preston North End, Bolton Wanderers, Everton, Burnley, Accrington and Blackburn Rovers, and six more, broadly, from the Midlands – Aston Villa, West Bromwich Albion, Wolverhampton Wanderers, Notts County, Derby County and Stoke. No southern club received an invitation simply because there was no professional football south of Birmingham. And McGregor was properly appointed as the first president.

The first simple rules were gradually improved and hardened to meet new problems, but, right from the start, clubs were obliged to play their strongest side in all matches. McGregor and his pioneers passionately believed in their new creation and were determined to make it work. The high court of history rightly applauds them.

The first programme of League matches took place on 8 September 1888 and the first League goal is reliably credited to Jack Gordon of Preston North End – the club whose form towered above everything in that first season. They won the League championship without losing a match and won the FA Cup without conceding a goal. One newspaper report of the time happily described them as 'the most perfect, most consistent team in the history of the game' – a claim that has never been sensibly repeated. How could it be? How can comparisons bridge a hundred years? Surely the only way Preston can be judged is by the margin of their superiority over their contemporaries; and North End's pre-eminence in 1888–9 has never been matched. They were well named The Invincibles.

Preston North End were simply ahead of their time. They played a major role in legalizing professionalism, enticing players from Scotland with guarantees of good jobs, and they turned the game itself from a vigorous exercise into something of a science. The celebrated James Crabtree of Burnley, Aston Villa and England, was to write: 'The three Preston half-backs were almost the first trio to realize the full importance of helping their forward line . . . it was axiomatic that when North End were attacking they had eight forwards at work.'

Their manager was William Sudell, the first outstanding member of a precarious profession. He was an astute businessman, a loyal boss and a flexible tactician who devised a playing format that made the best of his players' talents – including above all those of John Goodall, England's centre-forward, of whom that mighty Corinthian G.O. Smith said: 'A great player and a great gentleman. I've always been proud to count myself his friend.' Goodall, a Londoner who learnt the game in Scotland, has been described as the pioneer of scientific professional play.

Preston retained the championship in 1889–90 and then finished runners-up in the following three seasons. The Old Invincibles split up, and Preston have not been champions since. Their decline opened the way for Sunderland (who had replaced Stoke of the original twelve in 1890) and Aston Villa. Between them they were to win the title eight times by the turn of the century.

Sunderland, grandly known as 'the team of all the talents', were champions three times in four years; they brought new pride to the town and inspired a feeling for football in the north-east that still endures. They were the creation of their manager and match secretary Tom Watson, a hard and perceptive Newcastle man with an open admiration for Scottish players. His poaching raids across the border were so successful that he was personally threatened.

Watson knew a good player when he saw one, and among the best he brought south were the immensely popular John Campbell, a free-scoring centre-forward, a short and muscular dasher; John Edward Doig, known as 'the prince of goalkeepers', who covered his bald head with a cap held in place by an elastic band under his chin; and Hugh Wilson, a popular captain and peerless half-back. But Tom Watson himself was Sunderland's finest signing – a fact they quickly discovered when he joined Liverpool for four guineas a week (twice what Sunderland had been paying him) in 1896. Sunderland finished second from bottom in 1896–7 and, a few years later, Liverpool won the championship for the first time.

Before then, however, Aston Villa took command and their grip was one of iron. They won the championship five times in the last seven seasons of the century, won the FA Cup twice and in 1896–7 completed the League and Cup 'double'. Villa, remember, were William McGregor's own team – and their success inspired him to gentle tribute: 'If there is a club in the country which deserves to be dubbed the greatest (and the matter is one of some delicacy) few will deny the right of Aston Villa to share the highest niche of fame with even the most historic of other aspirants. For brilliancy and, at the same time, for consistency of achievement, for activity in philanthropic enterprise, for astuteness of management and for general alertness, the superiors of Aston Villa cannot be found.'

The names of the Villa players were household words: George Ramsay who had fashioned the club's style of play and whose dribbling was so good that the ball seemed a personal possession; auburn-haired Archie Hunter who was rated by McGregor as the finest centre-forward of all, an idol of the crowd who died at the age of 35; and all the heroes, of course, who completed the 'double' – among them Howard Spencer, the formidable James Crabtree, the two Cowans (James and John), John Devey, their richly talented captain, Fred Wheldon and winger Charlie Athersmith who is said to have played for much of one match holding up an umbrella in heavy rain. The story may owe nothing to fact, but we must cherish our legends.

The last years of the Victorian era saw the game make impressive strides. The League expanded, gingerly, to two Divisions of 18 clubs each. A southern club, Woolwich Arsenal, was elected for the first time. Promotion and relegation, goal nets and penalty kicks were introduced. Leagues of every size and standard sprouted up all over Britain, and travellers spread the word even further afield – to Europe, South America and every cranny and corner of a robust British Empire.

They were days of confidence, change and expansion.

MILESTONES *(Transfer fees approximate)*

1885	Professionalism legalized
1888	Football League founded
1891	Goal nets introduced
1891	Penalty kick introduced
1898	Promotion and relegation introduced
1905	First £1,000 transfer – Alf Common (Sunderland to Middlesbrough)
1922	First £5,000 transfer – Syd Puddefoot (West Ham United to Falkirk)
1925	New offside law
1928	First £10,000 transfer – David Jack (Bolton Wanderers to Arsenal)
1938	Laws of football re-written
1939	Compulsory numbering of players in League
1947	First £20,000 transfer – Tommy Lawton (Chelsea to Notts County)
1951	White ball first used
1956	First floodlit League match – Portsmouth *v* Newcastle United
1960	League Cup launched
1961	First £100,000 transfer involving a British club – Denis Law (Manchester City to Torino)
1961	Maximum wage removed
1963	'Retain and transfer' system ruled illegal in High Court
1965	Substitution – for injured players – allowed in League matches
1966	Substitution allowed for any reason
1973	Three-up, three-down promotion and relegation
1976	Goal difference replaces goal average when clubs equal on points
1979	First £500,000 transfer between British clubs – David Mills (Middlesbrough to West Bromwich Albion)
1979	First £1,000,000 transfer between British clubs – Trevor Francis (Birmingham City to Nottingham Forest)
1981	League football on Sundays
1981	Three points for win instead of two
1981	First £1,500,000 transfer between British clubs – Bryan Robson (West Bromwich Albion to Manchester United)
1982	League Cup sponsored – becomes Milk Cup
1983	Football League sponsored by Canon
1986	League Cup sponsored by Littlewoods
1986	Football League sponsored by *Today* newspaper
1986	First £2,000,000 transfers involving British players – Mark Hughes (Manchester United, £2,300,000) and Gary Lineker (Everton, £2,750,000) both to Barcelona
1987	End-of-season play-off matches for promotion and relegation
1987	First £3,000,000 transfer involving British player – Ian Rush (Liverpool to Juventus, £3,200,000)
1988	Football League Centenary

overleaf William McGregor
The founder of Football League

left Humour and information for a penny in 1900. And, top right of cover, Football Chat wrote happily of 'playing football for love, honour and charity'.

below Aston Villa's great League and FA Cup 'Double' side of 1896–7. Back row (l to r): G.B. Ramsay (secretary), J. Grierson (trainer), Howard Spencer, Jimmy Whitehouse, Mr Margoschis, Albert Evans, James Crabtree, J. Lees, C. Johnstone. Front row: Dr V. Jones, James Cowan, Charlie Athersmith, John Campbell, John Devey, Fred Wheldon, John Cowan, John Reynolds, F.W. Rinder (vice-chairman). Villa won the League championship five times in the last seven years of the nineteenth century.

right Royal Arsenal (later Woolwich Arsenal) – the first southern club to be elected to the League in 1893. Their shorts cost 3s 3d, their flannelette shirts 2s 5d and their russet calf boots 8s 6d.

below The Invincibles of Preston North End 1888–9. First champions of the Football League, without losing a match, and winners of the FA Cup without conceding a goal. Back row (l to r): G. Drummond, R. Howarth, Right Hon. R.W. Hanbury, Sir W.E.M. Tomlinson, D. Russell, R. Holmes, W. Sudell (manager), J. Graham, Dr Mills Roberts. Front row: J. Gordon, J. Ross, J. Goodall, F. Dewhurst, S. Thomson.

Everton – one of the most consistent Founder Members of the League. Champions once, runners-up twice and third twice between 1890–6. Goodison Park opened in 1892.

Most of the basic essentials in the process of photography were known by 1889, a year after the League's formation, but popular use of the action picture was still a thing of the future. Posed pictures and artist's impressions were the vogue.

right A studio picture of Ernie 'Nudger' Needham, the famous Sheffield United and England wing-half.

below An artist's view of Needham in action. Needham was only 5 ft 5 ins tall but he was a fearsome tackler, a quick, elusive runner and it was claimed he never had a bad game. He was in Sheffield United's first and only League championship side (1897–8) and was part of the smallest half-back line to win the title – Rabbi Howell, Tommy Morren and Needham who were all under 5 ft 6 ins. Needham also helped Sheffield United win the FA Cup in 1899 and 1902. He made 461 appearances for Sheffield United (1891–1913) and won 16 caps for England (1894–1902).

above William Isaiah 'Billy' Bassett of West Bromwich Albion (1886–99) and England (16 caps). Only 5 ft 5½ ins tall but the finest winger of his day and one of the great figures of Black Country football. Served Albion for 50 years as player, director and chairman.

NEEDHAM, THE SHEFFIELD CAPTAIN, MAKES SOME BRILLIANT DASHES

left Steve Bloomer of Derby County, Middlesbrough and England – one of the game's legendary figures, scorer of 353 goals in 598 League games (1892–1914) and known as 'Paleface'. Sometimes criticized for being selfish and looking too nonchalant. Don Davies of the *Manchester Guardian* (who died in the Munich air-crash in 1958) recalled that when, as a schoolboy, he watched Bloomer, he saw 'a portly individual with close-cropped hair and a great white moon of a face apparently bored to death by the proceedings. Near the end, it is true, Bloomer kicked disdainfully at a ball rolling towards him and through turning his back immediately was the only player on the field apparently who did not know he had scored. "A pure fluke" was the verdict of one observer to whom the "Ohs" and "Ahs" of admiration and the head-shakings of the elders in the crowd, seemed grossly overdue. But Bloomer in his prime walked to his place in an English Soccer side as uncontestably as Don Bradman later walked into Australia's cricket teams.' Bloomer scored 292 goals in 473 appearances for Derby (in two spells) and 61 in 125 games for Middlesbrough. He also scored 28 goals in 23 Home championship internationals – a record that stood for nearly 50 years.

right John Goodall of Preston North End, Derby County and England – centre-forward and star of Preston's Invincibles, first champions of the Football League. Has been described as the pioneer of scientific professional play. London-born but first made his reputation with Great Lever in Scotland. Joined Preston when they were already an outstanding side in 1886 and left soon after their famous 'double' season (1888–9) to become captain of Derby County. Won 14 caps for England (1888–98). Also played county cricket for Derbyshire. Goodall, a man of splendid temperament, observed: 'There is no game which is more calculated to rouse the evil passions than football, and therefore a great deal of restraint and self-control are absolutely necessary. A player must not regard it as a personal insult if the ball is taken from him or if he is the victim of a charge which, if heavy, is nevertheless legal. One might just as well expect a batsman to cherish a bitter hatred for the fieldsman who has just caught him brilliantly.' He was affectionately known as 'Johnny Allgood'.

right Harry Lockett – first secretary of the League in the first League office. Lockett did the job in an honorary capacity early on, in between running his own business at Stoke. But at the League's annual meeting in 1890 it was agreed he should be paid £30 for his first two years' work. The annual meeting also made his appointment official at £20 a year – which was increased to 30 guineas (£31.50) a year later. Lockett was secretary for 14 difficult years (1888–1902) and on his retirement he was replaced by Tom Charnley who worked for Preston North End – and Preston immediately became the League's headquarters.

Sunderland's 'team of all the talents' – League champions three times in four seasons (1892–3–5). Back row (l to r): W. Wallace (Finance Sec.), T. Dodds (trainer), R. McNeil, J.E. Doig, H. Wilson, D. Gow, A. McCreadie, Mr Jas Henderson, H. Reynolds (groundsman). Seated: Mr T. Potts, T. Watson (secretary-manager), W. Dunlop, J. Millar, J. Hannah, J. Harvie, Coun. J.P. Henderson (president), Coun. T. Marshall, Mr S. Wilson. Front: J. Auld, J. Gillespie, J. Campbell, J. Scott, H. Johnston.

above The first representative Football League team to play in Scotland, 1893. The English League beat the Scottish League 4–3 at Celtic Park. Back row (l to r): W. McGregor, T. Clare, J.J. Bentley, J. Southworth, C. Perry, R. Molyneux, W. Rowley, H. Lockett. Seated: W.I. Bassett, F. Geary, R. Howarth, H. Wood, J. Schofield. Front: I. Reynolds, E. Needham.

right The gold medal awarded to Herbert Rothwell, captain of Glossop North End who caused a major stir by winning promotion in their first season in the League (1898–9). Glossop and Manchester City were the first clubs to gain automatic promotion to Division One. Promotion and relegation had previously been decided by a series of 'Test' matches. Glossop (population 25,000) was probably the smallest town to have supported a First Division club – but they lasted only one season in Division One. They won only four of their 34 matches and finished bottom. They also finished bottom of Division Two in 1914–15 and did not apply for re-election after World War One. *right* T.T. Fitchie, an accomplished inside-forward who played for Woolwich Arsenal, Tottenham, Queen's Park and Scotland before joining Glossop.

far right A silver Vesta match case with enamelled decoration celebrating Aston Villa's League and Cup 'double' in 1897. The player is Villa's captain John Devey. The case fetched £380 at auction in December 1985.

above Charlie Athersmith of Aston Villa, Small Heath (Birmingham) and England – winger of great pace who played a major role in Aston Villa's sweeping success during the 1890s. Helped Villa win League championship five times and FA Cup twice in seven seasons. And in Villa's League and Cup 'double' season (1896–7) also played in all England's matches against Wales, Ireland and Scotland. Joined Villa from Unity Gas Depot in February 1891 and made 259 appearances for them before joining Small Heath (100 games, 1901–5). Twelve caps for England (1892–1900), many as right-wing partner of Steve Bloomer. Played in one match, in pouring rain, with raised umbrella lent by a spectator.

LEAGUE TABLES

1888–89

FOOTBALL LEAGUE

		P	W	D	L	F	A	Pts
1	Preston	22	18	4	0	74	15	40
2	Aston Villa	22	12	5	5	61	43	29
3	Wolves	22	12	4	6	50	37	28
4	Blackburn	22	10	6	6	66	45	26
5	Bolton	22	10	2	10	63	59	22
6	WBA	22	10	2	10	40	46	22
7	Accrington	22	6	8	8	48	48	20
8	Everton	22	9	2	11	35	46	20
9	Burnley	22	7	3	12	42	62	17
10	Derby	22	7	2	13	41	60	16
11	Notts County	22	5	2	15	39	73	12
12	Stoke	22	4	4	14	26	51	12

1889–90

FOOTBALL LEAGUE

		P	W	D	L	F	A	Pts
1	Preston	22	15	3	4	71	30	33
2	Everton	22	14	3	5	65	40	31
3	Blackburn	22	12	3	7	78	41	27
4	Wolves	22	10	5	7	51	38	25
5	WBA	22	11	3	8	47	50	25
6	Accrington	22	9	6	7	53	56	24
7	Derby	22	9	3	10	43	55	21
8	Aston Villa	22	7	5	10	43	51	19
9	Bolton	22	9	1	12	54	65	19
10	Notts County	22	6	5	11	43	51	17
11	Burnley	22	4	5	13	36	65	13
12	Stoke	22	3	4	15	27	69	10

1890–91

FOOTBALL LEAGUE

		P	W	D	L	F	A	Pts
1	Everton	22	14	1	7	63	29	29
2	Preston	22	12	3	7	44	23	27
3	Notts County	22	11	4	7	52	35	26
4	Wolves	22	12	2	8	39	50	26
5	Bolton	22	12	1	9	47	34	25
6	Blackburn	22	11	2	9	52	43	24
7	Sunderland	22	10	5	7	51	31	23*
8	Burnley	22	9	3	10	52	63	21
9	Aston Villa	22	7	4	11	45	58	18
10	Accrington	22	6	4	12	28	50	16
11	Derby	22	7	1	14	47	81	15
12	WBA	22	5	2	15	34	57	12

*Two points deducted for fielding Ned Doig against WBA on 20 September 1890 before the League had approved his registration from Arbroath.

1891–92

FOOTBALL LEAGUE

		P	W	D	L	F	A	Pts
1	Sunderland	26	21	0	5	93	36	42
2	Preston	26	18	1	7	61	31	37
3	Bolton	26	17	2	7	51	37	36
4	Aston Villa	26	15	0	11	89	56	30
5	Everton	26	12	4	10	49	49	28
6	Wolves	26	11	4	11	59	46	26
7	Burnley	26	11	4	11	49	45	26
8	Notts County	26	11	4	11	55	51	26
9	Blackburn	26	10	6	10	58	65	26
10	Derby	26	10	4	12	46	52	24
11	Accrington	26	8	4	14	40	78	20
12	WBA	26	6	6	14	51	58	18
13	Stoke	26	5	4	17	38	61	14
14	Darwen	26	4	3	19	38	112	11

1892–93

FIRST DIVISION

		P	W	D	L	F	A	Pts
1	Sunderland	30	22	4	4	100	36	48
2	Preston	30	17	3	10	57	39	37
3	Everton	30	16	4	10	74	51	36
4	Aston Villa	30	16	3	11	73	62	35
5	Bolton	30	13	6	11	56	55	32
6	Burnley	30	13	4	13	51	44	30
7	Stoke	30	12	5	13	58	48	29
8	WBA	30	12	5	13	58	69	29
9	Blackburn	30	8	13	9	47	56	29
10	Nottm Forest	30	10	8	12	48	52	28
11	Wolves	30	12	4	14	47	68	28
12	Wednesday	30	12	3	15	55	65	27
13	Derby	30	9	9	12	52	64	27
14	Notts County	30	10	4	16	53	61	24
15	Accrington	30	6	11	13	57	81	23
16	Newton Heath	30	6	6	18	50	85	18

SECOND DIVISION

		P	W	D	L	F	A	Pts
1	Small Heath	22	17	2	3	90	35	36
2	Sheff United	22	16	3	3	62	19	35
3	Darwen	22	14	2	6	60	36	30
4	Grimsby	22	11	1	10	42	41	23
5	Ardwick	22	9	3	10	45	40	21
6	Burton Swifts	22	9	2	11	47	47	20
7	Northwich Vic	22	9	2	11	42	58	20
8	Bootle	22	8	3	11	49	63	19
9	Lincoln	22	7	3	12	45	51	17
10	Crewe	22	6	3	13	42	69	15
11	Burslem PV	22	6	3	13	30	57	15
12	Walsall TS	22	5	3	14	37	75	13

1893–94

FIRST DIVISION

		P	W	D	L	F	A	Pts
1	Aston Villa	30	19	6	5	84	42	44
2	Sunderland	30	17	4	9	72	44	38
3	Derby	30	16	4	10	73	62	36
4	Blackburn	30	16	2	12	69	53	34
5	Burnley	30	15	4	11	61	51	34
6	Everton	30	15	3	12	90	57	33
7	Nottm Forest	30	14	4	12	57	48	32
8	WBA	30	14	4	12	66	59	32
9	Wolves	30	14	3	13	52	63	31
10	Sheff United	30	13	5	12	47	61	31
11	Stoke	30	13	3	14	65	79	29
12	Wednesday	30	9	8	13	48	57	26
13	Bolton	30	10	4	16	38	52	24
14	Preston	30	10	3	17	44	56	23
15	Darwen	30	7	5	18	37	83	19
16	Newton Heath	30	6	2	22	36	72	14

SECOND DIVISION

		P	W	D	L	F	A	Pts
1	Liverpool	28	22	6	0	77	18	50
2	Small Heath	28	21	0	7	103	44	42
3	Notts County	28	18	3	7	70	31	39
4	Newcastle	28	15	6	7	66	39	36
5	Grimsby	28	15	2	11	71	58	32
6	Burton Swifts	28	14	3	11	79	61	31
7	Burslem PV	28	13	4	11	66	64	30
8	Lincoln	28	11	6	11	59	58	28
9	Woolwich A	28	12	4	12	52	55	28
10	Walsall TS	28	10	3	15	51	61	23
11	Md Ironopolis	28	8	4	16	37	72	20
12	Crewe	28	6	7	15	42	73	19
13	Ardwick	28	8	2	18	47	71	18
14	Rotherham Twn	28	6	3	19	44	91	15
15	Northwich Vic	28	3	3	22	30	98	9

1894–95

FIRST DIVISION

		P	W	D	L	F	A	Pts
1	Sunderland	30	21	5	4	80	37	47
2	Everton	30	18	6	6	82	50	42
3	Aston Villa	30	17	5	8	82	43	39
4	Preston	30	15	5	10	62	46	35
5	Blackburn	30	11	10	9	59	49	32
6	Sheff United	30	14	4	12	57	55	32
7	Nottm Forest	30	13	5	12	50	56	31
8	Wednesday	30	12	4	14	50	55	28
9	Burnley	30	11	4	15	44	56	26
10	Bolton	30	9	7	14	61	62	25
11	Wolves	30	9	7	14	43	63	25
12	Small Heath	30	9	7	14	50	74	25
13	WBA	30	10	4	16	51	66	24
14	Stoke	30	9	6	15	50	67	24
15	Derby	30	7	9	14	45	68	23
16	Liverpool	30	7	8	15	51	70	22

SECOND DIVISION

		P	W	D	L	F	A	Pts
1	Bury	30	23	2	5	78	33	48
2	Notts County	30	17	5	8	75	45	39
3	Newton Heath	30	15	8	7	78	44	38
4	Leicester Fosse	30	15	8	7	72	53	38
5	Grimsby	30	18	1	11	79	52	37
6	Darwen	30	16	4	10	74	43	36
7	Burton Wand	30	14	7	9	67	39	35
8	Woolwich A	30	14	6	10	75	58	34
9	Man City	30	14	3	13	82	72	31
10	Newcastle	30	12	3	15	72	84	27
11	Burton Swifts	30	11	3	16	52	74	25
12	Rotherham T	30	11	2	17	55	62	24
13	Lincoln	30	10	0	20	52	92	20
14	Walsall TS	30	10	0	20	47	92	20
15	Burslem PV	30	7	4	19	39	77	18
16	Crewe	30	3	4	23	26	103	10

1895–96

FIRST DIVISION

		P	W	D	L	F	A	Pts
1	Aston Villa	30	20	5	5	78	45	45
2	Derby	30	17	7	6	68	35	41
3	Everton	30	16	7	7	66	43	39
4	Bolton	30	16	5	9	49	37	37
5	Sunderland	30	15	7	8	52	41	37
6	Stoke	30	15	0	15	56	47	30
7	Wednesday	30	12	5	13	44	53	29
8	Blackburn	30	12	5	13	40	50	29
9	Preston	30	11	6	13	44	48	28
10	Burnley	30	10	7	13	48	44	27
11	Bury	30	12	3	15	50	54	27
12	Sheff United	30	10	6	14	40	50	26
13	Nottm Forest	30	11	3	16	42	57	25
14	Wolves	30	10	1	19	61	65	21
15	Small Heath	30	8	4	18	39	79	20
16	WBA	30	6	7	17	30	59	19

SECOND DIVISION

		P	W	D	L	F	A	Pts
1	Liverpool	30	22	2	6	106	32	46
2	Man City	30	21	4	5	63	38	46
3	Grimsby	30	20	2	8	82	38	42
4	Burton Wand	30	19	4	7	69	40	42
5	Newcastle	30	16	2	12	73	50	34
6	Newton Heath	30	15	3	12	66	57	33
7	Woolwich A	30	14	4	12	59	42	32
8	Leicester Fosse	30	14	4	12	57	44	32
9	Darwen	30	12	6	12	72	67	30
10	Notts County	30	12	2	16	57	54	26
11	Burton Swifts	30	10	4	16	39	69	24
12	Loughborough	30	9	5	16	40	67	23
13	Lincoln	30	9	4	17	53	75	22
14	Burslem PV	30	7	4	19	43	78	18
15	Rotherham Tn	30	7	3	20	34	97	17
16	Crewe	30	5	3	22	30	95	13

1896–97

FIRST DIVISION

		P	W	D	L	F	A	Pts
1	Aston Villa	30	21	5	4	73	38	47
2	Sheff United	30	13	10	7	42	29	36
3	Derby	30	16	4	10	70	50	36
4	Preston	30	11	12	7	55	40	34
5	Liverpool	30	12	9	9	46	38	33
6	Wednesday	30	10	11	9	42	37	31
7	Everton	30	14	3	13	62	57	31
8	Bolton	30	12	6	12	40	43	30
9	Bury	30	10	10	10	39	44	30
10	Wolves	30	11	6	13	45	41	28
11	Nottm Forest	30	9	8	13	44	49	26
12	WBA	30	10	6	14	33	56	26
13	Stoke	30	11	3	16	48	59	25
14	Blackburn	30	11	3	16	35	62	25
15	Sunderland	30	7	9	14	34	47	23
16	Burnley	30	6	7	17	43	61	19

SECOND DIVISION

		P	W	D	L	F	A	Pts
1	Notts County	30	19	4	7	92	43	42
2	Newton Heath	30	17	5	8	56	34	39
3	Grimsby	30	17	4	9	66	45	38
4	Small Heath	30	16	5	9	69	47	37
5	Newcastle	30	17	1	12	56	52	35
6	Man City	30	12	8	10	58	50	32
7	Gainsborough	30	12	7	11	50	47	31
8	Blackpool	30	13	5	12	59	56	31
9	Leicester Fosse	30	13	4	13	59	56	30
10	Woolwich A	30	13	4	13	68	70	30
11	Darwen	30	14	0	16	67	61	28
12	Walsall	30	11	4	15	53	69	26
13	Loughborough	30	12	1	17	50	64	25
14	Burton Swifts	30	9	6	15	46	61	24
15	Burton Wand	30	9	2	19	31	67	20
16	Lincoln	30	5	2	23	27	85	12

1897–98

FIRST DIVISION

		P	W	D	L	F	A	Pts
1	Sheff United	30	17	8	5	56	31	42
2	Sunderland	30	16	5	9	43	30	37
3	Wolves	30	14	7	9	57	41	35
4	Everton	30	13	9	8	48	39	35
5	Wednesday	30	15	3	12	51	42	33
6	Aston Villa	30	14	5	11	61	51	33
7	WBA	30	11	10	9	44	45	32
8	Nottm Forest	30	11	9	10	47	49	31
9	Liverpool	30	11	6	13	48	45	28
10	Derby	30	11	6	13	57	61	28
11	Bolton	30	11	4	15	28	41	26
12	Preston NE	30	8	8	14	35	43	24
13	Notts County	30	8	8	14	36	46	24
14	Bury	30	8	8	14	39	51	24
15	Blackburn	30	7	10	13	39	54	24
16	Stoke	30	8	8	14	35	55	24

SECOND DIVISION

		P	W	D	L	F	A	Pts
1	Burnley	30	20	8	2	80	24	48
2	Newcastle	30	21	3	6	64	32	45
3	Man City	30	15	9	6	66	36	39
4	Newton Heath	30	16	6	8	64	35	38
5	Woolwich A	30	16	5	9	69	49	37
6	Small Heath	30	16	4	10	58	50	36
7	Leicester Fosse	30	13	7	10	46	35	33
8	Luton	30	13	4	13	68	50	30
9	Gainsborough	30	12	6	12	50	54	30
10	Walsall	30	12	5	13	58	58	29
11	Blackpool	30	10	5	15	49	61	25
12	Grimsby	30	10	4	16	52	62	24
13	Burton Swifts	30	8	5	17	38	69	21
14	Lincoln	30	6	5	19	43	82	17
15	Darwen	30	6	2	22	31	76	14
16	Loughborough	30	6	2	22	24	87	14

1898–99

FIRST DIVISION

		P	W	D	L	F	A	Pts
1	Aston Villa	34	19	7	8	76	40	45
2	Liverpool	34	19	5	10	49	33	43
3	Burnley	34	15	9	10	45	47	39
4	Everton	34	15	8	11	48	41	38
5	Notts County	34	12	13	9	47	51	37
6	Blackburn	34	14	8	12	60	52	36
7	Sunderland	34	15	6	13	41	41	36
8	Wolves	34	14	7	13	54	48	35
9	Derby	34	12	11	11	62	57	35
10	Bury	34	14	7	13	48	49	35
11	Nottm Forest	34	11	11	12	42	42	33
12	Stoke	34	13	7	14	47	52	33
13	Newcastle	34	11	8	15	49	48	30
14	WBA	34	12	6	16	42	57	30
15	Preston	34	10	9	15	44	47	29
16	Sheff United	34	9	11	14	45	51	29
17	Bolton	34	9	7	18	37	51	25
18	Wednesday	34	8	8	18	32	61	24

SECOND DIVISION

		P	W	D	L	F	A	Pts
1	Man City	34	23	5	6	92	35	52
2	Glossop NE	34	20	6	8	76	38	46
3	Leicester Fosse	34	18	9	7	64	42	45
4	Newton Heath	34	19	5	10	67	43	43
5	New Brighton	34	18	7	9	71	52	43
6	Walsall	34	15	12	7	79	36	42
7	Woolwich A	34	18	5	11	72	41	41
8	Small Heath	34	17	7	10	85	50	41
9	Burslem PV	34	17	5	12	56	34	39
10	Grimsby	34	15	5	14	71	60	35
11	Barnsley	34	12	7	15	52	56	31
12	Lincoln	34	12	7	15	51	56	31
13	Burton Swifts	34	10	8	16	51	70	28
14	Gainsborough	34	10	5	19	56	72	25
15	Luton	34	10	3	21	51	95	23
16	Blackpool	34	8	4	22	49	90	20
17	Loughborough	34	6	6	22	38	92	18
18	Darwen	34	2	5	27	22	141	9

1899–1900

FIRST DIVISION

		P	W	D	L	F	A	Pts
1	Aston Villa	34	22	6	6	77	35	50
2	Sheff United	34	18	12	4	63	33	48
3	Sunderland	34	19	3	12	50	35	41
4	Wolves	34	15	9	10	48	37	39
5	Newcastle	34	13	10	11	53	43	36
6	Derby	34	14	8	12	45	43	36
7	Man City	34	13	8	13	50	44	34
8	Nottm Forest	34	13	8	13	56	55	34
9	Stoke	34	10	10	14	37	45	34
10	Liverpool	34	14	5	15	49	45	33
11	Everton	34	13	7	14	47	49	33
12	Bury	34	13	6	15	40	44	32
13	WBA	34	11	8	15	43	51	30
14	Blackburn	34	13	4	17	49	61	30
15	Notts County	34	9	11	14	46	60	29
16	Preston	34	12	4	18	38	48	28
17	Burnley	34	11	5	18	34	54	27
18	Glossop NE	34	4	10	20	31	74	18

SECOND DIVISION

		P	W	D	L	F	A	Pts
1	Wednesday	34	25	4	5	84	22	54
2	Bolton	34	22	8	4	79	25	52
3	Small Heath	34	20	6	8	78	38	46
4	Newton Heath	34	20	4	10	63	27	44
5	Leicester Fosse	34	17	9	8	53	36	43
6	Grimsby	34	17	6	11	67	46	40
7	Chesterfield	34	16	6	12	65	60	38
8	Woolwich A	34	16	4	14	61	43	36
9	Lincoln	34	14	8	12	46	43	36
10	New Brighton	34	13	9	12	66	58	35
11	Burslem PV	34	14	6	14	39	49	34
12	Walsall	34	12	8	14	50	55	32
13	Gainsborough	34	9	7	18	47	75	25
14	Middlesbrough	34	8	8	18	39	69	24
15	Burton Swifts	34	9	6	19	43	84	24
16	Barnsley	34	8	7	19	46	79	23
17	Luton	34	5	8	21	40	75	18
18	Loughborough	34	1	6	27	18	100	8

1900–1

FIRST DIVISION

		P	W	D	L	F	A	Pts
1	Liverpool	34	19	7	8	59	35	45
2	Sunderland	34	15	13	6	57	26	43
3	Notts County	34	18	4	12	54	46	40
4	Nottm Forest	34	16	7	11	53	36	39
5	Bury	34	16	7	11	53	37	39
6	Newcastle	34	14	10	10	42	37	38
7	Everton	34	16	5	13	55	42	37
8	Wednesday	34	13	10	11	52	42	36
9	Blackburn	34	12	9	13	39	47	33
10	Bolton	34	13	7	14	39	55	33
11	Man City	34	13	6	15	48	58	32
12	Derby	34	12	7	15	55	42	31
13	Wolves	34	9	13	12	39	55	31
14	Sheff United	34	12	7	15	35	52	31
15	Aston Villa	34	10	10	14	45	51	30
16	Stoke	34	11	5	18	46	57	27
17	Preston	34	9	7	18	49	75	25
18	WBA	34	7	8	19	35	62	22

SECOND DIVISION

		P	W	D	L	F	A	Pts
1	Grimsby	34	20	9	5	60	33	49
2	Small Heath	34	19	10	5	57	24	48
3	Burnley	34	20	4	10	53	29	44
4	New Brighton	34	17	8	9	57	38	42
5	Glossop NE	34	15	8	11	51	33	38
6	Middlesbrough	34	15	7	12	50	40	37
7	Woolwich A	34	15	6	13	39	35	36
8	Lincoln	34	13	7	14	43	39	33
9	Burslem PV	34	11	11	12	45	47	33
10	Newton Heath	34	14	4	16	42	38	32
11	Leicester Fosse	34	11	10	13	39	37	32
12	Blackpool	34	12	7	15	33	58	31
13	Gainsborough	34	10	10	14	45	60	30
14	Chesterfield	34	9	10	15	46	58	28
15	Barnsley	34	11	5	18	47	60	27
16	Walsall	34	7	13	14	40	56	27
17	Stockport	34	11	3	20	38	68	25
18	Burton Swifts	34	8	4	22	34	66	20

TWO
The Edwardians
1901–1910

'I don't suppose the footballers of the future will ever have quite such riotous fun as their predecessors. But they may not be much the worse off for that. After all, it is easy to overdo the wild Bohemianism which characterized some of the footballers of the old school; and it must not be forgotten that there were often sore heads after a night out. There is every encouragement given today for the formation of character. There is a daily increasing tendency for clubs to look askance at men who have not a clean record. Clubs have begun to learn – nay, they have learned! – that it does not take many black sheep to lead the whole flock astray.'

W.I. 'Billy' Bassett, *the great West Bromwich Albion and England winger and later long-serving chairman of his club.*

League football moved into the twentieth century with a swagger. It was the people's game; and it was also big business. 'Working men,' complained one captain of industry, 'are too anxious to leave their work for the sake of seeing their favourite teams play football.'

Sixpence (2½p) got Edwardian man into most football grounds and from his place on the terrace, which was often a mound of earth reinforced by cinders or wooden sleepers, he saw the game take dramatic strides.

The outstanding side of the period was Newcastle United and their League accounts for 1904–5, when they very nearly managed the League and FA Cup 'double', show the kind of money that could be earned. Gate receipts and season tickets provided £17,780 and, after deducting wages and travelling costs, they finished with a profit of £5,487. Their Cup run was worth another £8,000 – and this at a time when half-a-crown would buy a five-course meal.

Newcastle won the League championship three times in five seasons and reached the FA Cup final at Crystal Palace five times in seven seasons, although they won the trophy only once. They were strong but fair, skilful but direct, a 'scientific' side that bristled with talent: Andy McCombie, 'a grand tackler and a sure kick', James 'Gentleman Jim' Howie who seemed to hop rather than run, 14-stone centre-forward Bill 'Cockles' Appleyard, Peter McWilliam and Colin Veitch, half-backs of wit and elegance, and the remarkable Bill McCracken, their Ireland full-back whose pace and cunning eventually led to a change in the offside law in 1925.

They were a side, above all, of colour and humour. They were practical jokers who would confuse officious ticket-collectors on trains by slipping through side-doors to be counted twice. 'How's this?' the inspector would ask. 'Twenty-two players but only 16 tickets?' They were superstitious and regarded the sight of a wedding on the way to a match as a sure omen of success, a funeral as a sign of failure. And on the way to the station after one match they persuaded the driver of their four-in-hand to drive so fast over rough and hilly roads that he was given a hefty fine by local magistrates.

It was a period strong in character and quality; a period, too, in which new names pushed to the fore – among them, significantly, Liverpool and Manchester United. Liverpool won their first League championships in 1901 and 1906, with sides that were durable and consistent rather than brilliant, and Manchester United earned their first title in 1908 – captained by the indomitable Charlie Roberts, the finest centre-half of his time, and inspired by Billy Meredith who was to football what W.G. Grace was to cricket. Meredith, with his pale face, cropped hair, slender frame and spindly legs, was a man apart, a winger of genius, an immortal – who was rarely without a toothpick in his mouth.

Meredith's career spanned 30 years (1894–1924) but the number of games he played, for Northwich Victoria, Manchester City, Manchester United, Manchester City again and Wales, is a matter of debate. His own claim, and he loved statistics, was 1,568 (470 goals); but what is certain is that he played in his last and forty-eighth international at the age of 45, and in an FA Cup semi-final when he was four months short of his fiftieth birthday: two lines that are still in the record books. He has been described as 'the Lloyd George of Welsh football', and 'a Matthews, Finney and Best of his day rolled into one'.

The north still dominated; but at least the south found a rare champion in 1901. Tottenham Hotspur won the FA Cup and thus became the first – and only – non-League club to win the trophy since the formation of the Football League. Spurs were members of the Southern League and their triumph gave the game in London fresh impetus and new status.

It was a remarkable achievement because Spurs had to beat four First Division sides: Proud Preston themselves, Bury who were the Cup-holders, West Bromwich Albion and, in the final, Sheffield United, champions once and runners-up twice in the previous four seasons. Sheffield United had nine full internationals in their side, including Ernest Needham, their captain, left-half and inspiration, one of the great men of his time, and Billy 'Fatty' Foulke in goal who at 6ft 2ins and 22 stone was a huge, loveable eccentric. Newspapers called him 'one of the curiosities of football' . . . 'a wonder to everyone who visits the classic grounds of the game'. Opponents who had been dangled from the ankles by the mighty Foulke had other names for him. Foulke's own comment was: 'I don't mind what they call me as long as it's not late for lunch.'

Spurs' success meant it was only a matter of time before they were elected to the League; they managed it in 1908 and immediately won promotion. By then, however, other London clubs had joined Woolwich Arsenal in breaking the monopoly of the north and midlands. The First and Second Divisions expanded to 20 clubs each in 1905 when Clapton Orient and, remarkably, Chelsea were elected.

Chelsea's ambition was matched only by their audacity. At the start of 1905 the club did not exist. Five months later, without having played a match, they were elected to the Second Division of the Football League.

H.A. 'Gus' Mears, the club's founder, started with a ground, the Stamford Bridge Athletic Ground, and a bright idea; the first meeting of the club was on 14 March; their first players were signed on 26 April 'subject to Chelsea being elected', and on 29 May they persuaded the League's annual meeting that 'you really cannot refuse us'. Players had been chosen for fame as well as quality – including the mountainous Foulke from Sheffield United – and the dividends were handsome. They lost their first League match at Stockport, but finished their first season in third position and were promoted the next.

Players all over the country were increasingly aware of their worth. They moved slowly but militantly – even threatening to strike – towards a strong union of their own. Their maximum wage of £208 a year, however, was still envied by most of the men who paid to watch them. Four pounds a week was twice what a works-foreman took home and nearly four times the average wage of a farm labourer.

Meanwhile, the transfer system was already causing emotive argument – and when Middlesbrough paid the first £1,000 fee for Alf Common, the skilful Sunderland and England inside-forward, the country divided on the issue. 'Where will it all end?' demanded one correspondent. 'Flesh and blood for sale' observed another. But Billy Bassett, the illustrious West Bromwich Albion and England winger who later became chairman of his club, defended the system stoutly: 'We can dismiss from our minds at once all the silly talk of silly people who say in a profoundly silly way that it is monstrous and a sin against morality that players should be bought and sold like cattle. They are not bought and sold as chattels. There is no law to compel any man to go where he does not desire to go . . . and who can say whether Common was a cheap or a dear man. I should say he was cheap because it was generally thought that he saved Middlesbrough from sinking into the Second League.'

An attempt was made later to introduce a ceiling for transfers of £350, but the regulation was neither wanted nor workable. It lasted less than four months. The men who ran English football were still learning.

THE GROWTH OF THE FOOTBALL LEAGUE

Divisions

	ONE	TWO	THREE (S)	THREE (N)	TOTAL CLUBS
1888–91	12				12
1891–92	14				14
1892–93	16	12			28
1893–94	16	15			31
1894–98	16	16			32
1898–05	18	18			36
1905–15	20	20			40
1919–20	22	22			44
1920–21	22	22	22*		66
1921–23	22	22	22	20	86
1923–50	22	22	22	22	88
1950–87	22	22	24†	24†	92
1987–88	21	23	24	24	92
1988–89	20	24	24	24	92

**Division Three.*

†In 1958 the clubs in Division Three (South) and Division Three (North) were reformed as Divisions Three and Four.

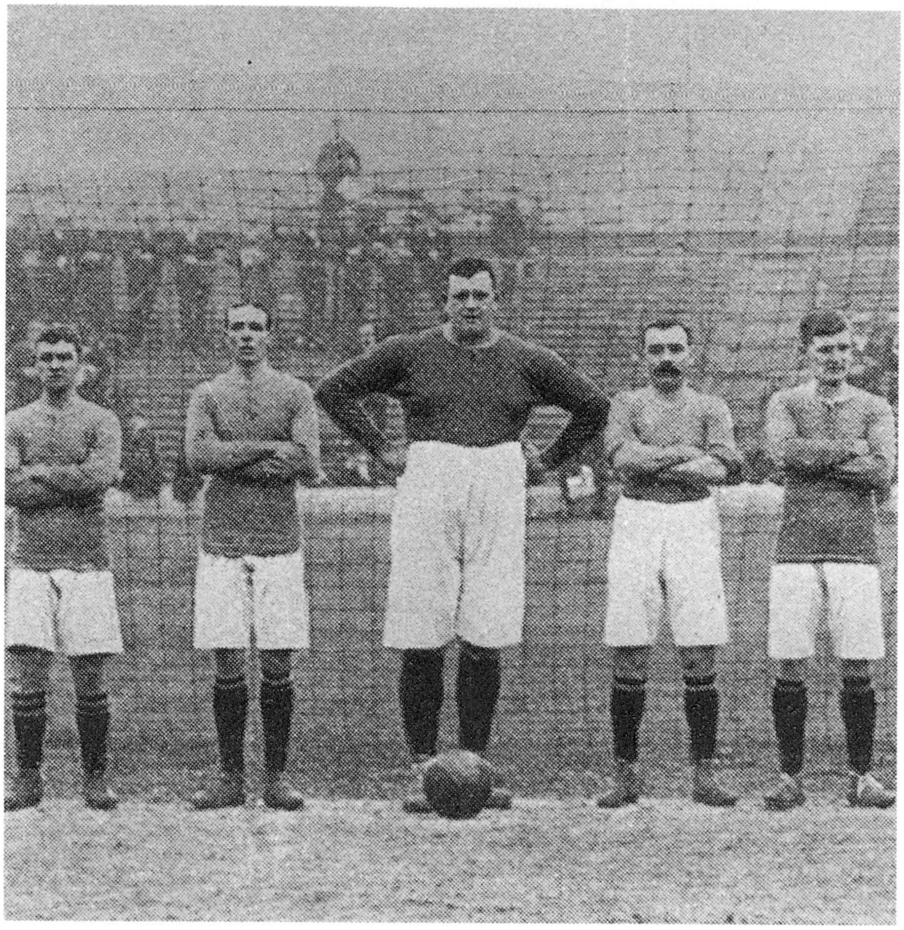

left Billy 'Fatty' Foulke (centre), 6 ft 2 ins and 22 stone, new captain and goalkeeper of the League's newest club, Chelsea, in 1905. At the start of the year Chelsea did not exist. Five months later, without having played a match, they were elected to the League – and the mountainous Foulke was an early import.

above Alternative view of Bill Foulke. He was remarkably agile and an expert at saving penalties – though opponents were known to admit that they sometimes shot straight at his stomach, his most vulnerable area, instead of keeping the ball low.

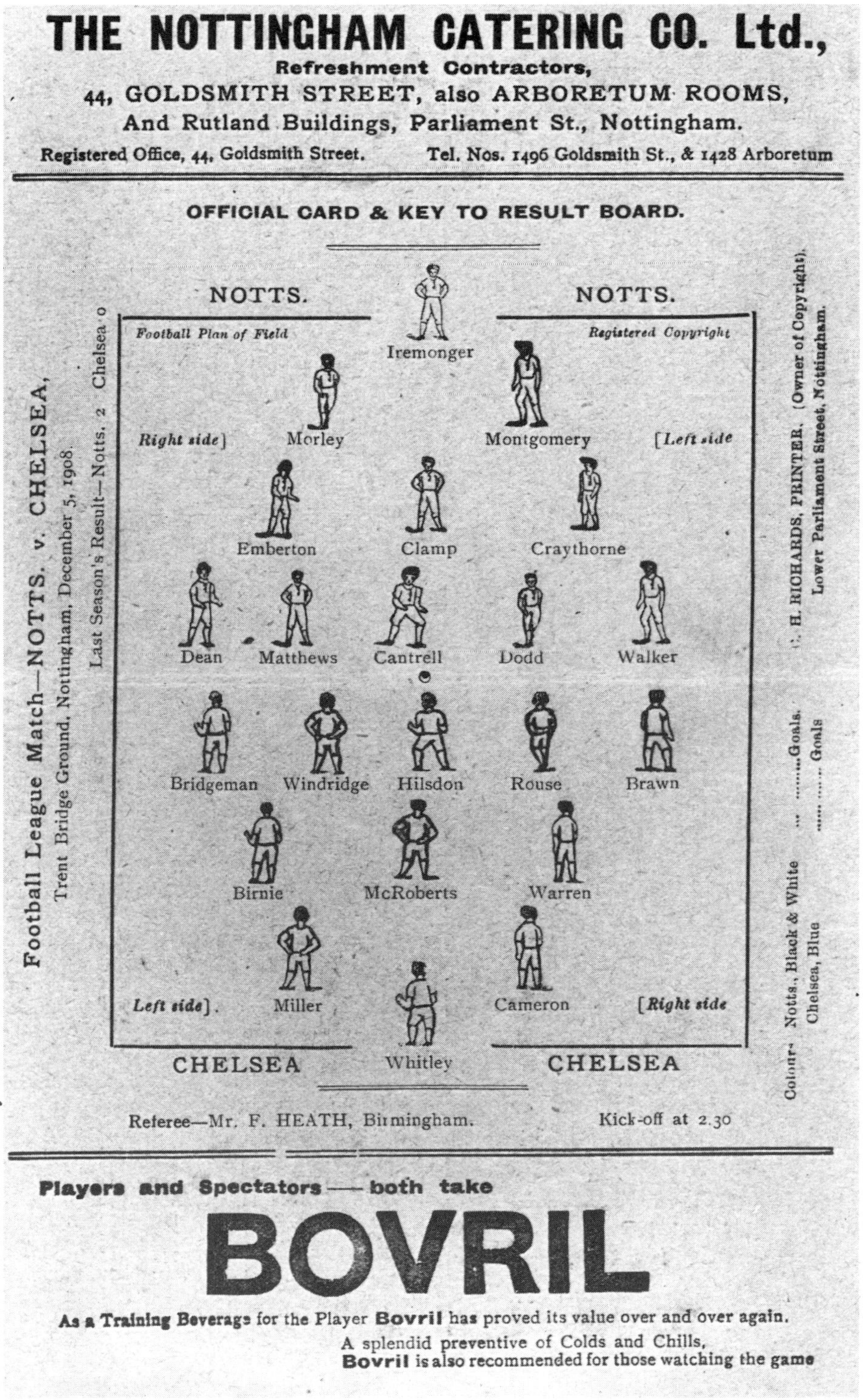

above Notts County v Chelsea, Division One, Trent Bridge Ground, 5 December 1908. Complete with 'plan of field'.

left Albert Iremonger, goalkeeper for Notts County and Lincoln City from 1905 to 1927, is believed to be the tallest man ever to play League football. He stood 6 ft 6 ins – and was an expert penalty-saver and rich humorist. Played 600 League games for Notts County and Lincoln City, 223 consecutively (1907–12). In action v Chelsea at Stamford Bridge, 1909.

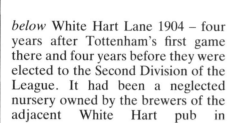

below White Hart Lane 1904 – four years after Tottenham's first game there and four years before they were elected to the Second Division of the League. It had been a neglected nursery owned by the brewers of the adjacent White Hart pub in Tottenham High Street – and the idea of thirsty football crowds next door appealed to them enormously. Spurs' first groundsman was John Over who had marked out the Oval when the first Test match in England was played there, against Australia, in 1880.

above Alf Common became the first player to be transferred for £1,000 when he moved from Sunderland to Middlesbrough in 1905. Society was shocked – but Common held off the spectre of relegation into Division Two for his new club.

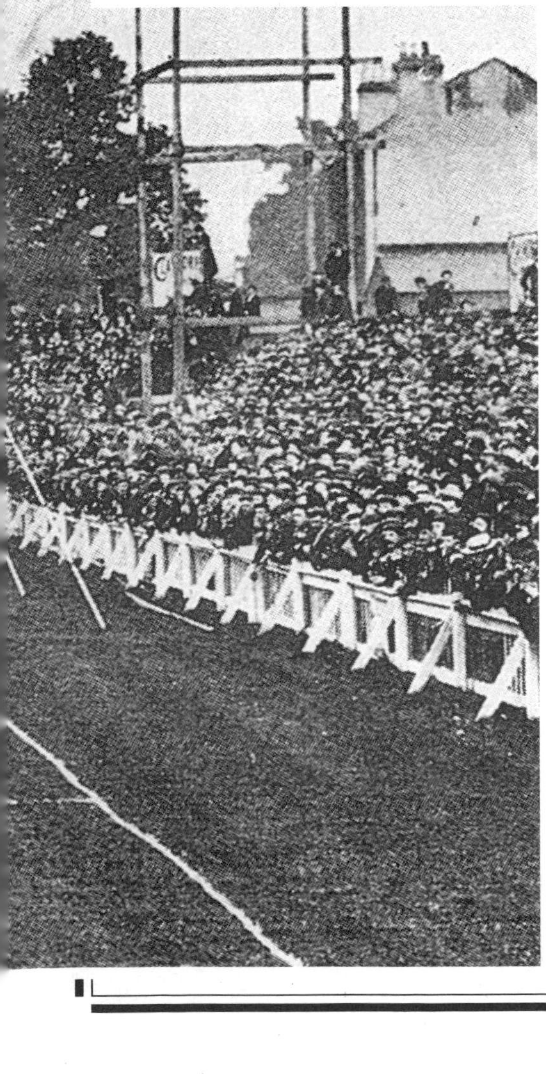

above Newcastle United at the highest point in their history. They won the League championship three times in five seasons (1905–7–9) and the FA Cup final was a regular engagement for them. A side of quality and character. Back row (l to r): McCracken, Pudan, McWilliam, Carr. Centre: J. Bell (vice-chairman), McCombie, Speedie, Willis, Lawrence, Rutherford, J.P. Oliver (director). Front: J.Q. McPherson (trainer), Veitch, Gosnell, Howie, Appleyard, Gardner, Wilson, F.G. Watt (secretary).

right Harry Makepeace – one of the rare breed who have played football and cricket for England. Skilful wing-half for Everton (1902–15), member of their FA Cup-winning side in 1906 and an England player four times (three v Scotland). A dour batsman for Lancashire and England – and his 43 first class centuries included 117 against Australia at Melbourne in 1920–21. Jack Sharp, his right-wing partner with Everton, was also a 'double' international.

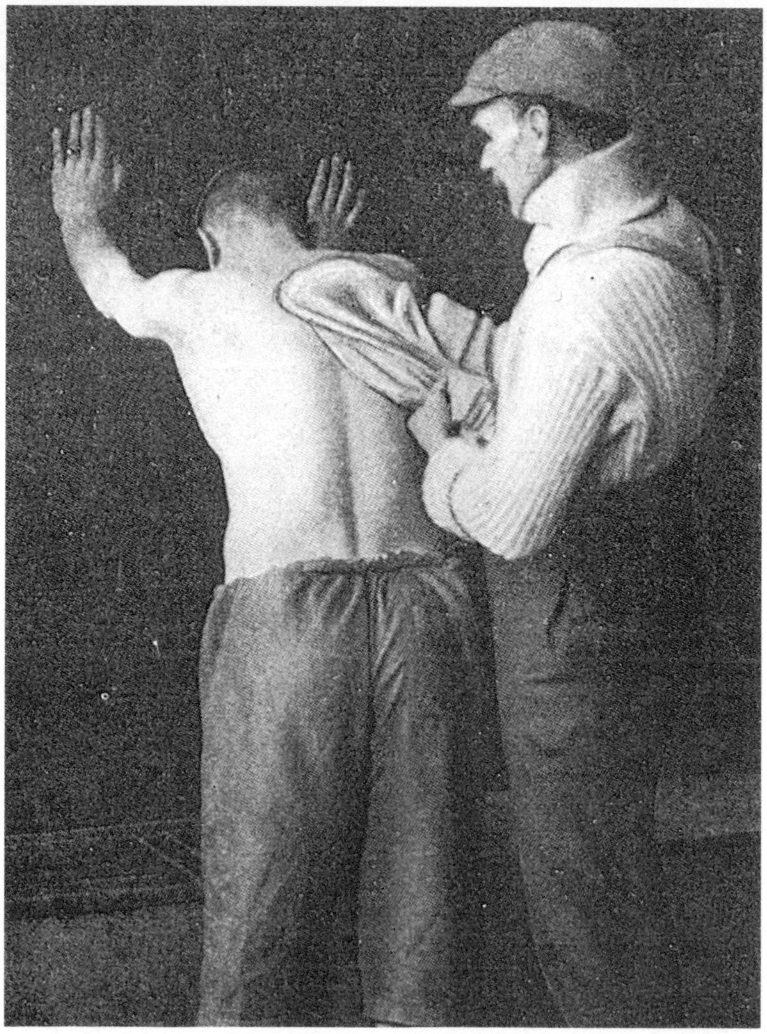

above West Bromwich Albion on a training stroll at the turn of the century. Caps, ties, waistcoats and watch-chains *de rigueur*. And after matches (*left*) a brisk rub down was considered essential.

168 *The Villa News and Record.* November 6, 1909

SCORING BOARD.

Arrangements have been made for showing the results of the most important matches played this afternoon. The Scoring Board is planned thus :—

A	B	C	D	E	F	G	H	J	K	L	N

The top figure in each square represents the home team.
M signifies match abandoned.
Key for to-day's matches as follows :—

		Half-time.	Final.			Half-time.	Final.
A	NOTTS COUNTY / PRESTON NORTH END			G	WOLVERHAMPTON W. / FULHAM		
B	SHEFFIELD UNITED / SHEFFIELD WED.			H	MIDDLESBROUGH / NOTTS FOREST		
C	MANCHESTER CITY / WEST BROMWICH A.			J	NEWCASTLE UNITED / TOTTENHAM HOTSPUR		
D	BLACKBURN ROVERS / SUNDERLAND			K	LEICESTER FOSSE / BIRMINGHAM		
E	BOLTON WANDERERS / MANCHESTER UNITED			L	CHELSEA / EVERTON		
F	LIVERPOOL / BURY			N	WOOLWICH ARSENAL / BRADFORD CITY		

NEXT WEEK!!! NEXT WEEK!!!

THE GREAT

LITTLE TICH.

JACK AND EVELYN,

Those favourite Society Entertainers,

Supported by TEN STAR TURNS.

BIRMINGHAM HIPPODROME.

November 6, 1909 *The Villa News and Record.* 169

FLETCHER'S CAFÉ, CORPORATION STREET. "The Caterers of the Midlands."

The most luxurious, largest, and up-to-date Café Restaurant in the Provinces.
Seating Accommodation, 800. Afternoon Teas a Speciality. Music All Day.

TEAMS FOR TO-DAY'S MATCH.

THE LEAGUE CHAMPIONSHIP.

Aston Villa v. Bristol City.

KICK-OFF AT 3 P.M.

ASTON VILLA.

RIGHT LEFT

CARTLIDGE (1)

LYONS (2) MILES (3)

LOGAN (4) BUCKLEY (5) TRANTER (6)

WALTERS (7) GERRISH (8) HAMPTON (9) BACHE (10) HALL (11)

Referee: Mr. T. P. CAMPBELL (Blackburn).
Linesmen: Messrs. A. OAKLEY (Wolverhampton) and W. MORTIMER (Windsor).

HARDY (12) BURTON (13) COWELL (14) HARDY (15) STANIFORTH (16)

SPEAR (17) WEDLOCK (18) MARR (19)

COTTLE (20) ANNAN (21)

CLAY (22)

LEFT RIGHT

BRISTOL CITY.

In the event of any alteration in the above teams, a board giving particulars will be sent round the ground.

Where to Dine! Fletcher's, Ltd. **"METROPOLE RESTAURANT"** (FULLY LICENSED), 35/36, HIGH STREET.
THE FRASCATI OF BIRMINGHAM.
Luncheons, Dinners, Teas, and Suppers.
...only on Draught and in Bottle. "Munich" and "Pilsener" Lager Beer on Draught.
The Ladies' Orchestra Plays Daily on the Balcony.

The Football Photographer.

ALBERT WILKES

(LATE ASTON VILLA),

Photographic Artist,

45, LEGGE ST., WEST BROMWICH.

Don't forget to drop a post card in summer time for particulars.
Groups and Parties a Speciality. The Finest Studio in the District.

Printed at the Colmore Press, Lionel Street, Birmingham, for the Aston Villa Football Club, Ltd., Proprietors, and published by them at their Offices, Trinity Road, Aston Manor, November 6th, 1909.

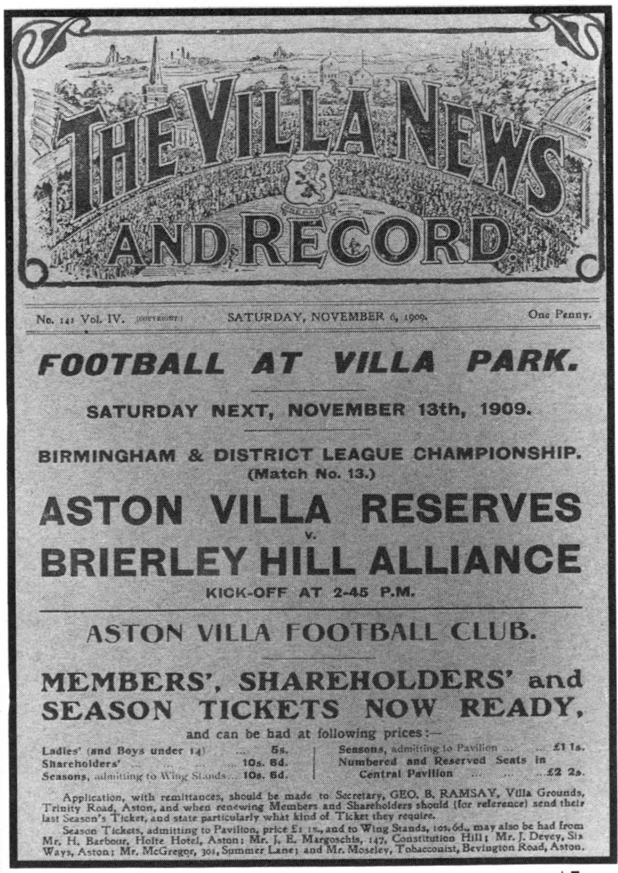

No. 141 Vol. IV. (COPYRIGHT) SATURDAY, NOVEMBER 6, 1909. One Penny.

FOOTBALL AT VILLA PARK.

SATURDAY NEXT, NOVEMBER 13th, 1909.

BIRMINGHAM & DISTRICT LEAGUE CHAMPIONSHIP.
(Match No. 13.)

ASTON VILLA RESERVES
v.
BRIERLEY HILL ALLIANCE

KICK-OFF AT 2-45 P.M.

ASTON VILLA FOOTBALL CLUB.

MEMBERS', SHAREHOLDERS' and SEASON TICKETS NOW READY,

and can be had at following prices:—

Ladies' (and Boys under 14) ... 5s.	Seasons, admitting to Pavilion ... ... £1 1s.
Shareholders' ... ... 10s. 6d.	Numbered and Reserved Seats in Central Pavilion ... ... £2 2s.
Seasons, admitting to Wing Stands ... 10s. 6d.	

Application, with remittances, should be made to Secretary, GEO. B. RAMSAY, Villa Grounds, Trinity Road, Aston, and when renewing Members and Shareholders should (for reference) send their last Season's Ticket, and state particularly what kind of Ticket they require.

Season Tickets, admitting to Pavilion, price £1 1s., and to Wing Stands, 10s. 6d., may also be had from Mr. H. Barbour, Holte Hotel, Aston; Mr. J. E. Margoschis, 147, Constitution Hill; Mr. J. Devey, Six Ways, Aston; Mr. McGregor, 301, Summer Lane; and Mr. Moseley, Tobacconist, Bevington Road, Aston.

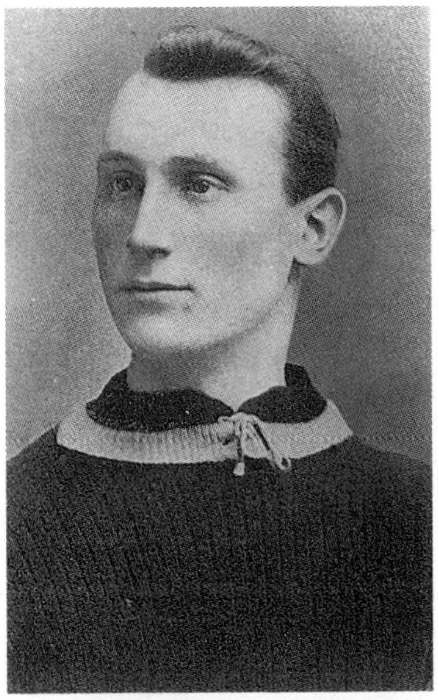

right Albert Wilkes – Aston Villa, Fulham, Chesterfield and England wing-half who became one of the best-known sports photographers of his time. He played five games for England – including the tragic match against Scotland at Ibrox in 1902 when part of the West Stand collapsed and 25 people were killed. He retired from football in 1909 and concentrated on photography until his death in 1936. His photographs figured on dozens of postcards – but here he is a postcard subject himself, one of a 'Birmingham Novelty Company' set issued in 1905.

left Billy Meredith – the brilliant 'Welsh wizard' – playing for Manchester United against Queen's Park Rangers in the first FA Charity Shield match at Stamford Bridge in 1908. United, the League champions, beat Rangers, the Southern League champions, by 4–0 in a replay.

right High technology. A boot-making machine, 1905, which – it was boasted – was 'practically a pair of hands which grips, clutches and pulls the uppers where it will and rivets where it likes.' It attached uppers to soles at the rate of 1,500 pairs a week.

below Football factory: one of the first. The game was becoming an industry – and dependent industries, employing large numbers of men, quickly mushroomed. Footballs were made by hand, cowhide was always used – described as 'practically waterproof' – and the stretching process was a trade secret. A ball made of badly stretched leather quickly lost its shape.

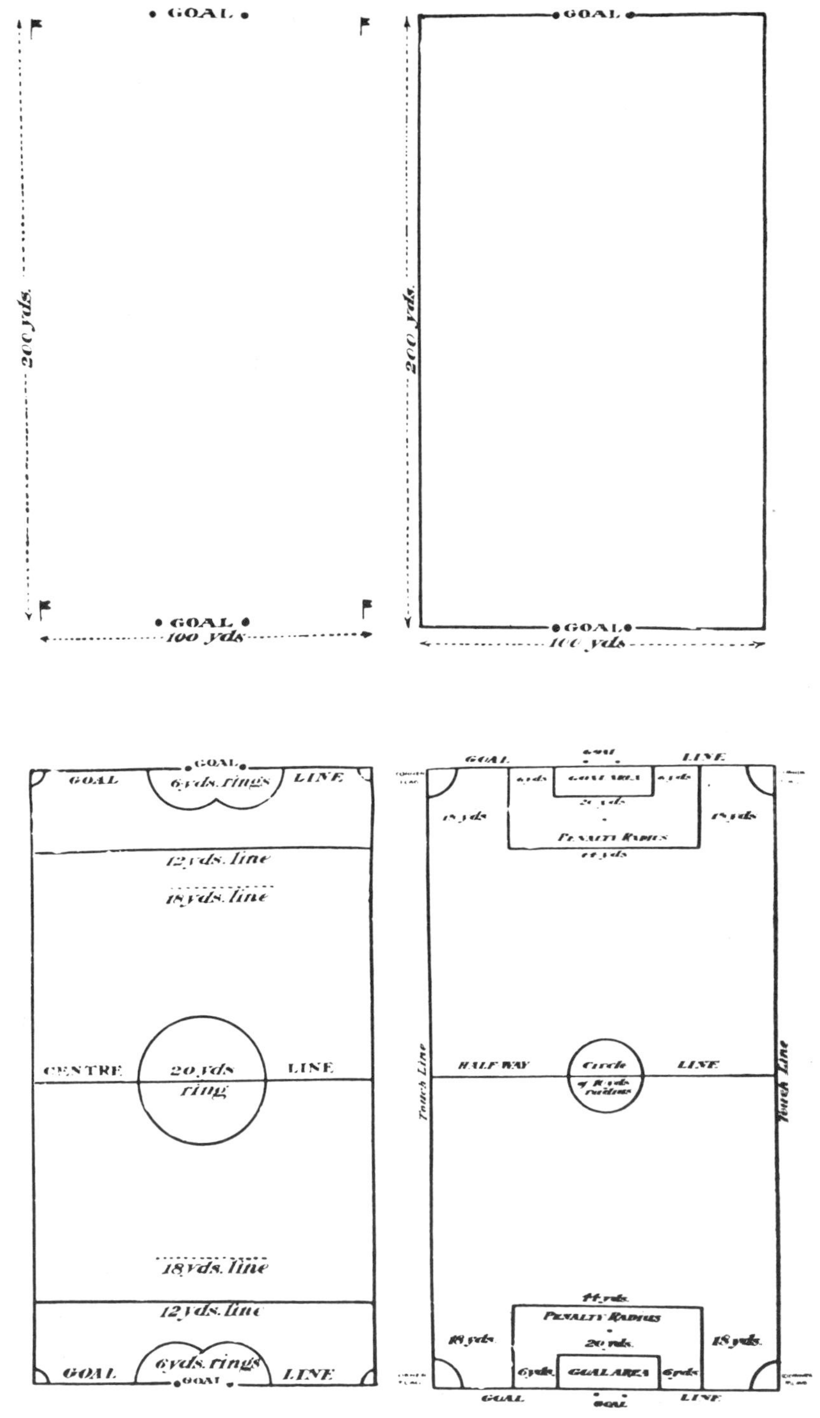

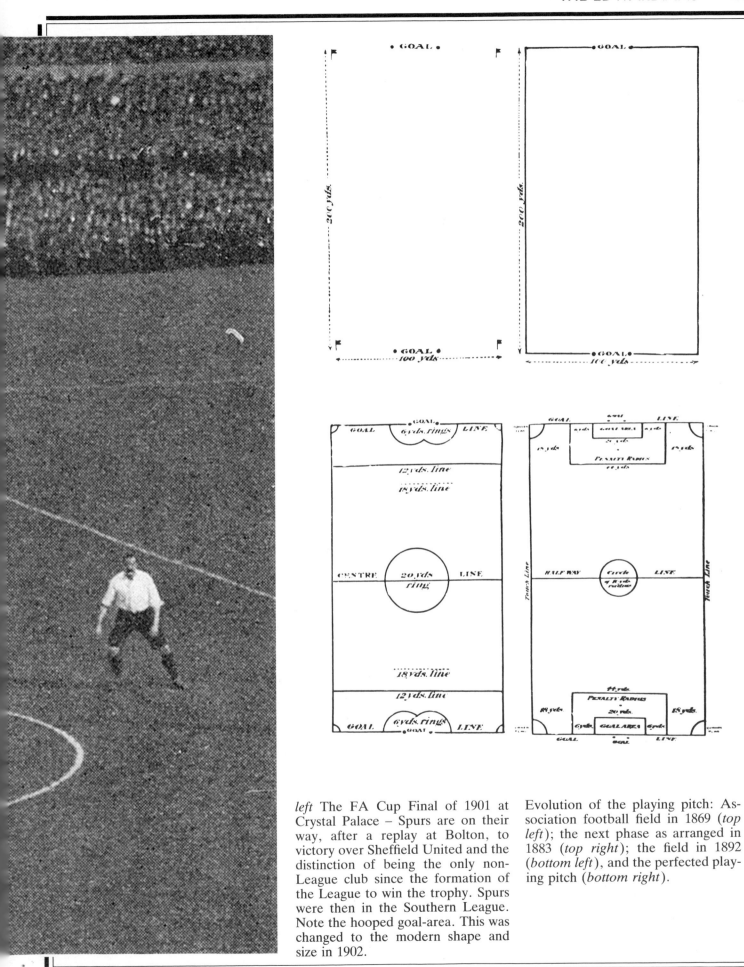

left The FA Cup Final of 1901 at Crystal Palace – Spurs are on their way, after a replay at Bolton, to victory over Sheffield United and the distinction of being the only non-League club since the formation of the League to win the trophy. Spurs were then in the Southern League. Note the hooped goal-area. This was changed to the modern shape and size in 1902.

Evolution of the playing pitch: Association football field in 1869 (*top left*); the next phase as arranged in 1883 (*top right*); the field in 1892 (*bottom left*), and the perfected playing pitch (*bottom right*).

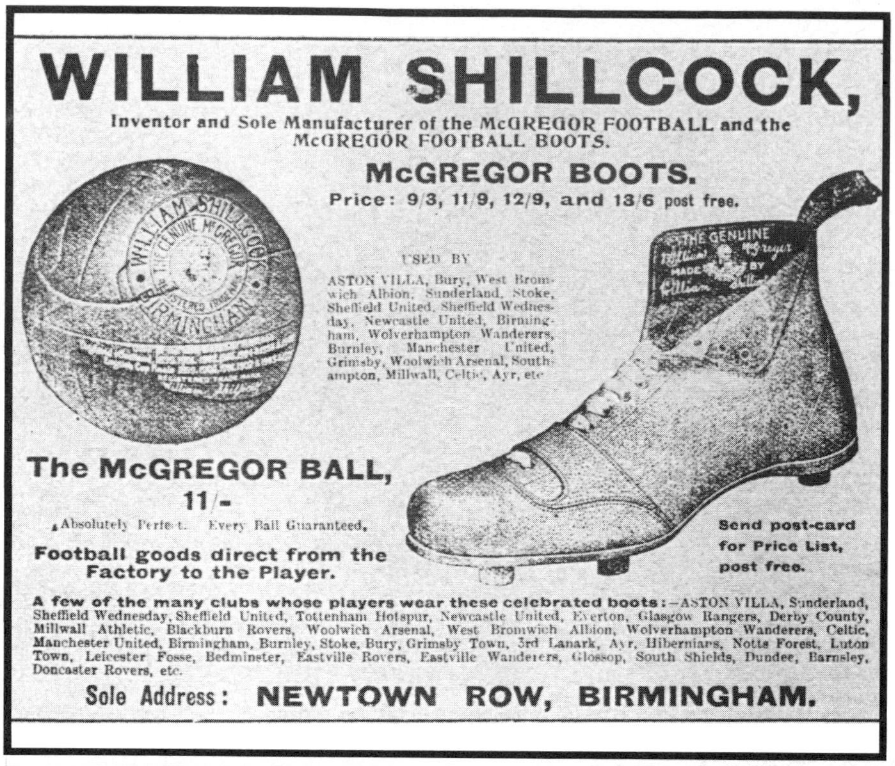

below Bramall Lane, home of Sheffield United Cricket and Football Club, in 1904 – soon after the main stand, with its endearing mock-Tudor gable, had been built. The gable was later destroyed in an air raid.

right Football League Management Committee 1903–4. Back row (l to r): W.W. Hart, J. McKenna, H.S. Radford. Front: William McGregor, T.H. Sidney, J.J. Bentley (president 1894–1910), John Lewis, Tom Charnley (secretary). John McKenna, one of the great figures in Liverpool FC's history, became League president in 1910 and remained so for 26 years – the longest-serving president of all. He was a strong disciplinarian and was known as 'Honest John'.

right Molineux – the classic home of Wolverhampton Wanderers in the early years of the century. Wolves, one of the League's original dozen, played their first game there against Aston Villa on 2 September 1889 – the start of the League's second season.

left The Recreation Ground, Saltergate, Chesterfield – with the town's famous crooked spire to the left of the grandstand. The picture was taken soon after Chesterfield joined the Second Division of the League in 1899. Chesterfield (founded 1866) are one of the League's oldest clubs.

above Leeds City in their first season as a League club, 1905–6. Back row (left to right): G. Swift, C. Morgan, D. Dooley, H. Bromage, J. Macdonald, H.B. Singleton, T. Thrupp (groundsman). Middle row: R. Watson, R. Ray (captain), G. Gillies (secretary/manager), R. Morriss, W. Clay. Front row: 'Roy' (the City dog), G.F. Parnell, J.F. Hargreaves, H. Stringfellow, E. Bintcliffe, J. Henderson, T. Drain. Leeds City remained members of the Second Division until October 1919 when they were expelled from the League for making illegal payments to players. They were unexpectedly successful in tournaments during World War One when more than 30 guest players, including many internationals, appeared for them. The club refused to present their books for examination and were immediately thrown out of the League. John McKenna, the League president, said: 'We will have no nonsense. The football stables must be cleansed.' Port Vale took over their fixtures. Herbert Chapman, who later led Huddersfield and Arsenal to outstanding success, was Leeds City's manager from 1912 – but he was manager of a munitions factory during the war and, although he was suspended for a short period, he may have been unaware of the full facts. A plan to move Huddersfield to Elland Road narrowly failed and a new club was formed . . . Leeds United.

THE FOOTBALL LEAGUE.

President:
J. J. BENTLEY

Programme of Music
AT THE
Commemoration
BANQUET.
IN THE
Venetian Chamber,
Holborn Restaurant,
ON
Tuesday, June 8th, 1909.

. . . ARTISTES . . .

Miss ROSA DALLOW — Miss MAY PETERS
Mr. HERBERT EMLYN — Mr. PETER DAWSON
Solo Violin ... ... Miss MARY LAW.
Recitation ... ... Mr. H. G. NORRIS.
At the Piano, Mr. DAVID RICHARDS.

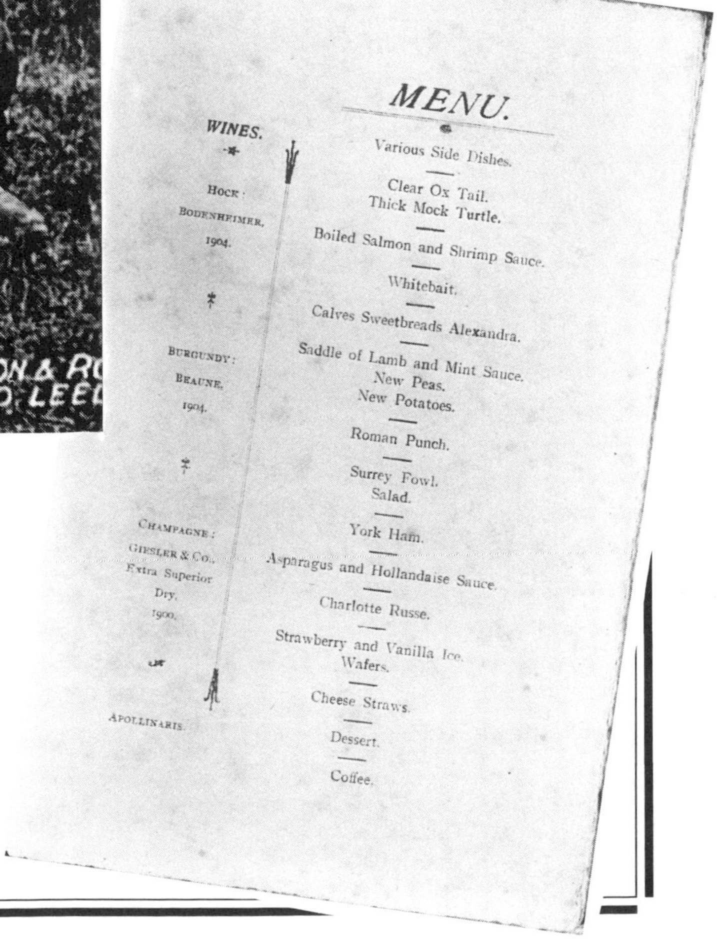

MENU.

WINES.

Hock: Bodenheimer, 1904.

Burgundy: Beaune, 1904.

Champagne: Giesler & Co., Extra Superior Dry, 1900.

Apollinaris.

Various Side Dishes.

Clear Ox Tail.
Thick Mock Turtle.

Boiled Salmon and Shrimp Sauce.

Whitebait.

Calves Sweetbreads Alexandra.

Saddle of Lamb and Mint Sauce.
New Peas.
New Potatoes.

Roman Punch.

Surrey Fowl.
Salad.

York Ham.

Asparagus and Hollandaise Sauce.

Charlotte Russe.

Strawberry and Vanilla Ice.
Wafers.

Cheese Straws.

Dessert.

Coffee.

right The Football League comes of age. Commemorative 'programme' and menu, Holborn restaurant, 8 June 1909.

LEAGUE TABLES

1901–2

FIRST DIVISION

		P	W	D	L	F	A	Pts
1	Sunderland	34	19	6	9	50	35	44
2	Everton	34	17	7	10	53	35	41
3	Newcastle	34	14	9	11	48	34	37
4	Blackburn	34	15	6	13	52	48	36
5	Nottm Forest	34	13	9	12	43	43	35
6	Derby	34	13	9	12	39	41	35
7	Bury	34	13	8	13	44	38	34
8	Aston Villa	34	13	8	13	42	40	34
9	Wednesday	34	13	8	13	48	52	34
10	Sheff United	34	13	7	14	53	48	33
11	Liverpool	34	10	12	12	42	38	32
12	Bolton	34	12	8	14	51	56	32
13	Notts County	34	14	4	16	51	57	32
14	Wolves	34	13	6	15	46	57	32
15	Grimsby	34	13	6	15	44	60	32
16	Stoke	34	11	9	14	45	55	31
17	Small Heath	34	11	8	15	47	45	30
18	Man City	34	11	6	17	42	58	28

SECOND DIVISION

		P	W	D	L	F	A	Pts
1	WBA	34	25	5	4	82	29	55
2	Middlesbrough	34	23	5	6	90	24	51
3	Preston NE	34	18	6	10	71	32	42
4	Woolwich A	34	18	6	10	50	26	42
5	Lincoln	34	14	13	7	45	35	41
6	Bristol City	34	17	6	11	52	35	40
7	Doncaster	34	13	8	13	49	58	34
8	Glossop NE	34	10	12	12	36	40	32
9	Burnley	34	10	10	14	41	45	30
10	Burton United	34	11	8	15	46	54	30
11	Barnsley	34	12	6	16	51	63	30
12	Burslem PV	34	10	9	15	43	59	29
13	Blackpool	34	11	7	16	40	56	29
14	Leicester Fosse	34	12	5	17	38	56	29
15	Newton Heath	34	11	6	17	38	53	28
16	Chesterfield	34	11	6	17	47	68	28
17	Stockport	34	8	7	19	36	72	23
18	Gainsborough	34	4	11	19	30	80	19

1902–3

FIRST DIVISION

		P	W	D	L	F	A	Pts
1	Wednesday	34	19	4	11	54	36	42
2	Aston Villa	34	19	3	12	61	40	41
3	Sunderland	34	16	9	9	51	36	41
4	Sheff United	34	17	5	12	58	44	39
5	Liverpool	34	17	4	13	68	49	38
6	Stoke	34	15	7	12	46	38	37
7	WBA	34	16	4	14	54	53	36
8	Bury	34	16	3	15	54	43	35
9	Derby	34	16	3	15	50	47	35
10	Nottm Forest	34	14	7	13	49	47	35
11	Wolves	34	14	5	15	48	57	33
12	Everton	34	13	6	15	45	47	32
13	Middlesbrough	34	14	4	16	41	50	32
14	Newcastle	34	14	4	16	41	51	32
15	Notts County	34	12	7	15	41	49	31
16	Blackburn	34	12	5	17	44	63	29
17	Grimsby	34	8	9	17	43	62	25
18	Bolton	34	8	3	23	37	73	19

SECOND DIVISION

		P	W	D	L	F	A	Pts
1	Man City	34	25	4	5	95	29	54
2	Small Heath	34	24	3	7	74	36	51
3	Woolwich A	34	20	8	6	66	30	48
4	Bristol City	34	17	8	9	59	38	42
5	Man United	34	15	8	11	53	38	38
6	Chesterfield	34	14	9	11	67	40	37
7	Preston	34	13	10	11	56	40	36
8	Barnsley	34	13	8	13	55	51	34
9	Burslem PV	34	13	8	13	57	62	34
10	Lincoln	34	12	6	16	46	53	30
11	Glossop NE	34	11	7	16	43	58	29
12	Gainsborough	34	11	7	16	41	59	29
13	Burton United	34	11	7	16	39	59	29
14	Blackpool	34	9	10	15	44	59	28
15	Leicester Fosse	34	10	8	16	41	65	28
16	Doncaster	34	9	7	18	35	72	25
17	Stockport	34	7	6	21	39	74	20
18	Burnley	34	6	8	20	30	77	20

1903–4

FIRST DIVISION

		P	W	D	L	F	A	Pts
1	Wednesday	34	20	7	7	48	28	47
2	Man City	34	19	6	9	71	45	44
3	Everton	34	19	5	10	59	32	43
4	Newcastle	34	18	6	10	58	45	42
5	Aston Villa	34	17	7	10	70	48	41
6	Sunderland	34	17	5	12	63	49	39
7	Sheff United	34	15	8	11	62	57	38
8	Wolves	34	14	8	12	44	66	36
9	Nottm Forest	34	11	9	14	57	57	31
10	Middlesbrough	34	9	12	13	46	47	30
11	Small Heath	34	11	8	15	39	52	30
12	Bury	34	7	15	12	40	53	29
13	Notts County	34	12	5	17	37	61	29
14	Derby	34	9	10	15	58	60	28
15	Blackburn	34	11	6	17	48	60	28
16	Stoke	34	10	7	17	54	57	27
17	Liverpool	34	9	8	17	49	62	26
18	WBA	34	7	10	17	36	60	24

SECOND DIVISION

		P	W	D	L	F	A	Pts
1	Preston	34	20	10	4	62	24	50
2	Woolwich A	34	21	7	6	91	22	49
3	Man United	34	20	8	6	65	33	48
4	Bristol City	34	18	6	10	73	41	42
5	Burnley	34	15	9	10	50	55	39
6	Grimsby	34	14	8	12	50	49	36
7	Bolton	34	12	10	12	59	41	34
8	Barnsley	34	11	10	13	38	57	32
9	Gainsborough	34	14	3	17	53	60	31
10	Bradford City	34	12	7	15	45	59	31
11	Chesterfield	34	11	8	15	37	45	30
12	Lincoln	34	11	8	15	41	58	30
13	Burslem PV	34	10	9	15	54	52	29
14	Burton United	34	11	7	16	45	61	29
15	Blackpool	34	11	5	18	40	67	27
16	Stockport	34	8	11	15	40	72	27
17	Glossop NE	34	10	6	18	57	64	26
18	Leicester Fosse	34	6	10	18	42	82	22

1904–5

FIRST DIVISION

		P	W	D	L	F	A	Pts
1	Newcastle	34	23	2	9	72	33	48
2	Everton	34	21	5	8	63	36	47
3	Man City	34	20	6	8	66	37	46
4	Aston Villa	34	19	4	11	63	43	42
5	Sunderland	34	16	8	10	60	44	40
6	Sheff United	34	19	2	13	64	56	40
7	Small Heath	34	17	5	12	54	38	39
8	Preston	34	13	10	11	42	37	36
9	Wednesday	34	14	5	15	61	57	33
10	Woolwich A	34	12	9	13	36	40	33
11	Derby	34	12	8	14	37	48	32
12	Stoke	34	13	4	17	40	58	30
13	Blackburn	34	11	5	18	40	51	27
14	Wolves	34	11	4	19	47	73	26
15	Middlesbrough	34	9	8	17	36	56	26
16	Nottm Forest	34	9	7	18	40	61	25
17	Bury	34	10	4	20	47	67	24
18	Notts County	34	5	8	21	36	69	18

SECOND DIVISION

		P	W	D	L	F	A	Pts
1	Liverpool	34	27	4	3	93	25	58
2	Bolton	34	27	2	5	87	32	56
3	Man United	34	24	5	5	81	30	53
4	Bristol City	34	19	4	11	66	45	42
5	Chesterfield	34	14	11	9	44	35	39
6	Gainsborough	34	14	8	12	61	58	36
7	Barnsley	34	14	5	15	38	56	33
8	Bradford City	34	12	8	14	45	49	32
9	Lincoln	34	12	7	15	42	40	31
10	WBA	34	13	4	17	56	48	30
11	Burnley	34	12	6	16	43	52	30
12	Glossop NE	34	10	10	14	37	46	30
13	Grimsby	34	11	8	15	33	46	30
14	Leicester Fosse	34	11	7	16	40	55	29
15	Blackpool	34	9	10	15	36	48	28
16	Burslem PV	34	10	7	17	47	72	27
17	Burton United	34	8	4	22	30	84	20
18	Doncaster	34	3	2	29	23	81	8

1905–6

FIRST DIVISION

		P	W	D	L	F	A	Pts
1	Liverpool	38	23	5	10	79	46	51
2	Preston NE	38	17	13	8	54	39	47
3	Wednesday	38	18	8	12	63	52	44
4	Newcastle	38	18	7	13	74	48	43
5	Man City	38	19	5	14	73	54	43
6	Bolton	38	17	7	14	81	67	41
7	Birmingham	38	17	7	14	65	59	41
8	Aston Villa	38	17	6	15	72	56	40
9	Blackburn	38	16	8	14	54	52	40
10	Stoke	38	16	7	15	54	55	39
11	Everton	38	15	7	16	70	66	37
12	Woolwich A	38	15	7	16	62	64	37
13	Sheff United	38	15	6	17	57	62	36
14	Sunderland	38	15	5	18	61	70	35
15	Derby	38	14	7	17	39	58	35
16	Notts County	38	11	12	15	55	71	34
17	Bury	38	11	10	17	57	74	32
18	Middlesbrough	38	10	11	17	56	71	31
19	Nottm Forest	38	13	5	20	58	79	31
20	Wolves	38	8	7	23	58	99	23

SECOND DIVISION

		P	W	D	L	F	A	Pts
1	Bristol City	38	30	6	2	83	28	66
2	Man United	38	28	6	4	90	28	62
3	Chelsea	38	22	9	7	90	37	53
4	WBA	38	22	8	8	79	36	52
5	Hull	38	19	6	13	67	54	44
6	Leeds City	38	17	9	12	59	47	43
7	Leicester Fosse	38	15	12	11	53	48	42
8	Grimsby	38	15	10	13	46	46	40
9	Burnley	38	15	8	15	42	53	38
10	Stockport	38	13	9	16	44	56	35
11	Bradford City	38	13	8	17	46	60	34
12	Barnsley	38	12	9	17	60	62	33
13	Lincoln	38	12	6	20	69	72	30
14	Blackpool	38	10	9	19	37	62	29
15	Gainsborough	38	12	4	22	44	57	28
16	Glossop NE	38	10	8	20	49	71	28
17	Burslem PV	38	12	4	22	49	82	28
18	Chesterfield	38	10	8	20	40	72	28
19	Burton United	38	10	6	22	34	67	26
20	Clapton Orient	38	7	7	24	35	78	21

1906–7

FIRST DIVISION

		P	W	D	L	F	A	Pts
1	Newcastle	38	22	7	9	74	46	51
2	Bristol City	38	20	8	10	66	47	48
3	Everton	38	20	5	13	70	46	45
4	Sheff United	38	17	11	10	57	55	45
5	Aston Villa	38	19	6	13	78	52	44
6	Bolton	38	18	8	12	59	47	44
7	Woolwich A	38	20	4	14	66	59	44
8	Man United	38	17	8	13	53	56	42
9	Birmingham	38	15	8	15	52	52	38
10	Sunderland	38	14	9	15	65	66	37
11	Middlesbrough	38	15	6	17	56	63	36
12	Blackburn	38	14	7	17	56	59	35
13	Wednesday	38	12	11	15	49	60	35
14	Preston	38	14	7	17	44	57	35
15	Liverpool	38	13	7	18	64	65	33
16	Bury	38	13	6	19	58	68	32
17	Man City	38	10	12	16	53	77	32
18	Notts County	38	8	15	15	46	50	31
19	Derby	38	9	9	20	41	59	27
20	Stoke	38	8	10	20	41	64	26

SECOND DIVISION

		P	W	D	L	F	A	Pts
1	Nottm Forest	38	28	4	6	74	36	60
2	Chelsea	38	26	5	7	80	34	57
3	Leicester Fosse	38	20	8	10	62	39	48
4	WBA	38	21	5	12	83	45	47
5	Bradford City	38	21	5	12	70	53	47
6	Wolves	38	17	7	14	66	53	41
7	Burnley	38	17	6	15	62	47	40
8	Barnsley	38	15	8	15	73	55	38
9	Hull	38	15	7	16	65	57	37
10	Leeds City	38	13	10	15	55	63	36
11	Grimsby	38	16	3	19	57	62	35
12	Stockport	38	12	11	15	42	52	35
13	Blackpool	38	11	11	16	33	51	33
14	Gainsborough	38	14	5	19	45	72	33
15	Glossop NE	38	13	6	19	53	79	32
16	Burslem PV	38	12	7	19	60	83	31
17	Clapton Orient	38	11	8	19	45	67	30
18	Chesterfield	38	11	7	20	50	66	29
19	Lincoln	38	12	4	22	46	73	28
20	Burton United	38	8	7	23	34	68	23

1907–8

FIRST DIVISION

		P	W	D	L	F	A	Pts
1	Man United	38	23	6	9	81	48	52
2	Aston Villa	38	17	9	12	77	59	43
3	Man City	38	16	11	11	62	54	43
4	Newcastle	38	15	12	11	65	54	42
5	Wednesday	38	19	4	15	73	64	42
6	Middlesbrough	38	17	7	14	54	45	41
7	Bury	38	14	11	13	58	61	39
8	Liverpool	38	16	6	16	68	61	38
9	Nottm Forest	38	13	11	14	59	62	37
10	Bristol City	38	12	12	14	58	61	36
11	Everton	38	15	6	17	58	64	36
12	Preston	38	12	12	14	47	53	36
13	Chelsea	38	14	8	16	53	62	36
14	Blackburn*	38	12	12	14	51	63	36
15	Woolwich A*	38	12	12	14	51	63	36
16	Sunderland	38	16	3	19	78	75	35
17	Sheff United	38	12	11	15	52	58	35
18	Notts County	38	13	8	17	39	51	34
19	Bolton	38	14	5	19	52	58	33
20	Birmingham	38	9	12	17	40	60	30

*equal

SECOND DIVISION

		P	W		L	F	A	Pts
1	Bradford City	38	24	6	8	90	42	54
2	Leicester Fosse	38	21	10	7	72	47	52
3	Oldham	38	22	6	10	76	42	50
4	Fulham	38	22	5	11	82	49	49
5	WBA	38	19	9	10	61	39	47
6	Derby	38	21	4	13	77	45	46
7	Burnley	38	20	6	12	67	50	46
8	Hull	38	21	4	13	73	62	46
9	Wolves	38	15	7	16	50	45	37
10	Stoke	38	16	5	17	57	52	37
11	Gainsborough	38	14	7	17	47	71	35
12	Leeds City	38	12	8	18	53	65	32
13	Stockport	38	12	8	18	48	67	32
14	Clapton Orient	38	11	10	17	40	65	32
15	Blackpool	38	11	9	18	51	58	31
16	Barnsley	38	12	6	20	54	68	30
17	Glossop NE	38	11	8	19	54	74	30
18	Grimsby	38	11	8	19	43	71	30
19	Chesterfield	38	6	11	21	46	92	23
20	Lincoln	38	9	3	26	46	83	21

1908–9

FIRST DIVISION

		P	W	D	L	F	A	Pts
1	Newcastle	38	24	5	9	65	41	53
2	Everton	38	18	10	10	82	57	46
3	Sunderland	38	21	2	15	78	63	44
4	Blackburn	38	14	13	11	61	50	41
5	Wednesday	38	17	6	15	67	61	40
6	Woolwich A	38	14	10	14	52	49	38
7	Aston Villa	38	14	10	14	58	56	38
8	Bristol City	38	13	12	13	45	58	38
9	Middlesbrough	38	14	9	15	59	53	37
10	Preston	38	13	11	14	48	44	37
11	Chelsea	38	14	9	15	56	61	37
12	Sheff United	38	14	9	15	51	59	37
13	Man United	38	15	7	16	58	68	37
14	Nottm Forest	38	14	8	16	66	57	36
15	Notts County	38	14	8	16	51	48	36
16	Liverpool	38	15	6	17	57	65	36
17	Bury	38	14	8	16	63	77	36
18	Bradford City	38	12	10	16	47	47	34
19	Man City	38	15	4	19	67	69	34
20	Leicester Fosse	38	8	9	21	54	102	25

SECOND DIVISION

		P	W	D	L	F	A	Pts
1	Bolton	38	24	4	10	59	28	52
2	Tottenham	38	20	11	7	67	32	51
3	WBA	38	19	13	6	56	27	51
4	Hull	38	19	6	13	63	39	44
5	Derby	38	16	11	11	55	41	43
6	Oldham	38	17	6	15	55	43	40
7	Wolves	38	14	11	13	56	48	39
8	Glossop NE	38	15	8	15	57	53	38
9	Gainsborough	38	15	8	15	49	70	38
10	Fulham	38	13	11	14	58	48	37
11	Birmingham	38	14	9	15	58	61	37
12	Leeds City	38	14	7	17	43	53	35
13	Grimsby	38	14	7	17	41	54	35
14	Burnley	38	13	7	18	51	58	33
15	Clapton Orient	38	12	9	17	37	49	33
16	Bradford PA	38	13	6	19	51	59	32
17	Barnsley	38	11	10	17	48	57	32
18	Stockport	38	14	3	21	39	71	31
19	Chesterfield	38	11	8	19	37	67	30
20	Blackpool	38	9	11	18	46	68	29

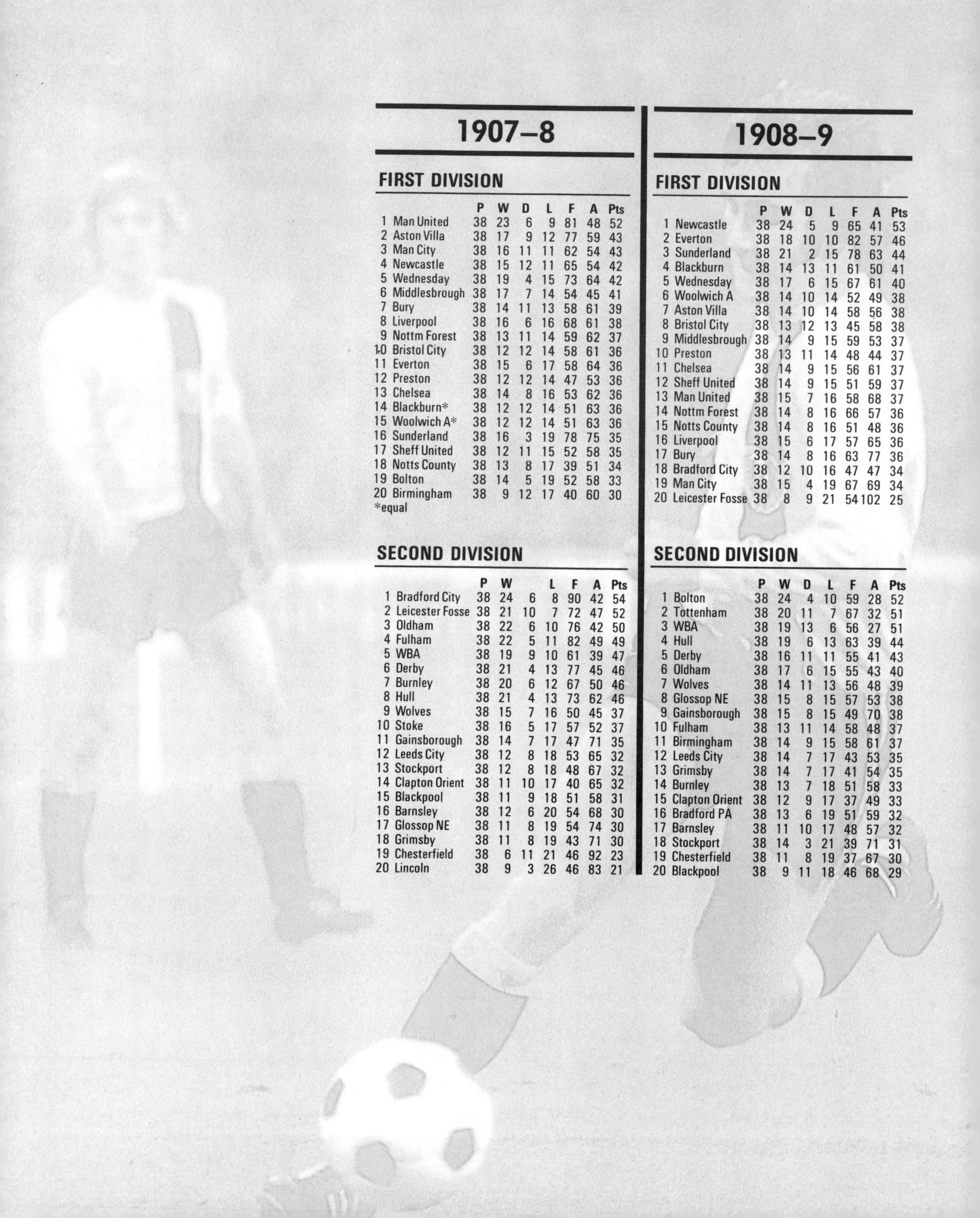

1909–10

FIRST DIVISION

		P	W	D	L	F	A	Pts
1	Aston Villa	38	23	7	8	84	42	53
2	Liverpool	38	21	6	11	78	57	48
3	Blackburn	38	18	9	11	73	55	45
4	Newcastle	38	19	7	12	70	56	45
5	Man United	38	19	7	12	69	61	45
6	Sheff United	38	16	10	12	62	41	42
7	Bradford City	38	17	8	13	64	47	42
8	Sunderland	38	18	5	15	66	51	41
9	Notts County	38	15	10	13	67	59	40
10	Everton	38	16	8	14	51	56	40
11	Wednesday	38	15	9	14	60	63	39
12	Preston	38	15	5	18	52	58	35
13	Bury	38	12	9	17	62	66	33
14	Nottm Forest	38	11	11	16	54	72	33
15	Tottenham	38	11	10	17	53	69	32
16	Bristol City	38	12	8	18	45	60	32
17	Middlesbrough	38	11	9	18	56	73	31
18	Woolwich A	38	11	9	18	37	67	31
19	Chelsea	38	11	7	20	47	70	29
20	Bolton	38	9	6	23	44	71	24

SECOND DIVISION

		P	W	D	L	F	A	Pts
1	Man City	38	23	8	7	81	40	54
2	Oldham	38	23	7	8	79	39	53
3	Hull City	38	23	7	8	80	46	53
4	Derby	38	22	9	7	72	47	53
5	Leicester Fosse	38	20	4	14	79	58	44
6	Glossop NE	38	18	7	13	64	57	43
7	Fulham	38	14	13	11	51	43	41
8	Wolves	38	17	6	15	64	63	40
9	Barnsley	38	16	7	15	62	59	39
10	Bradford PA	38	17	4	17	64	59	38
11	WBA	38	16	5	17	58	56	37
12	Blackpool	38	14	8	16	50	52	36
13	Stockport	38	13	8	17	50	47	34
14	Burnley	38	14	6	18	62	61	34
15	Lincoln	38	10	11	17	42	69	31
16	Clapton Orient	38	12	6	20	37	60	30
17	Leeds City	38	10	7	21	46	80	27
18	Gainsborough	38	10	6	22	33	75	26
19	Grimsby	38	9	6	23	50	77	24
20	Birmingham	38	8	7	23	42	78	23

1910–11

FIRST DIVISION

		P	W	D	L	F	A	Pts
1	Man United	38	22	8	8	72	40	52
2	Aston Villa	38	22	7	9	69	41	51
3	Sunderland	38	15	15	8	67	48	45
4	Everton	38	19	7	12	50	36	45
5	Bradford City	38	20	5	13	51	42	45
6	Wednesday	38	17	8	13	47	48	42
7	Oldham	38	16	9	13	44	41	41
8	Newcastle	38	15	10	13	61	43	40
9	Sheff United	38	15	8	15	49	43	38
10	Woolwich A	38	13	12	13	41	49	38
11	Notts County	38	14	10	14	37	45	38
12	Blackburn	38	13	11	14	62	54	37
13	Liverpool	38	15	7	16	53	53	37
14	Preston	38	12	11	15	40	49	35
15	Tottenham	38	13	6	19	52	63	32
16	Middlesbrough	38	11	10	17	49	63	32
17	Man City	38	9	13	16	43	58	31
18	Bury	38	9	11	18	43	71	29
19	Bristol City	38	11	5	22	43	66	27
20	Nottm Forest	38	9	7	22	55	75	25

SECOND DIVISION

		P	W	D	L	F	A	Pts
1	WBA	38	22	9	7	67	41	53
2	Bolton	38	21	9	8	69	40	51
3	Chelsea	38	20	9	9	71	35	49
4	Clapton Orient	38	19	7	12	44	35	45
5	Hull	38	14	16	8	55	39	44
6	Derby	38	17	8	13	73	52	42
7	Blackpool	38	16	10	12	49	38	42
8	Burnley	38	13	15	10	45	45	41
9	Wolves	38	15	8	15	51	52	38
10	Fulham	38	15	7	16	52	48	37
11	Leeds City	38	15	7	16	58	56	37
12	Bradford PA	38	14	9	15	53	55	37
13	Huddersfield	38	13	8	17	57	58	34
14	Glossop NE	38	13	8	17	48	62	34
15	Leicester Fosse	38	14	5	19	52	62	33
16	Birmingham	38	12	8	18	42	64	32
17	Stockport	38	11	8	19	47	79	30
18	Gainsborough	38	9	11	18	37	55	29
19	Barnsley	38	7	14	17	52	62	28
20	Lincoln	38	7	10	21	28	72	24

THREE
North Stars
1911–1915

'How glibly some people talk about football slavery! But how many of them would walk up to the members of a League team and tell them they are slaves? No, my friends, I'm not a slave. League football is the game of the people and it's not the slightest use a club relying wholly upon its local talent. The interest in the game would soon cease; and instead of huge flourishing concerns paying limit wages we should have the majority of clubs on the verge of bankruptcy.'

Albert Iremonger, *6 ft 5 ins Notts County goalkeeper, the tallest player of his time, writing in Leng's Football Handbook 1913–14.*

This was a little golden age of football. There were nearly 13,000 clubs and half a million players in England; and, at the top of the pyramid, the forty clubs of the Football League set a glossy example. The spirit of the game was strong and play was artistic and open.

No one was to know that soon the Great War would blanket Europe, Lord Kitchener would point his finger at the nation's young men and that for four years the art of kicking a ball for pay and pleasure would give way to the defence of freedom.

There was still time, however, for the north to emphasize its superiority. The last five championships before the war were won by Manchester United, Blackburn Rovers (twice), Sunderland and Everton – the first time that Blackburn, one of the League's original dozen clubs, had won the title.

Manchester United had a new address by now. They left their smokey old ground at Clayton without regret and moved to Old Trafford – a stately stadium that cost £60,000 and was the envy of football. It had a main stand with cushioned tip-up seats, towering terraces, broad gangways and regal dressing and bathing facilities for the players.

Old Trafford offered a glimpse of the future and United immediately responded by winning the championship in 1911. Billy Meredith and Charlie Roberts were still the cornerstones of the side, but the goals of Enoch 'Knocker' West, who had joined United from Nottingham Forest, were also hugely significant. 'Knocker' was a bull at large, a force of nature and no one enjoyed himself more when United, with a sense of style, celebrated their championship with a day at Chester races. But West was later banned for life for his part in a betting scandal – and United did not win the title again for 41 years.

Blackburn Rovers, too, will look back on this little period before the Great War with rare affection. They won the championship in 1912 and 1914 . . . their first and last titles. They were a resilient side that rarely had a poor day; and their main pillar and inspiration was a rock of man called Bob Crompton.

Crompton *was* Blackburn. He was born there, went to school there while Rovers were winning the FA Cup three years in succession in the mid-1880s and then, between 1896 and 1920, played 528 League games for them – and 41 more for England. He was a tall, straight man, broad-shouldered and broad-browed, who was everybody's idea of the model professional. He was a full back who was strong enough to have kicked any winger over any stand, but that was not his way. He was a marvellous craftsman, cool, perceptive and scrupulously fair. Blackburn is still proud of him.

It was Sunderland's turn for the championship again in 1913, and club historians have claimed that this was their best ever side. They also reached the final of the FA Cup in which they were beaten 1–0 by Aston Villa – the team that finished second to Sunderland in the League. Charlie Buchan, boney and angular but one of the game's finest inside-forwards, led the way with 27 League goals, and with Frank Cuggy and Jackie Mordue completed the famous 'Sunderland triangle'.

Buchan was respected as a man and as a player, a natural leader who influenced everyone around him. He was such an original thinker that some felt he was too clever by half, but when he moved to Arsenal in the later stages of his long career he formed a formidable partnership with perhaps the greatest manager of all, Herbert Chapman. But that story belongs to another decade: it was Sunderland who made Buchan and it is the people of Wearside who claim him. A year before Sunderland's championship, by the way, Buchan took a holiday in Canada. He sailed on the boat which followed the *Titanic*.

The period just before the Great War was strange and intense. The country seemed to sense that time was running out. There was social and political unrest, civil war threatened in Ireland and Mrs Pankhurst's suffragettes went to prison.

Oldham Athletic would have been champions in 1915 had they won their last game; they lost (to Liverpool) however and Everton made it by a point. But by now Germany had begun its match against the rest of the world and the decision of the football authorities to complete the 1914–15 season was not at all popular. A.F. Pollard, a historian, spoke for many in a letter to *The Times*: 'We view with indignation and alarm the persistence of Association Football clubs in doing their best for the enemy ... every club that employs a professional football player is bribing a much needed recruit to refrain from enlistment and every spectator who pays his gate money is contributing so much towards a German victory.'

In fact, League matches proved to be a useful recruiting platform. Military bands, speakers and posters were used – 'Do you want to be a Chelsea Die-Hard?' asked one poster. 'Join the 17th Battalion Middlesex Regt ... and follow the lead given by your favourite football players.'

Nearly half the country's professionals joined up quickly and by Christmas 1914 the Football Association was able to claim that football had provided more than 100,000 recruits. Gates were halved long before the end of the season.

Football's last big scene was the Cup Final between Sheffield United and Chelsea at Old Trafford – known as the Khaki Final because it was watched by so many men in uniform. Lord Derby presented the Cup to Sheffield United and his final words were inspired.

'You have played with one another and against one another for the Cup,' he said. 'It is now the duty of everyone to join with each other and play a sterner game for England.'

above Charlie Roberts – centre-half, king-pin and captain of Manchester United's first two League championship sides (1908 and 1911). Played 271 League games for United between 1904 and 1913 – and might have won more than three caps for England if he had not been so outspoken as chairman of the Players' Union. Pictured at Woolwich Arsenal's ground at Plumstead in 1912.

right Bob Crompton of Blackburn Rovers and England – outstanding full-back, model professional and great servant. He played 528 League games for Blackburn between 1896–1920 and inspired them to the League championships of 1912 and 1914. Crompton won 41 caps for England, 12 against Scotland.

above Bill McCracken of Distillery, Newcastle United and Ireland – the quick and astute right-back who is generally accepted as the man who forced the change in the offside law in 1925. Played more than 400 games for Newcastle, gained two League championship medals (1907 and 1909), won the first of his 15 caps in 1902 and the last in 1923 at the age of 40. Later managed Hull, Aldershot and Millwall and was still scouting after his ninetieth birthday.

right Tottenham before their First Division match with Everton in September 1912. Left to right: Middlemiss, Darnell, Bliss, Tattershall, Young, Collins, Lunn, Grimsdell, Lightfoot, Minter and Brittan. Arthur Grimsdell, fourth from right, one of Spurs' enduring heroes, made 316 League appearances between 1911–29 and won six caps for England. Behind him, in the picture, every spectator has a cap.

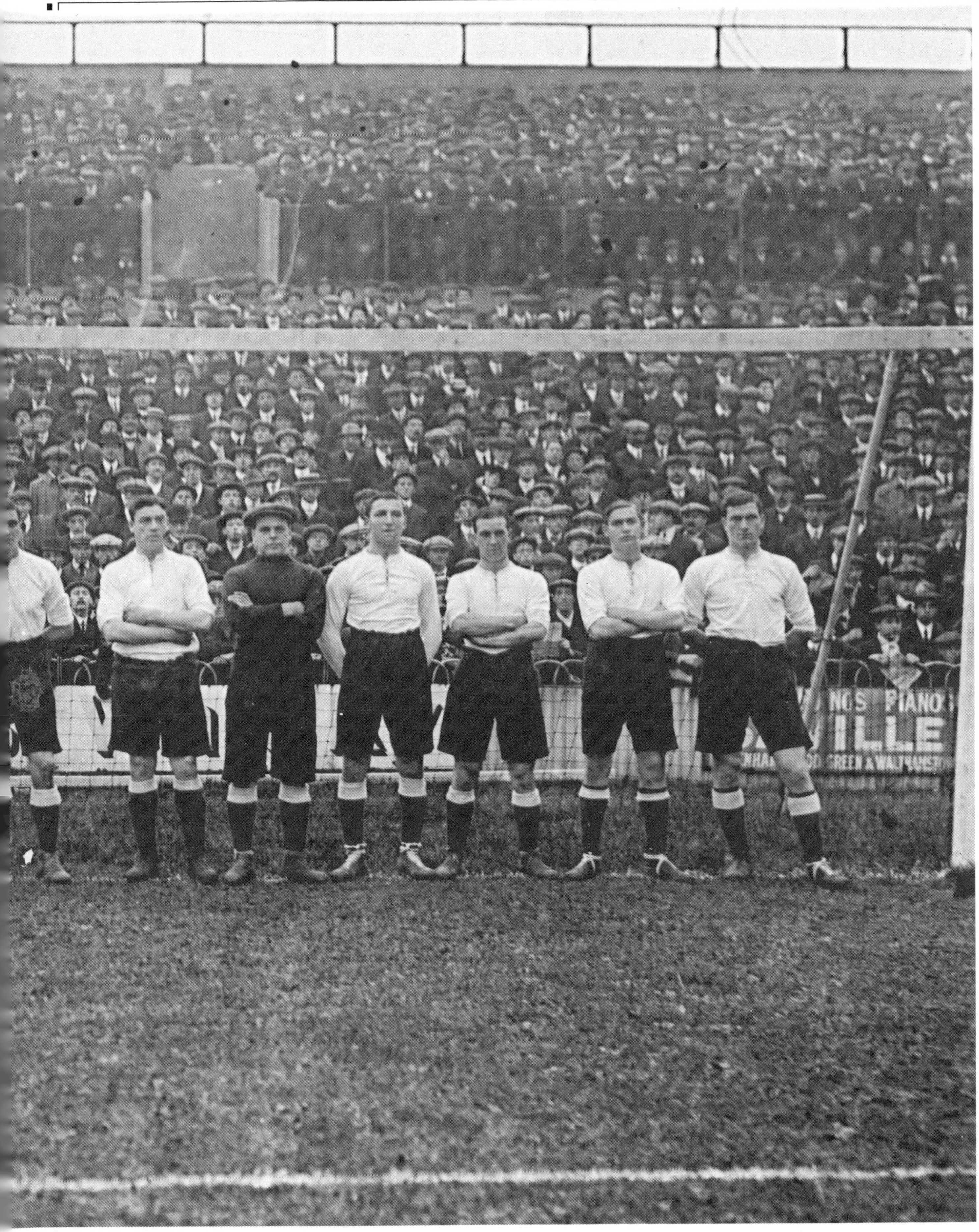

above Billy 'Fatty' Wedlock – Bristol City's greatest player. He played 413 matches for them (363 League) before retiring just before his fortieth birthday in 1920–1 and won 26 caps for England (1907–14). He helped Bristol City win promotion for the first time in 1906 and, although he was only 5 ft 4 ins tall, he was described as a half-back who was 'one of the world's wonders in getting the ball'.

left Sam Hardy who kept goal with matchless consistency for Chesterfield, Liverpool, Aston Villa, Nottingham Forest and England (21 caps) between 1903 and 1925. Made around 600 appearances for his four clubs, won a League championship medal with Liverpool (1906) and two FA Cup winners' medals with Aston Villa (1913 and 1920). He made his job look wonderfully easy.

Ask for
LAYMO
WH

above Harry Hampton – legendary Aston Villa centre-forward during the ten years before the First World War. Scored 213 goals for Villa, inspiring them to the 1910 League championship and two FA Cup Final triumphs (1905 and 1913). ''Appy 'Arry' was a forward of great dash and muscle who was loved by Villa fans – and hated by opposing goal-keepers who often found themselves charged into the net.

left A steamy day in Manchester in 1913 – and an ambulance man offers water to City fans.

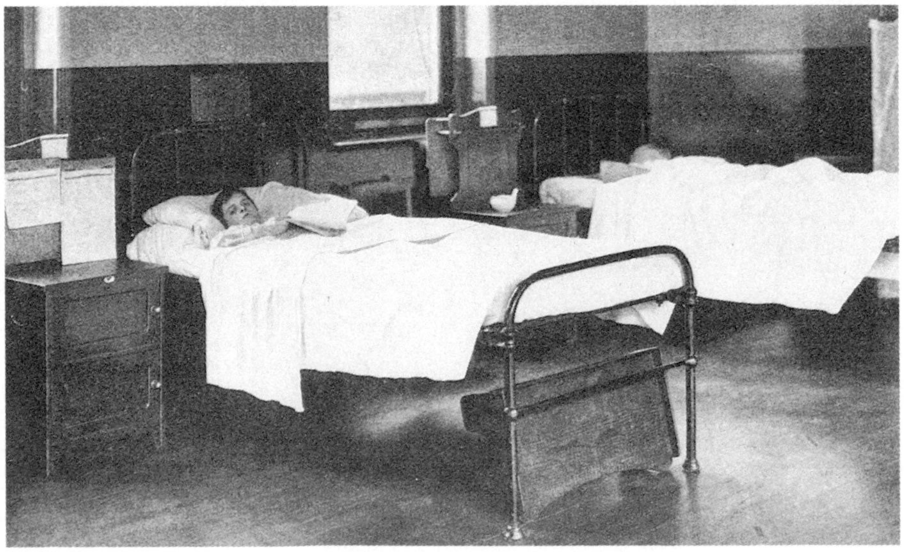

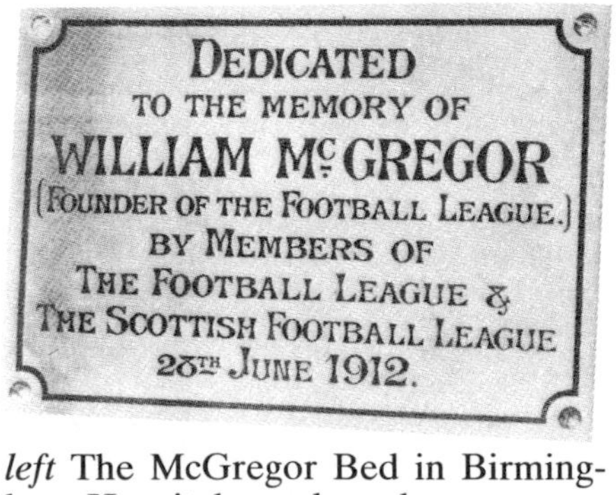
DEDICATED
TO THE MEMORY OF
WILLIAM M^C GREGOR
(FOUNDER OF THE FOOTBALL LEAGUE.)
BY MEMBERS OF
THE FOOTBALL LEAGUE &
THE SCOTTISH FOOTBALL LEAGUE
28TH JUNE 1912.

left The McGregor Bed in Birmingham Hospital – endowed as a memorial, after the League founder's death in 1911, by all the clubs of the Football League and the Scottish League.

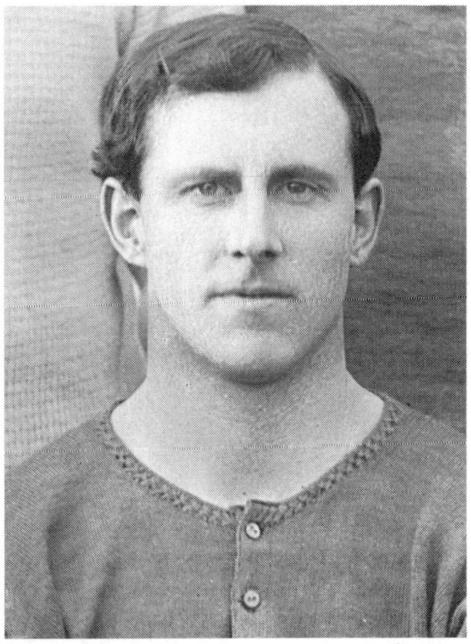

right Vivian Woodward of Tottenham, Chelsea and England – the great amateur centre-forward who would not even accept the cost of his bus fares to matches. He played in Spurs' first League match at White Hart Lane in 1908, helped them win promotion in their first season as a League club and then joined Chelsea because their ground was nearer his home. He played for Chelsea for six years (1909–15) and later became a director of the club. Made over 60 appearances for England (23 full internationals) and twice captained Great Britain's amateurs to Olympic victory (1908 and 1912). *left* Woodward (white shirt) rises high above Scotland's defence at Bramall Lane, Sheffield, in 1903. England 1 Scotland 2.

right Herbert Bamlett – one of the few referees to become League club managers. Bamlett is pictured in 1914 at the age of 32 when he became the youngest referee to control an FA Cup final (Burnley 1 Liverpool 0 at Crystal Palace). Soon afterwards he became manager of Oldham, but left Boundary Park in season 1919–20 to take charge of Wigan Borough. He moved to Middlesbrough in 1923 – where he discovered many outstanding players, including George Camsell – and then became manager of Manchester United in April 1927. He was a kind, knowledgeable man but United went through a bad spell (they lost twelve matches in succession at the start of the 1930–31 season) and 3,000 fans attended a meeting at Hulme Town Hall to express dissatisfaction. Bamlett resigned, after four years at Old Trafford, in April 1931. He was born in Gateshead-on-Tyne in March 1882 and died suddenly in October 1941.

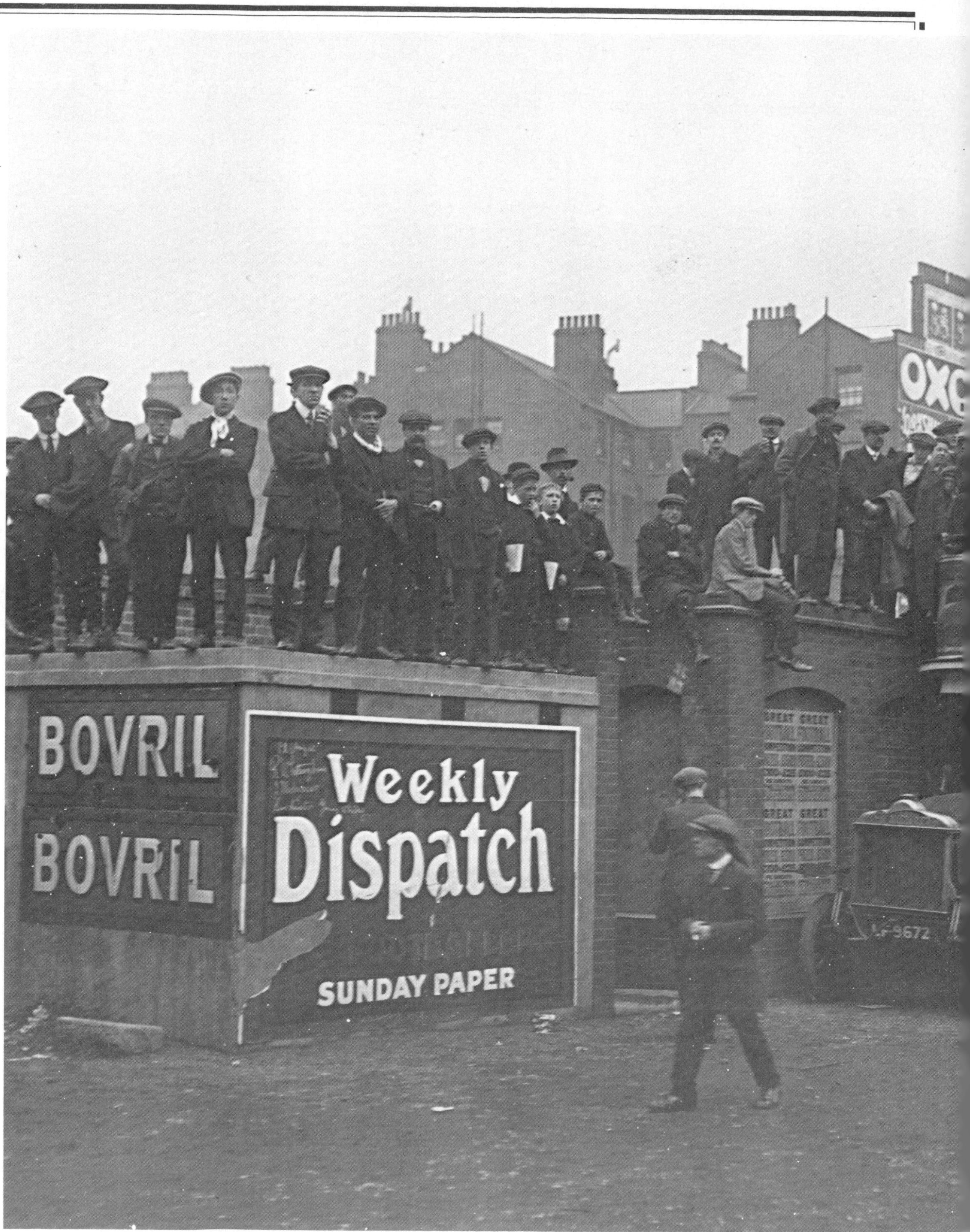
BOVRIL
BOVRIL
Weekly
Dispatch
SUNDAY PAPER
OXO

Room with a view at Stamford Bridge 1913: Chelsea v Spurs. Caps, trilbies and even a boater.

FOOTBALL OFFICIAL PROGRAMME

EVERTON

LIVERPOOL

VOL. 12—No. 27. REGISTERED. SATURDAY, FEBRUARY 13th, 1915. PRICE ONE PENNY.

Threlfall's Brewery Company

LIMITED

ASK FOR

"Blue Lab

On Draught or in Bottl

A Delightful Beer

ALSO

Their Extra Bottled Salford

IN FINE CONDITION

Joint enterprise: Liverpool and Everton joint programme, Saturday 13 February 1915. The only clubs to share a programme.

BEVINGTON HOUSE HOTEL for WORKING MEN, 6d. per Night, BEVINGTON BUSH.

Our Visitors.

CORNS CURED

QUALIFIED CHIROPODIST AND BOOT MAKER

T. SAYLE, 104 TUNNEL RD

R. NEILL, Gentlemen's Headwear Artist, High-Grade Goods at Moderate Prices. 20, Gt. Charlotte St.

Palais de Luxe Cinema, LIME STREET, LIVERPOOL.

The Most Famous Picture Theatre in the Kingdom

CRÊME DE LA CRÊME

THE WORLD'S GREATEST PICTURES

THE PICTURE HOUSE, Lime Street, Liverpool.

FINEST PICTURE THEATRE in the Kingdom.

CONTINUOUS PROGRAMME.

CREEDON'S, 10 ELLIOT ST., 211 LONDON ROAD, & 8 RICHMOND ST.

Unequalled for WINES, SPIRITS AND CIGARS.

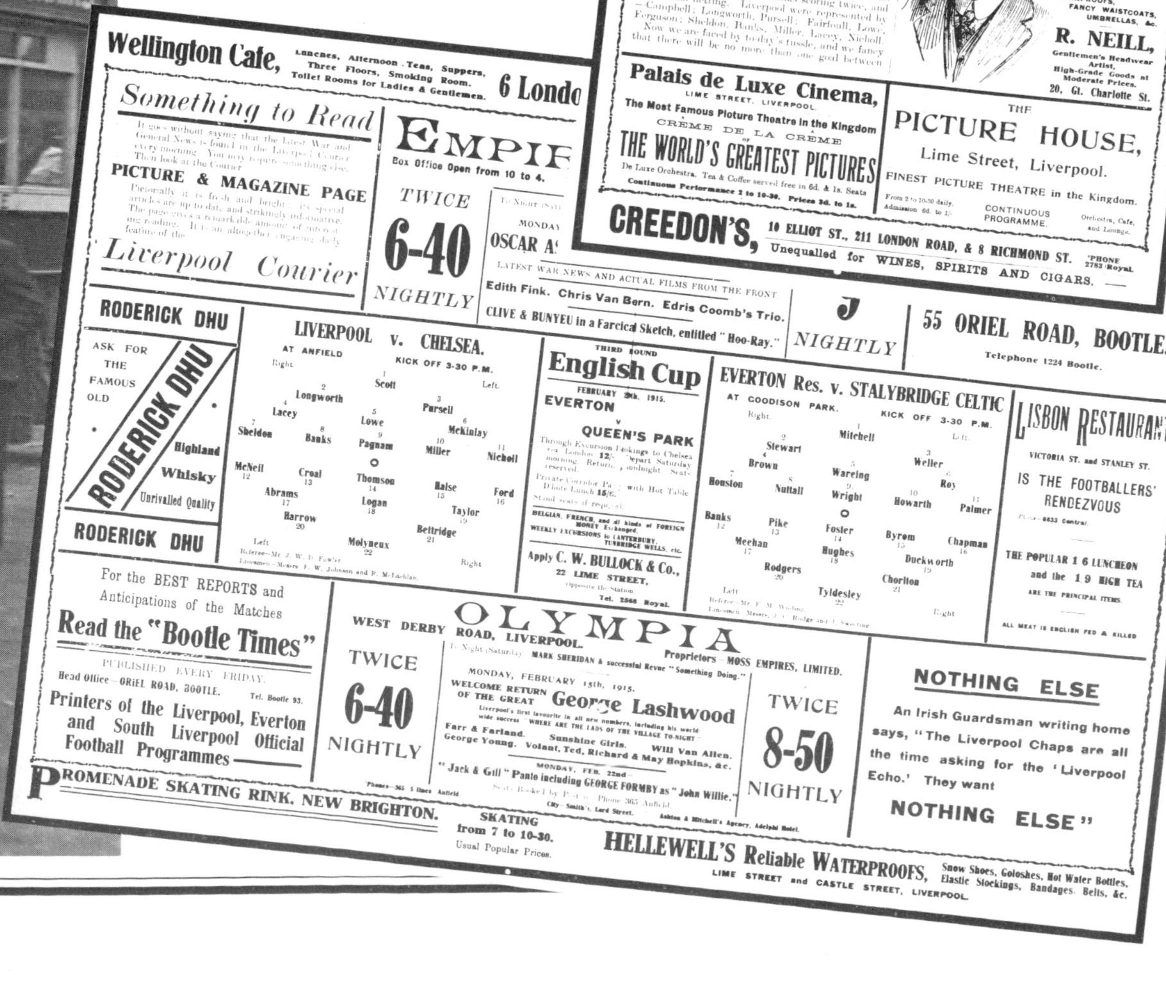
Wellington Cafe, Luncheons, Afternoon Teas, Suppers, Three Floors, Smoking Room. Toilet Rooms for Ladies & Gentlemen. 6 Londo

Something to Read

PICTURE & MAGAZINE PAGE

Liverpool Courier

EMPIR

Box Office Open from 10 to 4.

TWICE 6-40 NIGHTLY

OSCAR A

Edith Fink. Chris Van Bern. Edris Coomb's Trio.

CLIVE & BUNYEU in a Farcical Sketch, entitled "Hoo-Ray."

NIGHTLY

55 ORIEL ROAD, BOOTLE.

Telephone 1224 Bootle.

RODERICK DHU

ASK FOR THE FAMOUS OLD RODERICK DHU Highland Whisky Unrivalled Quality

RODERICK DHU

LIVERPOOL v. CHELSEA.

AT ANFIELD KICK OFF 3-30 P.M.

English Cup

EVERTON v QUEEN'S PARK

Apply C. W. BULLOCK & Co., 22 LIME STREET.

EVERTON Res. v. STALYBRIDGE CELTIC

AT GOODISON PARK. KICK OFF 3-30 P.M.

LISBON RESTAURANT

VICTORIA ST. and STANLEY ST.

IS THE FOOTBALLERS' RENDEZVOUS

THE POPULAR 1 6 LUNCHEON and the 1 9 HIGH TEA

For the BEST REPORTS and Anticipations of the Matches

Read the "Bootle Times"

PUBLISHED EVERY FRIDAY.

Printers of the Liverpool, Everton and South Liverpool Official Football Programmes

WEST DERBY ROAD, LIVERPOOL.

OLYMPIA

TWICE 6-40 NIGHTLY

MONDAY, FEBRUARY 15th, 1915.

WELCOME RETURN OF THE GREAT George Lashwood

Sunshine Girls. Will Van Allen.

TWICE 8-50 NIGHTLY

NOTHING ELSE

An Irish Guardsman writing home says, "The Liverpool Chaps are all the time asking for the 'Liverpool Echo.' They want NOTHING ELSE"

PROMENADE SKATING RINK, NEW BRIGHTON.

SKATING from 7 to 10-30.

HELLEWELL'S Reliable WATERPROOFS, LIME STREET and CASTLE STREET, LIVERPOOL.

above The Football League eleven which beat the Southern League 2–1 at Stoke, October 1911. Back row (players only, l to r): Hofton (Manchester United), Duckworth (Manchester United), Iremonger (Notts County), Pennington (West Bromwich). Middle: Simpson (Blackburn Rovers), Halse (Manchester United), Roberts (Manchester United), Buck (West Bromwich), Shearman (West Bromwich). Front: Hampton (Aston Villa), Hunter (Aston Villa). The League met the Southern League on only six occasions – the League winning four, losing one. And in 1920 the Southern League became the Third Division of the League.

above Derby County Division Two Champions' medal 1911–12. Enamel on 9ct gold. The medal is inscribed 'E. Scattergood' – Ted Scattergood, a goalkeeper who scored eight goals (seven from the penalty spot) during his career with Derby and Bradford Park Avenue, 1907–25. His other goal was scored for Bradford against Clapton Orient on Boxing Day 1921 when injury forced him to give up his regular position and he scored while in the outfield.

right Tommy Boyle of Barnsley, Burnley, Wrexham and England – centre-half and captain of the Burnley side that beat Liverpool 1–0 to win the FA Cup in 1914, the first final to be watched by a reigning monarch (George V) and the last to be played at Crystal Palace. Boyle was still inspiring Burnley in 1920–1 when they had a record unbeaten run of 30 First Division games to win their first League championship. Boyle was a popular personality, a dynamic captain and was noted for his mastery in the air; and with George Halley and William Watson he completed a half-back line that was considered the finest of its time. Made 349 League appearances (1906–24) and, as an attacking centre-half, scored 47 goals.

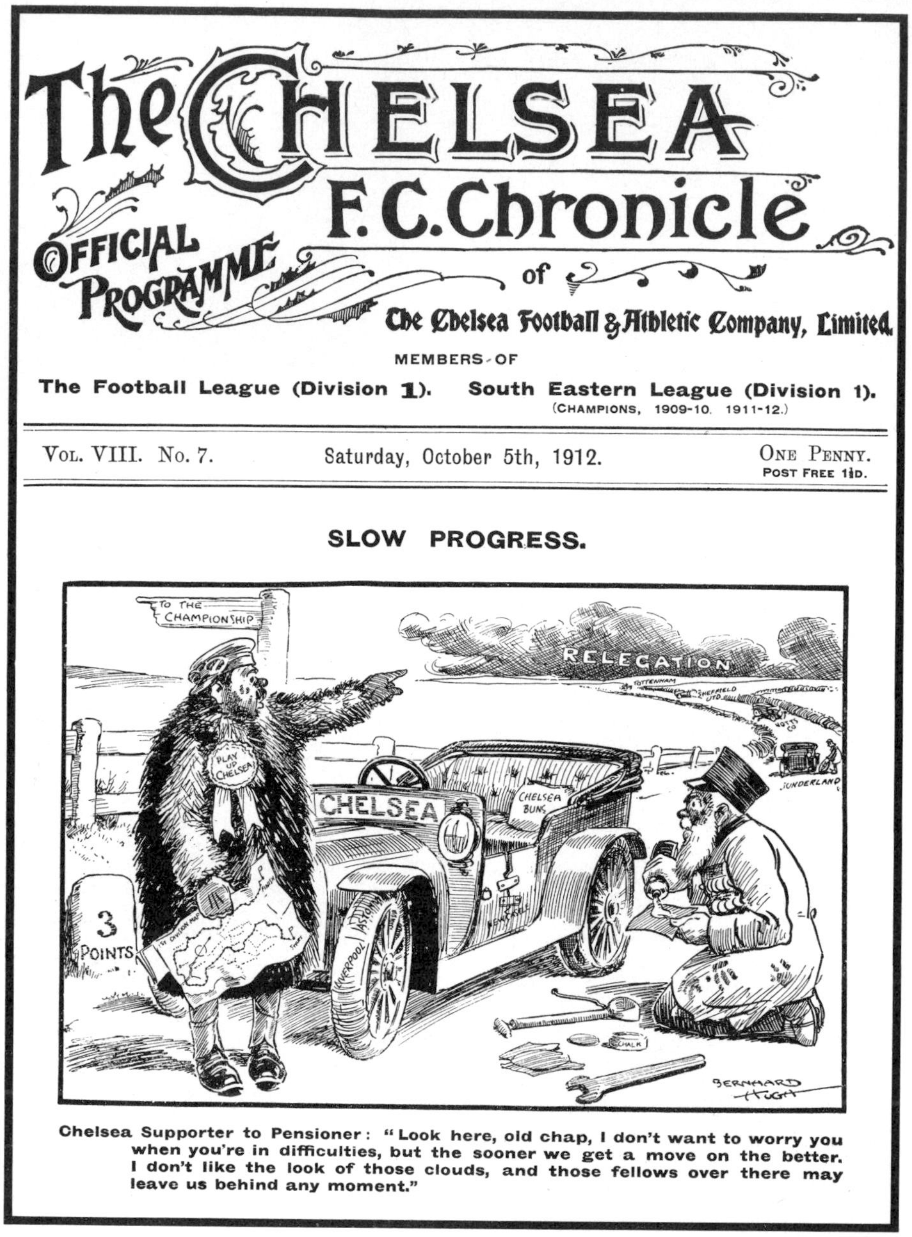

The CHELSEA F.C. Chronicle

OFFICIAL PROGRAMME of The Chelsea Football & Athletic Company, Limited.

MEMBERS OF

The Football League (Division 1). South Eastern League (Division 1).
(CHAMPIONS, 1909-10. 1911-12.)

VOL. VIII. No. 7. Saturday, October 5th, 1912. ONE PENNY. POST FREE 1½D.

SLOW PROGRESS.

Chelsea Supporter to Pensioner: "Look here, old chap, I don't want to worry you when you're in difficulties, but the sooner we get a move on the better. I don't like the look of those clouds, and those fellows over there may leave us behind any moment."

right

'On through the hail of slaughter,
Where gallant comrades fall,
Where blood is poured like water,
They drive the trickling ball.
The fear of death before them
Is but an empty name
True to the land that bore them
The Surreys play the game.'
'Touchstone', *Daily Mail*

The 8th Battalion The East Surrey Regiment attacking the Prussian Guards defending the Montauban Ridge on the Somme, 1 July 1916. Captain W.P. Nevill produced four footballs for his Company – and they dribbled and kicked them as they advanced across No Man's Land through heavy machine gun and mortar fire. Casualties were heavy – and Capt. Nevill was killed on enemy wire – but the ridge was captured. The East Surreys were awarded two DSOs, two MCs, two DCMs and one bar, and eight MMs.

above Chelsea v Sunderland, Saturday 5 October 1912.

left An ambulance car presented by the Football League during World War One.

LEAGUE TABLES

1911–12

FIRST DIVISION

		P	W	D	L	F	A	Pts
1	Blackburn	38	20	9	9	60	43	49
2	Everton	38	20	6	12	46	42	46
3	Newcastle	38	18	8	12	64	50	44
4	Bolton	38	20	3	15	54	43	43
5	Wednesday	38	16	9	13	69	49	41
6	Aston Villa	38	17	7	14	76	63	41
7	Middlesbrough	38	16	8	14	56	45	40
8	Sunderland	38	14	11	13	58	51	39
9	WBA	38	15	9	14	43	47	39
10	Woolwich A	38	15	8	15	55	59	38
11	Bradford City	38	15	8	15	46	50	38
12	Tottenham	38	14	9	15	53	53	37
13	Man United	38	13	11	14	45	60	37
14	Sheff United	38	13	10	15	63	56	36
15	Man City	38	13	9	16	56	58	35
16	Notts County	38	14	7	17	46	63	35
17	Liverpool	38	12	10	16	49	55	34
18	Oldham	38	12	10	16	46	54	34
19	Preston	38	13	7	18	40	57	33
20	Bury	38	6	9	23	32	59	21

SECOND DIVISION

		P	W	D	L	F	A	Pts
1	Derby	38	23	8	7	74	28	54
2	Chelsea	38	24	6	8	64	34	54
3	Burnley	38	22	8	8	77	41	52
4	Clapton Orient	38	21	3	14	61	44	45
5	Wolves	38	16	10	12	57	33	42
6	Barnsley	38	15	12	11	45	42	42
7	Hull	38	17	8	13	54	51	42
8	Fulham	38	16	7	15	66	58	39
9	Grimsby	38	15	9	14	48	55	39
10	Leicester Fosse	38	15	7	16	49	66	37
11	Bradford PA	38	13	9	16	44	45	35
12	Birmingham	38	14	6	18	55	59	34
13	Bristol City	38	14	6	18	41	60	34
14	Blackpool	38	13	8	17	32	52	34
15	Nottm Forest	38	13	7	18	46	48	33
16	Stockport	38	11	11	16	47	54	33
17	Huddersfield	38	13	6	19	50	64	32
18	Glossop NE	38	8	12	18	42	56	28
19	Leeds City	38	10	8	20	50	78	28
20	Gainsborough	38	5	13	20	30	64	23

1912–13

FIRST DIVISION

		P	W	D	L	F	A	Pts
1	Sunderland	38	25	4	9	86	43	54
2	Aston Villa	38	19	12	7	86	52	50
3	Wednesday	38	21	7	10	75	55	49
4	Man United	38	19	8	11	69	43	46
5	Blackburn	38	16	13	9	79	43	45
6	Man City	38	18	8	12	53	37	44
7	Derby	38	17	8	13	69	66	42
8	Bolton	38	16	10	12	62	63	42
9	Oldham	38	14	14	10	50	55	42
10	WBA	38	13	12	13	57	50	38
11	Everton	38	15	7	16	48	54	37
12	Liverpool	38	16	5	17	61	71	37
13	Bradford City	38	12	11	15	50	60	35
14	Newcastle	38	13	8	17	47	47	34
15	Sheff United	38	14	6	18	56	70	34
16	Middlesbrough	38	11	10	17	55	69	32
17	Tottenham	38	12	6	20	45	72	30
18	Chelsea	38	11	6	21	51	73	28
19	Notts County	38	7	9	22	28	56	23
20	Woolwich A	38	3	12	23	26	74	18

SECOND DIVISION

		P	W	D	L	F	A	Pts
1	Preston	38	19	15	4	56	33	53
2	Burnley	38	21	8	9	88	53	50
3	Birmingham	38	18	10	10	59	44	46
4	Barnsley	38	19	7	12	57	47	45
5	Huddersfield	38	17	9	12	66	40	43
6	Leeds City	38	15	10	13	70	64	40
7	Grimsby	38	15	10	13	51	50	40
8	Lincoln	38	15	10	13	50	52	40
9	Fulham	38	17	5	16	65	55	39
10	Wolves	38	14	10	14	56	54	38
11	Bury	38	15	8	15	53	57	38
12	Hull	38	15	6	17	60	56	36
13	Bradford PA	38	14	8	16	60	60	36
14	Clapton Orient	38	10	14	14	34	47	34
15	Leicester Fosse	38	13	7	18	50	65	33
16	Bristol City	38	9	15	14	46	72	33
17	Nottm Forest	38	12	8	18	58	59	32
18	Glossop NE	38	12	8	18	49	68	32
19	Stockport	38	8	10	20	56	78	26
20	Blackpool	38	9	8	21	39	69	26

1913–14

FIRST DIVISION

		P	W	D	L	F	A	Pts
1	Blackburn	38	20	11	7	78	42	51
2	Aston Villa	38	19	6	13	65	50	44
3	Oldham	38	17	9	12	55	45	43
4	Middlesbrough	38	19	5	14	77	60	43
5	WBA	38	15	13	10	46	42	43
6	Bolton	38	16	10	12	65	52	42
7	Sunderland	38	17	6	15	63	52	40
8	Chelsea	38	16	7	15	46	55	39
9	Bradford City	38	12	14	12	40	40	38
10	Sheff United	38	16	5	17	63	60	37
11	Newcastle	38	13	11	14	39	48	37
12	Burnley	38	12	12	14	61	53	36
13	Man City	38	14	8	16	51	53	36
14	Man United	38	15	6	17	52	62	36
15	Everton	38	12	11	15	46	55	35
16	Liverpool	38	14	7	17	46	62	35
17	Tottenham	38	12	10	16	50	62	34
18	Wednesday	38	13	8	17	53	70	34
19	Preston	38	12	6	20	52	69	30
20	Derby	38	8	11	19	55	71	27

SECOND DIVISION

		P	W	D	L	F	A	Pts
1	Notts County	38	23	7	8	77	36	53
2	Bradford PA	38	23	3	12	71	47	49
3	Arsenal	38	20	9	9	54	38	49
4	Leeds City	38	20	7	11	76	46	47
5	Barnsley	38	19	7	12	51	45	45
6	Clapton Orient	38	16	11	11	47	35	43
7	Hull	38	16	9	13	53	37	41
8	Bristol City	38	16	9	13	52	50	41
9	Wolves	38	18	5	15	51	52	41
10	Bury	38	15	10	13	39	40	40
11	Fulham	38	16	6	16	46	43	38
12	Stockport	38	13	10	15	55	57	36
13	Huddersfield	38	13	8	17	47	53	34
14	Birmingham	38	12	10	16	48	60	34
15	Grimsby	38	13	8	17	42	58	34
16	Blackpool	38	9	14	15	33	44	32
17	Glossop NE	38	11	6	21	51	67	28
18	Leicester Fosse	38	11	4	23	45	61	26
19	Lincoln	38	10	6	22	36	66	26
20	Nottm Forest	38	7	9	22	37	76	23

1914–15

FIRST DIVISION

		P	W	D	L	F	A	Pts
1	Everton	38	19	8	11	76	47	46
2	Oldham	38	17	11	10	70	56	45
3	Blackburn	38	18	7	13	83	61	43
4	Burnley	38	18	7	13	61	47	43
5	Man City	38	15	13	10	49	39	43
6	Sheff United	38	15	13	10	49	41	43
7	Wednesday	38	15	13	10	61	54	43
8	Sunderland	38	18	5	15	81	72	41
9	Bradford PA	38	17	7	14	69	65	41
10	Bradford City	38	13	14	11	55	49	40
11	WBA	38	15	10	13	49	43	40
12	Middlesbrough	38	13	12	13	62	74	38
13	Aston Villa	38	13	11	14	62	72	37
14	Liverpool	38	14	9	15	65	75	37
15	Newcastle	38	11	10	17	46	48	32
16	Notts County	38	9	13	16	41	57	31
17	Bolton	38	11	8	19	68	84	30
18	Man United	38	9	12	17	46	62	30
19	Chelsea	38	8	13	17	51	65	29
20	Tottenham	38	8	12	18	57	90	28

SECOND DIVISION

		P	W	D	L	F	A	Pts
1	Derby	38	23	7	8	71	33	53
2	Preston	38	20	10	8	61	42	50
3	Barnsley	38	22	3	13	51	51	47
4	Wolves	38	19	7	12	77	52	45
5	Arsenal	38	19	5	14	69	41	43
6	Birmingham	38	17	9	12	62	39	43
7	Hull	38	19	5	14	65	54	43
8	Huddersfield	38	17	8	13	61	42	42
9	Clapton Orient	38	16	9	13	50	48	41
10	Blackpool	38	17	5	16	58	57	39
11	Bury	38	15	8	15	61	56	38
12	Fulham	38	15	7	16	53	47	37
13	Bristol City	38	15	7	16	62	56	37
14	Stockport	38	15	7	16	54	60	37
15	Leeds City	38	14	4	20	65	64	32
16	Lincoln	38	11	9	18	46	65	31
17	Grimsby	38	11	9	18	48	76	31
18	Nottm Forest	38	10	9	19	43	77	29
19	Leicester Fosse	38	10	4	24	47	88	24
20	Glossop NE	38	6	6	26	31	87	18

FOUR
Expansion
1919–1930

Football 'turned you into a member of a new community, all brothers together for an hour and a half, for not only had you escaped from the clanking machinery of this lesser life, from work, wages, rent, doles, sick pay, insurance-cards, nagging wives, ailing children, bad bosses, idle workmen, but you had escaped with most of your mates and your neighbours, with half the town, and there you were, cheering together, thumping one another on the shoulders, swopping judgements like lords of the earth, having pushed your way through a turnstile into another and altogether more splendid kind of life, hurtling with Conflict and yet passionate and beautiful in its Art.'

J.B. Priestley
The Good Companions, 1928.

Football did not waste time after the muddy horror of the Great War. The First and Second Divisions of the League were immediately increased to 22 clubs each and, within a couple of years, there were two Third Divisions, first South, then North.

It was a solid platform for progress and change. Wembley Stadium – 'as big as the Biblical city of Jericho' declared one official – was built in 300 working days in north London to become the new home of the FA Cup final in 1923. The shape of the game itself was fundamentally changed by an alteration to the offside law in 1925. The transfer market became even bigger business with fees rising robustly to five figures. Bill 'Dixie' Dean of Everton smacked in goals with a regularity that has never been matched.

It was an age, however, that belonged to one man above all. The success, ideas and personality of Herbert Chapman revolutionized the game; but he was, more than anything else, a builder of winning football teams. Twice he created a side that was good enough to win the League championship in three consecutive seasons – first Huddersfield (1924–6) and then Arsenal (1933–5). Liverpool (1982–4) is the only other club, in a century of League football, to have managed this hat-trick.

Chapman was an ample and florid Yorkshireman whose moderate career as a player with Tottenham was notable only for the flamboyant yellow boots he wore. But as a manager he was years ahead of his time. He was an easy talker, a shrewd and tough businessman, an inspired motivator, a martinet but also an understanding father-figure, a realist who liked a gamble and a first-class publicist. He had a natural nose for talent and a rare ability to make the best of it.

Huddersfield, when he joined them in 1920, had little money, few resources and indifferent crowds in a town devoted to Rugby League. But Chapman bought perceptively, welded his assets together astutely and soon sent out one of the most successful League sides of all time. It was stubborn, disciplined and highly mobile with Clem Stephenson, once of Aston Villa, at the heart of everything. He was a stocky tactician without much pace but his passes were as sweet as stolen kisses. Later, too, there was Alex Jackson, handsome and irrepressible, one of Scotland's 'Wembley Wizards' who were to overwhelm England 5–1 in 1928.

Chapman led Huddersfield to their first two championships but then, before they began their third great season, he surprised the football world by joining Arsenal – and Arsenal, who had only just avoided relegation the previous season, finished as runners-up to Huddersfield. It was hardly a coincidence.

The year that Chapman left Huddersfield for Arsenal – 1925 – was also the year the offside law was changed. The number of opponents necessary to keep a player onside was reduced from three to two – an historic decision which has been the subject of heated debate ever since. Even then there were honest reservations. *Gamage's Association Football Annual*, the celebrated 'Green Book' and the best annual of its day, reported twelve months later: 'The change did not improve the quality of first-class football. It pleased the majority of the spectators because it provided them with more goals. But as the new rule tended to eliminate skill and to make pace a bigger fetish than ever, it was almost as common to see goals scored from bad play as from brilliant movements.' The number of League goals scored in the last season under the old law was 4,700. The first season under the new produced 6,373.

Chapman, inevitably, was the first manager to face the challenge. Arsenal plugged the holes in defence caused by the new law by using an extra defender. Their centre-half, instead of enjoying an attacking role in midfield, became a centre-back – the 'stopper' – and an inside-forward dropped back to make good the link between defence and attack. The day of the old formation 2–3–5 (two full-backs, three half-backs and five forwards) was over. Now it was 3–3–4. The shape of the game had changed.

The idea itself, however, came from Charlie Buchan and not Chapman. Chapman's first action as Arsenal manager had been to buy Buchan from Sunderland; and Buchan, that shrewdest of forwards, suggested before the first match of the 1925–6 season that Jack Butler, Arsenal's centre-half, should be used only as a defender. Chapman disagreed.

Buchan repeated his idea – without success – at every team meeting for the next five weeks. But in early October Arsenal were beaten 7–0 by Newcastle at St James's Park – and after the game Buchan said to Chapman: 'I want to go back to Sunderland. I'm not much use to Arsenal.' Chapman replied: 'Oh no, you're playing against West Ham on Monday. I know what you want and we'll have a special meeting to discuss it.' The meeting took place, immediately, in their Newcastle hotel; and Chapman, after a long discussion, agreed to experiment. Arsenal beat West Ham 4–0 at Upton Park two days later – and they were on their way to mighty deeds. It was Buchan's idea but it was Chapman who refined the system and made it work.

Arsenal's first major success was the FA Cup of 1930 and, in the final at Wembley, they beat Huddersfield 2–0 – Chapman's new creation getting the better of his old. Huddersfield were ageing while Arsenal were rising fast, and the following year they won the championship for the first time.

Buchan had retired by now, replaced by David Jack, a vital and elegant man who scored his goals with sharp-edged charm and even good manners; and the key role in midfield went to Alex James, an inside-forward of genius, an imp of a man with buttoned-down sleeves and famous baggy shorts. Jack of England moved from Bolton for £10,890, the first five-figure transfer fee, and James of Scotland from Preston for £9,000. The country raised its hands in horror at such extravagance. Chapman smiled at a couple of bargains. Chapman led his new Arsenal into the 1930s with huge and justified confidence – but that part of his story belongs to the next chapter.

One player Chapman desperately tried – and failed – to buy was a centre-forward whose place in the history of the game will always be secure. The player's name was William Ralph Dean – the immortal 'Dixie' Dean. He played for Tranmere Rovers, Everton, Notts County and England, and in a career which stretched from 1923 to 1939 he scored 473 goals (including 37 hat-tricks) in 502 League, FA Cup, representative and international matches. In one glorious season, 1927–8, aged just 21, Dean scored 60 League goals: a record which is now beyond reach and even comprehension. Everton became champions. They had no option.

Chapman went quietly to Goodison Park and offered Everton anything they wanted for Dean. It was an extraordinary offer and if Everton had asked for the moon, gift-wrapped, they would probably have got it. Everton's directors did not dare sell him, however, and in any case the immensely popular Dean was determined to stay at Goodison while he was in his prime. Even Chapman sometimes failed.

Dean was a burly light-heavyweight, 5ft 10in and 12 stone, and in the air he was a demon. Forty of his 60 League goals in 1927–8 are said to have been scored with his head – even though the first priority of every opposing side was to prevent the ball reaching his brow of steel.

The climax to the 1927–8 season was the stuff of fiction. Dean needed nine goals from the last three games to beat the 59 Second Division goals scored by George Camsell of Middlesbrough the previous year when confused defences were still coming to terms with the new offside law. Dean's task seemed impossible, but he obliged with style. He got two against Aston Villa, four at Burnley and then, against Arsenal of all teams in the final match, he completed his hat-trick just eight minutes from the end. *The Times* solemnly applauded 'this very brilliant player whose strength and good humour carried him through'.

Dean is often described as the best goalscorer the League has ever seen. His record makes the claim a fair one and, half a century and more later, his name is still part of everyday football talk on Merseyside.

Dixie died on the first day of March 1980 while watching Everton play Liverpool at Goodison Park. 'Where else?' asked his old friend Joe Mercer.

MOST LEAGUE GOALS IN CAREER

	GOALS
Arthur Rowley West Bromwich, Fulham and Shrewsbury – 1946–65	**434**
Dixie Dean Tranmere, Everton, Notts County – 1923–39	**379**
Jimmy Greaves Chelsea, Tottenham, West Ham – 1957–71	**357**
Steve Bloomer Derby, Middlesbrough and Derby again – 1892–1914	**352**
George Camsell Durham City and Middlesbrough – 1923–39	**348**

left Charlie Buchan scoring the only goal of the game for the Football League against the Scottish League at Highbury, March 1921. The Football League abandoned Inter-League fixtures in 1976. Full record since 1892: played 168, won 120, drawn 22, lost 26.

right Syd Puddefoot of West Ham, Falkirk, Blackburn, West Ham again and England – a strong, brave forward for whom Falkirk, surprisingly, paid West Ham the first £5,000 transfer fee in British football in February 1922. Puddefoot was born in West Ham and joined the Upton Park club in season 1912–13. He was the Second Division's leading scorer with 29 goals in 1920–1 and, after three years with Falkirk, moved to Blackburn and helped them win the FA Cup in 1928 (a major shock: Blackburn 3 Huddersfield 1). Two caps for England (1926).

below 'Pretty Play at Putney'.
J.B. Priestley described football as 'conflict and art' . . . artist Frank Reynolds saw it the same way, *Punch* 1921.

above Charlie Paynter and Syd King, 1923 – two of the great figures in West Ham's history. They joined the East London club in its first season in 1900, King as a full-back, Paynter as a winger, but injuries finished their playing careers almost immediately. Both stayed: King as secretary-manager from 1901 to 1932, Paynter as assistant-trainer from 1902, trainer in 1912, team-manager in 1932 and then secretary-manager until after World War Two – a career of nearly 50 years. The picture taken in the year that West Ham first won promotion to Division One and also took part in the first FA Cup final at Wembley: West Ham 0 Bolton 2. West Ham have had only five managers since they were founded: King, Paynter, Ted Fenton, Ron Greenwood and John Lyall.

left Elisha Scott of Liverpool and Ireland – the brave and agile goalkeeper Dixie Dean described as the best he ever faced. Scott played 429 League games for Liverpool over 22 years and was a member of their League championship sides in 1922 and 1923. His 31 caps for Ireland were spread over 17 seasons – the last when he was 42. His older brother William was a member of Everton's FA Cup-winning side in 1906.

above Jesse Pennington of West Bromwich Albion and England – distinguished left-back and club captain who played 455 League games in an 18-year career. Helped Albion win the Second Division championship in 1910–11 and the League championship, for the only time in the club's history, in 1919–20. Pennington, renowned for his sportsmanship, won 25 caps for England.

overleaf Constable George Scorey and his 13-year-old white horse 'Billy' pressing back part of the huge horde at the first FA Cup Final at Wembley, April 28 1923. Wembley had boasted it could take 127,000 . . . and 250,000 turned up. The start was delayed by 45 minutes but the good-humoured crowd dutifully sang the National Anthem when King George V arrived – and, inch by inch, 'Billy' and other horses slowly cleared the pitch. It is still known as the 'White Horse final' and, from that year on, Cup finals have been all-ticket. The final score was Bolton 2 West Ham 0. That night constable Scorey was asked by his girlfriend Kitty what sort of day he'd had. 'Oh, just ordinary, lass,' he said. 'Just ordinary.'

left Warney Cresswell of South Shields, Sunderland, Everton and England – full-back of unflappable authority who played 568 League games between 1919 and 1936. Moved from South Shields (then Second Division club) to Sunderland for record fee of £5,500 in 1922, helped Sunderland finish in top three in four seasons out of five, and then aided Everton to the League championships of 1928 and 1932 and the FA Cup in 1933. Seven caps for England between 1921 and 1930.

above George Camsell of Durham City, Middlesbrough and England who scored 344 League goals between 1923 and 1939. He scored 59 in 37 games for Middlesbrough in season 1926–7, still a Second Division record and bettered only by Dixie Dean's 60 in 1927–8. Middlesbrough scored 122 goals in 1926–7, also a Second Division record, and won promotion by an eight point margin. Camsell won nine caps for England (1929–36).

right Stan Seymour – 'Mr Newcastle'. He joined the club in 1920 and served the club as player, manager, director and chairman. He was a goalscoring left-winger who played a major part in Newcastle winning the FA Cup in 1924 (he scored the winning goal against Aston Villa) and the League championship in 1927. He joined the St James's Park board in 1938 and was honorary manager during the war and for several different periods after. He was a shrewd talent-spotter and brought players of the quality of Jackie Milburn, Joe Harvey, Charlie Wayman and Len Shackleton to the club – and led Newcastle to their Cup triumphs in 1951 and 1952, the first club to win the trophy in successive seasons in the twentieth century.

above Bolton Wanderers under pressure at Highbury, September 1925 – just after Herbert Chapman and Charlie Buchan had joined Arsenal. Left to right: Seddon (Bolton), Buchan (Arsenal), Greenhalgh (Bolton), Pym (Bolton's goalkeeper), Brain (Arsenal) and Haworth (Bolton). Arsenal finished runners-up in Division One; but Bolton won the Highbury match 3–2 and also the FA Cup – one of three times they won it in the 1920s.

right Nelson – champions of Division Three (North) 1923. Back row (l to r): Rigg, Braidwood, Birds, Wilson, Broadhead, Smith (trainer). Seated: Hoad, Lilley, McCullock, Eddleston, Wolstenhome, Hutchinson. Nelson experienced remarkable changes in fortune during their ten years (1921–31) in the League. They were promoted in their second season, relegated from Division Two in their third season and runners-up in Division Three (North) in their fourth. They scored 104 goals in 1926–7 but conceded 136 (a Third Division record) the following season. And in 1930–1 they lost all their away games – the only club to 'achieve' this in a season of at least 21 away games. They failed to win re-election in 1931 and were replaced by Chester.

above Tottenham laying down 3,000 bales of straw to protect the White Hart Lane pitch from frost before their Division One game with Aston Villa, December 1925. Five members of the groundstaff are all sporting caps and waistcoats.

Frank Barson of Barnsley, Aston Villa, Manchester United, Watford, Hartlepools United, Wigan Borough and England – attacking centre-half, greatly feared and much-suspended 'hard man' and one of football's most notorious characters between the wars. Barson, a former blacksmith, was always quick to seek retribution when a team-mate was fouled – and he often informed the referee first. More than once he had to be smuggled past angry fans. He was so powerful in the air that on Boxing Day 1921 he scored Aston Villa's winner against Sheffield United with a header from 30 yards. He helped Villa win the Cup in 1920 but Manchester United bought him for £5,000 in July 1922 just after they had been relegated to Division Two. United promised him a public house if they won promotion within three years. They made it (1925) but the story goes that when Barson opened the doors of his pub at Ardwick for the first time there was such a turn-out of fans that he decided within 15 minutes that the job was not for him – and, on the spot, gave the place to his head barman. The argumentative Barson hated flattery and could be rudely blunt, but he was a generous friend, an excellent youth coach and was popular in the dressing room. Billy Walker said of him: 'Frank did more than any other player to help me when I started with Villa – but he had no friends on the field.' Barson played 353 League games (1911–31) and won one cap for England in 1920. *right* Barson, in his Aston Villa days (1912–22) smiles broadly as he shakes hands with Billy Flint, the captain of Notts County. One reason for the cordiality may have been the bow-tied figure beside him – Jack 'Jimmy' Howcroft, the strongest and most respected referee of his day. Howcroft refereed the 1920 Cup final, and before the kick-off he went into the Villa dressing room and bluntly warned Barson that his first serious infringement would also be his last. Barson was impressed and did not put a foot wrong. But Barson never really changed: he was sent off in his last game of professional football.

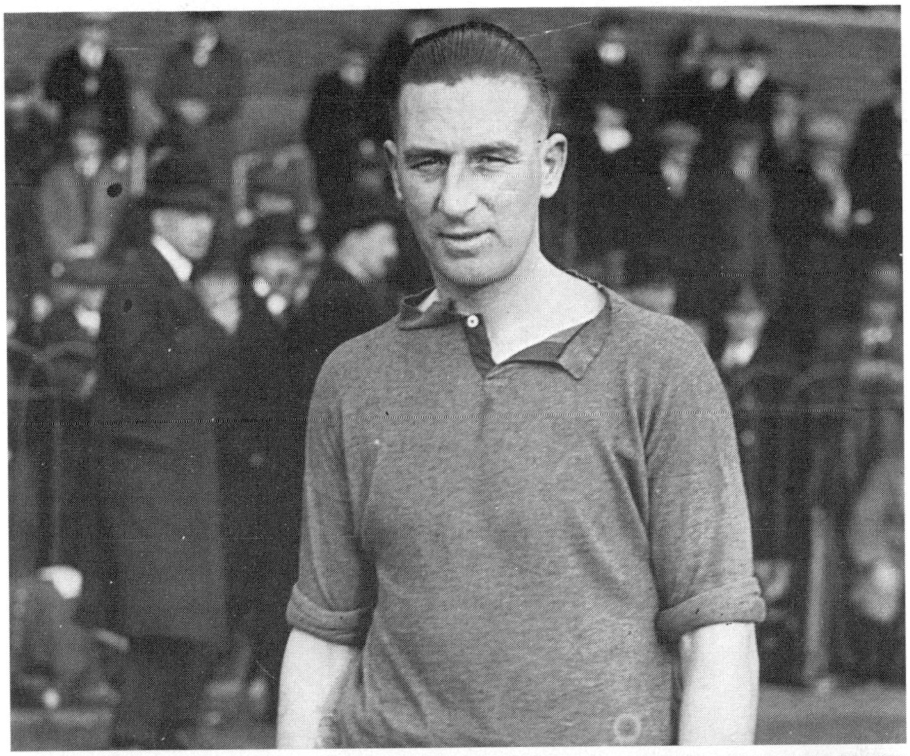

above Hughie Gallacher of Queen of the South, Airdrie, Newcastle, Chelsea, Derby, Notts County, Grimsby Town and Gateshead – often described as the greatest British centre-forward of all time. Here leading out Newcastle – with the approval of the law – during their League championship season of 1926–7. Only 5 ft 5 ins tall but astonishingly quick, brave, unpredictable and completely gifted. In football terms he was a genius. Scored 387 goals in 541 League games in England and Scotland and 22 in 20 internationals. Stormy, temperamental and restless off the field – but his wonderful skill was relished wherever he played. *right* Gallacher, in his Chelsea days, rises above the Arsenal defence at Stamford Bridge, November 1931.

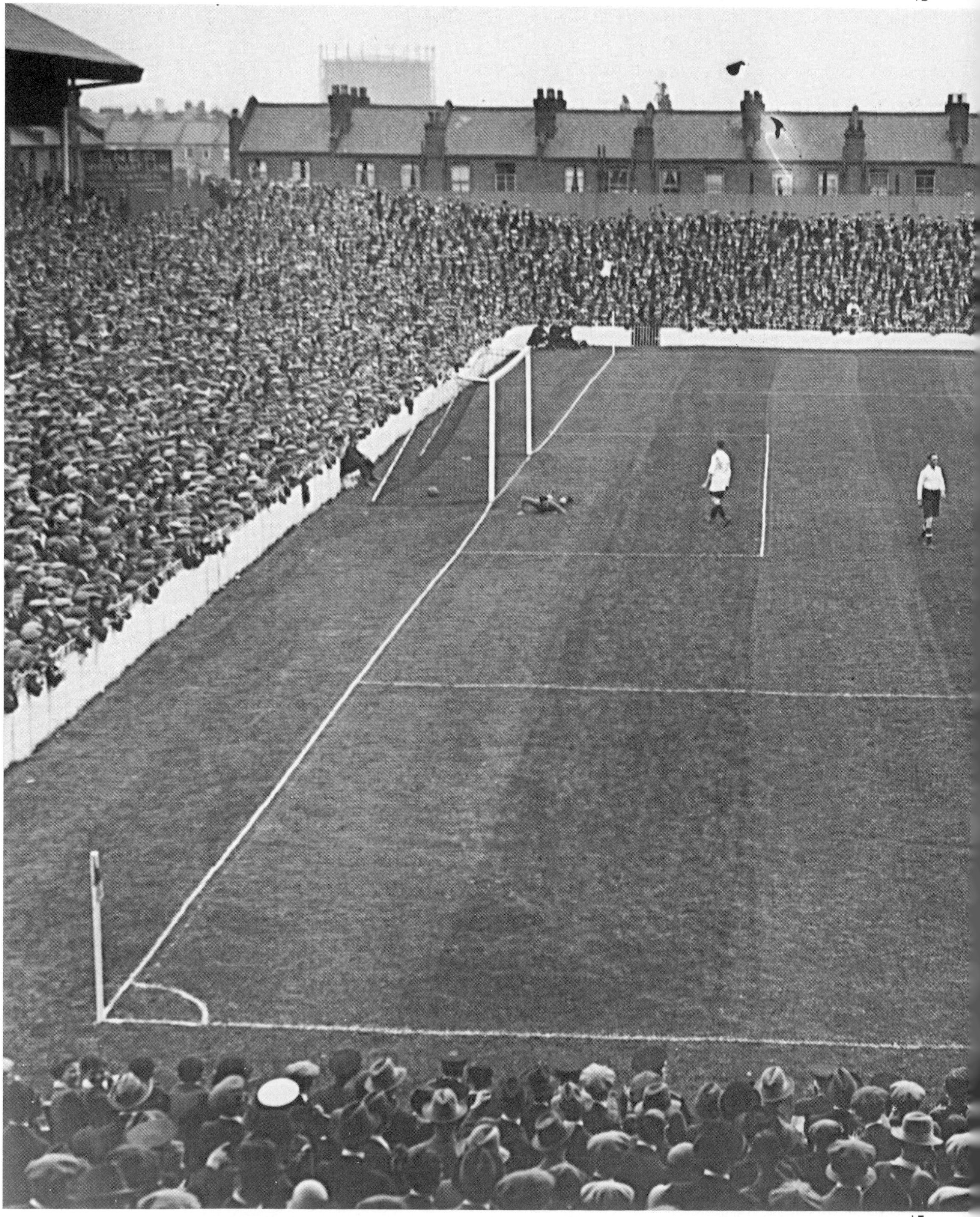

above Sam Wadsworth of Huddersfield and England – a renowned left-back and one of Huddersfield's cornerstones when they became the first club to win the League championship three seasons in succession (1924–5–6).

left The irrepressible Clem Stephenson, Huddersfield's captain, wheels away after scoring against Tottenham at White Hart Lane, Sept 1926. Huddersfield were beginning their defence of a championship they had won three seasons in succession – but in 1926–7 they finished runners-up, were second again the following season and have never since won the title.

inset Shield presented by the Football League to Huddersfield to mark their three successive League championships.

above Wadsworth is on right of second standing row – and Herbert Chapman is on left of seated row. Chapman led Huddersfield to their first two championships and then joined Arsenal in 1925.

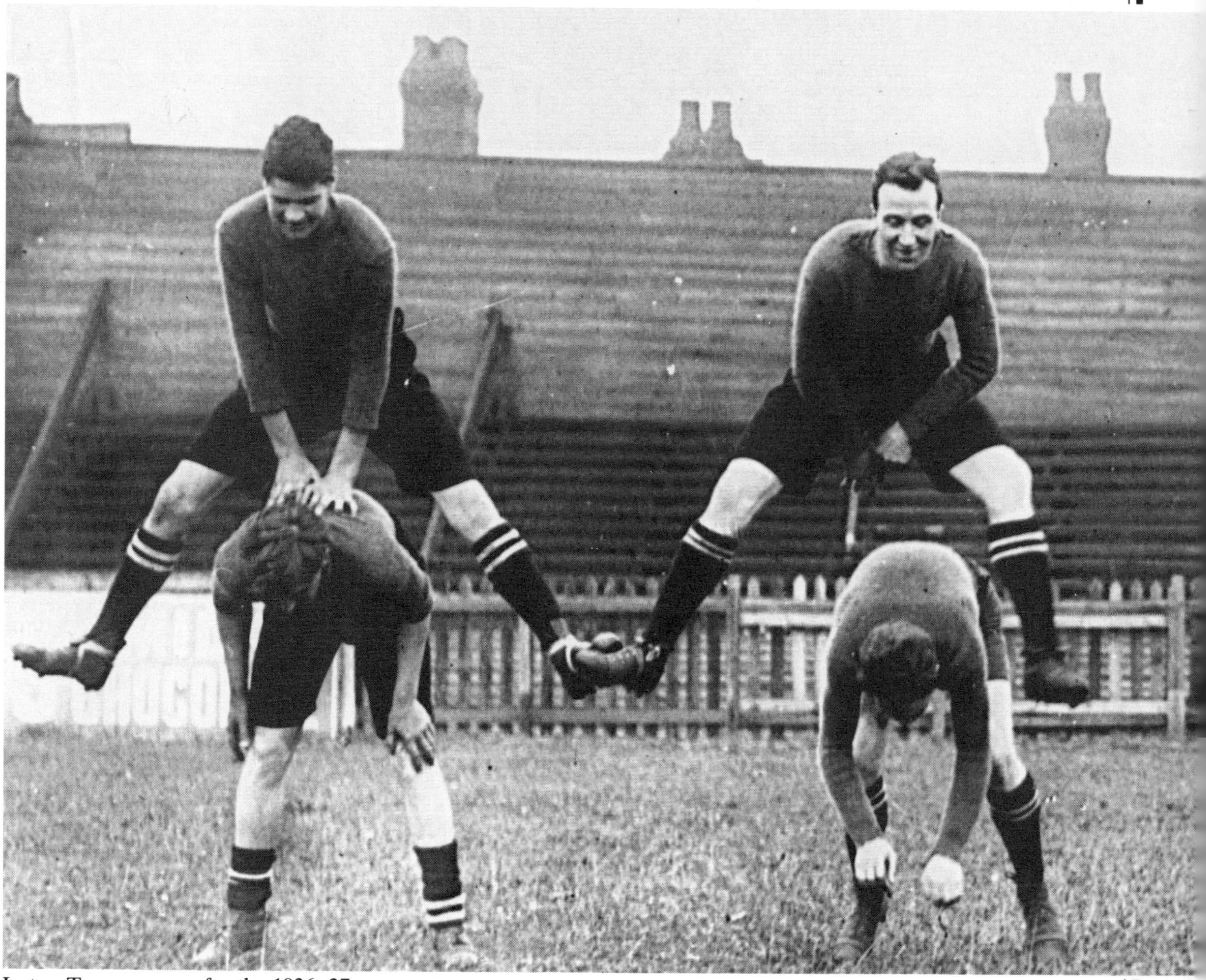

Luton Town prepare for the 1926–27 season – watched only by peeping chimnies. Jumping: Harkins, Gordon, Clarke, Moir. Bending: Wolstenholme, Black, Dennis and Pointon. Hopes are high – but they finished eighth in Division 3 South.

right Billy Walker of Aston Villa and England – an inside-forward of rare pace and stunning swerve who scored 213 goals (a club record he shares with Harry Hampton) in nearly 500 League games for Villa between 1919–34. Won 18 caps for England (1921–33). Inspiration of the Villa attack which scored 128 goals (a Division One record) in 1930–1 but only finished as runners-up. First player to score a hat-trick of penalties in a League game (v Bradford City, November 1921). Played in two FA Cup finals with Aston Villa (winners 1920, runners-up 1924), and later managed two other clubs to FA Cup success: Sheffield Wednesday in 1935 and Nottingham Forest in 1959. He was Forest's manager for 21 years (1939–60) and was a man of loyalty and high integrity.

Light relief at Plymouth Argyle's attractive Home Park during the Great Strike, June 1926. Police played Strikers – and Strikers won 2–1. But the 1920s were years of torment for Plymouth. They were runners-up for six consecutive seasons (1922 to 1927) in Third Division South from which only the champions were promoted, finished third in 1928, fourth in 1929 and then, at last, won the title in 1930. Eight seasons . . . the longest run of near misses in League history.

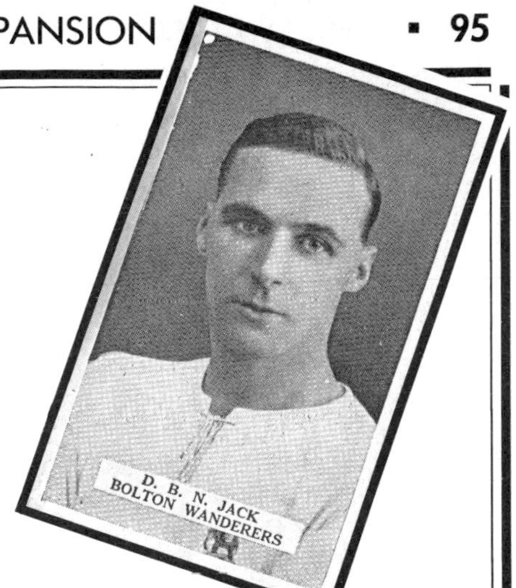

right David Bone Nightingale Jack of Bolton and England, for whom Arsenal paid £10,890 – the first five-figure transfer fee – in October 1928. Perhaps Arsenal's manager Herbert Chapman was impressed by the profile of Jack on the back of this cigarette card: 'Bolton Wanderers' inside-right to whom fell the honour of scoring the first goal in a Cup Final at Wembley (1923), was born at Bolton when his father, Mr Robert Jack, now manager of Plymouth Argyle, played on the Wanderers' left wing. David graduated in junior football at Plymouth and showed promise as a member of the Argyle team, but it was after his transfer to Bolton (1920) that his real talents were revealed. Superb and unorthodox in his methods, and a grand shot.' Bob Wall, who was to become Arsenal's secretary and one of football's most eminent administrators, was a 16-year-old who had just joined the club at the time of Jack's transfer to Arsenal. He often told the story of the signing: 'I was Chapman's personal assistant and on the day of the transfer he said to me: "Young Wall, come with me. I'll show you how to conduct a transfer. We are going to sign David Jack, the England inside-forward, from Bolton Wanderers. We are meeting their chairman and manager at the Euston Hotel. You are to sit with me, listen and not say a word. I'll do all the talking. Is that clear?" I nodded assent and hurried away to order a taxi. We arrived at the hotel half an hour before our appointment. Chapman immediately went into the lounge bar. He called the waiter, placed two pound notes in his hand and said "George, this is Mr Wall, my assistant. He will drink whisky and dry ginger. I will drink gin and tonic. We shall be joined by guests. They will drink whatever they like. But I want you to be careful of one thing. See that our guests are given double of everything, but Mr Wall's whisky and dry ginger will contain no whisky and my gin and tonic will contain no gin." When the Bolton pair arrived, Chapman ordered the drinks. We quickly downed ours and he called for the same again. The drinks continued to flow and our guests were soon in gay mood. Finally, when Chapman decided the time was opportune for talking business, they readily agreed to letting him sign Jack – and for £10,890, which we considered a bargain! Never did ginger ale and tonic water leave two persons so elated. "Wall," exclaimed Chapman, "that's your first lesson in football."'

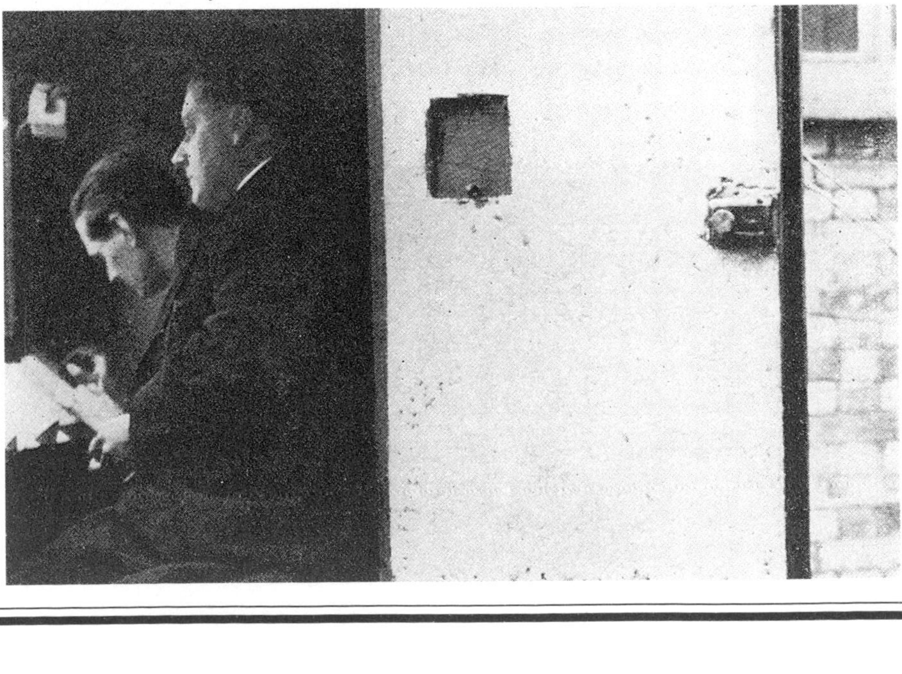

right George Allison – BBC Radio's first football commentator – at work with Derek ('Uncle Mac') McCulloch, 1927. McCulloch's job was to match the position of the ball on the field with a plan of the pitch, divided into numbered squares, in the *Radio Times* – and to place the ball for the listener by saying, for example, 'square two' or 'square seven'. The first match to be broadcast in England was the Division One game between Arsenal and Sheffield United on 22 January, 1927.

April 15, 1927.] —— RADIO TIMES —— 129

Broadcasting the Match of the Year.

THIS afternoon—Saturday, April 23—the broadcasting of sporting events will reach another landmark in its history. Listeners all over the country will be able to hear in their own homes the story, told from the ground during the actual progress of the game, of the match that packs the biggest arena in the country every year, on an occasion that is the red-letter day in the calendar of everyone who follows the national winter game.

Mr. G. F. ALLISON.

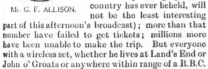

There will be 100,000 people in the Wembley Stadium (and to hear this vast crowd singing together before the kick-off, the largest demonstration of Community Singing this country has ever beheld, will not be the least interesting part of this afternoon's broadcast); more than that number have failed to get tickets; millions more have been unable to make the trip. But everyone with a wireless set, whether he lives at Land's End or John o' Groats or anywhere within range of a B.B.C. station, will be able to share in all the thrills of one of those days when football history is made.

THE CAUSE OF THE TROUBLE.

The actual broadcast promises to be as successful as any ever carried out. The two narrators, Mr. Allison and Mr. McCulloch, whose pictures you see inset, have been responsible for many previous football narratives, and the thrills of a big occasion have no terrors for them. The arrangements for transmission are unusually simple and compact. The portable sound-proof hut, which is becoming a familiar sight to match-goers, will at Wembley be situated at the right-hand end of the Press Gallery, which commands an unrivalled view of the field. There will be two microphones in the hut, and the control point for the engineers will be immediately behind, between the hut and the back wall of the Press Gallery. Thence two pairs of private lines run direct to Savoy Hill, where the messages will be dealt with in the ordinary way.

The broadcast, then, promises to be—like the Boat Race narrative—a worthy account of the match. And what a match it will be! Both teams have fine records in the earlier stages of the tournament, and won their way to Wembley by decisive victories against formidable opposition. Each has had to replay one match, and won the replay at home. Both play in the First Division of the League, where they are of almost equal standing; at the time of writing only one point separates them. All London will be backing the Arsenal, and Wales will be solid behind Cardiff City. No element of excitement seems to have been left out.

Mr. D. McCULLOCH.

First the Rugby Internationals; then the Grand National and the Boat Race; and now the Cup Final. Is it too much to claim that broadcasting has become as important to followers of sport as it has long been to music-lovers and to people who want to dance?

Aerofilms

This is the Wembley Stadium, packed with a cheering crowd of 100,000 people, as it will appear this afternoon when The Arsenal and Cardiff City are fighting for the Cup. The B.B.C. narrators will be at the top of the covered stand in the left-hand corner of the picture—just beside the domed tower in the foreground—and the sections numbered on the field are those that they will use in describing the course of the greatest game of the year.

above Common greatness: Charles Buchan of Arsenal and England and Jack Hobbs of Surrey and England meet in the London restaurant of the Daily News (later the News Chronicle) in January 1928. Buchan, 36 years old, retired at the end of the season and started work immediately as the Daily News' Football Correspondent, a post he held until 1956. Hobbs, who was 45 when the picture was taken, scored 98 centuries after he was 40 – his 197th and last when he was 51.

left Radio Times marks the first Radio commentary on an FA Cup final, Arsenal v Cardiff, Wembley 1927. *far right* King George V shakes hands with Fred Keenor, the Cardiff captain, before the start. *right* Hugh Ferguson, Cardiff's centre-forward, scores the goal which gave Cardiff victory by 1–0 – and the FA Cup left England for the first and only time.

THERE BEING NO NEWSPAPERS ON FRIDAY OR SATURDAY VERY FEW FOOTBALLERS KNEW HOW THEY HAD GOT ON.
ARE WE WINNING?
HOW SHOULD I KNOW. I CAN'T FIND A PRESSMAN.
TO A CERTAIN EXTENT ONLY THE GOALKEEPERS KNEW HOW THE GAME WAS GOING AND MOST OF THESE PEOPLE WERE AWFULLY QUIET ABOUT IT.
HOW MANY IS THAT?
— FOR INSTANCE NEWCASTLE UNITED HAD SIX GOALS SCORED AGAINST THEM ON CHRISTMAS DAY BUT ONE COULD HARDLY BLAME THE NEWCASTLE GOALKEEPER — FOR NOT REFERRING TO IT.
THEN ASTON VILLA WERE BEATEN BY 5–2 BUT THEIR GOALKEEPER GOT THEM ALL OUT — QUICKLY FROM THE BACK OF THE NET IN THE HOPE THAT NOBODY WAS COUNTING.
LOTS OF FOOTBALLERS WHOSE SIDE HAD BEEN BADLY BEATEN WENT HOME AND — REFUSED TO SAY A WORD TO THEIR PEOPLE IN CASE IT GOT INTO THE NEWSPAPERS.
CHELSEA PLAYED TWO MATCHES AGAINST BLACKPOOL AND DIDN'T WIN EITHER OF THEM.
EVERYBODY IN GT BRITAIN SEEMED TO KNOW ABOUT THIS. I THINK A BLACKPOOL DIRECTOR — RAN FROM TOWN TO TOWN AND TOLD EVERYBODY PUBLICLY.
TOM WEBSTER 25

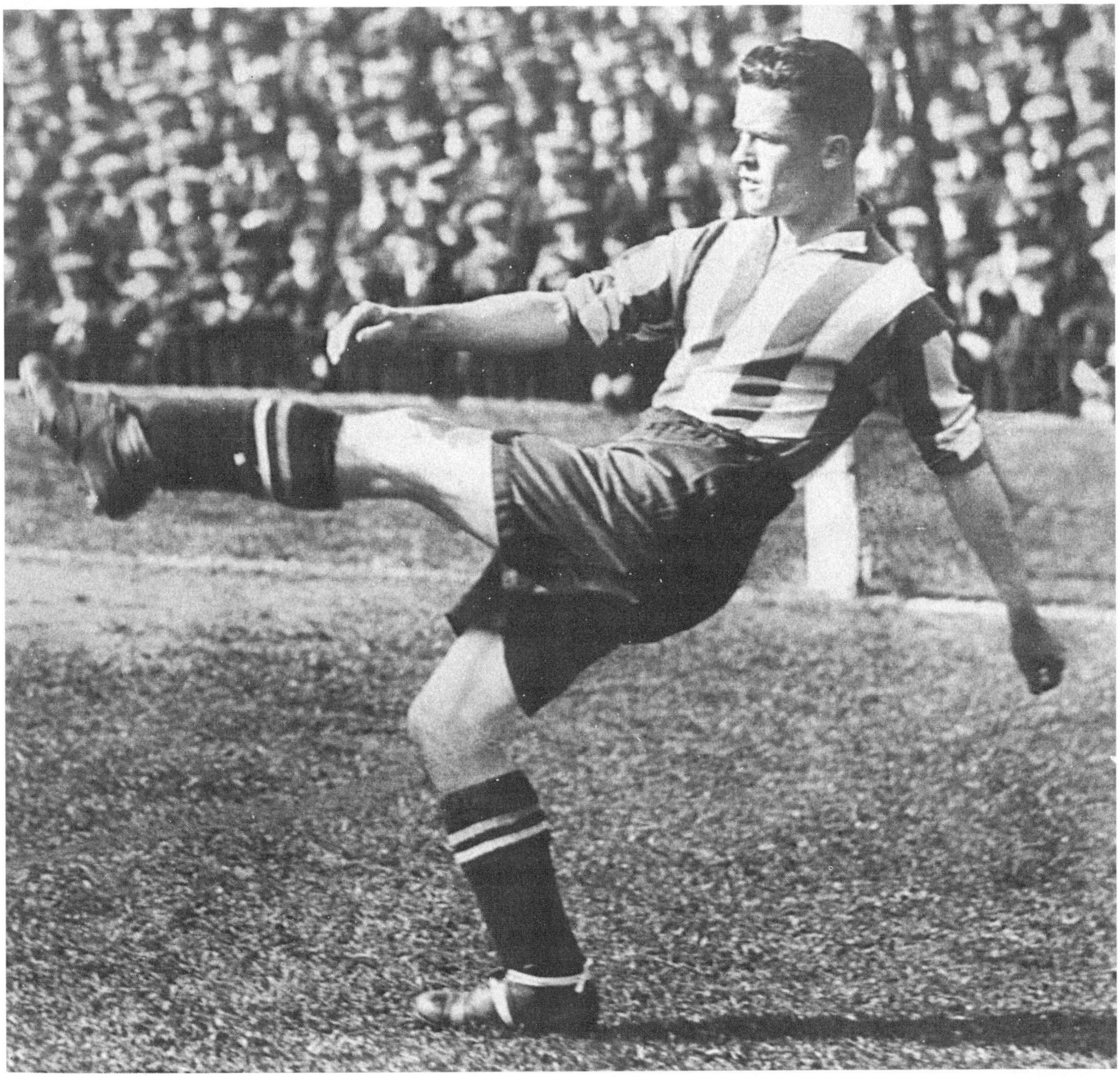

above Ernie Blenkinsop of Hull City, Sheffield Wednesday, Liverpool, Cardiff City and England – outstanding full-back of style and intelligence and a member of the powerful Sheffield Wednesday side which won the League championship in 1929 and 1930. Blenkinsop played for Wednesday for twelve years and won all his 26 caps for England while at Hillsborough.

right Ronnie Dix who became the youngest goalscorer in League history at the age of 15 years and 180 days when he scored for Bristol Rovers against Norwich in Third Division South in March 1928 – just one week after his debut.

left Tottenham v Wolverhampton Wanderers, Division Two, Saturday 8 September 1928. Spurs 3 Wolves 2.

above Brentford v Queen's Park Rangers, Division Three (Southern), Easter Monday 21 April 1930.

left Queen's Park Rangers v Crystal Palace, Division Three (Southern), Saturday 8 November 1930.

LEAGUE TABLES

1919–20

FIRST DIVISION

		P	W	D	L	F	A	Pts
1	WBA	42	28	4	10	104	47	60
2	Burnley	42	21	9	12	65	59	51
3	Chelsea	42	22	5	15	56	51	49
4	Liverpool	42	19	10	13	59	44	48
5	Sunderland	42	22	4	16	72	59	48
6	Bolton	42	19	9	14	72	65	47
7	Man City	42	18	9	15	71	62	45
8	Newcastle	42	17	9	16	44	39	43
9	Aston Villa	42	18	6	18	75	73	42
10	Arsenal	42	15	12	15	56	58	42
11	Bradford PA	42	15	12	15	60	63	42
12	Man United	42	13	14	15	54	50	40
13	Middlesbrough	42	15	10	17	61	65	40
14	Sheff United	42	16	8	18	59	69	40
15	Bradford City	42	14	11	17	54	63	39
16	Everton	42	12	14	16	69	68	38
17	Oldham	42	15	8	19	49	52	38
18	Derby	42	13	12	17	47	57	38
19	Preston	42	14	10	18	57	73	38
20	Blackburn	42	13	11	18	64	77	37
21	Notts County	42	12	12	18	56	74	36
22	Wednesday	42	7	9	26	28	64	23

SECOND DIVISION

		P	W	D	L	F	A	Pts
1	Tottenham	42	32	6	4	102	32	70
2	Huddersfield	42	28	8	6	97	38	64
3	Birmingham	42	24	8	10	85	34	56
4	Blackpool	42	21	10	11	65	47	52
5	Bury	42	20	8	14	60	44	48
6	Fulham	42	19	9	14	61	50	47
7	West Ham	42	19	9	14	47	40	47
8	Bristol City	42	13	17	12	46	43	43
9	South Shields	42	15	12	15	58	48	42
10	Stoke	42	18	6	18	60	54	42
11	Hull	42	18	6	18	78	72	42
12	Barnsley	42	15	10	17	61	55	40
13	Port Vale	42	16	8	18	59	62	40
14	Leicester	42	15	10	17	41	61	40
15	Clapton Orient	42	16	6	20	51	59	38
16	Stockport	42	14	9	19	52	61	37
17	Rotherham Co	42	13	8	21	51	83	34
18	Nottm Forest	42	11	9	22	43	73	31
19	Wolves	42	10	10	22	55	80	30
20	Coventry	42	9	11	22	35	73	29
21	Lincoln	42	9	9	24	44	101	27
22	Grimsby	42	10	5	27	34	75	25

1920–21

FIRST DIVISION

		P	W	D	L	F	A	Pts
1	Burnley	42	23	13	6	79	36	59
2	Man City	42	24	6	12	70	50	54
3	Bolton	42	19	14	9	77	53	52
4	Liverpool	42	18	15	9	63	35	51
5	Newcastle	42	20	10	12	66	45	50
6	Tottenham	42	19	9	14	70	48	47
7	Everton	42	17	13	12	66	55	47
8	Middlesbrough	42	17	12	13	53	53	46
9	Arsenal	42	15	14	13	59	63	44
10	Aston Villa	42	18	7	17	63	70	43
11	Blackburn	42	13	15	14	57	59	41
12	Sunderland	42	14	13	15	57	60	41
13	Man United	42	15	10	17	64	68	40
14	WBA	42	13	14	15	54	58	40
15	Bradford City	42	12	15	15	61	63	39
16	Preston	42	15	9	18	61	65	39
17	Huddersfield	42	15	9	18	42	49	39
18	Chelsea	42	13	13	16	48	58	39
19	Oldham	42	9	15	18	49	86	33
20	Sheff United	42	6	18	18	42	68	30
21	Derby	42	5	16	21	32	58	26
22	Bradford PA	42	8	8	26	43	76	24

SECOND DIVISION

		P	W	D	L	F	A	Pts
1	Birmingham	42	24	10	8	79	38	58
2	Cardiff	42	24	10	8	59	32	58
3	Bristol City	42	19	13	10	49	29	51
4	Blackpool	42	20	10	12	54	42	50
5	West Ham	42	19	10	13	51	30	48
6	Notts County	42	18	11	13	55	40	47
7	Clapton Orient	42	16	13	13	43	42	45
8	South Shields	42	17	10	15	61	46	44
9	Fulham	42	16	10	16	43	47	42
10	Wednesday	42	15	11	16	48	48	41
11	Bury	42	15	10	17	45	49	40
12	Leicester	42	12	16	14	39	46	40
13	Hull	42	10	20	12	43	53	40
14	Leeds	42	14	10	18	40	45	38
15	Wolves	42	16	6	20	49	66	38
16	Barnsley	42	10	16	16	48	50	36
17	Port Vale	42	11	14	17	43	49	36
18	Nottm Forest	42	12	12	18	48	55	36
19	Rotherham Co	42	12	12	18	37	53	36
20	Stoke	42	12	11	19	46	56	35
21	Coventry	42	12	11	19	39	70	35
22	Stockport	42	9	12	21	42	75	30

THIRD DIVISION

		P	W	D	L	F	A	Pts
1	Crystal Palace	42	24	11	7	70	34	59
2	Southampton	42	19	16	7	64	28	54
3	QPR	42	22	9	11	61	32	53
4	Swindon	42	21	10	11	73	49	52
5	Swansea	42	18	15	9	56	45	51
6	Watford	42	20	8	14	59	44	48
7	Millwall Ath	42	18	11	13	42	30	47
8	Merthyr Town	42	15	15	12	60	49	45
9	Luton	42	16	12	14	61	56	44
10	Bristol Rovers	42	18	7	17	68	57	43
11	Plymouth	42	11	21	10	35	34	43
12	Portsmouth	42	12	15	15	46	48	39
13	Grimsby	42	15	9	18	49	59	39
14	Northampton	42	15	8	19	59	75	38
15	Newport	42	14	9	19	43	64	37
16	Norwich	42	10	16	16	44	53	36
17	Southend	42	14	8	20	44	61	36
18	Brighton	42	14	8	20	42	61	36
19	Exeter	42	10	15	17	39	54	35
20	Reading	42	12	7	23	42	59	31
21	Brentford	42	9	12	21	42	67	30
22	Gillingham	42	8	12	22	34	74	28

1921–22

FIRST DIVISION

		P	W	D	L	F	A	Pts
1	Liverpool	42	22	13	7	63	36	57
2	Tottenham	42	21	9	12	65	39	51
3	Burnley	42	22	5	15	72	54	49
4	Cardiff	42	19	10	13	61	53	48
5	Aston Villa	42	22	3	17	74	55	47
6	Bolton	42	20	7	15	68	59	47
7	Newcastle	42	18	10	14	59	45	46
8	Middlesbrough	42	16	14	12	79	69	46
9	Chelsea	42	17	12	13	40	43	46
10	Man City	42	18	9	15	65	70	45
11	Sheff United	42	15	10	17	59	54	40
12	Sunderland	42	16	8	18	60	62	40
13	WBA	42	15	10	17	51	63	40
14	Huddersfield	42	15	9	18	53	54	39
15	Blackburn	42	13	12	17	54	57	38
16	Preston	42	13	12	17	42	65	38
17	Arsenal	42	15	7	20	47	56	37
18	Birmingham	42	15	7	20	48	60	37
19	Oldham	42	13	11	18	38	50	37
20	Everton	42	12	12	18	57	55	36
21	Bradford City	42	11	10	21	48	72	32
22	Man United	42	8	12	22	41	73	28

SECOND DIVISION

		P	W	D	L	F	A	Pts
1	Nottm Forest	42	22	12	8	51	30	56
2	Stoke	42	18	16	8	60	44	52
3	Barnsley	42	22	8	12	67	52	52
4	West Ham	42	20	8	14	52	39	48
5	Hull	42	19	10	13	51	41	48
6	South Shields	42	17	12	13	43	38	46
7	Fulham	42	18	9	15	57	38	45
8	Leeds	42	16	13	13	48	38	45
9	Leicester	42	14	17	11	39	34	45
10	Wednesday	42	15	14	13	47	50	44
11	Bury	42	15	10	17	54	55	40
12	Derby	42	15	9	18	60	64	39
13	Notts County	42	12	15	15	47	51	39
14	Crystal Palace	42	13	13	16	45	51	39
15	Clapton Orient	42	15	9	18	43	50	39
16	Rotherham Co	42	14	11	17	32	43	39
17	Wolves	42	13	11	18	44	49	37
18	Port Vale	42	14	8	20	43	57	36
19	Blackpool	42	15	5	22	44	57	35
20	Coventry	42	12	10	20	51	60	34
21	Bristol City	42	12	9	21	37	58	33
22	Bradford PA	42	12	9	21	46	62	33

THIRD DIVISION (NORTH)

		P	W	D	L	F	A	Pts
1	Stockport	38	24	8	6	60	21	56
2	Darlington	38	22	6	10	81	37	50
3	Grimsby	38	21	8	9	72	47	50
4	Hartlepools	38	17	8	13	52	39	42
5	Accrington	38	19	3	16	73	57	41
6	Crewe	38	18	5	15	60	56	41
7	Stalybridge Cel	38	18	5	15	62	63	41
8	Walsall	38	18	3	17	66	65	39
9	Southport	38	14	10	14	55	44	38
10	Ashington	38	17	4	17	59	66	38
11	Durham City	38	17	3	18	68	67	37
12	Wrexham	38	14	9	15	51	56	37
13	Chesterfield	38	16	3	19	48	67	35
14	Lincoln	38	14	6	18	48	59	34
15	Barrow	38	14	5	19	42	54	33
16	Nelson	38	13	7	18	48	66	33
17	Wigan Borough	38	11	9	18	46	72	31
18	Tranmere	38	9	11	18	51	61	29
19	Halifax	38	10	9	19	56	76	29
20	Rochdale	38	11	4	23	52	77	26

THIRD DIVISION (SOUTH)

		P	W	D	L	F	A	Pts
1	Southampton	42	23	15	4	68	21	61
2	Plymouth	42	25	11	6	63	24	61
3	Portsmouth	42	18	17	7	62	39	53
4	Luton	42	22	8	12	64	35	52
5	QPR	42	18	13	11	53	44	49
6	Swindon	42	16	13	13	72	60	45
7	Watford	42	13	18	11	54	48	44
8	Aberdare Ath	42	17	10	15	57	51	44
9	Brentford	42	16	11	15	52	43	43
10	Swansea	42	13	15	14	50	47	41
11	Merthyr Town	42	17	6	19	45	56	40
12	Millwall Ath	42	10	18	14	38	42	38
13	Reading	42	14	18	10	40	47	38
14	Bristol Rovers	42	14	10	18	52	67	38
15	Norwich	42	12	13	17	50	62	37
16	Charlton	42	13	11	18	43	56	37
17	Northampton	42	13	11	18	47	71	37
18	Gillingham	42	14	8	20	47	60	36
19	Brighton	42	13	9	20	45	51	35
20	Newport	42	11	12	19	44	61	34
21	Exeter	42	11	12	19	38	59	34
22	Southend	42	8	11	23	34	74	27

1922–23

FIRST DIVISION

		P	W	D	L	F	A	Pts
1	Liverpool	42	26	8	8	70	31	60
2	Sunderland	42	22	10	10	72	54	54
3	Huddersfield	42	21	11	10	60	32	53
4	Newcastle	42	18	12	12	45	37	48
5	Everton	42	20	7	15	63	59	47
6	Aston Villa	42	18	10	14	64	51	46
7	WBA	42	17	11	14	58	49	45
8	Man City	42	17	11	14	50	49	45
9	Cardiff	42	18	7	17	73	59	43
10	Sheff United	42	16	10	16	68	64	42
11	Arsenal	42	16	10	16	61	62	42
12	Tottenham	42	17	7	18	50	50	41
13	Bolton	42	14	12	16	50	58	40
14	Blackburn	42	14	12	16	47	62	40
15	Burnley	42	16	6	20	58	59	38
16	Preston	42	13	11	18	60	64	37
17	Birmingham	42	13	11	18	41	57	37
18	Middlesbrough	42	13	10	19	57	63	36
19	Chelsea	42	9	18	15	45	53	36
20	Nottm Forest	42	13	8	21	41	70	34
21	Stoke	42	10	10	22	47	67	30
22	Oldham	42	10	10	22	35	65	30

SECOND DIVISION

		P	W	D	L	F	A	Pts
1	Notts County	42	23	7	12	46	34	53
2	West Ham	42	20	11	11	63	38	51
3	Leicester	42	21	9	12	65	44	51
4	Man United	42	17	14	11	51	36	48
5	Blackpool	42	18	11	13	60	43	47
6	Bury	42	18	11	13	55	46	47
7	Leeds	42	18	11	13	43	36	47
8	Wednesday	42	17	12	13	54	47	46
9	Barnsley	42	17	11	14	62	51	45
10	Fulham	42	16	12	14	43	32	44
11	Southampton	42	14	14	14	40	40	42
12	Hull	42	14	14	14	43	45	42
13	South Shields	42	15	10	17	35	44	40
14	Derby	42	14	11	17	46	50	39
15	Bradford City	42	12	13	17	41	45	37
16	Crystal Palace	42	13	11	18	54	62	37
17	Port Vale	42	14	9	19	39	51	37
18	Coventry	42	15	7	20	46	63	37
19	Clapton Orient	42	12	12	18	40	50	36
20	Stockport	42	14	8	20	43	58	36
21	Rotherham Co	42	13	9	20	44	63	35
22	Wolves	42	9	9	24	42	77	27

THIRD DIVISION (NORTH)

	P	W	D	L	F	A	Pts
1 Nelson	38	24	3	11	61	41	51
2 Bradford PA	38	19	9	10	67	38	47
3 Walsall	38	19	8	11	51	44	46
4 Chesterfield	38	19	7	12	68	52	45
5 Wigan Borough	38	18	8	12	64	39	44
6 Crewe	38	17	9	12	48	38	43
7 Halifax	38	17	7	14	53	46	41
8 Accrington	38	17	7	14	59	65	41
9 Darlington	38	15	10	13	59	46	40
10 Wrexham	38	14	10	14	38	48	38
11 Stalybridge Cel	38	15	6	17	42	47	36
12 Rochdale	38	13	10	15	42	53	36
13 Lincoln	38	13	10	15	39	55	36
14 Grimsby	38	14	5	19	55	52	33
15 Hartlepools	38	10	12	16	48	54	32
16 Tranmere	38	12	8	18	49	59	32
17 Southport	38	12	7	19	32	46	31
18 Barrow	38	13	4	21	50	60	30
19 Ashington	38	11	8	19	51	77	30
20 Durham City	38	9	10	19	43	59	28

THIRD DIVISION (SOUTH)

	P	W	D	L	F	A	Pts
1 Bristol City	42	24	11	7	66	40	59
2 Plymouth	42	23	7	12	61	29	53
3 Swansea	42	22	9	11	78	45	53
4 Brighton	42	20	11	11	52	34	51
5 Luton	42	21	7	14	68	49	49
6 Portsmouth	42	19	8	15	58	52	46
7 Millwall Ath	42	14	18	10	45	40	46
8 Northampton	42	17	11	14	54	44	45
9 Swindon	42	17	11	14	62	56	45
10 Watford	42	17	10	15	57	54	44
11 QPR	42	16	10	16	54	49	42
12 Charlton	42	14	14	14	55	51	42
13 Bristol Rovers	42	13	16	13	35	36	42
14 Brentford	42	13	12	17	41	51	38
15 Southend	42	12	13	17	49	54	37
16 Gillingham	42	15	7	20	51	59	37
17 Merthyr Town	42	11	14	17	39	48	36
18 Norwich	42	13	10	19	51	71	36
19 Reading	42	10	14	18	36	55	34
20 Exeter	42	13	7	22	47	84	33
21 Aberdare Ath	42	9	11	22	42	70	29
22 Newport	42	8	11	23	40	70	27

1923–24

FIRST DIVISION

	P	W	D	L	F	A	Pts
1 Huddersfield	42	23	11	8	60	33	57
2 Cardiff	42	22	13	7	61	34	57
3 Sunderland	42	22	9	11	71	54	53
4 Bolton	42	18	14	10	68	34	50
5 Sheff United	42	19	12	11	69	49	50
6 Aston Villa	42	18	13	11	52	37	49
7 Everton	42	18	13	11	62	53	49
8 Blackburn	42	17	11	14	54	50	45
9 Newcastle	42	17	10	15	60	54	44
10 Notts County	42	14	14	14	44	49	42
11 Man City	42	15	12	15	54	71	42
12 Liverpool	42	15	11	16	49	48	41
13 West Ham	42	13	15	14	40	43	41
14 Birmingham	42	13	13	16	41	49	39
15 Tottenham	42	12	14	16	50	56	38
16 WBA	42	12	14	16	51	62	38
17 Burnley	42	12	12	18	55	60	36
18 Preston	42	12	10	20	52	67	34
19 Arsenal	42	12	9	21	40	63	33
20 Nottm Forest	42	10	12	20	42	64	32
21 Chelsea	42	9	14	19	31	53	32
22 Middlesbrough	42	7	8	27	37	60	22

SECOND DIVISION

	P	W	D	L	F	A	Pts
1 Leeds	42	21	12	9	61	35	54
2 Bury	42	21	9	12	63	35	51
3 Derby	42	21	9	12	75	42	51
4 Blackpool	42	18	13	11	72	47	49
5 Southampton	42	17	14	11	52	31	48
6 Stoke	42	14	18	10	44	42	46
7 Oldham	42	14	17	11	45	52	45
8 Wednesday	42	16	12	14	54	51	44
9 South Shields	42	17	10	15	49	50	44
10 Clapton Orient	42	14	15	13	40	36	43
11 Barnsley	42	16	11	15	57	61	43
12 Leicester	42	17	8	17	64	54	42
13 Stockport	42	13	16	13	44	52	42
14 Man United	42	13	14	15	52	44	40
15 Crystal Palace	42	13	13	16	53	65	39
16 Port Vale	42	13	12	17	50	66	38
17 Hull	42	10	17	15	46	51	37
18 Bradford City	42	11	15	16	35	48	37
19 Coventry	42	11	13	18	52	68	35
20 Fulham	42	10	14	18	45	56	34
21 Nelson	42	10	13	19	40	74	33
22 Bristol City	42	7	15	20	32	65	29

THIRD DIVISION (NORTH)

	P	W	D	L	F	A	Pts
1 Wolves	42	24	15	3	76	27	63
2 Rochdale	42	25	12	5	60	26	62
3 Chesterfield	42	22	10	10	70	39	54
4 Rotherham Co	42	23	6	13	70	43	52
5 Bradford PA	42	21	10	11	69	43	52
6 Darlington	42	20	8	14	70	53	48
7 Southport	42	16	14	12	44	42	46
8 Ashington	42	18	8	16	59	61	44
9 Doncaster	42	15	12	15	59	53	42
10 Wigan Borough	42	14	14	14	55	53	42
11 Grimsby	42	14	13	15	49	47	41
12 Tranmere	42	13	15	14	51	60	41
13 Accrington	42	16	8	18	48	61	40
14 Halifax	42	15	10	17	42	59	40
15 Durham City	42	15	9	18	59	60	39
16 Wrexham	42	10	18	14	37	44	38
17 Walsall	42	14	8	20	44	59	36
18 New Brighton	42	11	13	18	40	53	35
19 Lincoln	42	10	12	20	48	59	32
20 Crewe	42	7	13	22	32	58	27
21 Hartlepools	42	7	11	24	33	70	25
22 Barrow	42	8	9	25	35	80	25

THIRD DIVISION (SOUTH)

	P	W	D	L	F	A	Pts
1 Portsmouth	42	24	11	7	87	30	59
2 Plymouth	42	23	9	10	70	34	55
3 Millwall Ath	42	22	10	10	64	38	54
4 Swansea	42	22	8	12	60	48	52
5 Brighton	42	21	9	12	68	37	51
6 Swindon	42	17	13	12	58	44	47
7 Luton	42	16	14	12	50	44	46
8 Northampton	42	17	11	14	64	47	45
9 Bristol Rovers	42	15	13	14	52	46	43
10 Newport	42	17	9	16	56	64	43
11 Norwich	42	16	8	18	60	59	40
12 Aberdare Ath	42	12	14	16	45	58	38
13 Merthyr Town	42	11	16	15	45	65	38
14 Charlton	42	11	15	16	38	45	37
15 Gillingham	42	12	13	17	43	58	37
16 Exeter	42	15	7	20	37	52	37
17 Brentford	42	14	8	20	54	71	36
18 Reading	42	13	9	20	51	57	35
19 Southend	42	12	10	20	53	84	34
20 Watford	42	9	15	18	45	54	33
21 Bournemouth	42	11	11	20	40	65	33
22 QPR	42	11	9	22	37	77	31

1924–25

FIRST DIVISION

		P	W	D	L	F	A	Pts
1	Huddersfield	42	21	16	5	69	28	58
2	WBA	42	23	10	9	58	34	56
3	Bolton	42	22	11	9	76	34	55
4	Liverpool	42	20	10	12	63	55	50
5	Bury	42	17	15	10	54	51	49
6	Newcastle	42	16	16	10	61	42	48
7	Sunderland	42	19	10	13	64	51	48
8	Birmingham	42	17	12	13	49	53	46
9	Notts County	42	16	13	13	42	31	45
10	Man City	42	17	9	16	76	68	43
11	Cardiff	42	16	11	15	56	51	43
12	Tottenham	42	15	12	15	52	43	42
13	West Ham	42	15	12	15	62	60	42
14	Sheff United	42	13	13	16	55	63	39
15	Aston Villa	42	13	13	16	58	71	39
16	Blackburn	42	11	13	18	53	66	35
17	Everton	42	12	11	19	40	60	35
18	Leeds	42	11	12	19	46	59	34
19	Burnley	42	11	12	19	46	75	34
20	Arsenal	42	14	5	23	46	58	33
21	Preston	42	10	6	26	37	74	26
22	Nottm Forest	42	6	12	24	29	65	24

SECOND DIVISION

		P	W	D	L	F	A	Pts
1	Leicester	42	24	11	7	90	32	59
2	Man United	42	23	11	8	57	23	57
3	Derby	42	22	11	9	71	36	55
4	Portsmouth	42	15	18	9	58	50	48
5	Chelsea	42	16	15	11	51	37	47
6	Wolves	42	20	6	16	55	51	46
7	Southampton	42	13	18	11	40	36	44
8	Port Vale	42	17	8	17	48	56	42
9	South Shields	42	12	17	13	42	38	41
10	Hull	42	15	11	16	50	49	41
11	Clapton Orient	42	14	12	16	42	42	40
12	Fulham	42	15	10	17	41	56	40
13	Middlesbrough	42	10	19	13	36	44	39
14	Wednesday	42	15	8	19	50	56	38
15	Barnsley	42	13	12	17	46	59	38
16	Bradford City	42	13	12	17	37	50	38
17	Blackpool	42	14	9	19	65	61	37
18	Oldham	42	13	11	18	35	51	37
19	Stockport	42	13	11	18	37	57	37
20	Stoke	42	12	11	19	34	46	35
21	Crystal Palace	42	12	10	20	38	54	34
22	Coventry	42	11	9	22	45	84	31

THIRD DIVISION (NORTH)

		P	W	D	L	F	A	Pts
1	Darlington	42	24	10	8	78	33	58
2	Nelson	42	23	7	12	79	50	53
3	New Brighton	42	23	7	12	75	50	53
4	Southport	42	22	7	13	59	37	51
5	Bradford PA	42	19	12	11	84	42	50
6	Rochdale	42	21	7	14	75	53	49
7	Chesterfield	42	17	11	14	60	44	45
8	Lincoln	42	18	8	16	53	58	44
9	Halifax	42	16	11	15	56	52	43
10	Ashington	42	16	10	16	68	76	42
11	Wigan Borough	42	15	11	16	62	65	41
12	Grimsby	42	15	9	18	60	60	39
13	Durham City	42	13	13	16	50	68	39
14	Barrow	42	16	7	19	51	74	39
15	Crewe	42	13	13	16	53	78	39
16	Wrexham	42	15	8	19	53	61	38
17	Accrington	42	15	8	19	60	72	38
18	Doncaster	42	14	10	18	54	65	38
19	Walsall	42	13	11	18	44	53	37
20	Hartlepools	42	12	11	19	45	63	35
21	Tranmere	42	14	4	24	59	78	32
22	Rotherham Co	42	7	7	28	42	88	21

THIRD DIVISION (SOUTH)

		P	W	D	L	F	A	Pts
1	Swansea	42	23	11	8	68	35	57
2	Plymouth	42	23	10	9	77	38	56
3	Bristol City	42	22	9	11	60	41	53
4	Swindon	42	20	11	11	66	38	51
5	Millwall Ath	42	18	13	11	58	38	49
6	Newport	42	20	9	13	62	42	49
7	Exeter	42	19	9	14	59	48	47
8	Brighton	42	19	8	15	59	45	46
9	Northampton	42	20	6	16	51	44	46
10	Southend	42	19	5	18	51	61	43
11	Watford	42	17	9	16	38	47	43
12	Norwich	42	14	13	15	53	51	41
13	Gillingham	42	13	14	15	35	44	40
14	Reading	42	14	10	18	37	38	38
15	Charlton	42	13	12	17	46	48	38
16	Luton	42	10	17	15	49	57	37
17	Bristol Rovers	42	12	13	17	42	49	37
18	Aberdare Ath	42	14	9	19	54	67	37
19	QPR	42	14	8	20	42	63	36
20	Bournemouth	42	13	8	21	40	58	34
21	Brentford	42	9	7	26	38	91	25
22	Merthyr Town	42	8	5	29	35	77	21

1925–26

FIRST DIVISION

		P	W	D	L	F	A	Pts
1	Huddersfield	42	23	11	8	92	60	57
2	Arsenal	42	22	8	12	87	63	52
3	Sunderland	42	21	6	15	96	80	48
4	Bury	42	20	7	15	85	77	47
5	Sheff United	42	19	8	15	102	82	46
6	Aston Villa	42	16	12	14	86	76	44
7	Liverpool	42	14	16	12	70	63	44
8	Bolton	42	17	10	15	75	76	44
9	Man United	42	19	6	17	66	73	44
10	Newcastle	42	16	10	16	84	75	42
11	Everton	42	12	18	12	72	70	42
12	Blackburn	42	15	11	16	91	80	41
13	WBA	42	16	8	18	79	78	40
14	Birmingham	42	16	8	18	66	81	40
15	Tottenham	42	15	9	18	66	79	39
16	Cardiff	42	16	7	19	61	76	39
17	Leicester	42	14	10	18	70	80	38
18	West Ham	42	15	7	20	63	76	37
19	Leeds	42	14	8	20	64	76	36
20	Burnley	42	13	10	19	85	108	36
21	Man City	42	12	11	19	89	100	35
22	Notts County	42	13	7	22	54	74	33

SECOND DIVISION

		P	W	D	L	F	A	Pts
1	Wednesday	42	27	6	9	88	48	60
2	Derby	42	25	7	10	77	42	57
3	Chelsea	42	19	14	9	76	49	52
4	Wolves	42	21	7	14	84	60	49
5	Swansea	42	19	11	12	77	57	49
6	Blackpool	42	17	11	14	76	69	45
7	Oldham	42	18	8	16	74	62	44
8	Port Vale	42	19	6	17	79	69	44
9	South Shields	42	18	8	16	74	65	44
10	Middlesbrough	42	21	2	19	77	68	44
11	Portsmouth	42	17	10	15	79	74	44
12	Preston	42	18	7	17	71	84	43
13	Hull	42	16	9	17	63	61	41
14	Southampton	42	15	8	19	63	63	38
15	Darlington	42	14	10	18	72	77	38
16	Bradford City	42	13	10	19	47	66	36
17	Nottm Forest	42	14	8	20	51	73	36
18	Barnsley	42	12	12	18	58	84	36
19	Fulham	42	11	12	19	46	77	34
20	Clapton Orient	42	12	9	21	50	65	33
21	Stoke	42	12	8	22	54	77	32
22	Stockport	42	8	9	25	51	97	25

THIRD DIVISION (NORTH)

	P	W	D	L	F	A	Pts
1 Grimsby	42	26	9	7	91	40	61
2 Bradford PA	42	26	8	8	101	43	60
3 Rochdale	42	27	5	10	104	58	59
4 Chesterfield	42	25	5	12	100	54	55
5 Halifax	42	17	11	14	53	50	45
6 Hartlepools	42	18	8	16	82	73	44
7 Tranmere	42	19	6	17	73	83	44
8 Nelson	42	16	11	15	89	71	43
9 Ashington	42	16	11	15	70	62	43
10 Doncaster	42	16	11	15	80	72	43
11 Crewe	42	17	9	16	63	61	43
12 New Brighton	42	17	8	17	69	67	42
13 Durham City	42	18	6	18	63	70	42
14 Rotherham	42	17	7	18	69	92	41
15 Lincoln	42	17	5	20	66	82	39
16 Coventry	42	16	6	20	73	82	38
17 Wigan Borough	42	13	11	18	68	74	37
18 Accrington	42	17	3	22	81	105	37
19 Wrexham	42	11	10	21	63	92	32
20 Southport	42	11	10	21	62	92	32
21 Walsall	42	10	6	26	58	107	26
22 Barrow	42	7	4	31	50	98	18

THIRD DIVISION (SOUTH)

	P	W	D	L	F	A	Pts
1 Reading	42	23	11	8	77	52	57
2 Plymouth	42	24	8	10	107	67	56
3 Millwall	42	21	11	10	73	39	53
4 Bristol City	42	21	9	12	72	51	51
5 Brighton	42	19	9	14	84	73	47
6 Swindon	42	20	6	16	69	64	46
7 Luton	42	18	7	17	80	75	43
8 Bournemouth	42	17	9	16	75	91	43
9 Aberdare	42	17	8	17	74	66	42
10 Gillingham	42	17	8	17	53	49	42
11 Southend	42	19	4	19	78	73	42
12 Northampton	42	17	7	18	82	80	41
13 Crystal Palace	42	19	3	20	75	79	41
14 Merthyr Town	42	14	11	17	69	75	39
15 Watford	42	15	9	18	73	89	39
16 Norwich	42	15	9	18	58	73	39
17 Newport	42	14	10	18	64	74	38
18 Brentford	42	16	6	20	69	94	38
19 Bristol Rovers	42	15	6	21	66	69	36
20 Exeter	42	15	5	22	72	70	35
21 Charlton	42	11	13	18	48	68	35
22 QPR	42	6	9	27	37	84	21

1926–27

FIRST DIVISION

	P	W	D	L	F	A	Pts
1 Newcastle	42	25	6	11	96	58	56
2 Huddersfield	42	17	17	8	76	60	51
3 Sunderland	42	21	7	14	98	70	49
4 Bolton	42	19	10	13	84	62	48
5 Burnley	42	19	9	14	91	80	47
6 West Ham	42	19	8	15	86	70	46
7 Leicester	42	17	12	13	85	70	46
8 Sheff United	42	17	10	15	74	86	44
9 Liverpool	42	18	7	17	69	61	43
10 Aston Villa	42	18	7	17	81	83	43
11 Arsenal	42	17	9	16	77	86	43
12 Derby	42	17	7	18	86	73	41
13 Tottenham	42	16	9	17	76	78	41
14 Cardiff	42	16	9	17	55	65	41
15 Man United	42	13	14	15	52	64	40
16 Wednesday	42	15	9	18	75	92	39
17 Birmingham	42	17	4	21	64	73	38
18 Blackburn	42	15	8	19	77	96	38
19 Bury	42	12	12	18	68	77	36
20 Everton	42	12	10	20	64	90	34
21 Leeds	42	11	8	23	69	88	30
22 WBA	42	11	8	23	65	86	30

SECOND DIVISION

	P	W	D	L	F	A	Pts
1 Middlesbrough	42	27	8	7	122	60	62
2 Portsmouth	42	23	8	11	87	49	54
3 Man City	42	22	10	10	108	61	54
4 Chelsea	42	20	12	10	62	52	52
5 Nottm Forest	42	18	14	10	80	55	50
6 Preston	42	20	9	13	63	52	49
7 Hull	42	20	7	15	63	52	47
8 Port Vale	42	16	13	13	88	78	45
9 Blackpool	42	18	8	16	95	80	44
10 Oldham	42	19	6	17	74	84	44
11 Barnsley	42	17	9	16	88	87	43
12 Swansea	42	16	11	15	68	72	43
13 Southampton	42	15	12	15	60	62	42
14 Reading	42	16	8	18	64	72	40
15 Wolves	42	14	7	21	73	75	35
16 Notts County	42	15	5	22	70	96	35
17 Grimsby	42	11	12	19	74	91	34
18 Fulham	42	13	8	21	58	92	34
19 South Shields	42	11	11	20	71	96	33
20 Clapton Orient	42	12	7	23	60	96	31
21 Darlington	42	12	6	24	79	98	30
22 Bradford City	42	7	9	26	50	88	23

THIRD DIVISION (NORTH)

	P	W	D	L	F	A	Pts
1 Stoke	42	27	9	6	92	40	63
2 Rochdale	42	26	6	10	105	65	58
3 Bradford PA	42	24	7	11	101	59	55
4 Halifax	42	21	11	10	70	53	53
5 Nelson	42	22	7	13	104	75	51
6 Stockport	42	22	7	13	93	69	49*
7 Chesterfield	42	21	5	16	92	68	47
8 Doncaster	42	18	11	13	81	65	47
9 Tranmere	42	19	8	15	85	67	46
10 New Brighton	42	18	10	14	79	67	46
11 Lincoln	42	15	12	15	90	78	42
12 Southport	42	15	9	18	80	85	39
13 Wrexham	42	14	10	18	65	73	38
14 Walsall	42	14	10	18	68	81	38
15 Crewe	42	14	9	19	71	81	37
16 Ashington	42	12	12	18	60	90	36
17 Hartlepools	42	14	6	22	66	81	34
18 Wigan Borough	42	11	10	21	66	83	32
19 Rotherham	42	10	12	20	70	92	32
20 Durham City	42	12	6	24	58	105	30
21 Accrington	42	10	7	25	62	98	27
22 Barrow	42	7	8	27	34	117	22

*Two points deducted for fielding Joe Smith without FA permission on 26 March 1927.

THIRD DIVISION (SOUTH)

	P	W	D	L	F	A	Pts
1 Bristol City	42	27	8	7	104	54	62
2 Plymouth	42	25	10	7	95	61	60
3 Millwall	42	23	10	9	89	51	56
4 Brighton	42	21	11	10	79	50	53
5 Swindon	42	21	9	12	100	85	51
6 Crystal Palace	42	18	9	15	84	81	45
7 Bournemouth	42	18	8	16	78	66	44
8 Luton	42	15	14	13	68	66	44
9 Newport	42	19	6	17	57	71	44
10 Bristol Rovers	42	16	9	17	78	80	41
11 Brentford	42	13	14	15	70	61	40
12 Exeter	42	15	10	17	76	73	40
13 Charlton	42	16	8	18	60	61	40
14 QPR	42	15	9	18	65	71	39
15 Coventry	42	15	7	20	71	86	37
16 Norwich	42	12	11	19	59	71	35
17 Merthyr Town	42	13	9	20	63	80	35
18 Northampton	42	15	5	22	59	83	35
19 Southend	42	14	6	22	64	77	34
20 Gillingham	42	11	10	21	54	72	32
21 Watford	42	12	8	22	57	87	32
22 Aberdare Ath	42	9	7	26	62	101	25

1927–28

FIRST DIVISION

		P	W	D	L	F	A	Pts
1	Everton	42	20	13	9	102	66	53
2	Huddersfield	42	22	7	13	91	68	51
3	Leicester	42	18	12	12	96	72	48
4	Derby	42	17	10	15	96	83	44
5	Bury	42	20	4	18	80	80	44
6	Cardiff	42	17	10	15	70	80	44
7	Bolton	42	16	11	15	81	66	43
8	Aston Villa	42	17	9	16	78	73	43
9	Newcastle	42	15	13	14	79	81	43
10	Arsenal	42	13	15	14	82	86	41
11	Birmingham	42	13	15	14	70	75	41
12	Blackburn	42	16	9	17	66	78	41
13	Sheff United	42	15	10	17	79	86	40
14	Wednesday	42	13	13	16	81	78	39
15	Sunderland	42	15	9	18	74	76	39
16	Liverpool	42	13	13	16	84	87	39
17	West Ham	42	14	11	17	81	88	39
18	Burnley	42	16	7	19	82	98	39
19	Man United	42	16	7	19	72	87	39
20	Portsmouth	42	16	7	19	66	90	39
21	Tottenham	42	15	8	19	74	86	38
22	Middlesbrough	42	11	15	16	81	88	37

SECOND DIVISION

		P	W	D	L	F	A	Pts
1	Man City	42	25	9	8	100	59	59
2	Leeds	42	25	7	10	98	49	57
3	Chelsea	42	23	8	11	75	45	54
4	Preston	42	22	9	11	100	66	53
5	Stoke	42	22	8	12	78	59	52
6	Swansea	42	18	12	12	75	63	48
7	Oldham	42	19	8	15	75	51	46
8	WBA	42	17	12	13	90	70	46
9	Port Vale	42	18	8	16	68	57	44
10	Nottm Forest	42	15	10	17	83	84	40
11	Grimsby	42	14	12	16	69	83	40
12	Bristol City	42	15	9	18	76	79	39
13	Hull	42	12	15	15	41	54	39
14	Barnsley	42	14	11	17	65	85	39
15	Notts County	42	13	12	17	68	74	38
16	Wolves	42	13	10	19	63	91	36
17	Southampton	42	14	7	21	68	77	35
18	Reading	42	11	13	18	53	75	35
19	Blackpool	42	13	8	21	83	101	34
20	Clapton Orient	42	11	12	19	55	85	34
21	Fulham	42	13	7	22	68	89	33
22	South Shields	42	7	9	26	56	111	23

THIRD DIVISION (NORTH)

		P	W	D	L	F	A	Pts
1	Bradford PA	42	27	9	6	101	45	63
2	Lincoln	42	24	7	11	91	64	55
3	Stockport	42	23	8	11	89	51	54
4	Doncaster	42	23	7	12	80	44	53
5	Tranmere	42	22	9	11	105	72	53
6	Bradford City	42	18	12	12	85	60	48
7	Darlington	42	21	5	16	89	74	47
8	Southport	42	20	5	17	79	70	45
9	Accrington	42	18	8	16	76	67	44
10	New Brighton	42	14	14	14	72	62	42
11	Wrexham	42	18	6	18	64	67	42
12	Halifax	42	13	15	14	73	71	41
13	Rochdale	42	17	7	18	74	77	41
14	Rotherham	42	14	11	17	65	69	39
15	Hartlepools	42	16	6	20	69	81	38
16	Chesterfield	42	13	10	19	71	78	36
17	Crewe	42	12	10	20	77	86	34
18	Ashington	42	11	11	20	77	103	33
19	Barrow	42	10	11	21	54	102	31
20	Wigan Borough	42	10	10	22	56	97	30
21	Durham City	42	11	7	24	53	100	29
22	Nelson	42	10	6	26	76	136	26

THIRD DIVISION (SOUTH)

		P	W	D	L	F	A	Pts
1	Millwall	42	30	5	7	127	50	65
2	Northampton	42	23	9	10	102	64	55
3	Plymouth	42	23	7	12	85	54	53
4	Brighton	42	19	10	13	81	69	48
5	Crystal Palace	42	18	12	12	79	72	48
6	Swindon	42	19	9	14	90	69	47
7	Southend	42	20	6	16	80	64	46
8	Exeter	42	17	12	13	70	60	46
9	Newport	42	18	9	15	81	84	45
10	QPR	42	17	9	16	72	71	43
11	Charlton	42	15	13	14	60	70	43
12	Brentford	42	16	8	18	76	74	40
13	Luton	42	16	7	19	94	87	39
14	Bournemouth	42	13	12	17	72	79	38
15	Watford	42	14	10	18	68	78	38
16	Gillingham	42	13	11	18	62	81	37
17	Norwich	42	10	16	16	66	70	36
18	Walsall	42	12	9	21	75	101	33
19	Bristol Rovers	42	14	4	24	67	93	32
20	Coventry	42	11	9	22	67	96	31
21	Merthyr Town	42	9	13	20	53	91	31
22	Torquay	42	8	14	20	53	103	30

1928–29

FIRST DIVISION

		P	W	D	L	F	A	Pts
1	Wednesday	42	21	10	11	86	62	52
2	Leicester	42	21	9	12	96	67	51
3	Aston Villa	42	23	4	15	98	81	50
4	Sunderland	42	20	7	15	93	75	47
5	Liverpool	42	17	12	13	90	64	46
6	Derby	42	18	10	14	86	71	46
7	Blackburn	42	17	11	14	72	63	45
8	Man City	42	18	9	15	95	86	45
9	Arsenal	42	16	13	13	77	72	45
10	Newcastle	42	19	6	17	70	72	44
11	Sheff United	42	15	11	16	86	85	41
12	Man United	42	14	13	15	66	76	41
13	Leeds	42	16	9	17	71	84	41
14	Bolton	42	14	12	16	73	80	40
15	Birmingham	42	15	10	17	68	77	40
16	Huddersfield	42	14	11	17	70	61	39
17	West Ham	42	15	9	18	86	96	39
18	Everton	42	17	4	21	63	75	38
19	Burnley	42	15	8	19	81	103	38
20	Portsmouth	42	15	6	21	56	80	36
21	Bury	42	12	7	23	62	99	31
22	Cardiff	42	8	13	21	43	59	29

SECOND DIVISION

		P	W	D	L	F	A	Pts
1	Middlesbrough	42	22	11	9	92	57	55
2	Grimsby	42	24	5	13	82	61	53
3	Bradford PA	42	22	4	16	88	70	48
4	Southampton	42	17	14	11	74	60	48
5	Notts County	42	19	9	14	78	65	47
6	Stoke	42	17	12	13	74	51	46
7	WBA	42	19	8	15	80	79	46
8	Blackpool	42	19	7	16	92	76	45
9	Chelsea	42	17	10	15	64	65	44
10	Tottenham	42	17	9	16	75	81	43
11	Nottm Forest	42	15	12	15	71	70	42
12	Hull	42	13	14	15	58	63	40
13	Preston	42	15	9	18	78	79	39
14	Millwall	42	16	7	19	71	86	39
15	Reading	42	15	9	18	63	86	39
16	Barnsley	42	16	6	20	69	66	38
17	Wolves	42	15	7	20	77	81	37
18	Oldham	42	16	5	21	54	75	37
19	Swansea	42	13	10	19	62	75	36
20	Bristol City	42	13	10	19	58	72	36
21	Port Vale	42	15	4	23	71	86	34
22	Clapton Orient	42	12	8	22	45	72	32

THIRD DIVISION (NORTH)

		P	W	D	L	F	A	Pts
1	Bradford City	42	27	9	6	128	43	63
2	Stockport	42	28	6	8	111	58	62
3	Wrexham	42	21	10	11	91	69	52
4	Wigan Borough	42	21	9	12	82	49	51
5	Doncaster	42	20	10	12	76	66	50
6	Lincoln	42	21	6	15	91	67	48
7	Tranmere	42	22	3	17	79	77	47
8	Carlisle	42	19	8	15	86	77	46
9	Crewe	42	18	8	16	80	68	44
10	South Shields	42	18	8	16	83	74	44
11	Chesterfield	42	18	5	19	71	77	41
12	Southport	42	16	8	18	75	85	40
13	Halifax	42	13	13	16	63	62	39
14	New Brighton	42	15	9	18	64	71	39
15	Nelson	42	17	5	20	77	90	39
16	Rotherham	42	15	9	18	60	77	39
17	Rochdale	42	13	10	19	79	96	36
18	Accrington	42	13	8	21	68	82	34
19	Darlington	42	13	7	22	64	88	33
20	Barrow	42	10	8	24	64	93	28
21	Hartlepools	42	10	6	26	59	112	26
22	Ashington	42	8	7	27	45	115	23

THIRD DIVISION (SOUTH)

		P	W	D	L	F	A	Pts
1	Charlton	42	23	8	11	86	60	54
2	Crystal Palace	42	23	8	11	81	67	54
3	Northampton	42	20	12	10	96	57	52
4	Plymouth	42	20	12	10	83	51	52
5	Fulham	42	21	10	11	101	71	52
6	QPR	42	19	14	9	82	61	52
7	Luton	42	19	11	12	89	73	49
8	Watford	42	19	10	13	79	74	48
9	Bournemouth	42	19	9	14	84	77	47
10	Swindon	42	15	13	14	75	72	43
11	Coventry	42	14	14	14	62	57	42
12	Southend	42	15	11	16	80	75	41
13	Brentford	42	14	10	18	56	60	38
14	Walsall	42	13	12	17	73	79	38
15	Brighton	42	16	6	20	58	76	38
16	Newport	42	13	9	20	69	86	35
17	Norwich	42	14	6	22	69	81	34
18	Torquay	42	14	6	22	66	84	34
19	Bristol Rovers	42	13	7	22	60	79	33
20	Merthyr Town	42	11	8	23	55	103	30
21	Exeter	42	9	11	22	67	88	29
22	Gillingham	42	10	9	23	43	83	29

1929–30

FIRST DIVISION

		P	W	D	L	F	A	Pts
1	Sheff Wed	42	26	8	8	105	57	60
2	Derby	42	21	8	13	90	82	50
3	Man City	42	19	9	14	91	81	47
4	Aston Villa	42	21	5	16	92	83	47
5	Leeds	42	20	6	16	79	63	46
6	Blackburn	42	19	7	16	99	93	45
7	West Ham	42	19	5	18	86	79	43
8	Leicester	42	17	9	16	86	90	43
9	Sunderland	42	18	7	17	76	80	43
10	Huddersfield	42	17	9	16	63	69	43
11	Birmingham	42	16	9	17	67	62	41
12	Liverpool	42	16	9	17	63	79	41
13	Portsmouth	42	15	19	17	66	62	40
14	Arsenal	42	14	11	17	78	66	39
15	Bolton	45	15	9	18	74	74	39
16	Middlesbrough	42	16	6	20	82	84	38
17	Man United	42	15	8	19	67	88	38
18	Grimsby	42	15	7	20	73	89	37
19	Newcastle	42	15	7	20	71	92	37
20	Sheff United	42	15	6	21	91	96	36
21	Burnley	42	14	8	20	79	97	36
22	Everton	42	12	11	19	80	92	35

SECOND DIVISION

		P	W	D	L	F	A	Pts
1	Blackpool	42	27	4	11	98	67	58
2	Chelsea	42	22	11	9	74	46	55
3	Oldham	42	21	11	10	90	51	53
4	Bradford PA	42	19	12	11	91	70	50
5	Bury	42	22	5	15	78	67	49
6	WBA	42	21	5	16	105	73	47
7	Southampton	42	17	11	14	77	76	45
8	Cardiff	42	18	8	16	61	59	44
9	Wolves	42	16	9	17	77	79	41
10	Nottm Forest	42	13	15	14	55	69	41
11	Stoke	42	16	8	18	74	72	40
12	Tottenham	42	15	9	18	59	61	39
13	Charlton	42	14	11	17	59	63	39
14	Millwall	42	12	15	15	57	73	39
15	Swansea	42	14	9	19	57	61	37
16	Preston	42	13	11	18	65	80	37
17	Barnsley	42	14	8	20	56	71	36
18	Bradford City	42	12	12	18	60	77	36
19	Reading	42	12	11	19	54	67	35
20	Bristol City	42	13	9	20	61	83	35
21	Hull	42	14	7	21	51	78	35
22	Notts County	42	9	15	18	54	70	33

THIRD DIVISION (NORTH)

		P	W	D	L	F	A	Pts
1	Port Vale	42	30	7	5	103	37	67
2	Stockport	42	28	7	7	106	44	63
3	Darlington	42	22	6	14	108	73	50
4	Chesterfield	42	22	6	14	76	56	50
5	Lincoln	42	17	14	11	83	61	48
6	York	42	15	16	11	77	64	46
7	South Shields	42	18	10	14	77	74	46
8	Hartlepools	42	17	11	14	81	74	45
9	Southport	42	15	13	14	81	74	43
10	Rochdale	42	18	7	17	89	91	43
11	Crewe	42	17	8	17	82	71	42
12	Tranmere	42	16	9	17	83	86	41
13	New Brighton	42	16	8	18	69	79	40
14	Doncaster	42	15	9	18	62	69	39
15	Carlisle	42	16	7	19	90	101	39
16	Accrington	42	14	9	19	84	81	37
17	Wrexham	42	13	8	21	67	88	34
18	Wigan Borough	42	13	7	22	60	88	33
19	Nelson	42	13	7	22	51	80	33
20	Rotherham	42	11	8	23	67	113	30
21	Halifax	42	10	8	24	44	79	28
22	Barrow	42	11	5	26	41	98	27

THIRD DIVISION (SOUTH)

		P	W	D	L	F	A	Pts
1	Plymouth	42	30	8	4	98	38	68
2	Brentford	42	28	5	9	94	44	61
3	QPR	42	21	9	12	80	68	51
4	Northampton	42	21	8	13	82	58	50
5	Brighton	42	21	8	13	87	63	50
6	Coventry	42	19	9	14	88	73	47
7	Fulham	42	18	11	13	87	83	47
8	Norwich	42	18	10	14	88	77	46
9	Crystal Palace	42	17	12	13	81	74	46
10	Bournemouth	42	15	13	14	72	61	43
11	Southend	42	15	13	14	69	59	43
12	Clapton Orient	42	14	13	15	55	62	41
13	Luton	42	14	12	16	64	78	40
14	Swindon	42	13	12	17	73	83	38
15	Watford	42	15	8	19	60	73	38
16	Exeter	42	12	11	19	67	73	35
17	Walsall	42	13	8	21	71	78	34
18	Newport	42	12	10	20	74	85	34
19	Torquay	42	10	11	21	64	94	31
20	Bristol Rovers	42	11	8	23	67	93	30
21	Gillingham	42	11	8	23	51	80	30
22	Merthyr Town	42	6	9	27	60	135	21

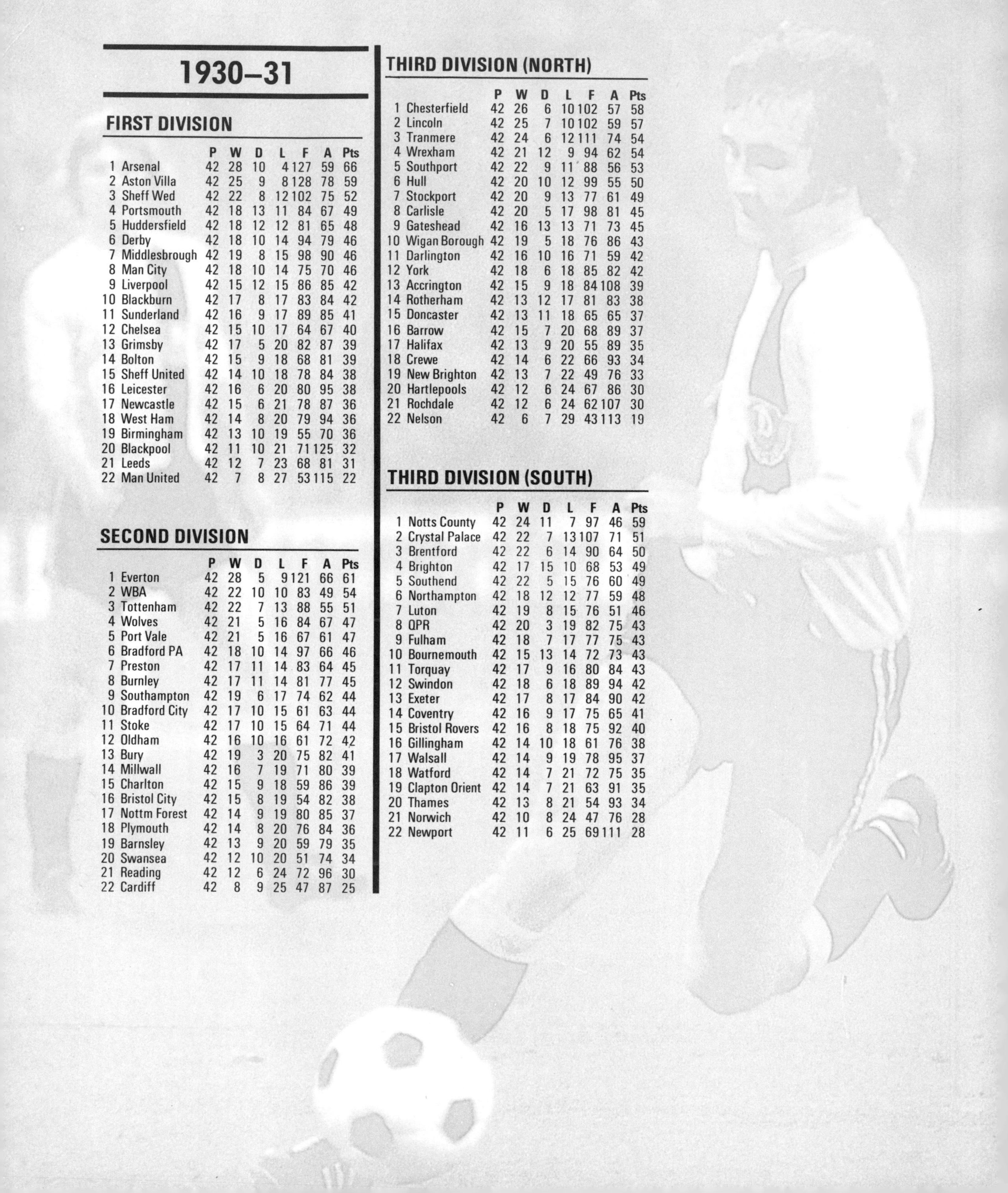

1930–31

FIRST DIVISION

		P	W	D	L	F	A	Pts
1	Arsenal	42	28	10	4	127	59	66
2	Aston Villa	42	25	9	8	128	78	59
3	Sheff Wed	42	22	8	12	102	75	52
4	Portsmouth	42	18	13	11	84	67	49
5	Huddersfield	42	18	12	12	81	65	48
6	Derby	42	18	10	14	94	79	46
7	Middlesbrough	42	19	8	15	98	90	46
8	Man City	42	18	10	14	75	70	46
9	Liverpool	42	15	12	15	86	85	42
10	Blackburn	42	17	8	17	83	84	42
11	Sunderland	42	16	9	17	89	85	41
12	Chelsea	42	15	10	17	64	67	40
13	Grimsby	42	17	5	20	82	87	39
14	Bolton	42	15	9	18	68	81	39
15	Sheff United	42	14	10	18	78	84	38
16	Leicester	42	16	6	20	80	95	38
17	Newcastle	42	15	6	21	78	87	36
18	West Ham	42	14	8	20	79	94	36
19	Birmingham	42	13	10	19	55	70	36
20	Blackpool	42	11	10	21	71	125	32
21	Leeds	42	12	7	23	68	81	31
22	Man United	42	7	8	27	53	115	22

SECOND DIVISION

		P	W	D	L	F	A	Pts
1	Everton	42	28	5	9	121	66	61
2	WBA	42	22	10	10	83	49	54
3	Tottenham	42	22	7	13	88	55	51
4	Wolves	42	21	5	16	84	67	47
5	Port Vale	42	21	5	16	67	61	47
6	Bradford PA	42	18	10	14	97	66	46
7	Preston	42	17	11	14	83	64	45
8	Burnley	42	17	11	14	81	77	45
9	Southampton	42	19	6	17	74	62	44
10	Bradford City	42	17	10	15	61	63	44
11	Stoke	42	17	10	15	64	71	44
12	Oldham	42	16	10	16	61	72	42
13	Bury	42	19	3	20	75	82	41
14	Millwall	42	16	7	19	71	80	39
15	Charlton	42	15	9	18	59	86	39
16	Bristol City	42	15	8	19	54	82	38
17	Nottm Forest	42	14	9	19	80	85	37
18	Plymouth	42	14	8	20	76	84	36
19	Barnsley	42	13	9	20	59	79	35
20	Swansea	42	12	10	20	51	74	34
21	Reading	42	12	6	24	72	96	30
22	Cardiff	42	8	9	25	47	87	25

THIRD DIVISION (NORTH)

		P	W	D	L	F	A	Pts
1	Chesterfield	42	26	6	10	102	57	58
2	Lincoln	42	25	7	10	102	59	57
3	Tranmere	42	24	6	12	111	74	54
4	Wrexham	42	21	12	9	94	62	54
5	Southport	42	22	9	11	88	56	53
6	Hull	42	20	10	12	99	55	50
7	Stockport	42	20	9	13	77	61	49
8	Carlisle	42	20	5	17	98	81	45
9	Gateshead	42	16	13	13	71	73	45
10	Wigan Borough	42	19	5	18	76	86	43
11	Darlington	42	16	10	16	71	59	42
12	York	42	18	6	18	85	82	42
13	Accrington	42	15	9	18	84	108	39
14	Rotherham	42	13	12	17	81	83	38
15	Doncaster	42	13	11	18	65	65	37
16	Barrow	42	15	7	20	68	89	37
17	Halifax	42	13	9	20	55	89	35
18	Crewe	42	14	6	22	66	93	34
19	New Brighton	42	13	7	22	49	76	33
20	Hartlepools	42	12	6	24	67	86	30
21	Rochdale	42	12	6	24	62	107	30
22	Nelson	42	6	7	29	43	113	19

THIRD DIVISION (SOUTH)

		P	W	D	L	F	A	Pts
1	Notts County	42	24	11	7	97	46	59
2	Crystal Palace	42	22	7	13	107	71	51
3	Brentford	42	22	6	14	90	64	50
4	Brighton	42	17	15	10	68	53	49
5	Southend	42	22	5	15	76	60	49
6	Northampton	42	18	12	12	77	59	48
7	Luton	42	19	8	15	76	51	46
8	QPR	42	20	3	19	82	75	43
9	Fulham	42	18	7	17	77	75	43
10	Bournemouth	42	15	13	14	72	73	43
11	Torquay	42	17	9	16	80	84	43
12	Swindon	42	18	6	18	89	94	42
13	Exeter	42	17	8	17	84	90	42
14	Coventry	42	16	9	17	75	65	41
15	Bristol Rovers	42	16	8	18	75	92	40
16	Gillingham	42	14	10	18	61	76	38
17	Walsall	42	14	9	19	78	95	37
18	Watford	42	14	7	21	72	75	35
19	Clapton Orient	42	14	7	21	63	91	35
20	Thames	42	13	8	21	54	93	34
21	Norwich	42	10	8	24	47	76	28
22	Newport	42	11	6	25	69	111	28

FIVE
Arsenal
1931–1939

'In an idle moment I set down this team of old players to amuse myself in comparing them with the chief players of today.

'Sam Hardy, Bob Crompton, Jesse Pennington, Ben Warren, Charlie Roberts, Ernest Needham, Jockie Simpson, Steve Bloomer, Albert Shepherd, George Holley, Fred Spiksley.

'It goes a long way to convince one that football has lost its personalities. We have now few of such giants. But I doubt very much whether the public would today be satisfied with the old football, with all its precision and deliberate accuracy. It does not fit modern tendencies. It would be out of tune with the bustle and excitement of everyday life. Spectators want a fast-moving spectacle, rapier-like attacks that have the spirit of adventure, and ever more goals. But I should do an injustice to the old-timers if I did not believe that they would have been able to accommodate themselves to modern requirements. Their natural ability would have ensured this.'

Herbert Chapman, *who made Huddersfield into the outstanding club of the 1920s and then Arsenal into the dominant force of the 1930s.*

Arsenal's dominance of the 1930s went far beyond their magnetic accumulation of trophies. A country crippled by recession and shamed by its dole queues saw the club as a symbol of the prosperity and privileges of London.

Herbert Chapman's team was loved by its own but cordially hated by just about everyone else. Arsenal were invincible, grandly untouchable and, always, the team to beat. Their success was even resented in other board-rooms where complacency and convention ruled; but this was just what the game needed. Envy became a stimulant. Arsenal's professionalism was studied and copied. The English game had a Highbury complex – and understandably so. Arsenal were League champions five times (1931, 1933–4–5 and 1938), runners-up in 1932 and third in 1937. They also won the FA Cup in 1930 and 1936 and were beaten finalists in 1932. The first 38 championships had belonged to the north and midlands but when, at last, the monopoly was broken Arsenal did the job properly.

There was no television then to flatter and project but Arsenal's players were household names. Alex James and David Jack, of course; Joe Hulme and Cliff 'Boy' Bastin, thunder and lightning on the wings; Herbie Roberts, the shy, red-headed giant who became Chapman's principal stopper; impeccable full-backs such as Tom Parker, George Male and Eddie Hapgood; and Ted Drake, a centre-forward who came later, a hammer who drove defences into the ground and who once scored seven goals against Aston Villa. Some cost a lot of money, others were conjured out of minor football, but all became essential components of a side that was horribly mean in defence and cruel in counter-attack.

Arsenal's football was sometimes described as 'smash and grab' and often they were called 'Lucky Arsenal', but Chapman was pointing the way to the future. His feeling for things to come was remarkable.

Chapman once visited an old friend in Austria and returned to talk excitedly about a night match he had watched. The pitch had been lit by the headlamps of 40 cars. 'Do you realize,' he asked, 'that if the same number of lights were up on 40-foot poles we could play football as if it was daylight?' Not long after, the Press were invited to watch an Arsenal practice match at night illuminated by dangling lanterns. Chapman got the publicity he wanted for an idea he was convinced would work. He later watched floodlit matches in Belgium and Holland – 'cricket with a white ball would have been possible,' he said. But authority was unimpressed, and it was nearly 20 years before the first official floodlit football match was played in England.

Chapman was also one of the first men to insist on first-class facilities for spectators. He tried out numbered shirts five years before there was approval from the Football League (in 1939); he advocated white balls and all-weather pitches; he experimented with independent time-keeping and goal judges; and, the biggest tribute of all to his gift for persuasion, he had the name of the local underground station changed from Gillespie Road to Arsenal.

Nothing about Chapman was grey or vague. He demanded power, loyalty, absolute obedience, punctuality at all times and devotion to club and profession. In return he was scrupulously fair and true to his word.

Chapman died, suddenly, in January 1934. Despite a chill, and against advice, he insisted on watching his third team play in a cutting wind at Guildford. 'I haven't seen the boys for a week or so,' he said. Pneumonia set in and three days later he was gone. Arsenal still won the championship that season; and the season after. There is a knowing smile on the face of the bust of Chapman which now stands in the main entrance hall at Highbury.

Chapman was succeeded as manager by one of the club's directors – George Allison. He was an experienced journalist who was best known as a broadcaster, the first regular BBC Radio football commentator, a pioneer in the field, a man whose rich voice (and habit of saying 'By Jove') was familiar to millions. Allison had no experience as a player but he stuck with Chapman's principles, made an ally of Tom Whittacker, the club's greatly respected trainer, and Arsenal kept on winning.

There are other clubs, however, who also remember the 1930s with pride. West Bromwich Albion won promotion from the Second Division and the FA Cup in 1931 – a unique double by what was known as 'the team of boys'. And Everton, that same year, began a remarkable run which saw them win the Second Division championship (121 goals, Dixie Dean 39), the First Division championship (116 goals, Dean 44) and the FA Cup (with Dean scoring in every round except the semi-final) in successive seasons.

Manchester City reached the Cup Final two years running with a stylish young Scot called Matt Busby at right-half – winning it in 1934 – and then became League champions for the first time in the Coronation year of 1937. Sunderland, too, with perhaps their last great side, won the championship in 1936 and the Cup a year later.

There was also one individual scoring record that even Dixie Dean never threatened. On Easter Monday 1936 Joe Payne of Luton scored ten goals against Bristol Rovers in a Third Division South match – a record which still stands and which is still celebrated by a Joe Payne Lounge at Kenilworth Road. Payne was a reserve wing-half but on that bitterly cold bank holiday afternoon he was sent out at centre-forward for the first time in his career. For 30 minutes nothing went right – and then for an hour nothing went wrong. His ten goals, one scored while he was on his backside, made him an instant national hero.

Luton and the modest Payne – who claimed it had been 'just one of those days' – resisted all manner of tempting offers in the next week or two, and their confidence in each other was justified. Payne scored 55 League goals (still a club record) the following season to help Luton win promotion. But then he moved on to Chelsea, West Ham and Millwall and, after a lot of injuries, he retired in 1948.

If only television could have been there to see Joe 'Ten Goal' Payne make his bit of history. But it wasn't until 1937 – a year later – that cameras first sent a football match into the homes of the nation.

The 1939–40 season opened on 26 August with Everton, the last champions before the Great War, again defending the title. Seven days later Poland was invaded and the world was at war once more. Many young men had played their last game of League football.

ARSENAL IN THE THIRTIES

1929–30	FA Cup winners
1930–31	League champions and FA Charity Shield winners
1931–32	League runners-up, FA Cup runners-up and FA Charity Shield winners
1932–33	League champions
1933–34	League champions and FA Charity Shield winners
1934–35	League champions and FA Charity Shield winners
1935–36	FA Cup winners
1936–37	Third in League
1937–38	League champions
1938–39	Fifth in League and FA Charity Shield winners

FOOTBALL LEAGUE GOALSCORERS: BEST IN SEASON

Division	Season		Goals	Games
1	1927–28	**Dixie Dean** (Everton)	60	39
2	1926–27	**George Camsell** (Middlesbrough)	59	37
3 (S)	1936–37	**Joe Payne** (Luton Town)	55	39
3 (N)	1936–37	**Ted Harston** (Mansfield Town)	55	41
3	1959–60	**Derek Reeves** (Southampton)	39	46
4	1960–61	**Terry Bly** (Peterborough United)	52	46

left Tom 'Pongo' Waring who scored 49 League goals for Aston Villa in season 1930–31 – a club record. Aston Villa scored 128 goals that season, still a First Division record, but only finished runners-up to Arsenal who scored a mere 127. Waring was bought by Villa from Tranmere Rovers for £4,700, then the highest fee paid for a Third Division player, and he won five caps for England in 1931 and 1932.

right Harry Hibbs of Birmingham and England – one of the finest goalkeepers of the inter-war period. Only 5 ft 9 ins tall but fearless, wonderfully agile and a master of position. England rarely looked beyond him between 1929 and 1936 (25 caps) but he never won any honours with Birmingham. He played nearly 400 League and Cup games for them but, in all that time, Birmingham never finished higher than ninth in Division One and lost the one FA Cup final they reached in 1931.

SATURDAY, MARCH 7th, 1931

THE
THAMES
ASSOCIATION FOOTBALL CLUB.

Price : ONE PENNY

Directors : Sir LOUIS W. DANE, G.C.I.E., C.S.I. (*Chairman*) ; CLANCY H. McKNIGHT, F.C.A. ; WRIGHT CUNDY ;
Major A. S. O'BRIEN ; W. REECE
Secretary : H. R. MILBANK. Manager : DAVID BUCHANAN.

THAMES v. TORQUAY UNITED

No. 35 FOOTBALL LEAGUE—Div. III. KICK-OFF at 3.15 P.M.

Half-Time Scores To-Day

	Home Club	*H.-T. Score*		*Away Club*	*H.-T. Score*
A	Bournemouth		v	Newport C.	
B	Clapton Orient		v	Brighton	
C	Coventry C.		v	Southend U.	
D	Fulham		v	Luton Town	
E	Norwich City		v	Northampt'n	
F	Notts. County		v	Exeter City	
G	Q.P. Rangers		v	Brentford	
H	Swindon T.		v	Bristol Rov.	
J	Walsall		v	Crystal Pal.	
K	Watford		v	Gillingham	
L	Arsenal		v	Huddersfield	
M	Blackpool		v	Chelsea	
N	Sheffield U.		v	West Ham	
P	Cardiff City		v	Southampt.	
Q	Charlton A.		v	Tottenham	
R	Everton		v	Reading	
S	West Brom A.		v	Millwall	
T	Plymouth		v	Bradford	

By Special Appointment Seedsmen to H.M. Edward VII

The Football Ground at this Stadium was reconstructed and returfed by
KENT & BRYDON, LTD., DARLINGTON
Seed Merchants and Landscape Contractors, Sports Ground Constructors.

above Thames were members of the League for only two seasons, 1930–32. They finished twentieth in Division Three (South) in their first season and bottom in their second with 23 points from 42 games. They did not apply for re-election and were replaced by Newport. Thames played at West Ham Stadium, Prince Regent's Lane, London E6; and the 469 who watched them beat Luton 1–0 on 6 December 1930 is believed to be the League's lowest gate for a Saturday afternoon game.

left 'Dixie' (William Ralph) Dean of Tranmere, Everton, Notts County and England – the natural starter for any argument about who was the best centre-forward in League history. Pictured in the last but one of his 16 games for England, against Spain at Highbury, 9 December 1931. England won 7–1 and Dean contributed his last – and 18th – international goal. The Spanish goalkeeper is the legendary Ricardo Zamora, known as the 'Man in Black', a cult figure who arrived at Highbury with an international reputation as the best 'keeper in the world. Dean and England humiliated him. 'Give it to Dixie' was a cry that followed Dean all his career – and his list of records show why: 60 League goals in season (1927–8); 100 in all games that same season; 200 goals in 199 League games by the age of 23; 300 in 310 League games, 362 in 400, 379 in 437 altogether; 37 hat-tricks and a grand total of 473 goals in 502 first class games (average 0.94 goals per game).

below left Dean heads his 60th League goal of the 1927–8 season. Believed to be the only surviving picture of a unique moment.

right Arthur Chandler, a swashbuckling centre-forward and great club servant, who scored 262 League goals for Leicester City between 1923–35: still a club record. The story goes that as he scored his fifth goal in one match at Filbert Street five white swans swooped low over the ground.

above Arsenal 1931 – champions of the League and, 43 years after the birth of the Football League, the first southern club to win the title. Their trophies and pride are reflected in the puddles. Back row (l to r): J. Shaw (assistant-manager), H. Cope, R. Robinson, W. Allison, J. Brain, C. Preedy, A. Haynes, H. Roberts, W. Harper, W. Seddon, D. Lewis, G. Male, R. Parkin, W. Milne (trainer). Second row: J. Williams, L. Thompson, W. Maycock, A. Baker, B. Diaper, C. Bastin, E. Hapgood, H. Lewis, R. John, J. Lambert. Seated: J. Hulme, T. Parker, H. Chapman (manager), T. Whittaker (chief trainer), D. Jack, C. Jones.

Arsenal at work and play. Cliff Bastin of England smashes a tennis ball, and Alex James of Scotland, minus shirt, punishes a football.

"THE EMPTY CHAIR"
Herbert Chapman's special seat in which he had always followed the games at Highbury.

THEIR TRIBUTE
The players wore black armlets i[n] yesterday's game.

left Herbert Chapman (centre) – builder of winning football teams, businessman, flamboyant publicist, strategist, psychologist, inspiring motivator, disciplinarian and innovator. Listening carefully: Bob John (left) and Alex James.

right A monument to Herbert Chapman's powers of persuasion. The master of Highbury had the name of the North London club's nearby Underground station changed from Gillespie Road to Arsenal. It took months of negotiation and all tickets and machines had to be altered.

bottom left Arsenal – and football – mourn the death of Herbert Chapman. January 1934.

left Albert Geldard of Bradford, Everton, Bolton and England who was once described by Tommy Lawton as 'the fastest thing on two legs – he could catch pigeons'. Geldard, an outside-right, became the youngest player ever to appear in a League game when he played for Bradford P.A. against Millwall in 1929 at the age of 15 years 158 days – a record equalled, to the day, by Ken Roberts of Wrexham in 1951. Geldard was a member of Everton's FA Cup-winning side in 1933 and won four caps between 1933 and 1938.

above Stamford Bridge: Chelsea v Arsenal, 12 October 1935, watched by a ground record crowd of 82,905. Painting by Charles Cundall, R.A., who worked on a special platform erected by the club. Oil on canvas (30″ × 47″).

left Stanley Rous – referee of the 1934 FA Cup Final between Manchester City and Portsmouth (2–1) – explaining the off-side law. Rous was appointed FA secretary the same year, was knighted in 1949 and became President of FIFA, the game's governing body, in 1961 (until 1974). He devised the diagonal system of refereeing, now used all over the world, actively encouraged the start of European football and, with Sir Walter Winterbottom, introduced organized coaching in England. One of the most influential administrators in the history of football, he died in 1986, aged 91.

left The great Steve Bloomer of England, who scored 291 goals in 475 games for Derby County between 1892–1914, assisted the club in various capacities until his death in 1938. He was always sure of an audience.

right Joe 'Ten Goal' Payne of Luton Town – the reserve wing-half who was sent out as a centre-forward against Bristol Rovers in a Third Division South match on Easter Monday 1936 and broke all individual League records by scoring ten. Luton won 12–0.

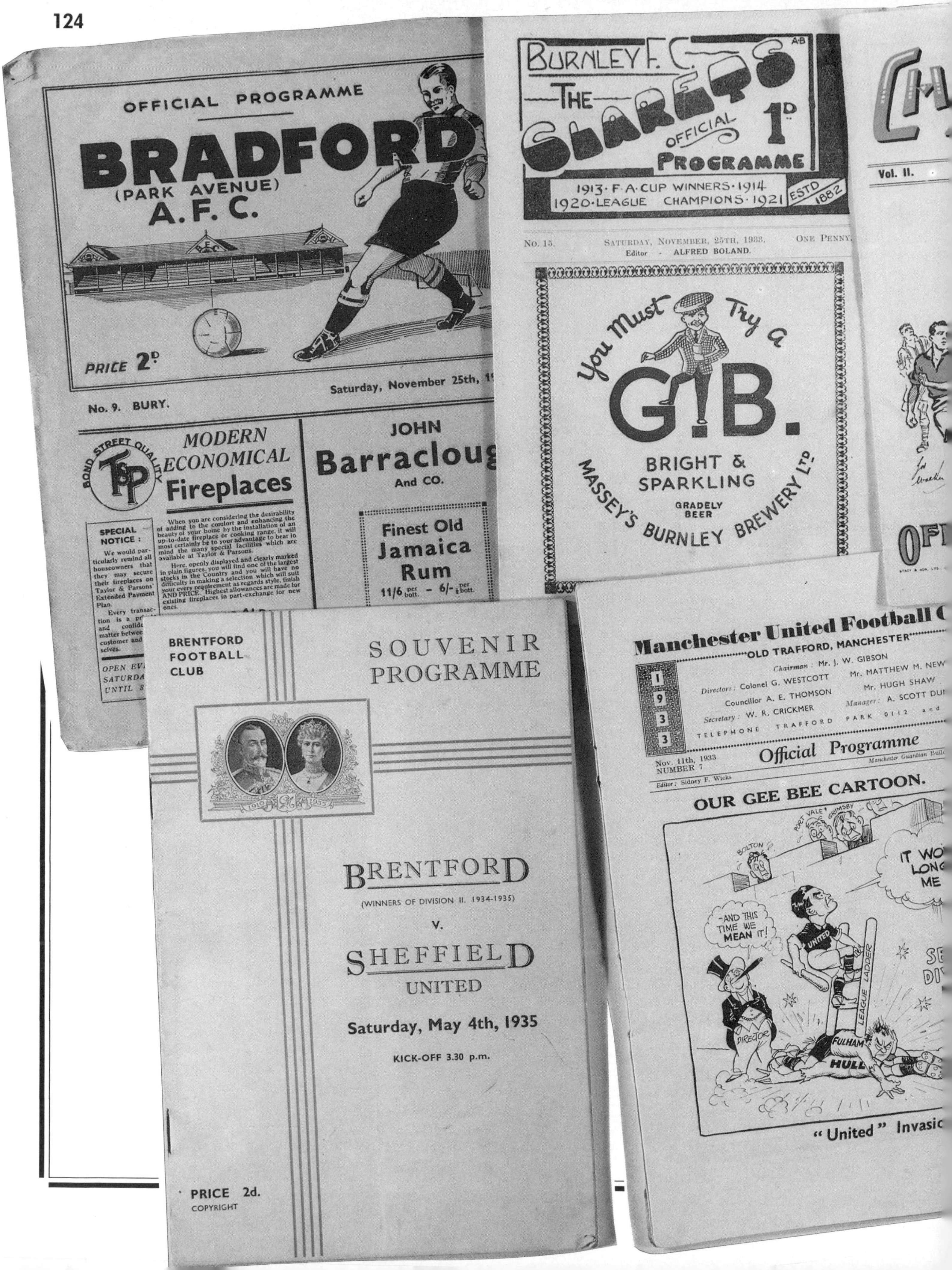

OFFICIAL PROGRAMME
BRADFORD
(PARK AVENUE)
A.F.C.
PRICE 2D.
Saturday, November 25th, 19
No. 9. BURY.
BOND STREET QUALITY
T&P
MODERN
ECONOMICAL
Fireplaces
SPECIAL NOTICE :
JOHN
Barracloug
And CO.
Finest Old
Jamaica
Rum
11/6 per bott. - 6/- ½ per bott.
BURNLEY F.C.
THE
CLARETS
OFFICIAL
1D
PROGRAMME
1913 · F.A. CUP WINNERS · 1914
1920 · LEAGUE CHAMPIONS · 1921
ESTD 1882
No. 15.
SATURDAY, NOVEMBER 25TH, 1933.
ONE PENNY.
Editor - ALFRED BOLAND.
You Must Try a
G.B.
BRIGHT &
SPARKLING
GRADELY
BEER
MASSEY'S BURNLEY BREWERY LTD.
Vol. II.
BRENTFORD
FOOTBALL
CLUB
SOUVENIR
PROGRAMME
1910
1935
BRENTFORD
(WINNERS OF DIVISION II. 1934-1935)
v.
SHEFFIELD
UNITED
Saturday, May 4th, 1935
KICK-OFF 3.30 p.m.
PRICE 2d.
COPYRIGHT
Manchester United Football C
OLD TRAFFORD, MANCHESTER
Chairman : Mr. J. W. GIBSON
Directors : Colonel G. WESTCOTT
Mr. MATTHEW M. NEW
Councillor A. E. THOMSON
Mr. HUGH SHAW
Secretary : W. R. CRICKMER
Manager : A. SCOTT DU
TELEPHONE TRAFFORD PARK 0112 and
1933
Nov. 11th, 1933
NUMBER 7
Official Programme
Editor : Sidney F. Wicks
OUR GEE BEE CARTOON.
PORT VALE
GRIMSBY
BOLTON
-AND THIS TIME WE MEAN IT!
UNITED
LEAGUE LADDER
DIRECTOR
FULHAM
HULL
"United" Invasio

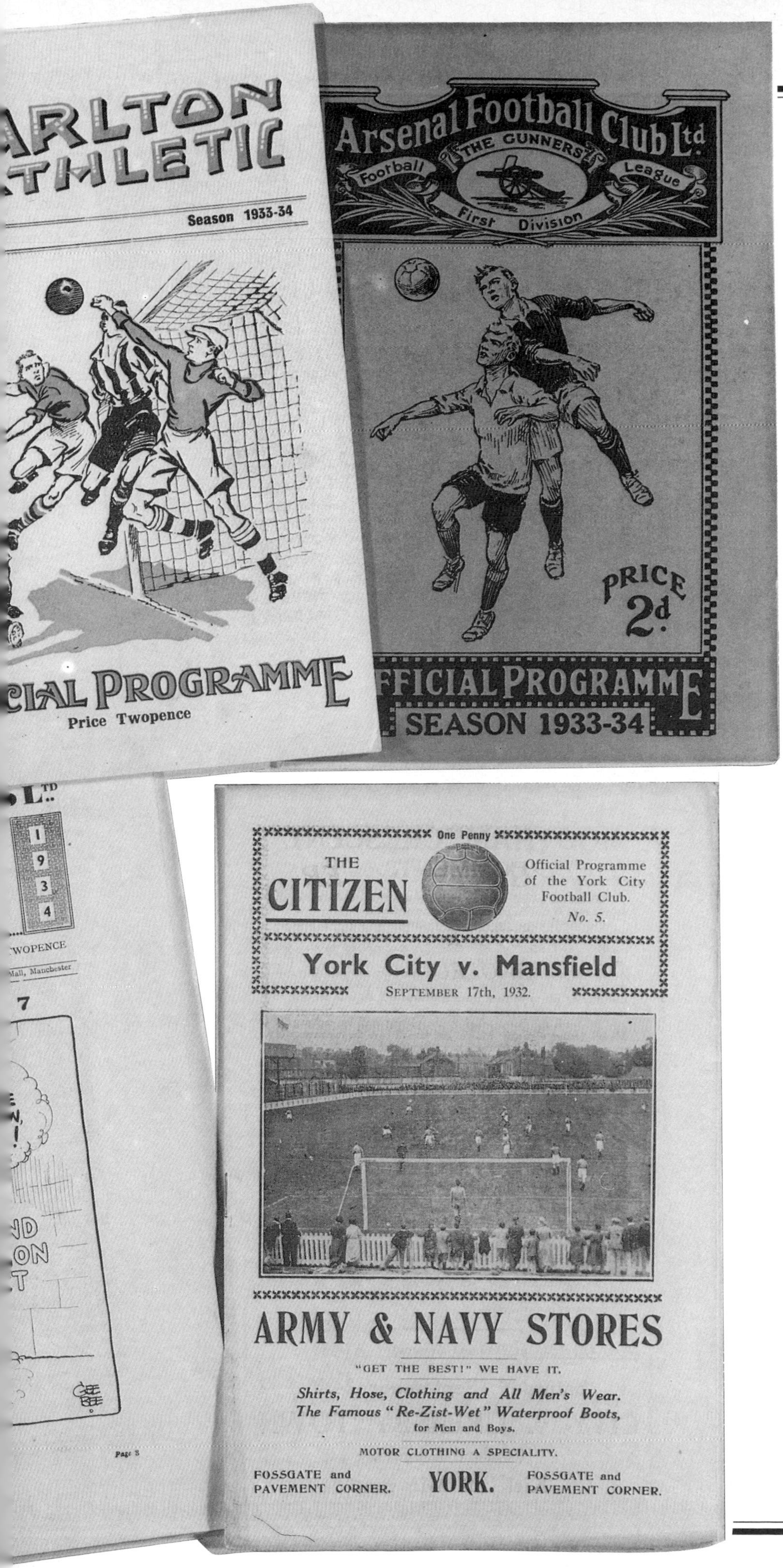

Programmes from the 'thirties. These are all now collectors' items.

above Coronation Loving Cup 1937 – to commemorate the Coronation of King George VI and Queen Elizabeth. Presented by Sir Francis Joseph, president of Stoke City, to each First Division club. The mould was then broken and Sir Francis requested clubs to fill the Loving Cup and drink a toast to their Majesties on 1 January every year. The ceremony endures; but dates vary and a more usual toast is Football, Friendships and the League. The makers of the Cup were Spode.

above Three thousand Stoke City supporters at a public protest meeting after Stanley Matthews had asked for a transfer: King's Hall, Stoke, February 1938. Another thousand fans were locked outside. The city was so incensed that work suffered in offices and factories. The meeting sent a deputation to meet Stoke's directors – and the problems between Matthews and his club were ironed out. Matthews played for Stoke between 1932–47, Blackpool 1947–61 and Stoke again 1961–65.

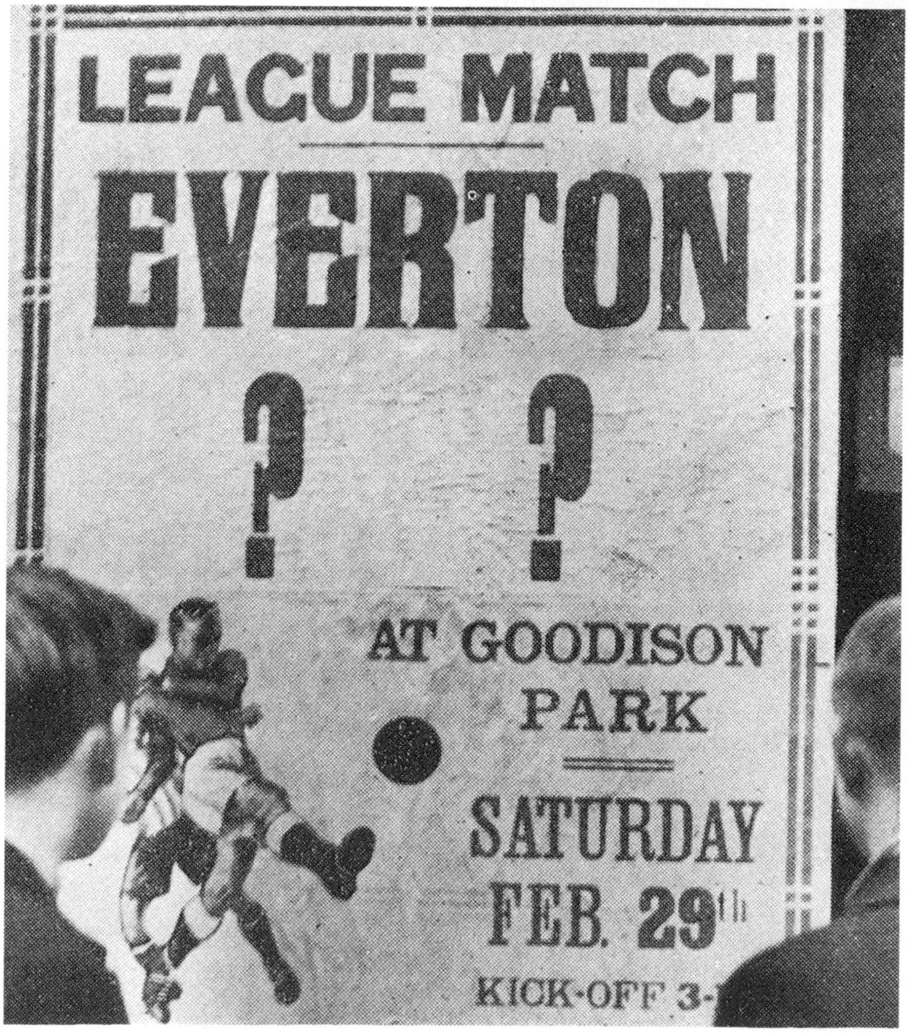

left The Football League decided pools promoters were a menace to the game in 1936 and attempted to sabotage coupons by withholding fixture lists. Names of opponents were filled in on posters like this only a day or so before a match. But a 'mole' began to leak details and posters such as 'Everton v ? ?' did not appeal to supporters. The scheme lasted three weeks.

left Matt Busby – with daughter Sheena – at the time of his transfer from Manchester City to Liverpool for £8,000 in March 1936. Busby will be remembered above all as an Olympian manager; but he was also a player of rare quality, a wing-half of great skill, intuition and composure. Joe Mercer remembers him as 'a players' player who influenced everything around him'. Busby helped Manchester City to the FA Cup Finals of 1933 and 1934; the first lost to Dixie Dean and Everton, the second won excitingly against Portsmouth. Busby played 202 League games for Manchester City (1929–36) and then 115 more for Liverpool before the war, by which time he was 30. He earned one full cap for Scotland (1934).

below Alex James of Arsenal – on his own. Three Manchester City defenders (Matt Busby on the left) can only wonder.

above Len Shackleton, 16 years old, 5 ft 2 ins tall and a 50-shilling-a-week, grass-clipping member of the Arsenal groundstaff, August 1938. A year later George Allison, Arsenal's manager, told him: 'Go back to Yorkshire and get a job. You will never make the grade as a professional footballer.' Shackleton grew up to play for Bradford Park Avenue, Newcastle, Sunderland and England, scored 126 goals in 384 League games and was widely regarded as one of the most brilliant and unorthodox inside-forwards of the years after World War Two.

right The Jubilee annual meeting of the Football League, Holborn Restaurant, London, 30 May 1938. The President was Charles E. Sutcliffe of Rawtenstall, a solicitor who served the League for 50 years. His proposal that £100,000 be raised as a Jubilee Fund, to assist players in need, was adopted.

above Souvenir programme for the Silver Jubilee of the Football League, 1938. Clubs played friendly games to mark the occasion and used the same programme – with a special insert in the centre for team news. Price threepence; proceeds to the League Jubilee Benevolent Fund.

above Bryn Jones of Wolves, Arsenal, Norwich and Wales – in Highbury red and white for the first time after his transfer from Wolves to Arsenal for a British record fee of £14,000 in August 1938. The fee was a sensation – 'it will never be surpassed' insisted one paper – but George Allison, Arsenal's manager, said: 'Bryn is a genius, a natural successor to Alex James at inside-forward.' Jones was a quiet and gentle man, however, and the enormous publicity he received undermined his form: he tried to give better than his best and was disappointing by his own standards. During the war and just after he found his real touch, a player of wonderful range and insight, but his most precious years were behind him. Bob Wall, later to become Arsenal's much-respected general manager, said: 'Bryn was only prevented from becoming a great player by the war.' Jones played 163 League games for Wolves, 71 for Arsenal, 23 for Norwich and won 17 caps for Wales (1935–49). He was also a member of a remarkable footballing family which included brother Ivor (Swansea, West Bromwich and Wales, 1919–26), brother Emlyn (Merthyr, Bournemouth, Everton, Southend and Barrow, 1927–38), nephew Cliff (Swansea, Spurs, Fulham and Wales, 1952–70), nephew Brin (Swansea, Newport, Bournemouth, Northampton and Watford, 1953–66) and nephew Ken (Southend, Swansea and Hereford and later an eminent journalist). Eight members of the Jones family played League football; and there was an unbroken sequence of 50 years in which there was always a member of the family registered as a League player.

above Stanley Matthews and Freddie Steele of Stoke City, January 1939. Matthews was a few days short of his 24th birthday and went on to play until he was 50. But Steele was depressed by a knee injury, personal problems and poor form and felt he would have to give up football. He was sent, as a last resort, to a psychiatrist who convinced him over several weeks that he was still an outstanding player – and Steele returned to score ten goals in five League games. Matthews observed later: 'I wouldn't have believed it possible if I hadn't seen it for myself.'

left The Unprofessional Footballer. Overcome by the excitement of a West Ham – Tottenham 'derby' at Upton Park in January 1939 a fan dashes onto the field and demonstrates the art of the clearance to a full house. West Ham and Spurs were then middle-order members of the Second Division.

left Many hands . . . light work. Ted Drake of Arsenal and England (right) and goalkeeper Vic Woodley of Chelsea and England in dispute at Highbury, February 1939. Arsenal 1 Chelsea 0. Drake fearlessly scored 136 goals for Arsenal in the six years before World War Two, once scoring seven against Aston Villa (1935), and won three League championship medals, an FA Cup Winners' medal and five caps for England. Drake, however, was to have his finest moment as a manager with Chelsea: he led them to their only League championship in 1955 to become the first man to play in and also manage a championship side. The impeccable Woodley made 252 First Division appearances for Chelsea before the war, helped Derby County win the FA Cup in 1946 and won 19 caps for England.

below Stanley Cullis (left) versus Tommy Lawton – Wolverhampton Wanderers versus Everton at Molineux, March 1939. Everton finished as champions, Wolves as runners-up – the last season before World War Two.

above The most famous shirt in English football. Stanley Matthews shuffles – a full-back lunges – and the 'wizard of dribble' is past him on the outside. And Matthews' speed meant he never had to beat a man twice.

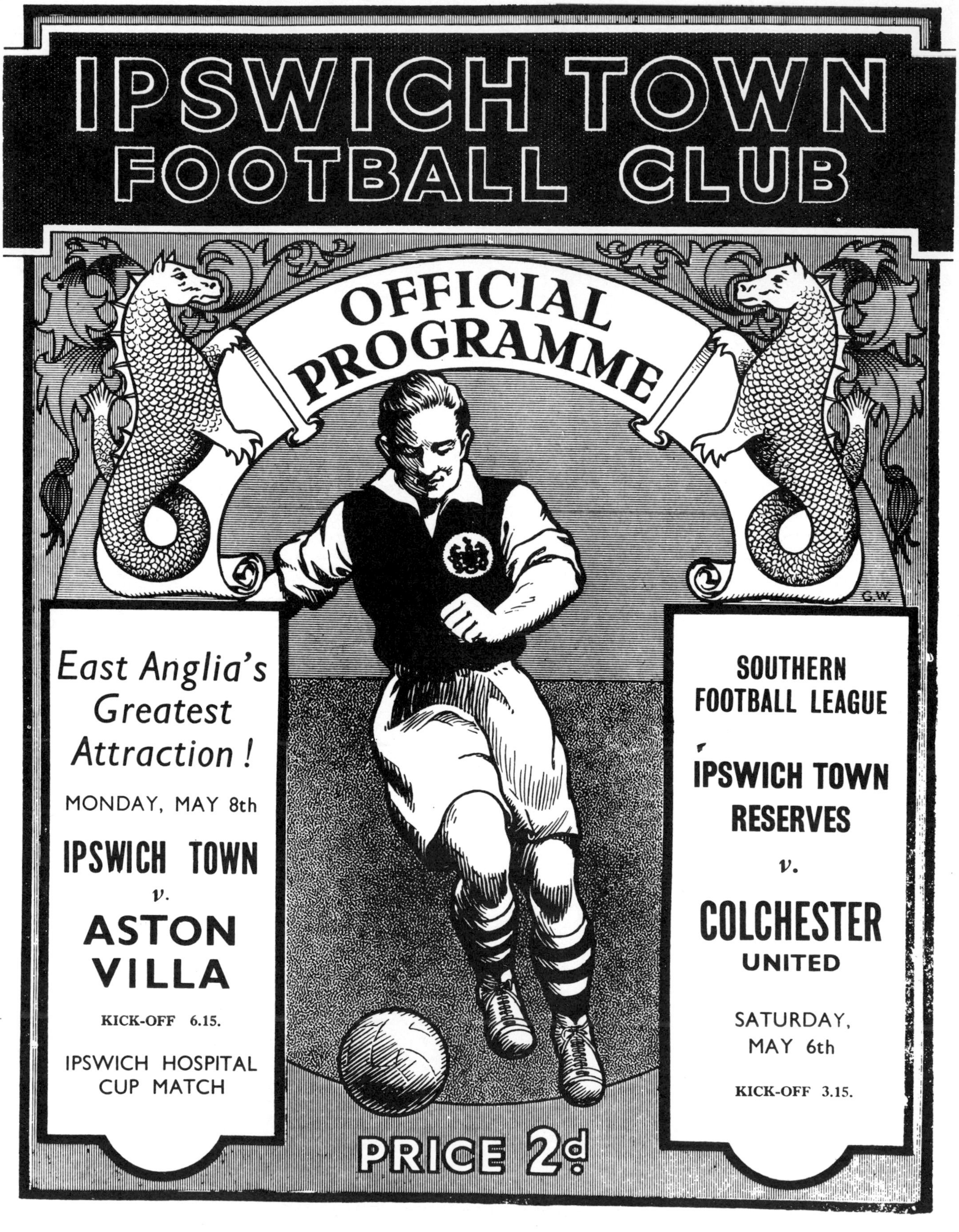

Ipswich Town's first season in the League, 1938–39.

Mercantile Credit League Centenary
100

The Football League
1888-1988

Mercantile Credit League Centenary
100

right Major Frank Buckley, one of the shrewdest and most innovative managers in League history, relaxing in April 1939 when Wolverhampton Wanderers finished runners-up in both League and Cup. Discoverer of talent, expert speculator in the transfer market and household name. Aggressive centre-half for Derby and England (one cap, 1914) and manager of Norwich, Blackpool, Wolves (1927–44), Notts County, Hull, Leeds and Walsall. Placed great emphasis on youth, hard running and versatility. His most celebrated years were with Wolves during the 1930s although they never finished higher than runners-up (1938 and 1939). But Buckley's business ability made Wolves £130,000 during the five years before World War Two – at a time when five figure transfer fees were considered immorally high – and he laid the foundations for the club's great period under Stan Cullis. Buckley was famous for his sensational 'monkey gland treatment' of players at Molineux (they were, in fact, injections against the common cold) and among the players he groomed were Bryn Jones and John Charles.

left Clothes maketh the manager, 1939. Scott Duncan, manager of Ipswich, left, and Jimmy Hogan, manager of Aston Villa, before a Cup replay. It was Ipswich's first season as a League club – and Aston Villa had won the Second Division championship the season before, 1937–8.

LEAGUE TABLES

1931–32

FIRST DIVISION

		P	W	D	L	F	A	Pts
1	Everton	42	26	4	12	116	64	56
2	Arsenal	42	22	10	10	90	48	54
3	Sheff Wed	42	22	6	14	96	82	50
4	Huddersfield	42	19	10	13	80	63	48
5	Aston Villa	42	19	8	15	104	72	46
6	WBA	42	20	6	16	77	55	46
7	Sheff United	42	20	6	16	80	75	46
8	Portsmouth	42	19	7	16	62	62	45
9	Birmingham	42	18	8	16	78	67	44
10	Liverpool	42	19	6	17	81	93	44
11	Newcastle	42	18	6	18	80	87	42
12	Chelsea	42	16	8	18	69	73	40
13	Sunderland	42	15	10	17	67	73	40
14	Man City	42	13	12	17	83	73	38
15	Derby	42	14	10	18	71	75	38
16	Blackburn	42	16	6	20	89	95	38
17	Bolton	42	17	4	21	72	80	38
18	Middlesbrough	42	15	8	19	64	89	38
19	Leicester	42	15	7	20	74	94	37
20	Blackpool	42	12	9	21	65	102	33
21	Grimsby	42	13	6	23	67	98	32
22	West Ham	42	12	7	23	62	107	31

SECOND DIVISION

		P	W	D	L	F	A	Pts
1	Wolves	42	24	8	10	115	49	56
2	Leeds	42	22	10	10	78	54	54
3	Stoke	42	19	14	9	69	48	52
4	Plymouth	42	20	9	13	100	66	49
5	Bury	42	21	7	14	70	58	49
6	Bradford PA	42	21	7	14	72	63	49
7	Bradford City	42	16	13	13	80	61	45
8	Tottenham	42	16	11	15	87	78	43
9	Millwall	42	17	9	16	61	61	43
10	Charlton	42	17	9	16	61	66	43
11	Nottm Forest	42	16	10	16	77	72	42
12	Man United	42	17	8	17	71	72	42
13	Preston	42	16	10	16	75	77	42
14	Southampton	42	17	7	18	66	77	41
15	Swansea	42	16	7	19	73	75	39
16	Notts County	42	13	12	17	75	75	38
17	Chesterfield	42	13	11	18	64	86	37
18	Oldham	42	13	10	19	62	84	36
19	Burnley	42	13	9	20	59	87	35
20	Port Vale	42	13	7	22	58	89	33
21	Barnsley	42	12	9	21	55	91	33
22	Bristol City	42	6	11	25	39	78	23

THIRD DIVISION (NORTH)

		P	W	D	L	F	A	Pts
1	Lincoln	40	26	5	9	106	47	57
2	Gateshead	40	25	7	8	94	48	57
3	Chester	40	21	8	11	78	60	50
4	Tranmere	40	19	11	10	107	58	49
5	Barrow	40	24	1	15	86	59	49
6	Crewe	40	21	6	13	95	66	48
7	Southport	40	18	10	12	58	53	46
8	Hull	40	20	5	15	82	53	45
9	York	40	18	7	15	76	81	43
10	Wrexham	40	18	7	15	64	69	43
11	Darlington	40	17	4	19	66	69	38
12	Stockport	40	13	11	16	55	53	37
13	Hartlepools	40	16	5	19	78	100	37
14	Accrington	40	15	6	19	75	80	36
15	Doncaster	40	16	4	20	59	80	36
16	Walsall	40	16	3	21	57	85	35
17	Halifax	40	13	8	19	61	87	34
18	Carlisle	40	11	11	18	64	79	33
19	Rotherham	40	14	4	22	63	72	32
20	New Brighton	40	8	8	24	38	76	24
21	Rochdale	40	4	3	33	48	135	11

22 Wigan Borough resigned from the League

THIRD DIVISION (SOUTH)

		P	W	D	L	F	A	Pts
1	Fulham	42	24	9	9	111	62	57
2	Reading	42	23	9	10	97	67	55
3	Southend	42	21	11	10	77	53	53
4	Crystal Palace	42	20	11	11	74	63	51
5	Brentford	42	19	10	13	68	52	48
6	Luton	42	20	7	15	95	70	47
7	Exeter	42	20	7	15	77	62	47
8	Brighton	42	17	12	13	73	58	46
9	Cardiff	42	19	8	15	87	73	46
10	Norwich	42	17	12	13	76	67	46
11	Watford	42	19	8	15	81	79	46
12	Coventry	42	18	8	16	108	97	44
13	QPR	42	15	12	15	79	73	42
14	Northampton	42	16	7	19	69	69	39
15	Bournemouth	42	13	12	17	70	78	38
16	Clapton Orient	42	12	11	19	77	90	35
17	Swindon	42	14	6	22	70	84	34
18	Bristol Rovers	42	13	8	21	65	92	34
19	Torquay	42	12	9	21	72	106	33
20	Mansfield	42	11	10	21	75	108	32
21	Gillingham	42	10	8	24	40	82	28
22	Thames	42	7	9	26	53	109	23

1932–33

FIRST DIVISION

		P	W	D	L	F	A	Pts
1	Arsenal	42	25	8	9	118	61	58
2	Aston Villa	42	23	8	11	92	67	54
3	Sheff Wed	42	21	9	12	80	68	51
4	WBA	42	20	9	13	83	70	49
5	Newcastle	42	22	5	15	71	63	49
6	Huddersfield	42	18	11	13	66	53	47
7	Derby	42	15	14	13	76	69	44
8	Leeds	42	15	14	13	59	62	44
9	Portsmouth	42	18	7	17	74	76	43
10	Sheff United	42	17	9	16	74	80	43
11	Everton	42	16	9	17	81	74	41
12	Sunderland	42	15	10	17	63	80	40
13	Birmingham	42	14	11	17	57	57	39
14	Liverpool	42	14	11	17	79	84	39
15	Blackburn	42	14	10	18	76	102	38
16	Man City	42	16	5	21	68	71	37
17	Middlesbrough	42	14	9	19	63	73	37
18	Chelsea	42	14	7	21	63	73	35
19	Leicester	42	11	13	18	75	89	35
20	Wolves	42	13	9	20	80	96	35
21	Bolton	42	12	9	21	78	92	33
22	Blackpool	42	14	5	23	69	85	33

SECOND DIVISION

		P	W	D	L	F	A	Pts
1	Stoke	42	25	6	11	78	39	56
2	Tottenham	42	20	15	7	96	51	55
3	Fulham	42	20	10	12	78	65	50
4	Bury	42	20	9	13	84	59	49
5	Nottm Forest	42	17	15	10	67	59	49
6	Man United	42	15	13	14	71	68	43
7	Millwall	42	16	11	15	59	57	43
8	Bradford PA	42	17	8	17	77	71	42
9	Preston	42	16	10	16	74	70	42
10	Swansea	42	19	4	19	50	54	42
11	Bradford City	42	14	13	15	65	61	41
12	Southampton	42	18	5	19	66	66	41
13	Grimsby	42	14	13	15	79	84	41
14	Plymouth	42	16	9	17	63	67	41
15	Notts County	42	15	10	17	67	78	40
16	Oldham	42	15	8	19	67	80	38
17	Port Vale	42	14	10	18	66	79	38
18	Lincoln	42	12	13	17	72	87	37
19	Burnley	42	11	14	17	67	79	36
20	West Ham	42	13	9	20	75	93	35
21	Chesterfield	42	12	10	20	61	84	34
22	Charlton	42	12	7	23	60	91	31

THIRD DIVISION (NORTH)

		P	W	D	L	F	A	Pts
1	Hull	42	26	7	9	100	45	59
2	Wrexham	42	24	9	9	106	51	57
3	Stockport	42	21	12	9	99	58	54
4	Chester	42	22	8	12	94	66	52
5	Walsall	42	19	10	13	75	58	48
6	Doncaster	42	17	14	11	77	79	48
7	Gateshead	42	19	9	14	78	67	47
8	Barnsley	42	19	8	15	92	80	46
9	Barrow	42	18	7	17	60	60	43
10	Crewe	42	20	3	19	80	84	43
11	Tranmere	42	17	8	17	70	66	42
12	Southport	42	17	7	18	70	67	41
13	Accrington	42	15	10	17	78	76	40
14	Hartlepools	42	16	7	19	87	116	39
15	Halifax	42	15	8	19	71	90	38
16	Mansfield	42	14	7	21	84	100	35
17	Rotherham	42	14	6	22	60	84	34
18	Rochdale	42	13	7	22	58	80	33
19	Carlisle	42	13	7	22	51	75	33
20	York	42	13	6	23	72	92	32
21	New Brighton	42	11	10	21	63	88	32
22	Darlington	42	10	8	24	66	109	28

THIRD DIVISION (SOUTH)

		P	W	D	L	F	A	Pts
1	Brentford	42	26	10	6	90	49	62
2	Exeter	42	24	10	8	88	48	58
3	Norwich	42	22	13	7	88	55	57
4	Reading	42	19	13	10	103	71	51
5	Crystal Palace	42	19	8	15	78	64	46
6	Coventry	42	19	6	17	106	77	44
7	Gillingham	42	18	8	16	72	61	44
8	Northampton	42	18	8	16	76	66	44
9	Bristol Rovers	42	15	14	13	61	56	44
10	Torquay	42	16	12	14	72	67	44
11	Watford	42	16	12	14	66	63	44
12	Brighton	42	17	8	17	66	65	42
13	Southend	42	15	11	16	65	82	41
14	Luton	42	13	13	16	78	78	39
15	Bristol City	42	12	13	17	83	90	37
16	QPR	42	13	11	18	72	87	37
17	Aldershot	42	13	10	19	61	72	36
18	Bournemouth	42	12	12	18	60	81	36
19	Cardiff	42	12	7	23	69	99	31
20	Clapton Orient	42	8	13	21	59	93	29
21	Newport	42	11	7	24	61	105	29
22	Swindon	42	9	11	22	60	105	29

1933–34

FIRST DIVISION

		P	W	D	L	F	A	Pts
1	Arsenal	42	25	9	8	75	47	59
2	Huddersfield	42	23	10	9	90	61	56
3	Tottenham	42	21	7	14	79	56	49
4	Derby	42	17	11	14	68	54	45
5	Man City	42	17	11	14	65	72	45
6	Sunderland	42	16	12	14	81	56	44
7	WBA	42	17	10	15	78	70	44
8	Blackburn	42	18	7	17	74	81	43
9	Leeds	42	17	8	17	75	66	42
10	Portsmouth	42	15	12	15	52	55	42
11	Sheff Wed	42	16	9	17	62	67	41
12	Stoke	42	15	11	16	58	71	41
13	Aston Villa	42	14	12	16	78	75	40
14	Everton	42	12	16	14	62	63	40
15	Wolves	42	14	12	16	74	86	40
16	Middlesbrough	42	16	7	19	68	80	39
17	Leicester	42	14	11	17	59	74	39
18	Liverpool	42	14	10	18	79	87	38
19	Chelsea	42	14	8	20	67	69	36
20	Birmingham	42	12	12	18	54	56	36
21	Newcastle	42	10	14	18	68	77	34
22	Sheff United	42	12	7	23	58	101	31

SECOND DIVISION

		P	W	D	L	F	A	Pts
1	Grimsby	42	27	5	10	103	59	59
2	Preston	42	23	6	13	71	52	52
3	Bolton	42	21	9	12	79	55	51
4	Brentford	42	22	7	13	85	60	51
5	Bradford PA	42	23	3	16	86	67	49
6	Bradford City	42	20	6	16	73	67	46
7	West Ham	42	17	11	14	78	70	45
8	Port Vale	42	19	7	16	60	55	45
9	Oldham	42	17	10	15	72	60	44
10	Plymouth	42	15	13	14	69	70	43
11	Blackpool	42	15	13	14	62	64	43
12	Bury	42	17	9	16	70	73	43
13	Burnley	42	18	6	18	60	72	42
14	Southampton	42	15	8	19	54	58	38
15	Hull	42	13	12	17	52	68	38
16	Fulham	42	15	7	20	48	67	37
17	Nottm Forest	42	13	9	20	73	74	35
18	Notts County	42	12	11	19	53	62	35
19	Swansea	42	10	15	17	51	60	35
20	Man United	42	14	6	22	59	85	34
21	Millwall	42	11	11	20	39	68	33
22	Lincoln	42	9	8	25	44	75	26

THIRD DIVISION (NORTH)

		P	W	D	L	F	A	Pts
1	Barnsley	42	27	8	7	118	61	62
2	Chesterfield	42	27	7	8	86	43	61
3	Stockport	42	24	11	7	115	52	59
4	Walsall	42	23	7	12	97	60	53
5	Doncaster	42	22	9	11	83	61	53
6	Wrexham	42	23	5	14	102	73	51
7	Tranmere	42	20	7	15	84	63	47
8	Barrow	42	19	9	14	116	94	47
9	Halifax	42	20	4	18	80	91	44
10	Chester	42	17	6	19	89	86	40
11	Hartlepools	42	16	7	19	89	93	39
12	York	42	15	8	19	71	74	38
13	Carlisle	42	15	8	19	66	81	38
14	Crewe	42	15	6	21	81	97	36
15	New Brighton	42	14	8	20	62	87	36
16	Darlington	42	13	9	20	70	101	35
17	Mansfield	42	11	12	19	81	88	34
18	Southport	42	8	17	17	63	90	33
19	Gateshead	42	12	9	21	76	110	33
20	Accrington	42	13	7	22	65	101	33
21	Rotherham	42	10	8	24	53	91	28
22	Rochdale	42	9	6	27	53	103	24

THIRD DIVISION (SOUTH)

		P	W	D	L	F	A	Pts
1	Norwich	42	25	11	6	88	49	61
2	Coventry	42	21	12	9	100	54	54
3	Reading	42	21	12	9	82	50	54
4	QPR	42	24	6	12	70	51	54
5	Charlton	42	22	8	12	83	56	52
6	Luton	42	21	10	11	83	61	52
7	Bristol Rovers	42	20	11	11	77	47	51
8	Swindon	42	17	11	14	64	68	45
9	Exeter	42	16	11	15	68	57	43
10	Brighton	42	15	13	14	68	60	43
11	Clapton Orient	42	16	10	16	75	69	42
12	Crystal Palace	42	16	9	17	71	67	41
13	Northampton	42	14	12	16	71	78	40
14	Aldershot	42	13	12	17	52	71	38
15	Watford	42	15	7	20	71	63	37
16	Southend	42	12	10	20	51	74	34
17	Gillingham	42	11	11	20	75	96	33
18	Newport	42	8	17	17	49	70	33
19	Bristol City	42	10	13	19	58	85	33
20	Torquay	42	13	7	22	53	93	33
21	Bournemouth	42	9	9	24	60	102	27
22	Cardiff	42	9	6	27	57	105	24

1934–35

FIRST DIVISION

		P	W	D	L	F	A	Pts
1	Arsenal	42	23	12	7	115	46	58
2	Sunderland	42	19	16	7	90	51	54
3	Sheff Wed	42	18	13	11	70	64	49
4	Man City	42	20	8	14	82	67	48
5	Grimsby	42	17	11	14	78	60	45
6	Derby	42	18	9	15	81	66	45
7	Liverpool	42	19	7	16	85	88	45
8	Everton	42	16	12	14	89	88	44
9	WBA	42	17	10	15	83	83	44
10	Stoke	42	18	6	18	71	70	42
11	Preston	42	15	12	15	62	67	42
12	Chelsea	42	16	9	17	73	82	41
13	Aston Villa	42	14	13	15	74	88	41
14	Portsmouth	42	15	10	17	71	72	40
15	Blackburn	42	14	11	17	66	78	39
16	Huddersfield	42	14	10	18	76	71	38
17	Wolves	42	15	8	19	88	94	38
18	Leeds	42	13	12	17	75	92	38
19	Birmingham	42	13	10	19	63	81	36
20	Middlesbrough	42	10	14	18	70	91	34
21	Leicester	42	12	9	21	61	86	33
22	Tottenham	42	10	10	22	54	93	30

SECOND DIVISION

		P	W	D	L	F	A	Pts
1	Brentford	42	26	9	7	93	48	61
2	Bolton	42	26	4	12	96	48	56
3	West Ham	42	26	4	12	80	63	56
4	Blackpool	42	21	11	10	79	57	53
5	Man United	42	23	4	15	76	55	50
6	Newcastle	42	22	4	16	89	68	48
7	Fulham	42	17	12	13	76	56	46
8	Plymouth	42	19	8	15	75	64	46
9	Nottm Forest	42	17	8	17	76	70	42
10	Bury	42	19	4	19	62	73	42
11	Sheff United	42	16	9	17	79	70	41
12	Burnley	42	16	9	17	63	73	41
13	Hull	42	16	8	18	63	74	40
14	Norwich	42	14	11	17	71	61	39
15	Bradford PA	42	11	16	15	55	63	38
16	Barnsley	42	13	12	17	60	83	38
17	Swansea	42	14	8	20	56	67	36
18	Port Vale	42	11	12	19	55	74	34
19	Southampton	42	11	12	19	46	75	34
20	Bradford City	42	12	8	22	50	68	32
21	Oldham	42	10	6	26	56	95	26
22	Notts County	42	9	7	26	46	97	25

THIRD DIVISION (NORTH)

		P	W	D	L	F	A	Pts
1	Doncaster	42	26	5	11	87	44	57
2	Halifax	42	25	5	12	76	67	55
3	Chester	42	20	14	8	91	58	54
4	Lincoln	42	22	7	13	87	58	51
5	Darlington	42	21	9	12	80	59	51
6	Tranmere	42	20	11	11	74	55	51
7	Stockport	42	22	3	17	90	72	47
8	Mansfield	42	19	9	14	75	62	47
9	Rotherham	42	19	7	16	86	73	45
10	Chesterfield	42	17	10	15	71	52	44
11	Wrexham	42	16	11	15	76	69	43
12	Hartlepools	42	17	7	18	80	78	41
13	Crewe	42	14	11	17	66	86	39
14	Walsall	42	13	10	19	81	72	36
15	York	42	15	6	21	76	82	36
16	New Brighton	42	14	8	20	59	76	36
17	Barrow	42	13	9	20	58	87	35
18	Accrington	42	12	10	20	63	89	34
19	Gateshead	42	13	8	21	58	96	34
20	Rochdale	42	11	11	20	53	71	33
21	Southport	42	10	12	20	55	85	32
22	Carlisle	42	8	7	27	51	102	23

THIRD DIVISION (SOUTH)

		P	W	D	L	F	A	Pts
1	Charlton	42	27	7	8	103	52	61
2	Reading	42	21	11	10	89	65	53
3	Coventry	42	21	9	12	86	50	51
4	Luton	42	19	12	11	92	60	50
5	Crystal Palace	42	19	10	13	86	64	48
6	Watford	42	19	9	14	76	49	47
7	Northampton	42	19	8	15	65	67	46
8	Bristol Rovers	42	17	10	15	73	77	44
9	Brighton	42	17	9	16	69	62	43
10	Torquay	42	18	6	18	81	75	42
11	Exeter	42	16	9	17	70	75	41
12	Millwall	42	17	7	18	57	62	41
13	QPR	42	16	9	17	63	72	41
14	Clapton Orient	42	15	10	17	65	65	40
15	Bristol City	42	15	9	18	52	68	39
16	Swindon	42	13	12	17	67	78	38
17	Bournemouth	42	15	7	20	54	71	37
18	Aldershot	42	13	10	19	50	75	36
19	Cardiff	42	13	9	20	62	82	35
20	Gillingham	42	11	13	18	55	75	35
21	Southend	42	11	9	22	65	78	31
22	Newport	42	10	5	27	54	112	25

1935–36

FIRST DIVISION

		P	W	D	L	F	A	Pts
1	Sunderland	42	25	6	11	109	74	56
2	Derby	42	18	12	12	61	52	48
3	Huddersfield	42	18	12	12	59	56	48
4	Stoke	42	20	7	15	57	57	47
5	Brentford	42	17	12	13	81	60	46
6	Arsenal	42	15	15	12	78	48	45
7	Preston	42	18	8	16	67	64	44
8	Chelsea	42	15	13	14	65	72	43
9	Man City	42	17	8	17	68	60	42
10	Portsmouth	42	17	8	17	54	67	42
11	Leeds	42	15	11	16	66	64	41
12	Birmingham	42	15	11	16	61	63	41
13	Bolton	42	14	13	15	67	76	41
14	Middlesbrough	42	15	10	17	84	70	40
15	Wolves	42	15	10	17	77	76	40
16	Everton	42	13	13	16	89	89	39
17	Grimsby	42	17	5	20	65	73	39
18	WBA	42	16	6	20	89	88	38
19	Liverpool	42	13	12	17	60	64	38
20	Sheff Wed	42	13	12	17	63	77	38
21	Aston Villa	42	13	9	20	81	110	35
22	Blackburn	42	12	9	21	55	96	33

SECOND DIVISION

		P	W	D	L	F	A	Pts
1	Man United	42	22	12	8	85	43	56
2	Charlton	42	22	11	9	85	58	55
3	Sheff United	42	20	12	10	79	50	52
4	West Ham	42	22	8	12	90	68	52
5	Tottenham	42	18	13	11	91	55	49
6	Leicester	42	19	10	13	79	57	48
7	Plymouth	42	20	8	14	71	57	48
8	Newcastle	42	20	6	16	88	79	46
9	Fulham	42	15	14	13	76	52	44
10	Blackpool	42	18	7	17	93	72	43
11	Norwich	42	17	9	16	72	65	43
12	Bradford City	42	15	13	14	55	65	43
13	Swansea	42	15	9	18	67	76	39
14	Bury	42	13	12	17	66	84	38
15	Burnley	42	12	13	17	50	59	37
16	Bradford PA	42	14	9	19	62	84	37
17	Southampton	42	14	9	19	47	65	37
18	Doncaster	42	14	9	19	51	71	37
19	Nottm Forest	42	12	11	19	69	76	35
20	Barnsley	42	12	9	21	54	80	33
21	Port Vale	42	12	8	22	56	106	32
22	Hull	42	5	10	27	47	111	20

THIRD DIVISION (NORTH)

	P	W	D	L	F	A	Pts
1 Chesterfield	42	24	12	6	92	39	60
2 Chester	42	22	11	9	100	45	55
3 Tranmere	42	22	11	9	93	58	55
4 Lincoln	42	22	10	8	91	51	53
5 Stockport	42	20	8	14	65	49	48
6 Crewe	42	19	9	14	80	76	47
7 Oldham	42	18	9	15	86	73	45
8 Hartlepools	42	15	12	15	57	61	42
9 Accrington	42	17	8	17	63	72	42
10 Walsall	42	16	9	17	79	59	41
11 Rotherham	42	16	9	17	69	66	41
12 Darlington	42	17	6	19	74	79	40
13 Carlisle	42	14	12	16	56	62	40
14 Gateshead	42	13	14	15	56	76	40
15 Barrow	42	13	12	17	58	65	38
16 York	42	13	12	17	62	95	38
17 Halifax	42	15	7	20	57	61	37
18 Wrexham	42	15	7	20	66	75	37
19 Mansfield	42	14	9	19	80	91	37
20 Rochdale	42	10	13	19	58	88	33
21 Southport	42	11	9	22	48	90	31
22 New Brighton	42	9	6	27	43	102	24

THIRD DIVISION (SOUTH)

	P	W	D	L	F	A	Pts
1 Coventry	42	24	9	9	102	45	57
2 Luton	42	22	12	8	81	45	56
3 Reading	42	26	2	14	87	62	54
4 QPR	42	22	9	11	84	53	53
5 Watford	42	20	9	13	80	54	49
6 Crystal Palace	42	22	5	15	96	74	49
7 Brighton	42	18	8	16	70	63	44
8 Bournemouth	42	16	11	15	60	56	43
9 Notts County	42	15	12	15	60	57	42
10 Torquay	42	16	9	17	62	62	41
11 Aldershot	42	14	12	16	53	61	40
12 Millwall	42	14	12	16	58	71	40
13 Bristol City	42	15	10	17	48	59	40
14 Clapton Orient	42	16	6	20	55	61	38
15 Northampton	42	15	8	19	62	90	38
16 Gillingham	42	14	9	19	66	77	37
17 Bristol Rovers	42	14	9	19	69	95	37
18 Southend	42	13	10	19	61	62	36
19 Swindon	42	14	8	20	64	73	36
20 Cardiff	42	13	10	19	60	73	36
21 Newport	42	11	9	22	60	111	31
22 Exeter	42	8	11	23	59	93	27

1936–37

FIRST DIVISION

	P	W	D	L	F	A	Pts
1 Man City	42	22	13	7	107	61	57
2 Charlton	42	21	12	9	58	49	54
3 Arsenal	42	18	16	8	80	49	52
4 Derby	42	21	7	14	96	90	49
5 Wolves	42	21	5	16	84	67	47
6 Brentford	42	18	10	14	82	78	46
7 Middlesbrough	42	19	8	15	74	71	46
8 Sunderland	42	19	6	17	89	87	44
9 Portsmouth	42	17	10	15	62	66	44
10 Stoke	42	15	12	15	72	57	42
11 Birmingham	42	13	15	14	64	60	41
12 Grimsby	42	17	7	18	86	81	41
13 Chelsea	42	14	13	15	52	55	41
14 Preston	42	14	13	15	56	67	41
15 Huddersfield	42	12	15	15	62	64	39
16 WBA	42	16	6	20	77	98	38
17 Everton	42	14	9	19	81	78	37
18 Liverpool	42	12	11	19	62	84	35
19 Leeds	42	15	4	23	60	80	34
20 Bolton	42	10	14	18	43	66	34
21 Man United	42	10	12	20	55	78	32
22 Sheff Wed	42	9	12	21	53	69	30

SECOND DIVISION

	P	W	D	L	F	A	Pts
1 Leicester	42	24	8	10	89	57	56
2 Blackpool	42	24	7	11	88	53	55
3 Bury	42	22	8	12	74	55	52
4 Newcastle	42	22	5	15	80	56	49
5 Plymouth	42	18	13	11	71	53	49
6 West Ham	42	19	11	12	73	55	49
7 Sheff United	42	18	10	14	66	54	46
8 Coventry	42	17	11	14	66	54	45
9 Aston Villa	42	16	12	14	82	70	44
10 Tottenham	42	17	9	16	88	66	43
11 Fulham	42	15	13	14	71	61	43
12 Blackburn	42	16	10	16	70	62	42
13 Burnley	42	16	10	16	57	61	42
14 Barnsley	42	16	9	17	50	64	41
15 Chesterfield	42	16	8	18	84	89	40
16 Swansea	42	15	7	20	50	65	37
17 Norwich	42	14	8	20	63	71	36
18 Nottm Forest	42	12	10	20	68	90	34
19 Southampton	42	11	12	19	53	77	34
20 Bradford PA	42	12	9	21	52	88	33
21 Bradford City	42	9	12	21	54	94	30
22 Doncaster	42	7	10	25	30	84	24

THIRD DIVISION (NORTH)

	P	W	D	L	F	A	Pts
1 Stockport	42	23	14	5	84	39	60
2 Lincoln	42	25	7	10	103	57	57
3 Chester	42	22	9	11	87	57	53
4 Oldham	42	20	11	11	77	59	51
5 Hull	42	17	12	13	68	69	46
6 Hartlepools	42	19	7	16	75	69	45
7 Halifax	42	18	9	15	68	63	45
8 Wrexham	42	16	12	14	71	57	44
9 Mansfield	42	18	8	16	91	76	44
10 Carlisle	42	18	8	16	65	68	44
11 Port Vale	42	17	10	15	58	64	44
12 York	42	16	11	15	79	70	43
13 Accrington	42	16	9	17	76	69	41
14 Southport	42	12	13	17	73	87	37
15 New Brighton	42	13	11	18	55	70	37
16 Barrow	42	13	10	19	70	86	36
17 Rotherham	42	14	7	21	78	91	35
18 Rochdale	42	13	9	20	69	86	35
19 Tranmere	42	12	9	21	71	88	33
20 Crewe	42	10	12	20	55	83	32
21 Gateshead	42	11	10	21	63	98	32
22 Darlington	42	8	14	20	66	96	30

THIRD DIVISION (SOUTH)

	P	W	D	L	F	A	Pts
1 Luton	42	27	4	11	103	53	58
2 Notts County	42	23	10	9	74	52	56
3 Brighton	42	24	5	13	74	43	53
4 Watford	42	19	11	12	85	60	49
5 Reading	42	19	11	12	76	60	49
6 Bournemouth	42	20	9	13	65	59	49
7 Northampton	42	20	6	16	85	68	46
8 Millwall	42	18	10	14	64	54	46
9 QPR	42	18	9	15	73	52	45
10 Southend	42	17	11	14	78	67	45
11 Gillingham	42	18	8	16	52	66	44
12 Clapton Orient	42	14	15	13	52	52	43
13 Swindon	42	14	11	17	75	73	39
14 Crystal Palace	42	13	12	17	62	61	38
15 Bristol Rovers	42	16	4	22	71	80	36
16 Bristol City	42	15	6	21	58	70	36
17 Walsall	42	13	10	19	62	84	36
18 Cardiff	42	14	7	21	54	87	35
19 Newport	42	12	10	20	67	98	34
20 Torquay	42	11	10	21	57	80	32
21 Exeter	42	10	12	20	59	88	32
22 Aldershot	42	7	9	26	50	89	23

1937–38

FIRST DIVISION

		P	W	D	L	F	A	Pts
1	Arsenal	42	21	10	11	77	44	52
2	Wolves	42	20	11	11	72	49	51
3	Preston	42	16	17	9	64	44	49
4	Charlton	42	16	14	12	65	51	46
5	Middlesbrough	42	19	8	15	72	65	46
6	Brentford	42	18	9	15	69	59	45
7	Bolton	42	15	15	12	64	60	45
8	Sunderland	42	14	16	12	55	57	44
9	Leeds	42	14	15	13	64	69	43
10	Chelsea	42	14	13	15	65	65	41
11	Liverpool	42	15	11	16	65	71	41
12	Blackpool	42	16	8	18	61	66	40
13	Derby	42	15	10	17	66	87	40
14	Everton	42	16	7	19	79	75	39
15	Huddersfield	42	17	5	20	55	68	39
16	Leicester	42	14	11	17	54	75	39
17	Stoke	42	13	12	17	58	59	38
18	Birmingham	42	10	18	14	58	62	38
19	Portsmouth	42	13	12	17	62	68	38
20	Grimsby	42	13	12	17	51	68	38
21	Man City	42	14	8	20	80	77	36
22	WBA	42	14	8	20	74	91	36

SECOND DIVISION

		P	W	D	L	F	A	Pts
1	Aston Villa	42	25	7	10	73	35	57
2	Man United	42	22	9	11	82	50	53
3	Sheff United	42	22	9	11	73	56	53
4	Coventry	42	20	12	10	66	45	52
5	Tottenham	42	19	6	17	76	54	44
6	Burnley	42	17	10	15	54	54	44
7	Bradford PA	42	17	9	16	69	56	43
8	Fulham	42	16	11	15	61	57	43
9	West Ham	42	14	14	14	53	52	42
10	Bury	42	18	5	19	63	60	41
11	Chesterfield	42	16	9	17	63	63	41
12	Luton	42	15	10	17	89	86	40
13	Plymouth	42	14	12	16	57	65	40
14	Norwich	42	14	11	17	56	75	39
15	Southampton	42	15	9	18	55	77	39
16	Blackburn	42	14	10	18	71	80	38
17	Sheff Wed	42	14	10	18	49	56	38
18	Swansea	42	13	12	17	45	73	38
19	Newcastle	42	14	8	20	51	58	36
20	Nottm Forest	42	14	8	20	47	60	36
21	Barnsley	42	11	14	17	50	64	36
22	Stockport	42	11	9	22	43	70	31

THIRD DIVISION (NORTH)

		P	W	D	L	F	A	Pts
1	Tranmere	42	23	10	9	81	41	56
2	Doncaster	42	21	12	9	74	49	54
3	Hull	42	20	13	9	80	43	53
4	Oldham	42	19	13	10	67	46	51
5	Gateshead	42	20	11	11	84	59	51
6	Rotherham	42	20	10	12	68	56	50
7	Lincoln	42	19	8	15	66	50	46
8	Crewe	42	18	9	15	71	53	45
9	Chester	42	16	12	14	77	72	44
10	Wrexham	42	16	11	15	58	63	43
11	York	42	16	10	16	70	68	42
12	Carlisle	42	15	9	18	57	67	39
13	New Brighton	42	15	8	19	60	61	38
14	Bradford City	42	14	10	18	66	69	38
15	Port Vale	42	12	14	16	65	73	38
16	Southport	42	12	14	16	53	82	38
17	Rochdale	42	13	11	18	67	78	37
18	Halifax	42	12	12	18	44	66	36
19	Darlington	42	11	10	21	54	79	32
20	Hartlepools	42	10	12	20	53	80	32
21	Barrow	42	11	10	21	41	71	32
22	Accrington	42	11	7	24	45	75	29

THIRD DIVISION (SOUTH)

		P	W	D	L	F	A	Pts
1	Millwall	42	23	10	9	83	37	56
2	Bristol City	42	21	13	8	68	40	55
3	QPR	42	22	9	11	80	47	53
4	Watford	42	21	11	10	73	43	53
5	Brighton	42	21	9	12	64	44	51
6	Reading	42	20	11	11	71	63	51
7	Crystal Palace	42	18	12	12	67	47	48
8	Swindon	42	17	10	15	49	49	44
9	Northampton	42	17	9	16	51	57	43
10	Cardiff	42	15	12	15	67	54	42
11	Notts County	42	16	9	17	50	50	41
12	Southend	42	15	10	17	70	68	40
13	Bournemouth	42	14	12	16	56	57	40
14	Mansfield	42	15	9	18	62	67	39
15	Bristol Rovers	42	13	13	16	46	61	39
16	Newport	42	11	16	15	43	52	38
17	Exeter	42	13	12	17	57	70	38
18	Aldershot	42	15	5	22	39	59	35
19	Clapton Orient	42	13	7	22	42	61	33
20	Torquay	42	9	12	21	38	73	30
21	Walsall	42	11	7	24	52	88	29
22	Gillingham	42	10	6	26	36	77	26

1938–39

FIRST DIVISION

	P	W	D	L	F	A	Pts
1 Everton	42	27	5	10	88	52	59
2 Wolves	42	22	11	9	88	39	55
3 Charlton	42	22	6	14	75	59	50
4 Middlesbrough	42	20	9	13	93	74	49
5 Arsenal	42	19	9	14	55	41	47
6 Derby	42	19	8	15	66	55	46
7 Stoke	42	17	12	13	71	68	46
8 Bolton	42	15	15	12	67	58	45
9 Preston	42	16	12	14	63	59	44
10 Grimsby	42	16	11	15	61	69	43
11 Liverpool	42	14	14	14	62	63	42
12 Aston Villa	42	15	11	16	71	60	41
13 Leeds	42	16	9	17	59	67	41
14 Man United	42	11	16	15	57	65	38
15 Blackpool	42	12	14	16	56	68	38
16 Sunderland	42	13	12	17	54	67	38
17 Portsmouth	42	12	13	17	47	70	37
18 Brentford	42	14	8	20	53	74	36
19 Huddersfield	42	12	11	19	58	64	35
20 Chelsea	42	12	9	21	64	80	33
21 Birmingham	42	12	8	22	62	84	32
22 Leicester	42	9	11	22	48	82	29

SECOND DIVISION

	P	W	D	L	F	A	Pts
1 Blackburn	42	25	5	12	94	60	55
2 Sheff United	42	20	14	8	69	41	54
3 Sheff Wed	42	21	11	10	88	59	53
4 Coventry	42	21	8	13	62	45	50
5 Man City	42	21	7	14	96	72	49
6 Chesterfield	42	20	9	13	69	52	49
7 Luton	42	22	5	15	82	66	49
8 Tottenham	42	19	9	14	67	62	47
9 Newcastle	42	18	10	14	61	48	46
10 WBA	42	18	9	15	89	72	45
11 West Ham	42	17	10	15	70	52	44
12 Fulham	42	17	10	15	61	55	44
13 Millwall	42	14	14	14	64	53	42
14 Burnley	42	15	9	18	50	56	39
15 Plymouth	42	15	8	19	49	55	38
16 Bury	42	12	13	17	65	74	37
17 Bradford PA	42	12	11	19	61	82	35
18 Southampton	42	13	9	20	56	82	35
19 Swansea	42	11	12	19	50	83	34
20 Nottm Forest	42	10	11	21	49	82	31
21 Norwich	42	13	5	24	50	91	31
22 Tranmere	42	6	5	31	39	99	17

THIRD DIVISION (NORTH)

	P	W	D	L	F	A	Pts
1 Barnsley	42	30	7	5	94	34	67
2 Doncaster	42	21	14	7	87	47	56
3 Bradford City	42	22	8	12	89	56	52
4 Southport	42	20	10	12	75	54	50
5 Oldham	42	22	5	15	76	59	49
6 Chester	42	20	9	13	88	70	49
7 Hull	42	18	10	14	83	74	46
8 Crewe	42	19	6	17	82	70	44
9 Stockport	42	17	9	16	91	77	43
10 Gateshead	42	14	14	14	74	67	42
11 Rotherham	42	17	8	17	64	64	42
12 Halifax	42	13	16	13	52	54	42
13 Barrow	42	16	9	17	66	65	41
14 Wrexham	42	17	7	18	66	79	41
15 Rochdale	42	15	9	18	92	82	39
16 New Brighton	42	15	9	18	68	73	39
17 Lincoln	42	12	9	21	66	92	33
18 Darlington	42	13	7	22	62	92	33
19 Carlisle	42	13	7	22	64	111	33
20 York	42	12	8	22	66	92	32
21 Hartlepools	42	12	7	23	55	94	31
22 Accrington	42	7	6	29	49	103	20

THIRD DIVISION (SOUTH)

	P	W	D	L	F	A	Pts
1 Newport	42	22	11	9	58	45	55
2 Crystal Palace	42	20	12	10	71	52	52
3 Brighton	42	19	11	12	68	49	49
4 Watford	42	17	12	13	62	51	46
5 Reading	42	16	14	12	69	59	46
6 QPR	42	15	14	13	68	49	44
7 Ipswich	42	16	12	14	62	52	44
8 Bristol City	42	16	12	14	61	63	44
9 Swindon	42	18	8	16	72	77	44
10 Aldershot	42	16	12	14	53	66	44
11 Notts County	42	17	9	16	59	54	43
12 Southend	42	16	9	17	61	64	41
13 Cardiff	42	15	11	16	61	65	41
14 Exeter	42	13	14	15	65	82	40
15 Bournemouth	42	13	13	16	52	58	39
16 Mansfield	42	12	15	15	44	62	39
17 Northampton	42	15	8	19	51	58	38
18 Port Vale	42	14	9	19	52	58	37
19 Torquay	42	14	9	19	54	70	37
20 Clapton Orient	42	11	13	18	53	55	35
21 Walsall	42	11	11	20	68	69	33
22 Bristol Rovers	42	10	13	19	55	61	33

SIX
Boom Years
1946–1950

'I was manager of Manchester United, a very raw young manager. I sat in the directors' box and a director sat behind me. During the game he leaned forward and said in a voice that people around him could hear: "Why didn't you do so-and-so?" "Shall I turn round and give him a blast?" I asked myself. But my judgement said: "No. Wait." I waited for the first convenient moment. Convenient? It was in the 'gents'. I said to him: "Never dare to say anything like that to me when other people can hear you." And I put it on the agenda for the next board meeting: "Interference by directors."'

Sir Matt Busby, *on his early days at Old Trafford.*

League football returned on Saturday, 31 August 1946 after a break of seven years; and a country tired of war and austerity was waiting for it. The game offered excitement, a sign of normality and the promise of a better tomorrow in one heady and irresistible package.

Huge crowds shuffled their way onto the terraces . . . men in ill-fitting demob suits, men who wanted to make up for lost years, men with a few shillings to spare for the first time in their lives, men whose memories of pre-war football had grown steadily brighter in foxhole and desert. A few women, yes, but football was essentially a male preserve.

Crowds in that first season after World War II totalled 35,604,606 – and they kept on growing until, toweringly, they reached 41,271,414 in 1948–9. The aggregate over four seasons was nearly 157 million. Football provided men with purpose and dignity for the price (1s 3d – 6p) of a couple of square feet on the terraces. It was so popular that absenteeism became a problem, especially in mid-week, and many employers quickly plumped for staggered hours. Even the winter of 1947, so cruel that it is described as the worst of the century, did nothing to chill interest.

Few seemed to care – or even notice – that the standard of football was not always very good. Seven years is a long time in the life of a footballer, and many of the stars of the 1930s were past their best after the war. Untried youngsters were sent out in famous shirts as clubs searched for new talent and balanced combinations. But it did not matter. The game was back – and answering a call from the nation.

The League championship's first move after the war was a short one – across the green acres of Stanley Park which separates the stadiums of Goodison Park and Anfield. Everton won the title in 1939, and Liverpool in 1947 for the fifth time.

Liverpool won most games, conceded fewest goals and suddenly realized that in a young chap called Billy Liddell they had someone rather special. He became a bull of a winger who played 492 League games for Liverpool and who fired in shots with either foot that made goalkeepers feel they were being attacked by cannons. He also happened to be a youth worker, an accountant, a lay preacher and – before he finished playing – Justice of the Peace. For two decades Liddell of Liverpool and Scotland was something much more than another Saturday hero.

Some players straddled the war with success and Joe Mercer of England was among them. Mercer joined Everton in the days of Dixie Dean and, at right-half, was a cornerstone of the side that won the championship in 1939. Then, after the war, he joined a grateful Arsenal who were now in debt and worried sick about relegation: they made him captain and hoped for a couple of good seasons from him. But Mercer always gave more than expected. He played on for eight years – having 'just one more' after another – and inspired them to two championships (1948 and 1953) and two Cup Finals (with a 1950 victory over Liverpool). Mercer, too, was special. He had a wonderful lop-sided smile and a pair of legs as full of twists and angles as a spiral staircase. The legs often hurt him, but the smile – and the man – enriched the game.

Portsmouth finished seven places and 14 points behind Arsenal in 1948 but then – with the Fratton Park terraces chiming 'Play up Pom-pey . . . Pom-pey play up' – they suddenly produced a team good enough to win the title in 1949 and again in 1950. They were so good during this one high-water period in the club's history that – like Arsenal in the 1930s – the rest of the country disliked them.

Pompey were a unit without basic weakness and, week in, week out, they played to the ceiling of their ability. They were without any galactic stars but they did have a lot of very good players. Their attack was given point by Doug Reid, a big, raw-boned Scot, Ike Clarke, Jack Froggatt and the scurrying figure of Peter Harris on the right-wing – but the essential strength of the side was its half-back line. Reg Flewin glued the defence together while Jimmy Scoular provided blood and thunder to the right and Jimmy Dickinson craft and variety to the left. Dickinson, a quiet but immensely loyal man, played 764 League games for Portsmouth and 48 times for England. He was the type of player that managers dream about.

But by now there was a new power in the land. Matt Busby took over as manager of Manchester United in October 1945, and he got things right from the start. United were obliged to share Maine Road with Manchester City for a season or two because Old Trafford had been blitzed; but Busby inherited some wonderful players, Johnny Carey, Charlie Mitten, Jack Rowley, Allenby Chilton and Stan Pearson among them, and he quickly got them into shape and a hungry frame of mind. United were runners-up in four of the first five seasons after the war and beat Blackpool 4–2 at Wembley in 1948 in what is still regarded as the finest footballing FA Cup final of them all. Remarkably, though, Busby and United were just beginning.

These were years when stars were seen – and allowed – to be stars. Tackling was hard and marking could be close but defence was not yet an applied science. There was still a long way to go before managers would start programming their defenders to smother and outnumber forwards. It was a different age with different priorities.

It meant, happily, that the packed terraces of the late 1940s were able to relish the virtuosity of men like the peerless Tommy Lawton, Peter Doherty and the silver-haired Raich Carter who together helped Derby County win the first FA Cup final after the war; Wilf Mannion; Len Shackleton, the self-confessed Clown Prince of Soccer and an artful dodger of genius; Denis Compton, almost as gifted at football as he was at cricket; Stan Mortensen and, most of all perhaps, Stanley Matthews, the 'Wizard of Dribble' whose career of 33 years took him past his fiftieth birthday and whose finest moment would come in the Coronation Year of 1953.

left Frank Swift of Manchester City and England – one of the game's finest and most popular goalkeepers. Showman, humorist, mimic and crowd-puller. 'Big Swifty' helped City win the FA Cup in 1934, the League championship for the first time in 1937 and the Second Division championship in 1947. He won 19 caps for England, two as captain, and retired in 1949 to become a journalist. He died in the Munich air-crash in 1958.

above Frank Swift as a special constable in Manchester early in World War Two. 'But on my very first day of traffic point duty,' he later recalled, 'I got everything so muddled that, on the advice of a colleague, I walked away leaving the traffic to sort itself out. I felt at that moment how many full-backs must have felt when playing against Stanley Matthews.'

left Horatio Stratton 'Raich' Carter of Sunderland, Derby County, Hull and England – described by Charles Buchan as 'the greatest inside-forward of his generation: he stood out in every game he played.' And Willie Watson, an England international at football and cricket, said he never knew for sure how good Carter was – 'You can only judge a player when you've seen him under pressure and I never saw him under pressure. He carried empty space around with him like an umbrella.' Carter, who in his maturer years as a player had distinctive silver hair, was a master technician, a strategist of natural authority and an expert at punishing weaknesses. He and Stanley Matthews formed an England right-wing pair of stunning virtuosity. Carter scored 213 goals in 451 League games: 248 games (121 goals) for Sunderland (1932–45), 67 (34) for Derby (1945–8), 136 (58) for Hull (1948–52). He helped Sunderland win the League championship in 1936 and the FA Cup (as captain at the age of 23) in 1937. He formed a brilliant inside-forward partnership with Peter Doherty of Northern Ireland in Derby's FA Cup-winning team in 1946 and then, as player-manager, inspired Hull to the championship of Division Three North in 1949. Won 13 caps for England (1934–47).

left Bevin Boy 1945. Nat Lofthouse was a miner before he became one of post-war football's most formidable centre-forwards for Bolton and England. His Saturdays started before 4 am and continued with eight hours of wagon pushing down the pit before he turned to football. But his pitwork made him tough and accustomed to hard work.

below Moscow Dynamo take the field at Stamford Bridge in November 1945 – complete with famous long shorts and bouquets of flowers. 'They are not nearly good enough to play our professionals,' wrote one critic. But, in front of a crowd of 85,000, Dynamo played beautifully, drew 3–3 with a Chelsea side that included Tommy Lawton and were unlucky not to win. They then beat Cardiff of the Third Division 10–1 and, in pea-soup fog, overcame Arsenal 4–3 – with Stanley Matthews and Stan Mortensen, the celebrated Blackpool forwards, 'guesting' for the North London club. The Dynamos left an indelible memory.

left Higher education. Tufts of grass, cracked concrete, torn pants and scuffed boots – the type of 'school' in which many League players learnt the game. The tutor is Wilf Mannion of Middlesbrough and England – an inside-forward of memorable verve and invention who scored two goals and was outstanding in Great Britain's 6–1 victory over the Rest of Europe in 1947. Won 26 caps for England and scored 100 goals in 357 League games for Middlesbrough and, briefly, Hull.

bottom left Johnny Carey (right) of Manchester United, Republic of Ireland and Northern Ireland – one of the most versatile and impeccably mannered of all footballers. 'Gentleman John' played in every position for United except outside-left but climbed his loftiest peaks as a right-back of great style and composure. He led United to their memorable FA Cup Final triumph in 1948 – they were twice down to Stanley Matthews' Blackpool but fought back to win 4–2 – and then to their 1952 League championship, United's first title for 41 years. He captained the Rest of Europe against Britain in 1947 and had the curious and unique distinction of captaining both Irelands – a situation made possible by his service in the British Army. Played 306 League games for United (1936–53), 29 games for the Republic of Ireland and seven for Northern Ireland. Footballer of the Year 1949. When he retired he was invited to the Old Trafford boardroom where it was formally recorded in the minute-book that Carey 'had covered his career with glory and set a shining example to all who follow him.' Later managed Blackburn, Everton, Leyton Orient and Nottingham Forest. Picture: Highbury 1948 – and Carey is challenged by Arsenal winger Ian McPherson who as an RAF Mosquito pilot during the war earned a double DFC.

right Denis Compton, one of the great all-round sporting heroes: Middlesex and England cricketer of genius and Arsenal footballer of high merit. Neville Cardus said he was a batsman 'who pulled science by the beard like a cheeky schoolboy' – and Arsenal colleague Bernard Joy said he was a left-winger 'who was a devil on his day'. Compton played for Arsenal before and after the war (1932–52) and was a member of their FA Cup-winning side in 1950. Compton was 32 years old then and playing his last game for the club; and during the interval of an exhausting final in heavy rain he looked drained. But someone produced a large brandy for him – and 18 minutes into the second half Compton provided the long and accurate centre which led to Arsenal's second and decisive goal against Liverpool. Compton also played in twelve wartime internationals and was alongside Stanley Matthews, Raich Carter, Tommy Lawton and Jimmy Hagan in the England attack that beat Scotland 8–0 at Maine Road in October 1943. But, above all, Compton was a cricketer of unconventional brilliance: he scored 38,942 first-class runs (123 centuries) and in his finest season (1947) he shattered records by scoring 3,816 runs with 18 centuries and twelve half-centuries. Serious knee trouble sustained while playing football curtailed his career. His elder brother Leslie was an indomitable centre-half who played 253 League games for Arsenal (1932–52) and became the oldest player to make his debut for England when he played against Wales in 1950 at the age of 38 years 2 months. 'Big Les' also played cricket for Middlesex.

right William Cuff, chairman of Everton and president of the Football League during the diffficult war years, addressing the 1947 annual meeting of the League. On the left is Fred Howarth, League secretary from 1933 to 1957 – only the third man to hold the post.

above Portsmouth celebrate their Golden Jubilee at Fratton Park in December 1948. Field Marshal Montgomery, the club's president, shakes the hand of Peter Harris who is on the left of Jimmy Dickinson. Portsmouth marked the occasion with a reunion of old players, a civic reception, a 4–1 victory over Arsenal – and the League championships of 1949 and 1950. Dickinson (764 between 1946–65) and Harris (479 between 1946–59) played 1,243 League games between them – all for Portsmouth. Harris scored 194 goals, still a club record.

right The start of the 1948–9 season during which a record 41,271,414 people watched League football. Part of a huge Highbury crowd which saw Manchester United, the FA Cup holders, beat Arsenal, the League champions, by 1–0 on the opening Saturday. Receipts for the game were around £7,500; and Arsenal finished the season with a profit of £59,125 – a record, at the time, for any League club.

left Billy Liddell of Liverpool and Scotland – a left-winger and later centre-forward of wonderfully harnessed power and speed whose influence and example were so outstanding that Liverpool were often nicknamed 'Liddellpool'. Scored 216 goals in 492 League games (1946–60) and won 28 caps. He and Stanley Matthews were the only players to play for Britain against the Rest of Europe in both 1947 and 1955 – Britain scoring six in each game. A colleague said of Liddell: 'He was a gentleman who scared defenders stiff.'

above Stan Mortensen of Blackpool and England – also known as 'the Blackpool Bombshell' and 'the Electric Eel' – cutting between Bill Pavitt and Harry Freeman of Fulham at Craven Cottage, February 1950. Mortensen was a match-winner who always seemed to know the quickest, shortest and most unexpected route to goal, a forward of boundless energy and determination. Scored 197 goals in 320 League games for Blackpool; and contributed a hat-trick to Blackpool's 4–3 extra-time victory over Bolton in the 'Stanley Matthews' Cup final of 1953. Scored four goals in his first international (against Portugal in Lisbon 1947, 10–0) and, altogether, scored 24 goals in 25 games for England. Member of an England forward line which is still recited like a litany: Matthews, Mortensen, Lawton, Mannion, Finney. Later played for Hull and Southport.

2

above Neil Franklin of Stoke, Santa Fe (Colombia), Hull, Crewe and Stockport – a centre-half of distinction and high skill who played in 27 consecutive internationals for England after World War Two. No one challenged his place. Just before the 1950 World Cup he joined the Santa Fe club in Bogota who promised him handsome payment – but he returned in a few months and, after suspension, joined Hull. Played 323 League games between 1946 and 1957.

left Wolverhampton Wanderers and Middlesbrough begin the 1949–50 season with sunshine, high hope and a full house. Jimmy Mullen (centre) – described by Billy Wright as 'one of the finest wingers I've seen' – is in full stride. Wolves finished as runners-up on goal average to Portsmouth.

above E.A. 'Ted' Croker, Charlton Athletic defender, 1950, who became secretary of the Football Association in September 1973. Croker, as a former professional footballer and then a successful businessman, brought new experience and a personable new image to the Lancaster Gate post at a time of great change and increasing problems in the game. His brother Peter played in Charlton's FA Cup-winning side in 1947 (1–0 v Burnley).

below Willie Watson – versatile forward/wing-half for Huddersfield, Sunderland and England (four caps, 1950 and 1951) and outstanding left-hand batsman for Yorkshire, Leicestershire and England (23 Tests).

36
EVERTON
FOOTBALL CLUB
SEASON 1948 1949
GOODISON PARK
FOOTBALL LEAGUE—1st Division.
EVERTON
versus
BLACKPOOL
AT GOODISON PARK.
SATURDAY, MARCH 5th, 1949
KICK-OFF 3.15 p.m.
C. F. Lello
Vol. 7
PRICE 1D
OFFICIAL PROGRAMME
RTH-EAST
IGLAND
stle - Sunderland
sbrough - York
ton - Stockton
by
ESS COACHES
from
COACH STATION
& NIGHT
ERVICE
D & ORANGE
NE : SLOane 0202
th to mouth...
SHOOT, MAN, SHOOT! AND DON'T MEANDER, THERE'S NO TIME NOW FOR
AFRIKANDER
BRITAIN'S MOST FAMOUS MIXTURE 3/4½ PER OZ.
FULHA
White Shirts, Black Knickers.
R
HINTON
2 LEWIN
4 QUESTED
5 TAYLOR
8 THOMAS, R.
7 THOMAS, S.
9 STEVENS
Referee— Mr. H. BRYAN (Tipton)
11 ELLIOTT
9 AINSLE
10 DOWNIE
6 LAYTON
GREENWO
3 FARRELL
FARR
L
BRADFO
Red, Amber & Black Shirts, White Knickers.
Patrons will be advised of any change in t
WASHABLE
CHINA & GLASS PAINTING COLOURS
ART ENAMELS HAND CUT
DECORAT
MATERIA
ENAMEL
PATTERN
J.
37, FU
OFFICIAL PROGRAMME
HULL CITY A.F.C.
PRICE 3D.
HULL CITY A·F·C
v.
HALIFAX TOWN
BOOTHFERRY PARK · SATURDAY, 5th FEBRUARY, 1949
KICK-OFF 3.0 p.m.
OFFICIAL PROGRAMME
GRIMSBY TOWN F
SECOND DIVISIO
Town v SW
Saturday, Dec. 9th, 1
IS YOUR PROBL
BUILDING
THEN CONSULT
F. A.
OLD MAR
GRIMSB
TELEPHONE 55014
Richardsons & Coppin, Ltd.,

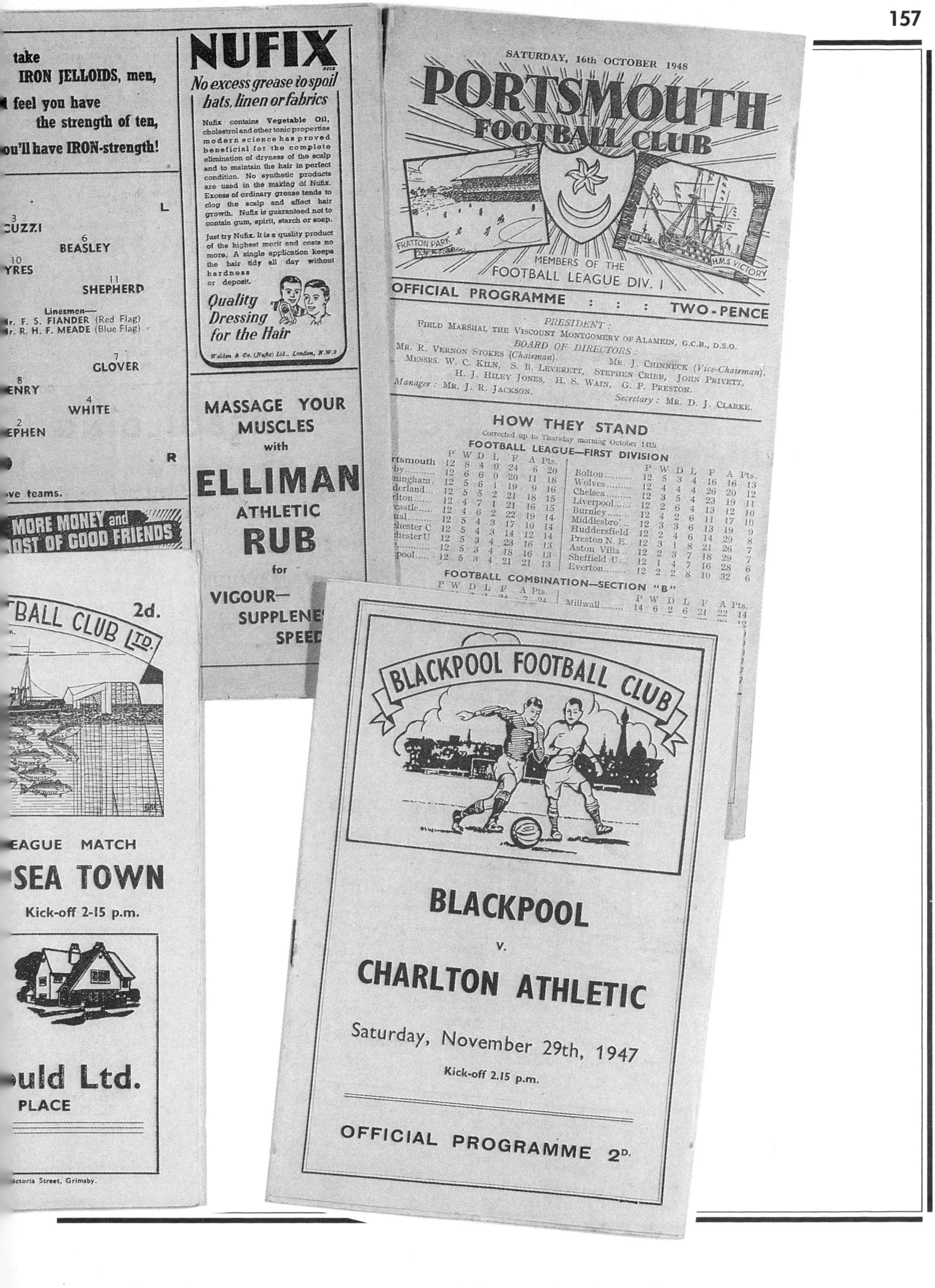
take
IRON JELLOIDS, men,
feel you have
the strength of ten,
ou'll have IRON-strength!
NUFIX
No excess grease to spoil
hats, linen or fabrics
Nufix contains Vegetable Oil, cholestrol and other tonic properties modern science has proved beneficial for the complete elimination of dryness of the scalp and to maintain the hair in perfect condition. No synthetic products are used in the making of Nufix. Excess of ordinary grease tends to clog the scalp and affect hair growth. Nufix is guaranteed not to contain gum, spirit, starch or soap.
Just try Nufix. It is a quality product of the highest merit and costs no more. A single application keeps the hair tidy all day without hardness or deposit.
Quality Dressing for the Hair
Walden & Co. (Nufix) Ltd., London, N.W.9
MASSAGE YOUR MUSCLES with
ELLIMAN
ATHLETIC
RUB
for
VIGOUR—
SUPPLENES
SPEED
3 CUZZI
6 BEASLEY
10 YRES
11 SHEPHERD
Linesmen—
r. F. S. FIANDER (Red Flag)
r. R. H. F. MEADE (Blue Flag)
7 GLOVER
8 ENRY
4 WHITE
2 EPHEN
L
R
ve teams.
MORE MONEY and
OST OF GOOD FRIENDS
SATURDAY, 16th OCTOBER 1948
PORTSMOUTH
FOOTBALL CLUB
FRATTON PARK
H.M.S. VICTORY
MEMBERS OF THE
FOOTBALL LEAGUE DIV. I
OFFICIAL PROGRAMME : : : TWO-PENCE
PRESIDENT :
FIELD MARSHAL THE VISCOUNT MONTGOMERY OF ALAMEIN, G.C.B., D.S.O.
BOARD OF DIRECTORS :
MR. R. VERNON STOKES (Chairman). MR. J. CHINNECK (Vice-Chairman).
MESSRS. W. C. KILN, S. B. LEVERETT, STEPHEN CRIBB, JOHN PRIVETT, H. J. HILEY JONES, H. S. WAIN, G. F. PRESTON.
Manager : MR. J. R. JACKSON. Secretary : MR. D. J. CLARKE.
HOW THEY STAND
Corrected up to Thursday morning October 14th
FOOTBALL LEAGUE—FIRST DIVISION
FOOTBALL COMBINATION—SECTION "B"
TBALL CLUB LTD.
2d.
EAGUE MATCH
SEA TOWN
Kick-off 2-15 p.m.
uld Ltd.
PLACE
ictoria Street, Grimsby.
BLACKPOOL FOOTBALL CLUB
BLACKPOOL
v.
CHARLTON ATHLETIC
Saturday, November 29th, 1947
Kick-off 2.15 p.m.
OFFICIAL PROGRAMME 2D.

LEAGUE TABLES

1946–47

FIRST DIVISION

		P	W	D	L	F	A	Pts
1	Liverpool	42	25	7	10	84	52	57
2	Man United	42	22	12	8	95	54	56
3	Wolves	42	25	6	11	98	56	56
4	Stoke	42	24	7	11	90	53	55
5	Blackpool	42	22	6	14	71	70	50
6	Sheff United	42	21	7	14	89	75	49
7	Preston	42	18	11	13	76	74	47
8	Aston Villa	42	18	9	15	67	53	45
9	Sunderland	42	18	8	16	65	66	44
10	Everton	42	17	9	16	62	67	43
11	Middlesbrough	42	17	8	17	73	68	42
12	Portsmouth	42	16	9	17	66	60	41
13	Arsenal	42	16	9	17	72	70	41
14	Derby	42	18	5	19	73	79	41
15	Chelsea	42	16	7	19	69	84	39
16	Grimsby	42	13	12	17	61	82	38
17	Blackburn	42	14	8	20	45	53	36
18	Bolton	42	13	8	21	57	69	34
19	Charlton	42	11	12	19	57	71	34
20	Huddersfield	42	13	7	22	53	79	33
21	Brentford	42	9	7	26	45	88	25
22	Leeds	42	6	6	30	45	90	18

SECOND DIVISION

		P	W	D	L	F	A	Pts
1	Man City	42	26	10	6	78	35	62
2	Burnley	42	22	14	6	65	29	58
3	Birmingham	42	25	5	12	74	33	55
4	Chesterfield	42	18	14	10	58	44	50
5	Newcastle	42	19	10	13	95	62	48
6	Tottenham	42	17	14	11	65	53	48
7	WBA	42	20	8	14	88	75	48
8	Coventry	42	16	13	13	66	59	45
9	Leicester	42	18	7	17	69	64	43
10	Barnsley	42	17	8	17	84	86	42
11	Nottm Forest	42	15	10	17	69	74	40
12	West Ham	42	16	8	18	70	76	40
13	Luton	42	16	7	19	71	73	39
14	Southampton	42	15	9	18	69	76	39
15	Fulham	42	15	9	18	63	74	39
16	Bradford PA	42	14	11	17	65	77	39
17	Bury	42	12	12	18	80	78	36
18	Millwall	42	14	8	20	56	79	36
19	Plymouth	42	14	5	23	79	96	33
20	Sheff Wed	42	12	8	22	67	88	32
21	Swansea	42	11	7	24	55	83	29
22	Newport	42	10	3	29	61	133	23

THIRD DIVISION (NORTH)

		P	W	D	L	F	A	Pts
1	Doncaster	42	33	6	3	123	40	72
2	Rotherham	42	29	6	7	114	53	64
3	Chester	42	25	6	11	95	51	56
4	Stockport	42	24	2	16	78	53	50
5	Bradford City	42	20	10	12	62	47	50
6	Rochdale	42	19	10	13	80	64	48
7	Wrexham	42	17	12	13	65	51	46
8	Crewe	42	17	9	16	70	74	43
9	Barrow	42	17	7	18	54	62	41
10	Tranmere	42	17	7	18	66	77	41
11	Hull	42	16	8	18	49	53	40
12	Lincoln	42	17	5	20	86	87	39
13	Hartlepools	42	15	9	18	64	73	39
14	Gateshead	42	16	6	20	62	72	38
15	York	42	14	9	19	67	81	37
16	Carlisle	42	14	9	19	70	93	37
17	Darlington	42	15	6	21	68	80	36
18	New Brighton	42	14	8	20	57	77	36
19	Oldham	42	12	8	22	55	80	32
20	Accrington	42	14	4	24	56	92	32
21	Southport	42	7	11	24	53	85	25
22	Halifax	42	8	6	28	43	92	22

THIRD DIVISION (SOUTH)

		P	W	D	L	F	A	Pts
1	Cardiff	42	30	6	6	93	30	66
2	QPR	42	23	11	8	74	40	57
3	Bristol City	42	20	11	11	94	56	51
4	Swindon	42	19	11	12	84	73	49
5	Walsall	42	17	12	13	74	59	46
6	Ipswich	42	16	14	12	61	53	46
7	Bournemouth	42	18	8	16	72	54	44
8	Southend	42	17	10	15	71	60	44
9	Reading	42	16	11	15	83	74	43
10	Port Vale	42	17	9	16	68	63	43
11	Torquay	42	15	12	15	52	61	42
12	Notts County	42	15	10	17	63	63	40
13	Northampton	42	15	10	17	72	75	40
14	Bristol Rovers	42	16	8	18	59	69	40
15	Exeter	42	15	9	18	60	69	39
16	Watford	42	17	5	20	61	76	39
17	Brighton	42	13	12	17	54	72	38
18	Crystal Palace	42	13	11	18	49	62	37
19	Leyton Orient	42	12	8	22	54	75	32
20	Aldershot	42	10	12	20	48	78	32
21	Norwich	42	10	8	24	64	100	28
22	Mansfield	42	9	10	23	48	96	28

1947–48

FIRST DIVISION

		P	W	D	L	F	A	Pts
1	Arsenal	42	23	13	6	81	32	59
2	Man United	42	19	14	9	81	48	52
3	Burnley	42	20	12	10	56	43	52
4	Derby	42	19	12	11	77	57	50
5	Wolves	42	19	9	14	83	70	47
6	Aston Villa	42	19	9	14	65	57	47
7	Preston	42	20	7	15	67	68	47
8	Portsmouth	42	19	7	16	68	50	45
9	Blackpool	42	17	10	15	57	41	44
10	Man City	42	15	12	15	52	47	42
11	Liverpool	42	16	10	16	65	61	42
12	Sheff United	42	16	10	16	65	70	42
13	Charlton	42	17	6	19	57	66	40
14	Everton	42	17	6	19	52	66	40
15	Stoke	42	14	10	18	41	55	38
16	Middlesbrough	42	14	9	19	71	73	37
17	Bolton	42	16	5	21	46	58	37
18	Chelsea	42	14	9	19	53	71	37
19	Huddersfield	42	12	12	18	51	60	36
20	Sunderland	42	13	10	19	56	67	36
21	Blackburn	42	11	10	21	54	72	32
22	Grimsby	42	8	6	28	45	111	22

SECOND DIVISION

		P	W	D	L	F	A	Pts
1	Birmingham	42	22	15	5	55	24	59
2	Newcastle	42	24	8	10	72	41	56
3	Southampton	42	21	10	11	71	53	52
4	Sheff Wed	42	20	11	11	66	53	51
5	Cardiff	42	18	11	13	61	58	47
6	West Ham	42	16	14	12	55	53	46
7	WBA	42	18	9	15	63	58	45
8	Tottenham	42	15	14	13	56	43	44
9	Leicester	42	16	11	15	60	57	43
10	Coventry	42	14	13	15	59	52	41
11	Fulham	42	15	10	17	47	46	40
12	Barnsley	42	15	10	17	62	64	40
13	Luton	42	14	12	16	56	59	40
14	Bradford PA	42	16	8	18	68	72	40
15	Brentford	42	13	14	15	44	61	40
16	Chesterfield	42	16	7	19	54	55	39
17	Plymouth	42	9	20	13	40	58	38
18	Leeds	42	14	8	20	62	72	36
19	Nottm Forest	42	12	11	19	54	60	35
20	Bury	42	9	16	17	58	68	34
21	Doncaster	42	9	11	22	40	66	29
22	Millwall	42	9	11	22	44	74	29

THIRD DIVISION (SOUTH)

		P	W	D	L	F	A	Pts
1	QPR	42	26	9	7	74	37	61
2	Bournemouth	42	24	9	9	76	35	57
3	Walsall	42	21	9	12	70	40	51
4	Ipswich	42	23	3	16	67	61	49
5	Swansea	42	18	12	12	70	52	48
6	Notts County	42	19	8	15	68	59	46
7	Bristol City	42	18	7	17	77	65	43
8	Port Vale	42	16	11	15	63	54	43
9	Southend	42	15	13	14	51	58	43
10	Reading	42	15	11	16	56	58	41
11	Exeter	42	15	11	16	55	63	41
12	Newport	42	14	13	15	61	73	41
13	Crystal Palace	42	13	13	16	49	49	39
14	Northampton	42	14	11	17	58	72	39
15	Watford	42	14	10	18	57	79	38
16	Swindon	42	10	16	16	41	46	36
17	Leyton Orient	42	13	10	19	51	73	36
18	Torquay	42	11	13	18	63	62	35
19	Aldershot	42	10	15	17	45	67	35
20	Bristol Rovers	42	13	8	21	71	75	34
21	Norwich	42	13	8	21	61	76	34
22	Brighton	42	11	12	19	43	73	34

THIRD DIVISION (NORTH)

		P	W	D	L	F	A	Pts
1	Lincoln	42	26	8	8	81	40	60
2	Rotherham	42	25	9	8	95	49	59
3	Wrexham	42	21	8	13	74	54	50
4	Gateshead	42	19	11	12	75	57	49
5	Hull	42	18	11	13	59	48	47
6	Accrington	42	20	6	16	62	59	46
7	Barrow	42	16	13	13	49	40	45
8	Mansfield	42	17	11	14	57	51	45
9	Carlisle	42	18	7	17	88	77	43
10	Crewe	42	18	7	17	61	63	43
11	Oldham	42	14	13	15	63	64	41
12	Rochdale	42	15	11	16	48	72	41
13	York	42	13	14	15	65	60	40
14	Bradford City	42	15	10	17	65	66	40
15	Southport	42	14	11	17	60	63	39
16	Darlington	42	13	13	16	54	70	39
17	Stockport	42	13	12	17	63	67	38
18	Tranmere	42	16	4	22	54	72	36
19	Hartlepools	42	14	8	20	51	73	36
20	Chester	42	13	9	20	64	67	35
21	Halifax	42	7	13	22	43	76	27
22	New Brighton	42	8	9	25	38	81	25

1948–49

FIRST DIVISION

		P	W	D	L	F	A	Pts
1	Portsmouth	42	25	8	9	84	42	58
2	Man United	42	21	11	10	77	44	53
3	Derby	42	22	9	11	74	55	53
4	Newcastle	42	20	12	10	70	56	52
5	Arsenal	42	18	13	11	74	44	49
6	Wolves	42	17	12	13	79	66	46
7	Man City	42	15	15	12	47	51	45
8	Sunderland	42	13	17	12	49	58	43
9	Charlton	42	15	12	15	63	67	42
10	Aston Villa	42	16	10	16	60	76	42
11	Stoke	42	16	9	17	66	68	41
12	Liverpool	42	13	14	15	53	43	40
13	Chelsea	42	12	14	16	69	68	38
14	Bolton	42	14	10	18	59	68	38
15	Burnley	42	12	14	16	43	50	38
16	Blackpool	42	11	16	15	54	67	38
17	Birmingham	42	11	15	16	36	38	37
18	Everton	42	13	11	18	41	63	37
19	Middlesbrough	42	11	12	19	46	57	34
20	Huddersfield	42	12	10	20	40	69	34
21	Preston	42	11	11	20	62	75	33
22	Sheff United	42	11	11	20	57	78	33

SECOND DIVISION

		P	W	D	L	F	A	Pts
1	Fulham	42	24	9	9	77	37	57
2	WBA	42	24	8	10	69	39	56
3	Southampton	42	23	9	10	69	36	55
4	Cardiff	42	19	13	10	62	47	51
5	Tottenham	42	17	16	9	72	44	50
6	Chesterfield	42	15	17	10	51	45	47
7	West Ham	42	18	10	14	56	58	46
8	Sheff Wed	42	15	13	14	63	56	43
9	Barnsley	42	14	12	16	62	61	40
10	Luton	42	14	12	16	55	57	40
11	Grimsby	42	15	10	17	72	76	40
12	Bury	42	17	6	19	67	76	40
13	QPR	42	14	11	17	44	62	39
14	Blackburn	42	15	8	19	53	63	38
15	Leeds	42	12	13	17	55	63	37
16	Coventry	42	15	7	20	55	64	37
17	Bradford PA	42	13	11	18	65	78	37
18	Brentford	42	11	14	17	42	53	36
19	Leicester	42	10	16	16	62	79	36
20	Plymouth	42	12	12	18	49	64	36
21	Nottm Forest	42	14	7	21	50	54	35
22	Lincoln	42	8	12	22	53	91	28

THIRD DIVISION (NORTH)

		P	W	D	L	F	A	Pts
1	Hull	42	27	11	4	93	28	65
2	Rotherham	42	28	6	8	90	46	62
3	Doncaster	42	20	10	12	53	40	50
4	Darlington	42	20	6	16	83	74	46
5	Gateshead	42	16	13	13	69	58	45
6	Oldham	42	18	9	15	75	67	45
7	Rochdale	42	18	9	15	55	53	45
8	Stockport	42	16	11	15	61	56	43
9	Wrexham	42	17	9	16	56	62	43
10	Mansfield	42	14	14	14	52	48	42
11	Tranmere	42	13	15	14	46	57	41
12	Crewe	42	16	9	17	52	74	41
13	Barrow	42	14	12	16	41	48	40
14	York	42	15	9	18	74	74	39
15	Carlisle	42	14	11	17	60	77	39
16	Hartlepools	42	14	10	18	45	58	38
17	New Brighton	42	14	8	20	46	58	36
18	Chester	42	11	13	18	57	56	35
19	Halifax	42	12	11	19	45	62	35
20	Accrington	42	12	10	20	55	64	34
21	Southport	42	11	9	22	45	64	31
22	Bradford City	42	10	9	23	48	77	29

THIRD DIVISION (SOUTH)

		P	W	D	L	F	A	Pts
1	Swansea	42	27	8	7	87	34	62
2	Reading	42	25	5	12	77	50	55
3	Bournemouth	42	22	8	12	69	48	52
4	Swindon	42	18	15	9	64	56	51
5	Bristol Rovers	42	19	10	13	61	51	48
6	Brighton	42	15	18	9	55	55	48
7	Ipswich	42	18	9	15	78	77	45
8	Millwall	42	17	11	14	63	64	45
9	Torquay	42	17	11	14	65	70	45
10	Norwich	42	16	12	14	67	49	44
11	Notts County	42	19	5	18	102	68	43
12	Exeter	42	15	10	17	63	76	40
13	Port Vale	42	14	11	17	51	54	39
14	Walsall	42	15	8	19	56	64	38
15	Newport	42	14	9	19	68	92	37
16	Bristol City	42	11	14	17	44	62	36
17	Watford	42	10	15	17	41	54	35
18	Southend	42	9	16	17	41	46	34
19	Leyton Orient	42	11	12	19	58	80	34
20	Northampton	42	12	9	21	51	62	33
21	Aldershot	42	11	11	20	48	59	33
22	Crystal Palace	42	8	11	23	38	76	27

1949–50

FIRST DIVISION

		P	W	D	L	F	A	Pts
1	Portsmouth	42	22	9	11	74	38	53
2	Wolves	42	20	13	9	76	49	53
3	Sunderland	42	21	10	11	83	62	52
4	Man United	42	18	14	10	69	44	50
5	Newcastle	42	19	12	11	77	55	50
6	Arsenal	42	19	11	12	79	55	49
7	Blackpool	42	17	15	10	46	35	49
8	Liverpool	42	17	14	11	64	54	48
9	Middlesbrough	42	20	7	15	59	48	47
10	Burnley	42	16	13	13	40	40	45
11	Derby	42	17	10	15	69	61	44
12	Aston Villa	42	15	12	15	61	61	42
13	Chelsea	42	12	16	14	58	65	40
14	WBA	42	14	12	16	47	53	40
15	Huddersfield	42	14	9	19	52	73	37
16	Bolton	42	10	14	18	45	59	34
17	Fulham	42	10	14	18	41	54	34
18	Everton	42	10	14	18	42	66	34
19	Stoke	42	11	12	19	45	75	34
20	Charlton	42	13	6	23	53	65	32
21	Man City	42	8	13	21	36	68	29
22	Birmingham	42	7	14	21	31	67	28

SECOND DIVISION

		P	W	D	L	F	A	Pts
1	Tottenham	42	27	7	8	81	35	61
2	Sheff Wed	42	18	16	8	67	48	52
3	Sheff United	42	19	14	9	68	49	52
4	Southampton	42	19	14	9	64	48	52
5	Leeds	42	17	13	12	54	45	47
6	Preston	42	18	9	15	60	49	45
7	Hull	42	17	11	14	64	72	45
8	Swansea	42	17	9	16	53	49	43
9	Brentford	42	15	13	14	44	49	43
10	Cardiff	42	16	10	16	41	44	42
11	Grimsby	42	16	8	18	74	73	40
12	Coventry	42	13	13	16	55	55	39
13	Barnsley	42	13	13	16	64	67	39
14	Chesterfield	42	15	9	18	43	47	39
15	Leicester	42	12	15	15	55	65	39
16	Blackburn	42	14	10	18	55	60	38
17	Luton	42	10	18	14	41	51	38
18	Bury	42	14	9	19	60	65	37
19	West Ham	42	12	12	18	53	61	36
20	QPR	42	11	12	19	40	57	34
21	Plymouth	42	8	16	18	44	65	32
22	Bradford PA	42	10	11	21	51	77	31

THIRD DIVISION (NORTH)

		P	W	D	L	F	A	Pts
1	Doncaster	42	19	17	6	66	38	55
2	Gateshead	42	23	7	12	87	54	53
3	Rochdale	42	21	9	12	68	41	51
4	Lincoln	42	21	9	12	60	39	51
5	Tranmere	42	19	11	12	51	48	49
6	Rotherham	42	19	10	13	80	59	48
7	Crewe	42	17	14	11	68	55	48
8	Mansfield	42	18	12	12	66	54	48
9	Carlisle	42	16	15	11	68	51	47
10	Stockport	42	19	7	16	55	52	45
11	Oldham	42	16	11	15	58	63	43
12	Chester	42	17	6	19	70	79	40
13	Accrington	42	16	7	19	57	62	39
14	New Brighton	42	14	10	18	45	63	38
15	Barrow	42	14	9	19	47	53	37
16	Southport	42	12	13	17	51	71	37
17	Darlington	42	11	13	18	56	69	35
18	Hartlepools	42	14	5	23	52	79	33
19	Bradford City	42	12	8	22	61	76	32
20	Wrexham	42	10	12	20	39	54	32
21	Halifax	42	12	8	22	58	85	32
22	York	42	9	13	20	52	70	31

THIRD DIVISION (SOUTH)

		P	W	D	L	F	A	Pts
1	Notts County	42	25	8	9	95	50	58
2	Northampton	42	20	11	11	72	50	51
3	Southend	42	19	13	10	66	48	51
4	Nottm Forest	42	20	9	13	67	39	49
5	Torquay	42	19	10	13	66	63	48
6	Watford	42	16	13	13	45	35	45
7	Crystal Palace	42	15	14	13	55	54	44
8	Brighton	42	16	12	14	57	69	44
9	Bristol Rovers	42	19	5	18	51	51	43
10	Reading	42	17	8	17	70	64	42
11	Norwich	42	16	10	16	65	63	42
12	Bournemouth	42	16	10	16	57	56	42
13	Port Vale	42	15	11	16	47	42	41
14	Swindon	42	15	11	16	59	62	41
15	Bristol City	42	15	10	17	60	61	40
16	Exeter	42	14	11	17	63	75	39
17	Ipswich	42	12	11	19	57	86	35
18	Leyton Orient	42	12	11	19	53	85	35
19	Walsall	42	9	16	17	61	62	34
20	Aldershot	42	13	8	21	48	60	34
21	Newport	42	13	8	21	67	98	34
22	Millwall	42	14	4	24	55	63	32

1950–51

FIRST DIVISION

	P	W	D	L	F	A	Pts
1 Tottenham	42	25	10	7	82	44	60
2 Man United	42	24	8	10	74	40	56
3 Blackpool	42	20	10	12	79	53	50
4 Newcastle	42	18	13	11	62	53	49
5 Arsenal	42	19	9	14	73	56	47
6 Middlesbrough	42	18	11	13	76	65	47
7 Portsmouth	42	16	15	11	71	68	47
8 Bolton	42	19	7	16	64	61	45
9 Liverpool	42	16	11	15	53	59	43
10 Burnley	42	14	14	14	48	43	42
11 Derby	42	16	8	18	81	75	40
12 Sunderland	42	12	16	14	63	73	40
13 Stoke	42	13	14	15	50	59	40
14 Wolves	42	15	8	19	74	61	38
15 Aston Villa	42	12	13	17	66	68	37
16 WBA	42	13	11	18	53	61	37
17 Charlton	42	14	9	19	63	80	37
18 Fulham	42	13	11	18	52	68	37
19 Huddersfield	42	15	6	21	64	92	36
20 Chelsea	42	12	8	22	53	65	32
21 Sheff Wed	42	12	8	22	64	83	32
22 Everton	42	12	8	22	48	86	32

SECOND DIVISION

	P	W	D	L	F	A	Pts
1 Preston	42	26	5	11	91	49	57
2 Man City	42	19	14	9	89	61	52
3 Cardiff	42	17	16	9	53	45	50
4 Birmingham	42	20	9	13	64	53	49
5 Leeds	42	20	8	14	63	55	48
6 Blackburn	42	19	8	15	65	66	46
7 Coventry	42	19	7	16	75	59	45
8 Sheff United	42	16	12	14	72	62	44
9 Brentford	42	18	8	16	75	74	44
10 Hull	42	16	11	15	74	70	43
11 Doncaster	42	15	13	14	64	68	43
12 Southampton	42	15	13	14	66	73	43
13 West Ham	42	16	10	16	68	69	42
14 Leicester	42	15	11	16	68	58	41
15 Barnsley	42	15	10	17	74	68	40
16 QPR	42	15	10	17	71	82	40
17 Notts County	42	13	13	16	61	60	39
18 Swansea	42	16	4	22	54	77	36
19 Luton	42	9	14	19	57	70	32
20 Bury	42	12	8	22	60	86	32
21 Chesterfield	42	9	12	21	44	69	30
22 Grimsby	42	8	12	22	61	95	28

THIRD DIVISION (NORTH)

	P	W	D	L	F	A	Pts
1 Rotherham	46	31	9	6	103	41	71
2 Mansfield	46	26	12	8	78	48	64
3 Carlisle	46	25	12	9	79	50	62
4 Tranmere	46	24	11	11	83	62	59
5 Lincoln	46	25	8	13	89	58	58
6 Bradford PA	46	23	8	15	90	72	54
7 Bradford City	46	21	10	15	90	63	52
8 Gateshead	46	21	8	17	84	62	50
9 Crewe	46	19	10	17	61	60	48
10 Stockport	46	20	8	18	63	63	48
11 Rochdale	46	17	11	18	69	62	45
12 Scunthorpe	46	13	18	15	58	57	44
13 Chester	46	17	9	20	62	64	43
14 Wrexham	46	15	12	19	55	71	42
15 Oldham	46	16	8	22	73	73	40
16 Hartlepools	46	16	7	23	64	66	39
17 York	46	12	15	19	66	77	39
18 Darlington	46	13	13	20	59	77	39
19 Barrow	46	16	6	24	51	76	38
20 Shrewsbury	46	15	7	24	43	74	37
21 Southport	46	13	10	23	56	72	36
22 Halifax	46	11	12	23	50	69	34
23 Accrington	46	11	10	25	42	101	32
24 New Brighton	46	11	8	27	40	90	30

THIRD DIVISION (SOUTH)

	P	W	D	L	F	A	Pts
1 Nottm Forest	46	30	10	6	110	40	70
2 Norwich	46	25	14	7	82	45	64
3 Reading	46	21	15	10	88	53	57
4 Plymouth	46	24	9	13	85	55	57
5 Millwall	46	23	10	13	80	57	56
6 Bristol Rovers	46	20	15	11	64	42	55
7 Southend	46	21	10	15	92	69	52
8 Ipswich	46	23	6	17	69	58	52
9 Bournemouth	46	22	7	17	65	57	51
10 Bristol City	46	20	11	15	64	59	51
11 Newport	46	19	9	18	77	70	47
12 Port Vale	46	16	13	17	60	65	45
13 Brighton	46	13	17	16	71	79	43
14 Exeter	46	18	6	22	62	85	42
15 Walsall	46	15	10	21	52	62	40
16 Colchester	46	14	12	20	63	76	40
17 Swindon	46	18	4	24	55	67	40
18 Aldershot	46	15	10	21	56	88	40
19 Leyton Orient	46	15	8	23	53	75	38
20 Torquay	46	14	9	23	64	81	37
21 Northampton	46	10	16	20	55	67	36
22 Gillingham	46	13	9	24	69	101	35
23 Watford	46	9	11	26	54	88	29
24 Crystal Palace	46	8	11	27	33	84	27

SEVEN
Messrs Busby and Cullis
1951–1960

'Playing in Italy is just like going into one of the Services. If you try to kick against everything then you are in for a miserable time. If you take the attitude that you are in and you might as well enjoy yourself, in spite of the rules and regulations, then the chances are you won't have such a bad time. You must tell yourself you are getting well paid and put up with strictness and soul-destroying defensive football. Then you will have a fine time.'

John Charles *of Leeds, Juventus, Roma, Cardiff and Wales – who helped Juventus win the Italian championship three times and the Italian Cup twice between 1958 and 1961 and was idolized as 'the gentle giant'.*

The 'fifties were the most stirring and restless years in the history of football. Old notions were challenged and new ideas accepted: but it was a period that also knew terrible sadness. The Football League shared it all.

The dream of competitive European football became a reality; some talented Hungarians proved that English football still had much to learn; floodlights gave the game an exciting extra dimension; Stanley Matthews won his FA Cup winners' medal at last; Wolves and Manchester United each won the League championship three times – and United, in one of football's darkest hours, perished in the slush and ice of a West German airport.

Nothing touched the inner heart of the nation more than the Munich disaster. The date and even the minute – four minutes past three on Thursday, 6 February 1958 – are remembered by countless thousands. Twenty-three people were killed: among them eight players – the essence of a champion side which had been returning from a European Cup match in Yugoslavia. The eight players who died were Roger Byrne, Geoff Bent, Eddie Colman, Mark Jones, Bill Whelan, Tommy Taylor, David Pegg and a giant young prodigy called Duncan Edwards, a First Division player at 15, an England international at 17, who hung courageously onto life for 15 days after the crash. Edwards had been the very spirit of his time.

A fine team of journalists also died, eight again, and among them was Frank Swift ('Big Swifty') who had kept goal for Manchester City for two decades and for England after Hitler's war. He was a mischievous giant with a gift for mimicry and hands so big they were known as 'the frying pans'. He was the first of the modern goalkeepers and many still argue he was also the best.

Some, incredibly, survived. Bobby Charlton went on to win 106 caps for England and Matt Busby, the father of the Busby Babes, lived to build an enduring memorial to those who died. Busby, a remarkable man of dignity, compassion and charm but also iron resolve, had already led United to three championships – 1952, 1956 and 1957 – and if his young side had been allowed to mature they might have dominated English football for a generation.

Yet there was one manager who matched Busby's achievements in the 'fifties: Stanley Cullis of Wolverhampton Wanderers also led his club to three League championships – 1954, 1958 and 1959. But there were essential differences between the two men.

Busby was a cunning strategist but he had a burning faith in natural talent. He gave his players guidelines . . . and freedom. He wanted them to have fun and give pleasure. Cullis was one of the game's regimental sergeant majors, an autocrat whose confidence was bullet-proof and whose criticism, it was said, could strip paint at twenty paces. Cullis as a player had been an outstanding centre-half with Wolves and England, an expert craftsman with a touch that was almost delicate. Cullis the manager, however, was committed to pace and stamina. He insisted that the ball should be hoisted into the opposition penalty area with a minimum of delay – and then kept there. Elaboration was a sin, the short pass a capital crime. 'Our forwards,' he once said, 'are not encouraged to parade their ability in ostentatious fashion.' Some critics called it 'kick and rush'

– but Wolves, under Cullis, enjoyed the best years in their history.

No player was better equipped to make Cullis's plan work on the field than Billy Wright who played First Division football for Wolves for 14 years, first at wing-half, then centre-half, and became the first man to win a hundred caps for England. Wright, with his fair hair, disarming smile and modest manner, was captain of club and country and every schoolboy's idea of a sporting hero. Wright was no conjurer with the ball; but he relished conflict and did the obvious wonderfully well. Wright captained England against Hungary at Wembley in November 1953 and then, a year later, led Wolves to famous floodlit victories over Moscow Spartak and Honved, the champions-elect of Hungary, at Molineux. Here were milestones in the history of the European game.

Hungary won the match at Wembley by 6–3, the first time that England had lost there to Continental opposition, but it was the difference between the sides in concept and technique that mattered most of all. Hungary, inspired by the great Ferenc Puskas, won with such style and authority that English football was forced to accept that it might not be the best in the world – a belief which had helped sustain the nation through two wars and a corrosive recession.

A year later, however, Wolves made their contribution to the argument in two magnificent floodlit games which must formally be described as 'friendlies'. First they beat Moscow Spartak, the Russian champions, by 4–0 and then they overcame Honved of Budapest by 3–2. Honved had six of the Hungarian side, including Puskas, which had beaten England at Wembley – but Wolves, in their distinctive strip of old gold and black, were unstoppable. And afterwards, in a dressing room full of noise and emotion, Stan Cullis pointed at his players and said: 'There they are. The champions of the world.' The morning papers could hardly wait. Wolves were world champions . . . and that was that.

The claim proved a perfect catalyst. Gabriel Hanot, editor of the French daily sports paper *L'Equipe*, had long championed the idea of a European tournament for clubs and now he followed up hard. He faced official indifference, conservative argument and maddening frustration but, in the early summer of 1955, FIFA and UEFA gave their formal blessing.

Chelsea, who had won the 1955 League championship (their first title) under Ted Drake, were invited to take part; but time was short, the new project was regarded with some suspicion, the interests of the domestic game were considered paramount, and Chelsea – at the League's request – declined the invitation. But a year later Manchester United, the new League champions, led English football across the English Channel. Matt Busby had no doubts. 'Challenges,' he said, 'should be met, not avoided.'

There were other men and teams who made an indelible print on the 'fifties. Spurs won the championships of the Second and First Divisions in successive seasons (1950 and 1951) and, at the same time, they startled convention with a method that was different, effective and attractive – known as 'push and run'. Arthur Rowe, Tottenham's manager, a distinctive man and an original thinker, told his players to 'make it simple, make it quick' and they did so, brilliantly. Their style was based on guarded possession, high mobility, accuracy at speed and the short pass. It was the antithesis of the Wolves' way – but there is room enough for all styles in the Football League.

No player meant more to his time than Stanley Matthews: he was, simply, a national institution. He played his first game for Stoke on 19 March 1932 and his last – a First Division match at the age of 50 years and five days – for Stoke again on 6 February 1965. His first game for England was in 1934 at the age of 19 and his last and 54th in 1957 when he was 42. Matthews was the 'Wizard of Dribble', the 'King of Soccer' and the 'Ageless Wonder'. He was also the first and only professional footballer to be knighted while he was still playing, the first to be named Footballer of the Year (an award he won again 16 years later) and the first to be voted European Footballer of the Year. He became the oldest man to play First Division football, to score a League goal and to score a Cup goal. But facts and records are only half the legend. The other half is about an ability to dribble past opponents that has known no equal. Matthews, with his impassive face and slightly bowed legs, made full-backs all over the world feel like a child who has been invited to guess which hand the sweet is in – and then discovered it was in neither. He would politely invite a tackle and then dismiss his opponent with sleight of head, shoulder and foot, severe control, exquisite balance and a stunning change of pace, standing start to fast lane in the blink of an eye. His repertoire of tricks never changed but nor were they ever rumbled. Matthews was a work of art.

Matthews' career spanned four decades but he is remembered for one match above all – the FA Cup final of 1953, the cornucopic year of the Coronation, the ascent of Everest, Gordon Richards' Derby, England's Ashes and a record seventh League championship for Arsenal. Matthews had been to Wembley twice before with Blackpool – in the middle phase of his career – but a winner's medal eluded him. He was 38 and the whole country shared his hopes and fears. The rest, as they say, is history. Bolton led Blackpool by 3–1 with little more than 20 minutes to go but Matthews, suddenly, theatrically, took the game by the throat. His bemusing swerves and centres like open invitations unhinged the Bolton defence, the brilliant Stan Mortensen completed a hat-trick and then, with less than a minute to go, Matthews picked his way along the right wing once more to lay on the winner for Bill Perry. Blackpool 4 Bolton 3 . . . to be known, henceforth, as the 'Matthews final'.

The first floodlit League game was between Portsmouth and Newcastle at Fratton Park on 22 February 1956 – and, even though the kick-off was delayed for nearly half an hour because of fuse failure, the public liked what it saw. Football at night with a white ball seemed quicker and more dramatic. The clubs themselves discovered that mid-week football after dark was an important source of new income and a way, too, of easing congestion when there was bad weather. It was a whole new ball game.

Some clubs had been ahead of the field, among them Arsenal, Tottenham, Wolves and Newcastle, but now pylons popped up on the corners of grounds all over the country – and they threw light on other changes. Players even looked different. The days of long baggy shorts and heavily armoured footwear were gone and, instead, players wore lightweight strips and supple cut-away boots. Everton even used electricity underground; in 1958 they becamc the first club to use under-soil heating. The modern game was taking shape.

above Matt Busby versus Stanley Cullis: first as players (pictured at the start of an England v Scotland wartime international) and then as managers. Cullis happily admitted that Busby was the player on whom he modelled his own play – but as a manager Cullis had very different ideas.

right Bloomfield Road, 15 September 1951. The sun shines, the terraces and car-parks are full and the message on top of the West Stand urges the world to be joyful. But Blackpool lose 0–3 to Aston Villa. The railway sidings have now been replaced by one of the biggest car-parks in Britain.

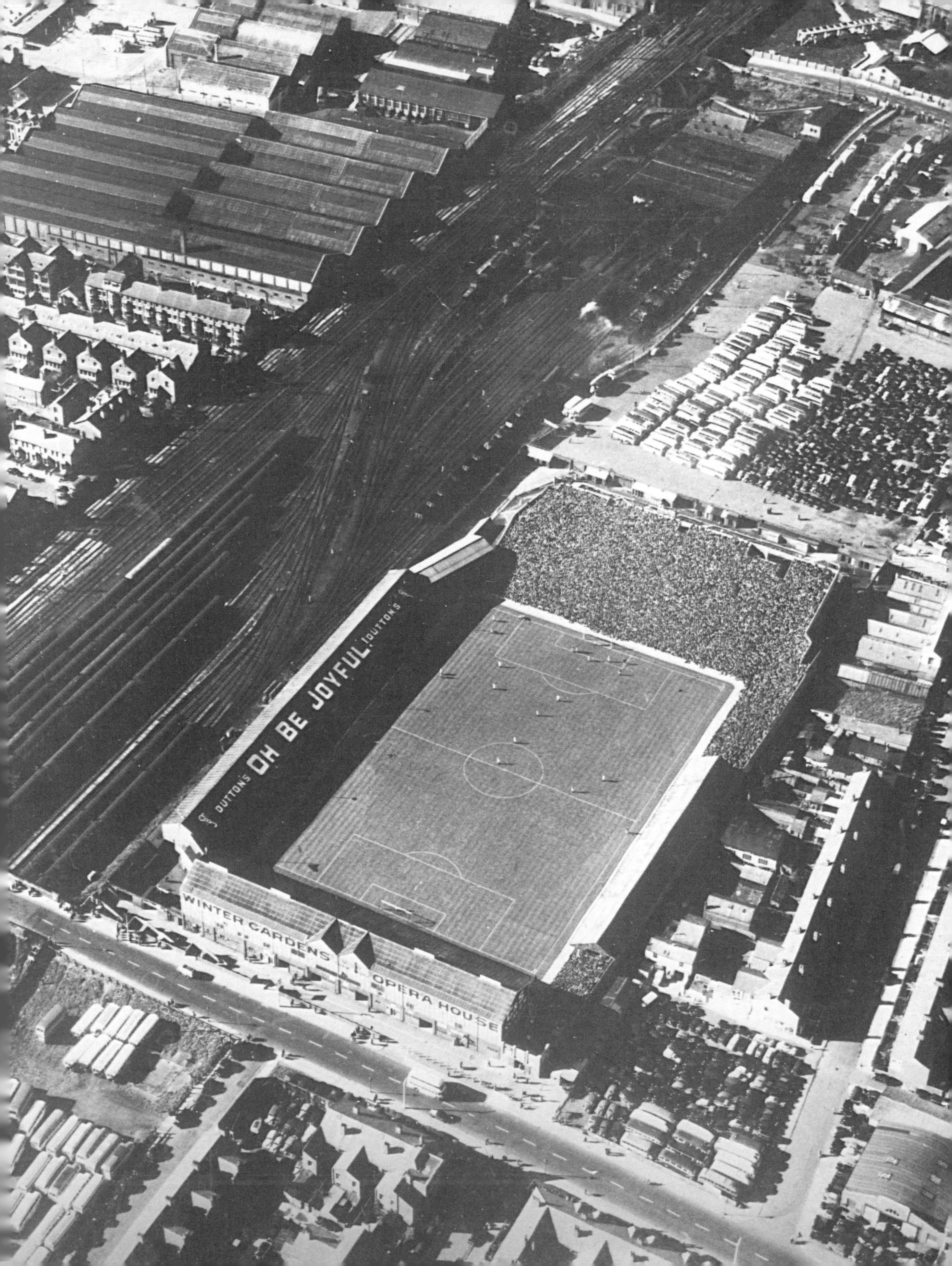
DUTTON'S OH BE JOYFUL DUTTON'S
WINTER GARDENS
OPERA HOUSE

"There is Some Corner of a Foreign Field . . ."
On it, Manchester United (left) and Tottenham Hotspur stand to attention while the National Anthems are played. Twenty-five thousand spectators have come to root, the largest crowd ever seen at a soccer match in the States.

THE MANGLING OF THE MANCS

Photographed by LARRY FRIED

On the hottest day of the year at New York's Yankee Stadium (capacity 75,000 and one-third full) Tottenham Hotspur gained a 7-1 victory over Manchester United after the finest exhibition of soccer ever seen in the United States. American critics were puzzled by the result, pointing out that United had only four corners given against them, while Spurs had nine

I AM not expecting to see Harry the Horse propping up a pillar of the 'El' at the corner of Jerome Avenue and 161st Street in the Bronx one hot Sunday afternoon when the mercury is breasting the nineties and the Yanks are out in Cleveland busy slaughtering the Indians.

"What gives so far from Broadway?" I enquire curiously.

"I should of stood in bed," he mutters savagely through his toothpick. "Here am I strolling past Yankee Stadium wishing I have the price of a ticket to Cleveland when I hear a great yell going up. I am puzzled because it sounds very much like 'Up the Yanks!' And here I am thinking the Yankees are out in Cleveland engaging the Redlegs of that

"Don't Be Without Your Favour"
Fifty cents for a genuine Spurs pennant, as carried (or so it's claimed) at White Hart Lane. Business is good.

The Film Star Fan
Herbert Marshall explains the game to his wife. A United fan, he has plenty to explain.

They pl

34

above Football League tribute to Baseball, Yankee Stadium, New York, June 1952. In the top right picture, Ron Burgess (Tottenham), left, and Johnny Carey (Manchester United) place a wreath before memorials to baseball immortals Babe Ruth and Lou Gehrig. A crowd of 25,000 saw Spurs beat United 7–1 in what was described as 'the finest exhibition of Soccer ever seen in the USA'. United had just won the 1952 League championship with Spurs as runners-up. Spurs completed the most successful overseas tour ever undertaken by a League club: Played ten, won ten, 85 goals for, six against.

right Tommy Lawton – playing his first Second Division game for Brentford shortly after being transferred from Notts County, Griffin Park on 15 March 1952. He had delighted crowds and humbled defences with Burnley, Everton, Chelsea, Notts County and England – but, even though he was 33 years old, he was still big news and still everybody's idea of a perfect centre-forward. He soon became Brentford's player-manager but then – a major sensation – he moved back to the First Division with Arsenal for the last three seasons of his playing career. Arsenal wanted someone to give them glamour, confidence and goals: and Lawton did not let them down. Lawton began his League career with Burnley when he was 16 – too young to sign professional forms – and scored a hat-trick against Tottenham four days after his 17th birthday. Stardom was inevitable and before his 18th birthday he moved to Everton for £6,500 – the chosen successor to Dixie Dean. He headed the First Division scoring list in the last two seasons before the war, scoring 34 goals in 38 League games to help Everton win the championship in 1939. He joined Chelsea after the war and then moved to Notts County who, despite being a Third Division club, paid the first transfer fee of £20,000 for him: a record sum which proved a gilt-edged investment. Meadow Lane gates tripled to more than 30,000. There was no one quite like Lawton in English football from the late 1930s until the mid-1950s – a classic centre-forward who was fast, brave, intelligent, a good team-man

The Rival Captains Pay Homage to the Immortals
eath before memorials to baseball stars Babe Ruth and Lou Gehrig to a trumpet
Below: British war veterans, now American citizens, lead the parade.

above Friends, team-mates and men with important futures: Jimmy Hill and Ron Greenwood at Brentford 1951. Each played more than 300 League games – Hill as an inside-forward for Brentford and Fulham (1949–60), Greenwood as a centre-half for Bradford Park Avenue, Brentford, Chelsea (League championship medal 1955) and Fulham (1946–56). Hill as chairman of the PFA, was instrumental in removing the maximum wage, and managed Coventry from the Third Division to the First (Second Division champions 1967) before beginning an influential television career. Greenwood managed West Ham for 16 years, leading them to triumphs in the FA Cup (1964) and the European Cup Winners' Cup (1965) before becoming a highly respected manager of England for five years (1977–82). They were men of vision, courage and high standards.

and a lethal finisher who was supreme in the air. Sam Bartram, a fine and loyal goalkeeper, often told the story of how he waited on his line in one match while Lawton rose for a centre. Lawton kept on climbing – reached the sort of height that most men are happy to leave to the birds – and then shouted: 'Top left-hand corner Barty'. Forehead met ball . . . and the ball, indeed, was in the top left corner. 'And I hadn't moved a muscle,' Sam would add. Lawton scored 231 goals in 390 League games (1936–56) and 22 in his 23 full internationals for England (1939–49). His dark good looks, splendid temperament and majestic talent made him a natural hero. The goalkeeper frustrating Lawton in the picture is Johnny King of Swansea.

above Cartoonist George Green's view of important Second Division matters, 1953–4. Everton beat Oldham, just promoted, by 3–1 at home and 4–0 at Boundary Park in their last game of the season to make sure of going up. Oldham were relegated – and did not return to Division Two for 20 years.

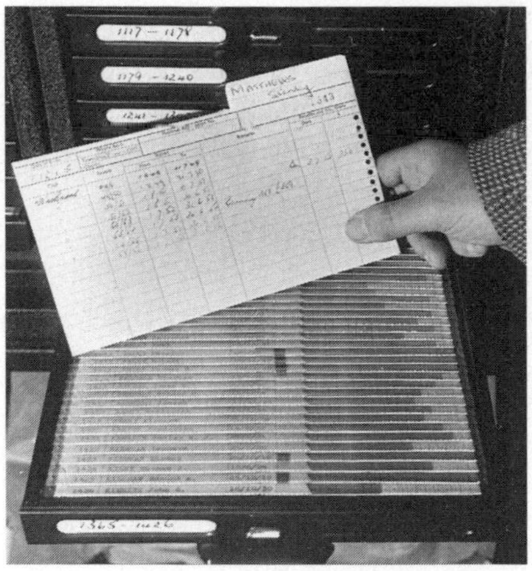

above Stanley Matthews' registration card at League headquarters in 1955 . . . confirming he was born on 1 February 1915, had a benefit worth £750 in 1952 and was safely signed by Blackpool until 30 June 1956.

above right Stanley Matthews, control tight, balance perfect, on the way to his precious FA Cup-winners' medal at Wembley in 1953. The Blackpool winger eases his way past Malcolm Barrass of Bolton – and Blackpool, 3–1 down with 20 minutes to go, fight back heroically to win 4–3.

right Jimmy Glazzard of Huddersfield heading one of his four goals in an 8–2 win over Everton in Division Two in April 1953. Huddersfield were promoted and the following season finished third in Division One – their highest position since World War Two – with Glazzard the First Division's leading scorer with 29. Everton themselves were promoted in 1953–4 and have been members of Division One ever since. Glazzard scored 142 goals in 299 League games for Huddersfield.

above Albert Leake, airborne, scores one of Port Vale's three goals against Bradford City in 1953–4: a matchless season for the Vale Park club – and for the Midlands. Port Vale won the Third Division North championship by a margin of eleven points and also reached the semi-finals of the FA Cup. Wolverhampton Wanderers won the League championship, West Bromwich went near to completing the 'double' (FA Cup winners and Division One runners-up) and Leicester City won the Second Division championship. But many felt Port Vale were 'the team of the season'. They conceded only 21 goals in their 46 League games (a record at the time); kept a clean sheet in 35 of their 54 League and Cup games; were the only side in the League unbeaten at home, and were the first Third Division club since the war to reach the FA Cup semi-finals. Their manager was Freddie Steele, the former Stoke and England forward, and eight of their players were born locally. Their average home gate was 20,000.

left

'Boots – boots – boots – boots,
Movin' up an' down again.'

Rudyard Kipling

This picture could have been taken in any boot-room in any club in the country in the 1950s – but, in fact, it belonged to Wolves.

above Jack Kelsey of Arsenal on a foggy day in London town, January 1954. The match, against Aston Villa, had to be stopped. The brave and athletic Kelsey played 327 League games for Arsenal – and two months after the picture was taken he was married and capped by Wales for the first of his 41 internationals (1954–62).

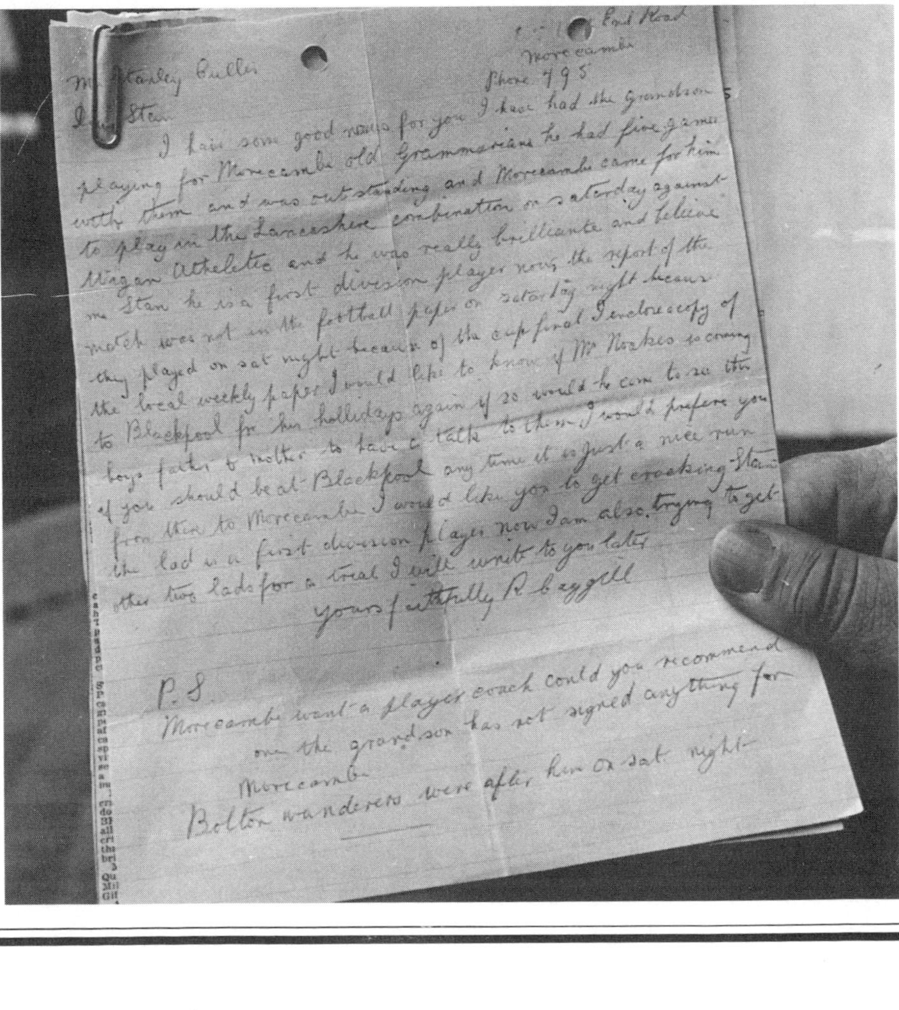

Rd Road
Morecambe
Mr Stanley Cullis
Phone 795
Dear Stan
I have some good news for you I have had the Grandson
playing for Morecambe old Grammarians he had five games
with them and was outstanding and Morecambe came for him
to play in the Lancashire combination on saturday against
Wigan Athletic and he was really brilliante and believe
me Stan he is a first division player now the report of the
match was not in the football paper on saturday night becaus
they played on sat night because of the cup final I enclose a copy of
the local weekly paper I would like to know if Mr Noakes is coming
to Blackpool for his hollidays again if so would he come to see the
boys father & mother to have a talk to them I would prefere you
if you should be at Blackpool any time it is just a nice run
from there to Morecambe I would like you to get cracking Stan
the lad is a first division player now I am also trying to get
other two lads for a trial I will write to you later
yours faithfully R Baggell

P.S.
Morecambe want a player coach could you recommend
one the grandson has not signed anything for
Morecambe
Bolton wanderers were after him on sat night

right Up to seventy letters a day were received by Stan Cullis, the manager of Wolves, and his scouts as they searched the country for young talent. This one had a 1952 post-mark. 'Dear Stan, I have some good news for you. I have had the grand-son playing for Morecombe Old Grammarians . . . and he was really brilliant and believe me Stan he is a First Division player right now . . . I would like you to get cracking . . . yours faithfully . . . PS. Bolton Wanderers were after him on Saturday night.' Cullis estimated that the number of young players watched by Wolves' representatives each year ran into five figures.

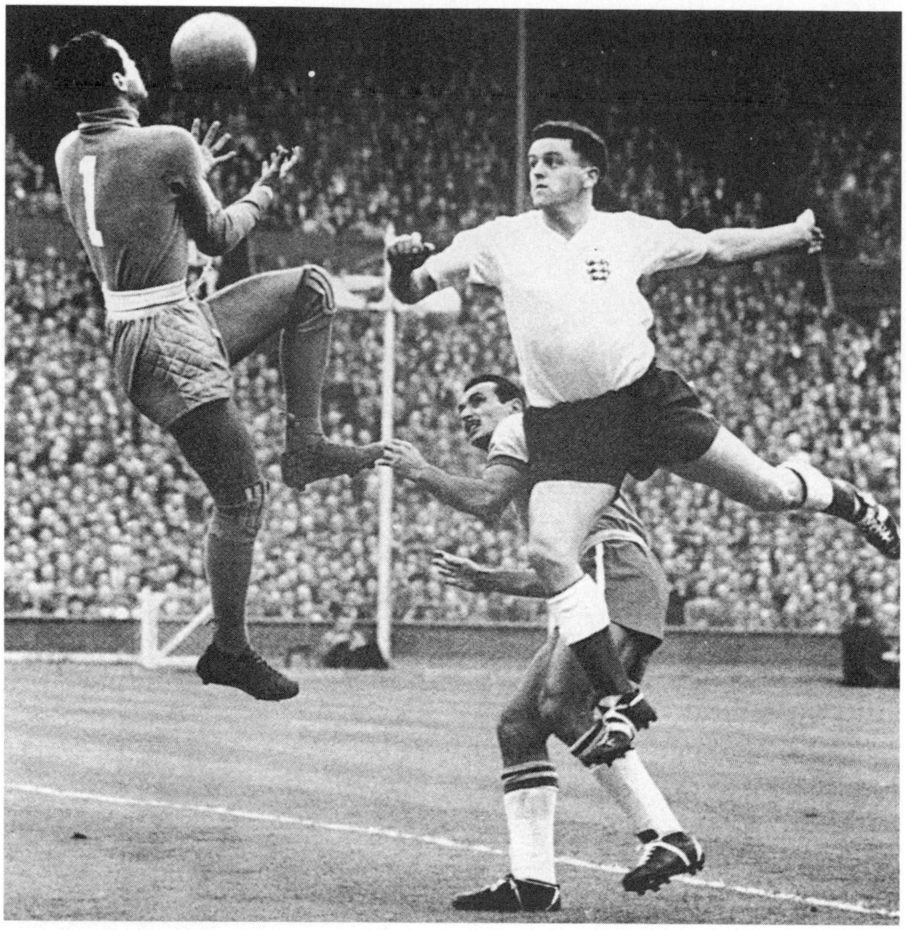

above left Tommy Taylor of Manchester United spearheading the England side which beat Brazil 4–2 (Taylor 2) at Wembley in May 1956. It was 20 months before the Munich air-crash and Taylor, a centre-forward of fire and mobility, was in his prime. He moved from Barnsley for £29,999 in 1953 and scored 112 goals in 163 League games for United. Won 19 caps for England.

below left Cliff Holton of Arsenal is challenged by Aston Villa's Dave Hickson (in number nine shirt) at Highbury, October 1955. Holton was renowned for his shooting power – the 'hot shot' of his day – and scored 292 goals in 570 League games for Arsenal, Watford, Northampton, Crystal Palace, Charlton and Orient between 1950 and 1967. His distinctions are numerous. He was the subject of the first hire-purchase transfer when he moved from Arsenal to Watford in 1958; and no Watford player has scored more League goals in a season than Holton's 42 for them in 1959–60 (Division Four). He also became Northampton's best over a season by scoring 36 in 1961–2 (Division Three). And Holton is the only League player known to have scored a hat-trick on consecutive days. He scored three for Watford against Chester (4–2) on Good Friday 1960, and got three more the following day against Gateshead (5–0) in Division Four.

above One of the few Hungarian shots at Wembley 1953 which did not produce a goal. England 3 Hungary 6 – but Gil Merrick (Birmingham) turns this attempt past a post. England players (in white shirts, l to r): Billy Wright (Wolves), Jimmy Dickinson (Portsmouth) and, behind net, Alf Ramsey (Spurs). A game which obliged England to accept they were no longer the overlords of football.

left Billy Wright is congratulated by Stanley Cullis after Wolves' 4–0 victory over Moscow Spartak at Molineux, November 1954. Wolves' success against Spartak and the outstanding Honved of Hungary were dramatic floodlit triumphs which persuaded Cullis to describe his side as 'the champions of the world' – a claim which incensed influential figures on the other side of the channel and played an important part in the birth of the European Cup in 1955.

left Jackie Milburn of Newcastle and England – one of the most revered of all Tyneside heroes. He was 'Wor Jackie' to a generation of Geordies and his initials, splendidly, were J.E.T. Milburn scored 179 goals in 354 League games for Newcastle (1946–57) and, above all, he led them from the front to three FA Cup Final triumphs in five years (1951–52–55). He started at inside-forward, moved to the right-wing and then became a centre-forward; but, wherever he played, his tearaway runs, his verve, his cleanness of style and the dramatic power of his shooting always identified him. Milburn was a player who changed the course of games. He succeeded Tommy Lawton as England's centre-forward and scored ten goals in 13 internationals. Milburn was a charming and modest man who lived easily with his immense popularity – but, then, he was one of the Milburns of Ashington ... the family which also produced George Milburn (Leeds and Chesterfield), Jack Milburn (Leeds and Bradford City), Jimmy Milburn (Leeds and Bradford Park Avenue) and Stan Milburn (Chesterfield, Leicester and Rochdale). And Cissie Milburn was the mother of a couple of likely lads called Jackie and Bobby Charlton.

left Harold Bell, the Tranmere Rovers centre-half, who did not miss a single game for nine seasons after World War Two – a League record of 401 consecutive matches that may never be beaten. The loyal and durable Bell played 595 League games in 14 seasons – and the highest position Tranmere managed in his time was fourth in Division Three North.

Stanley Matthews: the one and only.

above The Duncan Edwards' window in the Parish Church of St Francis in Dudley, Worcestershire – the home-town of the young Manchester United and England wing-half who died in the Munich air-crash, February 1958.

below Lost outposts: Workington v Barrow. Workington (in red) were League members from 1951 to 1977 when they were replaced by Wimbledon – and Barrow were League members for 50 years before their eleventh application for re-election was refused in 1972 and Hereford took their place. Workington's record win was 9–1 against Barrow in the League Cup, September 1964.

right The march of the football magazine – with (centre) the Football League Review, 1965–73, which was the first weekly magazine published by a professional football league.

below It needs more than footballers to win a trophy. The Swindon 'team' – full version – that won the League Cup in 1969. Back row (l to r): J. Conley (youth manager), L. Trollope (scout), M. Owen (chief scout), three members of Swindon Town Girls, E. Buckley (youth team attendant). E. Davies (groundsman), J. Wheeler (maintenance man). Second row: Members of Swindon Town Girls. Third row: R.A. Morse (secretary), Mrs C. Moss (shorthand typist), R. Jefferies (assistant secretary), A.W. Done (director), C.J. Green (director), F. Plyer (director), H. Williams (director), R. Fricker (vice-chairman), W.J. Castle (president), H.E. Lane (chairman), F.L. Collings (director), K.H. Wilmer (director), M.W. Earle (director), Dr J. Nicholas (director). Fourth row: R. Thomas, J. Butler, W. Penman, J. Smith, R. Smart, D. Heath, C. Jones, S. Harland, F. Burrows, D. Rogers, P. Downsborough, J. Trollope, P. Noble, O. Dawson. Fifth row: B. Lowes, T. Hubbard, J. Bailey, R. Desmeules, V. Mascia, D. Dangerfield, K. Allen, D. Claypole, K. Morgan, R. Handrick, V. Stroud, P. Aldworth, R. Jones, M. Blick. Front: H. Cousins (trainer), D. Williams (manager).

above Tony Book, captain of Manchester City, with (l to r) the League championship trophy (won in 1968), the FA Cup (1969) and the FA Charity Shield (1968). Book was also voted joint Footballer of the Year with Dave Mackay (Derby County) in 1969 – the only time the award has been shared.

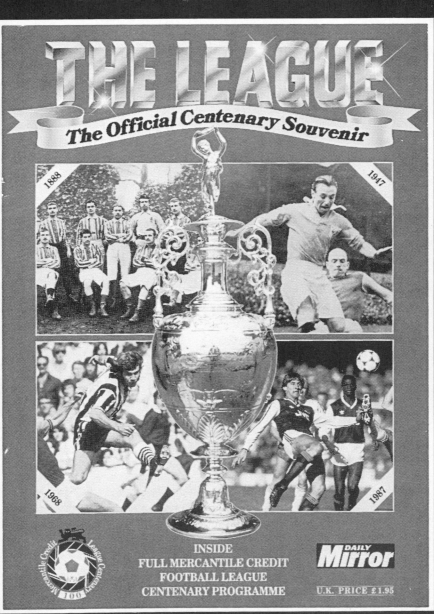

right Neil McBain, manager of Watford, reminding new players that a ball is round at the start of the 1957–8 season. McBain, born in 1895, has a line all to himself in the record books: in March 1947 – at the age of 52 years 4 months – he became the oldest player to appear in a League game. He was manager of New Brighton at the time and played as an emergency goalkeeper against Hartlepools in Division Three North. New Brighton lost 3–0.

left Arthur Rowley of West Bromwich Albion, Fulham, Leicester and Shrewsbury – the highest goalscorer in League history. Scored 434 goals in 619 League games between 1946 and 1965 – four for WBA, 27 for Fulham, 251 for Leicester (1950–58) and 152 for Shrewsbury. No other Football League player has passed the 400 milestone.

right Craven Cottage, October 1956 – big crowd, gentle Thames breeze, lots of laughter, a Fulham side of character including Roy Bentley, Jimmy Hill, Trevor 'Tosh' Chamberlain, Roy Dwight, Eddie Lowe – and Johnny Haynes of England (centre) to provide inspiration. Fulham even got the right result: 3–1. Haynes was an inside-forward for whom football was a game of grand strategy, a perfectionist and an expert at the long pass. He played 594 League games (145 goals) for Fulham between 1952–70 and won 56 caps for England, 22 of them as captain. And when the maximum wage was removed in 1961 Haynes became the League's first £100 a week footballer.

above Don Revie of Leicester, Hull, Manchester City, Sunderland, Leeds and England – a skilful and innovative inside-forward and later outstanding manager of Leeds and – less notably – of England. Originator of the 'Revie' deep-lying centre-forward plan based on the style of the 1953 Hungarians. Helped Manchester City to two FA Cup Finals – the first lost to Newcastle in 1955, the second won against Birmingham in 1956. 1955 Footballer of the Year. Played 474 League games and scored 100 goals between 1946–61. Six caps (1955–7).

above left Tom Finney of Preston and England – the 'Preston Plumber' attempting to turn on the water at Stamford Bridge, August 1956. Finney was universally admired as a player, professional and man. He spent his career playing with consummate skill and modest loyalty for his home town, mostly as a winger but later as a centre-forward, and earned one of the sincerest and most famous of all testimonials from Bill Shankly. 'Finney,' said Shankly, 'would have been great in any team, in any match and in any age – even if he had been wearing an overcoat.' Finney scored 187 goals in 433 League games (1946–60) and 30 goals in 76 internationals for England. Twice Footballer of the Year, in 1954 and 1957.

1-5 DOWN AFTER 62 MINUTES, CHARLTON FIGHT

10 MEN MAKE SOCC

Big Game Specials

WONDER GOAL BY TOMMY HARMER

Chelsea 2, Spurs 4 : by ALAN HOBY

THIS was the greatest London derby I have seen. Right from the first whistle we had a ceaseless flow of super-Soccer from the Tottenham masters. We had the goal of the season from that spry, sly wizard Tommy Harmer, when he glided like a white-shirted wraith past six Chelsea defenders.

We had a brave and brilliant goalkeeping display from Reg Matthews as, time and again, he ran out of goal to hurl himself at shots which looked certain winners.

Finally, we had two impudently opportunistic scoring efforts from the most improved centre forward in the country, Bobby Smith.

What made this tense, flaring struggle so fascinating was the contrast in styles. It was the Artists versus the Fighters.

On the sanded, skidding pitch Spurs stroked the greasy ball to one another with precision passes. Time and again Harmer the "Charmer," and Professor Danny Blanchflower carved open the Chelsea defence.

But for bad luck and Reg Matthews, Spurs would have had a bucketful.

Then, in the 10th minute, Spurs right wing flier Terry Medwin raced away and centred. Centre-half Mortimore, harried by Smith, miskicked wildly back, and there was that man Smith flinging himself after the ball and heading it home.

Five minutes later from a corner, Blanchflower slipped a crafty return pass to Medwin, who let fly. The Welshman's drive hit Peter Sillett and cannoned crazily into the net.

Two up, and by half-time it could have been four, five, or six.

But in the second half Chelsea came out fighting. And now we saw the brilliant worth of Maurice Norman, a towering centre half.

With goalkeeper Ted Ditchburn never really himself after the ball had hit him on the chin early in the game, Chelsea came at Tottenham like snapping terriers—and 15 minutes after half-time the alert McNichol stabbed the ball into the net after Ditchburn had missed a high one.

Another time Hopkins kicked off the line. It looked as if Spurs were about to wilt when suddenly we had two cracking goals in two minutes.

First, Harmer called for the ball in the 25th minute—and was given it by Brooks.

Controlling it with the outside of his right foot, Harmer beat five men in a crazy dribble before saucily flicking the ball round Matthews with the inside of his boot. Pure magic.

A minute later Chelsea's tough little left back Bellett hit the ball a terrific belt from 30 yards and, like a brown flash, it was in the net. 3—2.

But I must be Spurs' lucky mascot. . . . Each time I have watched them this … won!

In the 44th … Matthews had kno… with a string of … Brooks, Smith an… Smith scored Spu… Harmer's gem of a …

Last-seconds goa

by JAMES CONNOLLY

AMAZING, incredible, fantastic . . . call it what you will, but never in the history of the Football League can there have been anything to match 10-men-Charlton's last seconds' 7—6 defeat of Huddersfield at the Valley yesterday—*AFTER BEING 1—5 DOWN WITH ONLY 28 MINUTES TO GO!*

The crowd swarmed on to the pitch at the end, crying for left-winger Johnny Summers, who grabbed five second-half goals in the greatest rally of all time.

Breathless and excited, Summers and his happy Charlton colleagues clambered into the directors' box and got a wonderful hand from the cheering fans.

Charlton lost their skipper and centre half, Derek Ufton, with a dislocated shoulder after 15 minutes.

Down 2—0 at the interval, the Charlton plight looked hopeless when Huddersfield swept to a 5—1 lead with 28 minutes left to play. Massie, Bain (2), McGarry and Ledger had scored for Huddersfield, and Summers for Charlton.

Unbelievable

Then came the unbelievable comeback. Twenty-seven minutes to go—centre-forward Johnny Ryan rallied Charlton with a fine goal . . . 26 minutes to go—Summers got them really confident with another . . . 16 minutes to go—Summers scored again.

Twelve minutes to go—Summers made it 5—5 . . . six minutes to go—Summers put Charlton in front for the first time . . . three minutes to go—Howard

LAWTON SIGNS —FOR CUP TIES

TOMMY LAWTON, Notts County manager, can play again in Cup ties and friendlies. But manager Lawton will not be eligible for County's third round tie with Tranmere on January 4.

After weeks of negotiation, Kettering agreed to transfer Lawton the player, but not until 6 o'clock last night, so Tommy fails to qualify for the next round under the 14-day rule.

Lawton cannot play in the League, having already accepted the money due to him from the Players' Provident Fund.

The price Lawton paid for his own transfer was not disclosed, but part of the deal is a floodlight friendly between Notts County and Kettering at Meadow-lane later in the season.

Luton after

Bolton 1, … AYNHAM, … his net in … Bolton. Not … mad…

ICK TO BEAT HUDDERSFIELD 7-6

CER HISTORY

wins fantastic match

give lesson
arly shock

2: by
ton goalke
ond minut
vere they b
though

HERD beats Fraser to score Arsenal's third goal in the match with Sunderland at Highbury.

RALLY EARNS

GREGORY'S GOAL ONLY

left Division Two: Saturday 21 December 1957.

below John Charles (second right) scoring one of his last goals for Leeds United before joining Juventus of Turin for a British record transfer fee of £65,000 in the summer of 1957. Charles scored twice in Leeds' 3–1 Easter Monday victory over Sunderland at Elland Road and finished the season as Division One's top scorer with 38 goals. *below left* Charles, a year earlier, receiving a cup of champagne from manager Raich Carter after Leeds had won promotion from Division Two. Charles, who played for Leeds, Juventus, Roma, Cardiff and Wales, was magnificently – almost unfairly – gifted. He was a noble physical speciman (nearly 6 ft 2 in, 13½ stone) and his talent was prodigious. His touch was sensitive, his control precise, his finishing cruel and, above all, he was a grandmaster in the air. His range was so great that managers were often unsure where to play him: he was outstanding anywhere. And to all this he added such a lovely temperament that during his five years in Italy he was known as 'Il buon gigante' – the Gentle Giant. He was never sent off or reported or cautioned. His greatest years were undoubtedly in Italy where he was lionized as he helped Juventus to three championships (scoring 93 goals in 155 League games – a sensational scoring rate in the land of defence) and two Cups. Italy's gain was British football's loss, but Charles still won 38 caps for Wales (1950–65). He scored 153 goals in 308 League games for Leeds (1948–57, 1962) and the 42 League goals he scored for them in 1953–4 is still a club record. He finished his League career by scoring 18 goals in 70 games for Cardiff (1963–6) – though by that time his years of punishment in Italy were beginning to take toll. Mel Charles, John's younger brother, played 377 League games for Swansea, Arsenal, Cardiff and Port Vale, and won 31 caps for Wales (1955–63).

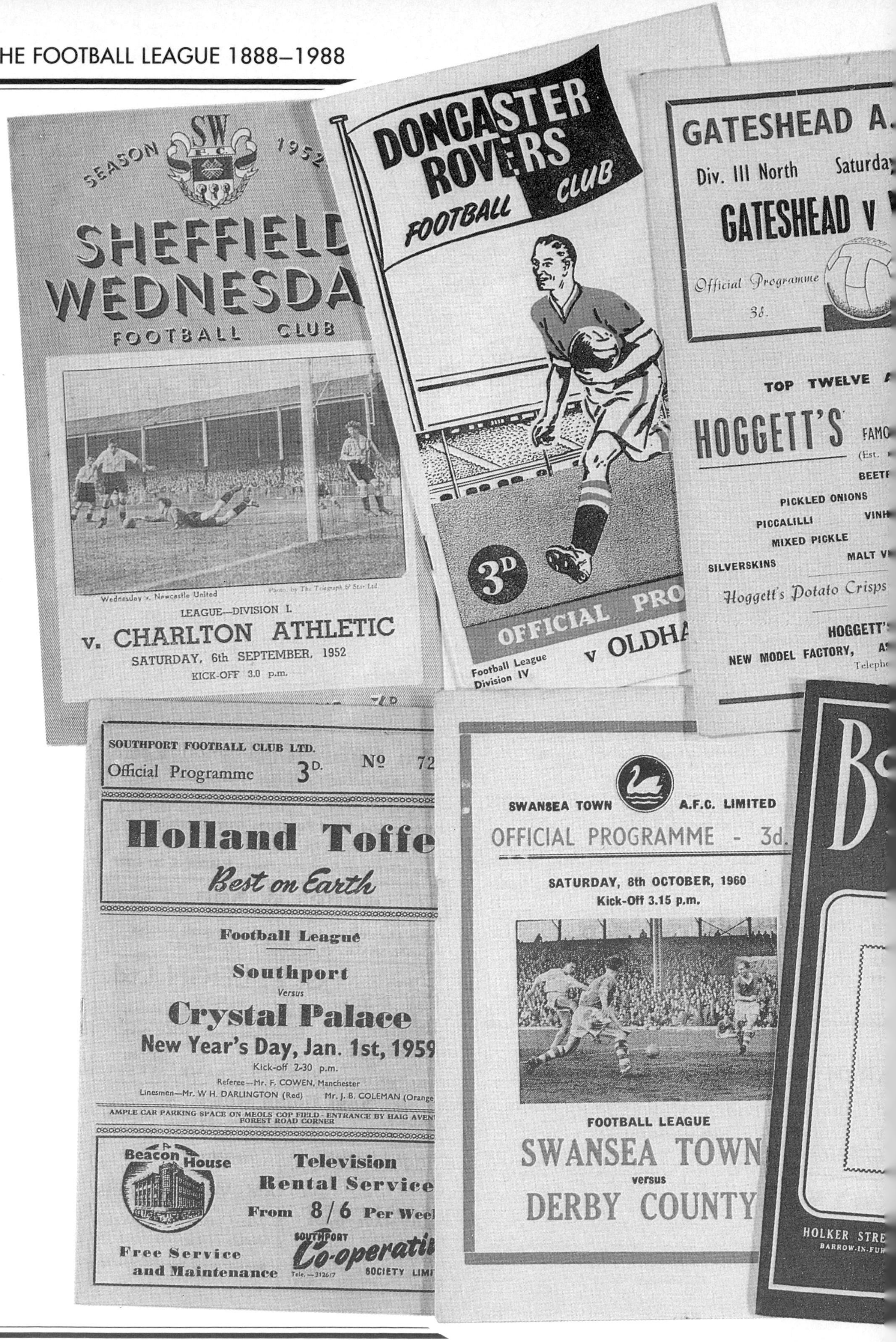
SEASON 1952
SW F.C.
SHEFFIELD WEDNESDAY
FOOTBALL CLUB
Wednesday v. Newcastle United
LEAGUE—DIVISION I.
v. CHARLTON ATHLETIC
SATURDAY, 6th SEPTEMBER, 1952
KICK-OFF 3.0 p.m.
DONCASTER ROVERS
FOOTBALL CLUB
3D
OFFICIAL PRO
Football League Division IV
v OLDHA
GATESHEAD A.
Div. III North
GATESHEAD v
Official Programme
TOP TWELVE
HOGGETT'S
PICKLED ONIONS
PICCALILLI
MIXED PICKLE
SILVERSKINS
MALT
Hoggett's Potato Crisps
NEW MODEL FACTORY,
SOUTHPORT FOOTBALL CLUB LTD.
Official Programme 3D. №
Holland Toffe
Best on Earth
Football League
Southport
Versus
Crystal Palace
New Year's Day, Jan. 1st, 1959
Kick-off 2-30 p.m.
Referee—Mr. F. COWEN, Manchester
Linesmen—Mr. W. H. DARLINGTON (Red) Mr. J. B. COLEMAN (Orange
Beacon House
Television
Rental Service
From 8/6 Per Weel
Free Service
and Maintenance
SOUTHPORT Co-operati
SOCIETY LIMI
SWANSEA TOWN A.F.C. LIMITED
OFFICIAL PROGRAMME - 3d.
SATURDAY, 8th OCTOBER, 1960
Kick-Off 3.15 p.m.
FOOTBALL LEAGUE
SWANSEA TOWN
versus
DERBY COUNTY
HOLKER STRE

C. Ltd.
28th, 1957
XHAM
Season 1957-58
SEASON
PRODUCTS
POMPY SAUCE
SWEET PICKLE
ll at 3d. per packet
GATESHEAD
LUTON TOWN F.C.
DIVISION 1
TOWN
ton Wan.
rphy
"tambour"
ll away out
Richard
R. WILLIAMS
the VILLA news and record
3D
T DIVISION
h 1956
off 2.15 p.m.
FOOTBALL LEAGUE DIVISION ONE
4D
SATURDAY
26th NOVEMBER 1960
Kick-off 3 p.m.
CONSILIO ET ANIMIS
OFFICIAL PROGRAMME
SHEFFIELD WEDNESDAY
versus
ASTON VILLA
Hillsbo
rrow F.C.
TELEPHONE:
Barrow 2091
Dalton 175
Whitehaven 723
AS. KENDALL
5, Cavendish Street
ROW-IN-FURNESS
Tudor Square
TON-IN-FURNESS
STREET Whitehaven
Official Programm
Albion NEWS & PROGRAMME
West Bromwich Albion Football Club, Limited
President: Mr. W. W. Hackett, C.B.E., J.P.
Directors:
Major H. Wilson Keys, M.C., T.D. (Chairman)
Mr. W. H. Thursfield, J.P. (Vice-Chairman)
Mr. J. W. Gaunt, junr., Mr. T. W. Glidden,
Mr. S. R. Shephard, J.P. and Mr. L. Prichards
Secretary: Mr. E. Smith
Team Manager: Mr. G. V. Clark
Ground: The Hawthorns, West Bro
Vol. 51 No. 11 (Copyright) · October 10th, 1959
ALBION v. FULHAM
BRISTOL CITY F.C.
ENGLISH LEAGUE
THIRD DIV. SOUTH
Vol. 7 No. 20
SATURDAY, FEBRUARY 6th, 1954
K.O. 3 p.m.
BRISTOL CITY v. LEYTON ORIENT
PRICE
3D
FOOTBALL LEAGUE—THIRD DIVISION (SOUTH)
Beer is Best!
GEORGES'
Yes!
THE COUNTY TYRE SERVICE (Bristol) LTD.
23-25 NELSON PARADE, BRISTOL 3
Telephone Bristol 61061 & 61062 Also at Cardiff & Swansea

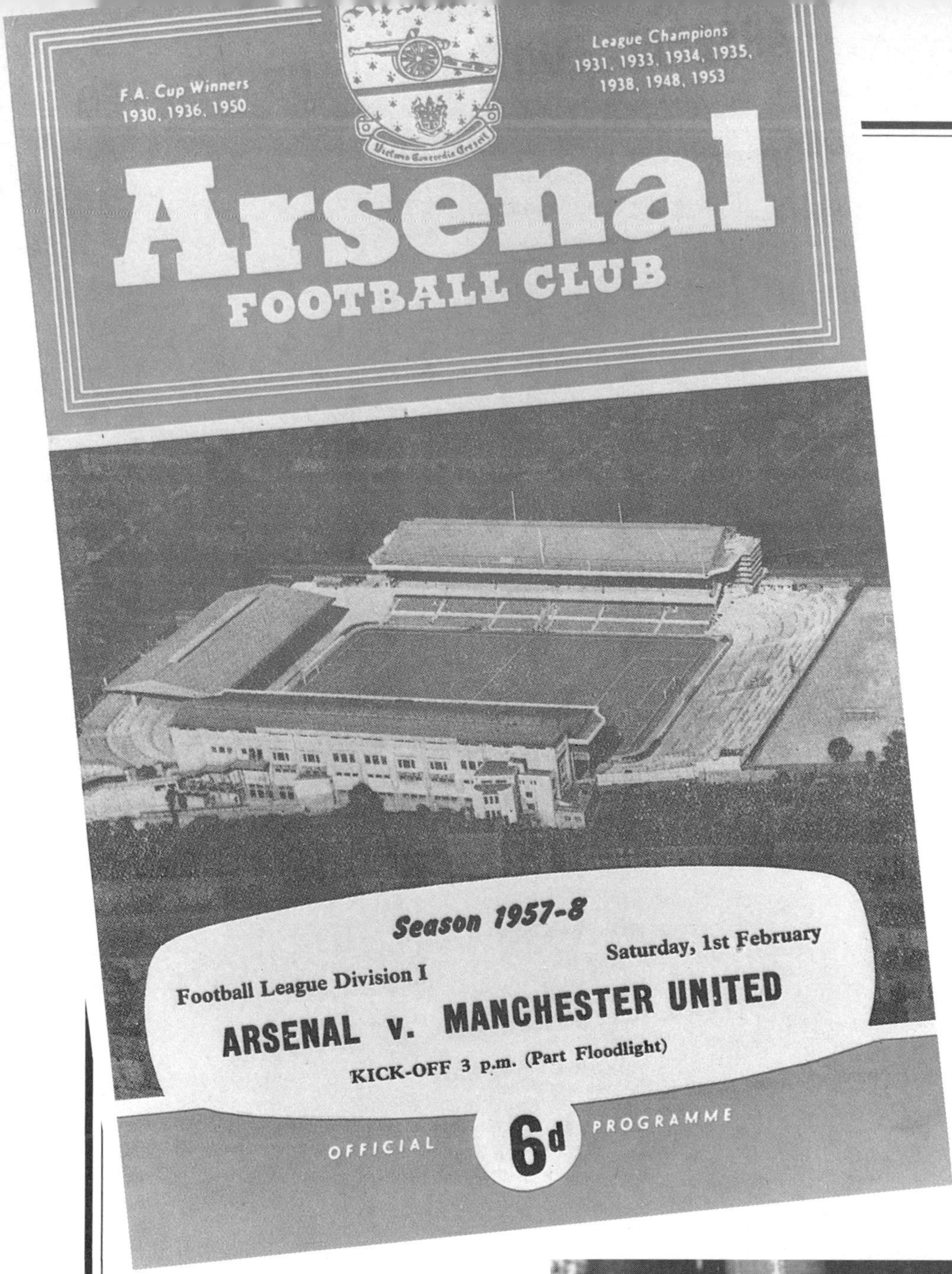

left Manchester United's last League game before the Munich disaster. February 1958; and United won an unforgettable match 5–4.

right Duncan Edwards' instructional book – published after the celebrated young Manchester United and England wing-half had died in the Munich air-crash, February 1958. Stanley Paul Ltd, who published the book in the following June, explained in an introduction: 'On the eve of his departure with the Manchester United team for Yugoslavia he passed his manuscript over to us with almost boyish enthusiasm. When the news of the disaster at Munich first reached us we considered cancelling the publication of the book but, after consultation with the relatives of Duncan, we have decided that the book should be published as a permanent record of his great faith in, and love for, the game of Soccer. In addition, everyone concerned has agreed that all the profits from the book shall be devoted to the Lord Mayor of Manchester's Fund for the dependents of those who lost their lives in the Munich crash.' Joining Edwards on the front-cover: Stanley Matthews (left) and Billy Wright.

right Matt Busby talks to his attentive Manchester United players before their European Cup quarter-final against Red Star in Belgrade, February 1958 – their last match before the Munich air disaster.

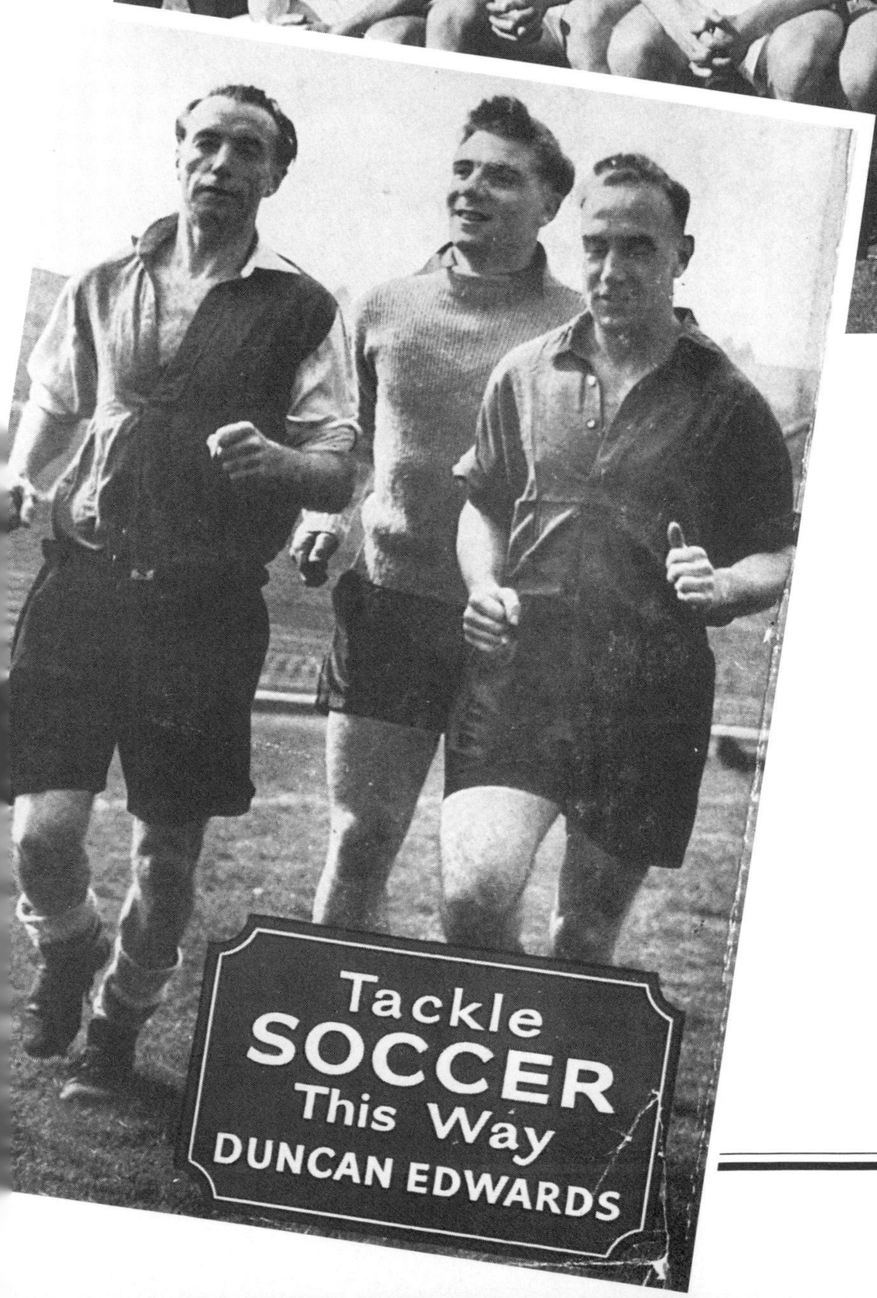

above The 'Busby Babes' of Manchester United – the side destroyed in the Munich air disaster, February 1958. Back row (l to r): trainer Tom Curry, Duncan Edwards, Mark Jones, Ray Wood (survived), Bobby Charlton (survived), Bill Foulkes (survived), Matt Busby (survived). Front row: John Berry (survived), Bill Whelan, Roger Byrne, David Pegg, Eddie Colman. Twenty-three people were killed altogether – including eight players and eight journalists.

above League football's boom stretched well into the 'fifties. The average aggregate attendance for the ten seasons after World War Two was 34,702,608. Behaviour was faultless, fans were mixed – and their pleasure apparent.

right Christmas in the 1950s meant return fixtures, tight schedules, awkward trips and self-discipline for professional footballers. Example: West Bromwich beat Newcastle 1–0 at the Hawthorns on Christmas Day 1956 – and then lost 5–2 at St James's Park on Boxing Day. Here West Bromwich prepare to travel: Bobby Robson (left) has his back to the camera, Don Howe can be seen over Robson's right shoulder and manager Vic Buckingham is on the right.

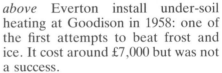

above Everton install under-soil heating at Goodison in 1958: one of the first attempts to beat frost and ice. It cost around £7,000 but was not a success.

left Nat Lofthouse of Bolton and England – a brave, combative and immensely consistent centre-forward known as the 'Lion of Vienna' for a stunning breakaway goal he scored for England in Austria in 1952. Scored 255 goals in 452 League games for Bolton (1946–60) and 30 goals in 33 internationals. Scored in every round of the FA Cup in 1953 – including one in the 'Stanley Matthews final'. Matthews got his winners' medal and the adulation but Lofthouse was the Footballer of the Year in 1953. And he scored the two Bolton goals that beat Manchester United in the 1958 FA Cup Final – three months after the Munich air disaster.

above The Football League's headquarters at Lytham St Annes, Lancashire. Previously a private hotel, it was bought for £11,000 in 1959 and modifications costing £40,000 took six months. The League's previous headquarters were in Starkie Street, Preston.

below Burnley clinching the 1959–60 League championship by winning their last game of the season against Manchester City at Maine Road. Burnley won 2–1 – and Ray Pointer, centre, starts to celebrate their first goal by Brian Pilkington (not in picture). It was Burnley's second title (the first in 1920–21) and, under the management of Harry Potts, they won it with style and discipline – finishing a point ahead of Wolves, two ahead of Spurs.

above Pools girls checking millions of coupons – in search of the lucky few who have hit the jackpot. Pools were started soon after World War One, and by the 1950s had become one of the nation's top ten industries, employing over 100,000 people. The first £100,000 winner came in 1950, £200,000 in 1957, £300,000 in 1959. But it was not until 1959 that the Football League established copyright in their fixtures and began to receive payment from the Pools Promoters.

LEAGUE TABLES

1951–52

FIRST DIVISION

		P	W	D	L	F	A	Pts
1	Man United	42	23	11	8	95	52	57
2	Tottenham	42	22	9	11	76	51	53
3	Arsenal	42	21	11	10	80	61	53
4	Portsmouth	42	20	8	14	68	58	48
5	Bolton	42	19	10	13	65	61	48
6	Aston Villa	42	19	9	14	79	70	47
7	Preston	42	17	12	13	74	54	46
8	Newcastle	42	18	9	15	98	73	45
9	Blackpool	42	18	9	15	64	64	45
10	Charlton	42	17	10	15	68	63	44
11	Liverpool	42	12	19	11	57	61	43
12	Sunderland	42	15	12	15	70	61	42
13	WBA	42	14	13	15	74	77	41
14	Burnley	42	15	10	17	56	63	40
15	Man City	42	13	13	16	58	61	39
16	Wolves	42	12	14	16	73	73	38
17	Derby	42	15	7	20	63	80	37
18	Middlesbrough	42	15	6	21	64	88	36
19	Chelsea	42	14	8	20	52	72	36
20	Stoke	42	12	7	23	49	88	31
21	Huddersfield	42	10	8	24	49	82	28
22	Fulham	42	8	11	23	58	77	27

SECOND DIVISION

		P	W	D	L	F	A	Pts
1	Sheff Wed	42	21	11	10	100	66	53
2	Cardiff	42	20	11	11	72	54	51
3	Birmingham	42	21	9	12	67	56	51
4	Nottm Forest	42	18	13	11	77	62	49
5	Leicester	42	19	9	14	78	64	47
6	Leeds	42	18	11	13	59	57	47
7	Everton	42	17	10	15	64	58	44
8	Luton	42	16	12	14	77	78	44
9	Rotherham	42	17	8	17	73	71	42
10	Brentford	42	15	12	15	54	55	42
11	Sheff United	42	18	5	19	90	76	41
12	West Ham	42	15	11	16	67	77	41
13	Southampton	42	15	11	16	61	73	41
14	Blackburn	42	17	6	19	54	63	40
15	Notts County	42	16	7	19	71	68	39
16	Doncaster	42	13	12	17	55	60	38
17	Bury	42	15	7	20	67	69	37
18	Hull	42	13	11	18	60	70	37
19	Swansea	42	12	12	18	72	76	36
20	Barnsley	42	11	14	17	59	72	36
21	Coventry	42	14	6	22	59	82	34
22	QPR	42	11	12	19	52	81	34

THIRD DIVISION (NORTH)

		P	W	D	L	F	A	Pts
1	Lincoln	46	30	9	7	121	52	69
2	Grimsby	46	29	8	9	96	45	66
3	Stockport	46	23	13	10	74	40	59
4	Oldham	46	24	9	13	90	61	57
5	Gateshead	46	21	11	14	66	49	53
6	Mansfield	46	22	8	16	73	60	52
7	Carlisle	46	19	13	14	62	57	51
8	Bradford PA	46	19	12	15	74	64	50
9	Hartlepools	46	21	8	17	71	65	50
10	York	46	18	13	15	73	52	49
11	Tranmere	46	21	6	19	76	71	48
12	Barrow	46	17	12	17	57	61	46
13	Chesterfield	46	17	11	18	65	66	45
14	Scunthorpe	46	14	16	16	65	74	44
15	Bradford City	46	16	10	20	61	68	42
16	Crewe	46	17	8	21	63	82	42
17	Southport	46	15	11	20	53	71	41
18	Wrexham	46	15	9	22	63	73	39
19	Chester	46	15	9	22	72	85	39
20	Halifax	46	14	7	25	61	97	35
21	Rochdale	46	11	13	22	47	79	35
22	Accrington	46	10	12	24	61	92	32
23	Darlington	46	11	9	26	64	103	31
24	Workington	46	11	7	28	50	91	29

THIRD DIVISION (SOUTH)

		P	W	D	L	F	A	Pts
1	Plymouth	46	29	8	9	107	53	66
2	Reading	46	29	3	14	112	60	61
3	Norwich	46	26	9	11	89	50	61
4	Millwall	46	23	12	11	74	53	58
5	Brighton	46	24	10	12	87	63	58
6	Newport	46	21	12	13	77	76	54
7	Bristol Rovers	46	20	12	14	89	53	52
8	Northampton	46	22	5	19	93	74	49
9	Southend	46	19	10	17	75	66	48
10	Colchester	46	17	12	17	56	77	46
11	Torquay	46	17	10	19	86	98	44
12	Aldershot	46	18	8	20	78	89	44
13	Port Vale	46	14	15	17	50	66	43
14	Bournemouth	46	16	10	20	69	75	42
15	Bristol City	46	15	12	19	58	69	42
16	Swindon	46	14	14	18	51	68	42
17	Ipswich	46	16	9	21	63	74	41
18	Leyton Orient	46	16	9	21	55	68	41
19	Crystal Palace	46	15	9	22	61	80	39
20	Shrewsbury	46	13	10	23	62	86	36
21	Watford	46	13	10	23	57	81	36
22	Gillingham	46	11	13	22	71	81	35
23	Exeter	46	13	9	24	65	86	35
24	Walsall	46	13	5	28	55	94	31

1952–53

FIRST DIVISION

		P	W	D	L	F	A	Pts
1	Arsenal	42	21	12	9	97	64	54
2	Preston	42	21	12	9	85	60	54
3	Wolves	42	19	13	10	86	63	51
4	WBA	42	21	8	13	66	60	50
5	Charlton	42	19	11	12	77	63	49
6	Burnley	42	18	12	12	67	52	48
7	Blackpool	42	19	9	14	71	70	47
8	Man United	42	18	10	14	69	72	46
9	Sunderland	42	15	13	14	68	82	43
10	Tottenham	42	15	11	16	78	69	41
11	Aston Villa	42	14	13	15	63	61	41
12	Cardiff	42	14	12	16	54	46	40
13	Middlesbrough	42	14	11	17	70	77	39
14	Bolton	42	15	9	18	61	69	39
15	Portsmouth	42	14	10	18	74	83	38
16	Newcastle	42	14	9	19	59	70	37
17	Liverpool	42	14	8	20	61	82	36
18	Sheff Wed	42	12	11	19	62	72	35
19	Chelsea	42	12	11	19	56	66	35
20	Man City	42	14	7	21	72	87	35
21	Stoke	42	12	10	20	53	66	34
22	Derby	42	11	10	21	59	74	32

SECOND DIVISION

		P	W	D	L	F	A	Pts
1	Sheff United	42	25	10	7	97	55	60
2	Huddersfield	42	24	10	8	84	33	58
3	Luton	42	22	8	12	84	49	52
4	Plymouth	42	20	9	13	65	60	49
5	Leicester	42	18	12	12	89	74	48
6	Birmingham	42	19	10	13	71	66	48
7	Nottm Forest	42	18	8	16	77	67	44
8	Fulham	42	17	10	15	81	71	44
9	Blackburn	42	18	8	16	68	65	44
10	Leeds	42	14	15	13	71	63	43
11	Swansea	42	15	12	15	78	81	42
12	Rotherham	42	16	9	17	75	74	41
13	Doncaster	42	12	16	14	58	64	40
14	West Ham	42	13	13	16	58	60	39
15	Lincoln	42	11	17	14	64	71	39
16	Everton	42	12	14	16	71	75	38
17	Brentford	42	13	11	18	59	76	37
18	Hull	42	14	8	20	57	69	36
19	Notts County	42	14	8	20	60	88	36
20	Bury	42	13	9	20	53	81	35
21	Southampton	42	10	13	19	68	85	33
22	Barnsley	42	5	8	29	47	108	18

THIRD DIVISION (NORTH)

	P	W	D	L	F	A	Pts
1 Oldham	46	22	15	9	77	45	59
2 Port Vale	46	20	18	8	67	35	58
3 Wrexham	46	24	8	14	86	66	56
4 York	46	20	13	13	60	45	53
5 Grimsby	46	21	10	15	75	59	52
6 Southport	46	20	11	15	63	60	51
7 Bradford PA	46	19	12	15	75	61	50
8 Gateshead	46	17	15	14	76	60	49
9 Carlisle	46	18	13	15	82	68	49
10 Crewe	46	20	8	18	70	68	48
11 Stockport	46	17	13	16	82	69	47
12 Chesterfield*	46	18	11	17	65	63	47
13 Tranmere*	46	21	5	20	65	63	47
14 Halifax	46	16	15	15	68	68	47
15 Scunthorpe	46	16	14	16	62	56	46
16 Bradford City	46	14	18	14	75	80	46
17 Hartlepools	46	16	14	16	57	61	46
18 Mansfield	46	16	14	16	55	62	46
19 Barrow	46	16	12	18	66	71	44
20 Chester	46	11	15	20	64	85	37
21 Darlington	46	14	6	26	58	96	34
22 Rochdale	46	14	5	27	62	83	33
23 Workington	46	11	10	25	55	91	32
24 Accrington	46	8	11	27	39	89	27

*Equal

THIRD DIVISION (SOUTH)

	P	W	D	L	F	A	Pts
1 Bristol Rovers	46	26	12	8	92	46	64
2 Millwall	46	24	14	8	82	44	62
3 Northampton	46	26	10	10	109	70	62
4 Norwich	26	25	10	11	99	55	60
5 Bristol City	46	22	15	9	95	61	59
6 Coventry	46	19	12	15	77	62	50
7 Brighton	46	19	12	15	81	75	50
8 Southend	46	18	13	15	69	74	49
9 Bournemouth	46	19	9	18	74	69	47
10 Watford	46	15	17	14	62	63	47
11 Reading	46	19	8	19	69	64	46
12 Torquay	46	18	9	19	87	88	45
13 Crystal Palace	46	15	13	18	66	82	43
14 Leyton Orient	46	16	10	20	68	73	42
15 Newport	46	16	10	20	70	82	42
16 Ipswich	46	13	15	18	60	69	41
17 Exeter	46	13	14	19	61	71	40
18 Swindon	46	14	12	20	64	79	40
19 Aldershot	46	12	15	19	61	77	39
20 Gillingham	46	12	15	19	55	74	39
21 QPR	46	12	15	19	61	82	39
22 Colchester	46	12	14	20	59	76	38
23 Shrewsbury	46	12	12	22	68	91	36
24 Walsall	46	7	10	29	56	118	24

1953–54

FIRST DIVISION

	P	W	D	L	F	A	Pts
1 Wolves	42	25	7	10	96	56	57
2 WBA	42	22	9	11	86	63	53
3 Huddersfield	42	20	11	11	78	61	51
4 Man United	42	18	12	12	73	58	48
5 Bolton	42	18	12	12	75	60	48
6 Blackpool	42	19	10	13	80	69	48
7 Burnley	42	21	4	17	78	67	46
8 Chelsea	42	16	12	14	74	68	44
9 Charlton	42	19	6	17	75	77	44
10 Cardiff	42	18	8	16	51	71	44
11 Preston	42	19	5	18	87	58	43
12 Arsenal	42	15	13	14	75	73	43
13 Aston Villa	42	16	9	17	70	68	41
14 Portsmouth	42	14	11	17	81	89	39
15 Newcastle	42	14	10	18	72	77	38
16 Tottenham	42	16	5	21	65	76	37
17 Man City	42	14	9	19	62	77	37
18 Sunderland	42	14	8	20	81	89	36
19 Sheff Wed	42	15	6	21	70	91	36
20 Sheff United	42	11	11	20	69	90	33
21 Middlesbrough	42	10	10	22	60	91	30
22 Liverpool	42	9	10	23	68	97	28

SECOND DIVISION

	P	W	D	L	F	A	Pts
1 Leicester	42	23	10	9	97	60	56
2 Everton	42	20	16	6	92	58	56
3 Blackburn	42	23	9	10	86	50	55
4 Nottm Forest	42	20	12	10	86	59	52
5 Rotherham	42	21	7	14	80	67	49
6 Luton	42	18	12	12	64	59	48
7 Birmingham	42	18	11	13	78	58	47
8 Fulham	42	17	10	15	98	85	44
9 Bristol Rovers	42	14	16	12	64	58	44
10 Leeds	42	15	13	14	89	81	43
11 Stoke	42	12	17	13	71	60	41
12 Doncaster	42	16	9	17	59	63	41
13 West Ham	42	15	9	18	67	69	39
14 Notts County	42	13	13	16	54	74	39
15 Hull	42	16	6	20	64	66	38
16 Lincoln	42	14	9	19	65	83	37
17 Bury	42	11	14	17	54	72	36
18 Derby	42	12	11	19	64	82	35
19 Plymouth	42	9	16	17	65	82	34
20 Swansea	42	13	8	21	58	82	34
21 Brentford	42	10	11	21	40	78	31
22 Oldham	42	8	9	25	40	89	25

THIRD DIVISION (NORTH)

	P	W	D	L	F	A	Pts
1 Port Vale	46	26	17	3	74	21	69
2 Barnsley	46	24	10	12	77	57	58
3 Scunthorpe	46	21	15	10	77	56	57
4 Gateshead	46	21	13	12	74	55	55
5 Bradford City	46	22	9	15	60	55	53
6 Chesterfield	46	19	14	13	76	64	52
7 Mansfield	46	20	11	15	88	67	51
8 Wrexham	46	21	9	16	81	68	51
9 Bradford PA	46	18	14	14	77	68	50
10 Stockport	46	18	11	17	77	67	47
11 Southport	46	17	12	17	63	60	46
12 Barrow	46	16	12	18	72	71	44
13 Carlisle	46	14	15	17	83	71	43
14 Tranmere	46	18	7	21	59	70	43
15 Accrington	46	16	10	20	66	74	42
16 Crewe	46	14	13	19	49	67	41
17 Grimsby	46	16	9	21	51	77	41
18 Hartlepools	46	13	14	19	59	65	40
19 Rochdale	46	15	10	21	59	77	40
20 Workington	46	13	14	19	59	80	40
21 Darlington	46	12	14	20	50	71	38
22 York	46	12	13	21	64	86	37
23 Halifax	46	12	10	24	44	73	34
24 Chester	46	11	10	25	48	67	32

THIRD DIVISION (SOUTH)

	P	W	D	L	F	A	Pts
1 Ipswich	46	27	10	9	82	51	64
2 Brighton	46	26	9	11	86	61	61
3 Bristol City	46	25	6	15	88	66	56
4 Watford	46	21	10	15	85	69	52
5 Northampton	46	20	11	15	82	55	51
6 Southampton	46	22	7	17	76	63	51
7 Norwich	46	20	11	15	73	66	51
8 Reading	46	20	9	17	86	73	49
9 Exeter	46	20	8	18	68	58	48
10 Gillingham	46	19	10	17	61	66	48
11 Leyton Orient	46	18	11	17	79	73	47
12 Millwall	46	19	9	18	74	77	47
13 Torquay	46	17	12	17	81	88	46
14 Coventry	46	18	9	19	61	56	45
15 Newport	46	19	6	21	61	81	44
16 Southend	46	18	7	21	69	71	43
17 Aldershot	46	17	9	20	74	86	43
18 QPR	46	16	10	20	60	68	42
19 Bournemouth	46	16	8	22	67	70	40
20 Swindon	46	15	10	21	67	70	40
21 Shrewsbury	46	14	12	20	65	76	40
22 Crystal Palace	46	14	12	20	60	86	40
23 Colchester	46	10	10	26	50	78	30
24 Walsall	46	9	8	29	40	87	26

1954–55

FIRST DIVISION

	P	W	D	L	F	A	Pts
1 Chelsea	42	20	12	10	81	57	52
2 Wolves	42	19	10	13	89	70	48
3 Portsmouth	42	18	12	12	74	62	48
4 Sunderland	42	15	18	9	64	54	48
5 Man United	42	20	7	15	84	74	47
6 Aston Villa	42	20	7	15	72	73	47
7 Man City	42	18	10	14	76	69	46
8 Newcastle	42	17	9	16	89	77	43
9 Arsenal	42	17	9	16	69	63	43
10 Burnley	42	17	9	16	51	48	43
11 Everton	42	16	10	16	62	68	42
12 Huddersfield	42	14	13	15	63	68	41
13 Sheff United	42	17	7	18	70	86	41
14 Preston	42	16	8	18	83	64	40
15 Charlton	42	15	10	17	76	75	40
16 Tottenham	42	16	8	18	72	73	40
17 WBA	42	16	8	18	76	96	40
18 Bolton	42	13	13	16	62	69	39
19 Blackpool	42	14	10	18	60	64	38
20 Cardiff	42	13	11	18	62	76	37
21 Leicester	42	12	11	19	74	86	35
22 Sheff Wed	42	8	10	24	63	100	26

SECOND DIVISION

	P	W	D	L	F	A	Pts
1 Birmingham	42	22	10	10	92	47	54
2 Luton	42	23	8	11	88	53	54
3 Rotherham	42	25	4	13	94	64	54
4 Leeds	42	23	7	12	70	53	53
5 Stoke	42	21	10	11	69	46	52
6 Blackburn	42	22	6	14	114	79	50
7 Notts County	42	21	6	15	74	71	48
8 West Ham	42	18	10	14	74	70	46
9 Bristol Rovers	42	19	7	16	75	70	45
10 Swansea	42	17	9	16	86	83	43
11 Liverpool	42	16	10	16	92	96	42
12 Middlesbrough	42	18	6	18	73	82	42
13 Bury	42	15	11	16	77	72	41
14 Fulham	42	14	11	17	76	79	39
15 Nottm Forest	42	16	7	19	58	62	39
16 Lincoln	42	13	10	19	68	79	36
17 Port Vale	42	12	11	19	48	71	35
18 Doncaster	42	14	7	21	58	95	35
19 Hull	42	12	10	20	44	69	34
20 Plymouth	42	12	7	23	57	82	31
21 Ipswich	42	11	6	25	57	92	28
22 Derby	42	7	9	26	53	82	23

THIRD DIVISION (NORTH)

	P	W	D	L	F	A	Pts
1 Barnsley	46	30	5	11	86	46	65
2 Accrington	46	25	11	10	96	67	61
3 Scunthorpe	46	23	12	11	81	53	58
4 York	46	24	10	12	92	63	58
5 Hartlepools	46	25	5	16	64	49	55
6 Chesterfield	46	24	6	16	81	70	54
7 Gateshead	46	20	12	14	65	69	52
8 Workington	46	18	14	14	68	55	50
9 Stockport	46	18	12	16	84	70	48
10 Oldham	46	19	10	17	74	68	48
11 Southport	46	16	16	14	47	44	48
12 Rochdale	46	17	14	15	69	66	48
13 Mansfield	46	18	9	19	65	71	45
14 Halifax	46	15	13	18	63	67	43
15 Darlington	46	14	14	18	62	73	42
16 Bradford PA	46	15	11	20	56	70	41
17 Barrow	46	17	6	23	70	89	40
18 Wrexham	46	13	12	21	65	77	38
19 Tranmere	46	13	11	22	55	70	37
20 Carlisle	46	15	6	25	78	89	36
21 Bradford City	46	13	10	23	47	55	36
22 Crewe	46	10	14	22	68	91	34
23 Grimsby	46	13	8	25	47	78	34
24 Chester	46	12	9	25	44	77	33

THIRD DIVISION (SOUTH)

	P	W	D	L	F	A	Pts
1 Bristol City	46	30	10	6	101	47	70
2 Leyton Orient	46	26	9	11	89	47	61
3 Southampton	46	24	11	11	75	51	59
4 Gillingham	46	20	15	11	77	66	55
5 Millwall	46	20	11	15	72	68	51
6 Brighton	46	20	10	16	76	63	50
7 Watford	46	18	14	14	71	62	50
8 Torquay	46	18	12	16	82	82	48
9 Coventry	46	18	11	17	67	59	47
10 Southend	46	17	12	17	83	80	46
11 Brentford	46	16	14	16	82	82	46
12 Norwich	46	18	10	18	60	60	46
13 Northampton	46	19	8	19	73	81	46
14 Aldershot	46	16	13	17	75	71	45
15 QPR	46	15	14	17	69	75	44
16 Shrewsbury	46	16	10	20	70	78	42
17 Bournemouth	46	12	18	16	57	65	42
18 Reading	46	13	15	18	65	73	41
19 Newport	46	11	16	19	60	73	38
20 Crystal Palace	46	11	16	19	52	80	38
21 Swindon	46	11	15	20	46	64	37
22 Exeter	46	11	15	20	47	73	37
23 Walsall	46	10	14	22	75	86	34
24 Colchester	46	9	13	24	53	91	31

1955–56

FIRST DIVISION

	P	W	D	L	F	A	Pts
1 Man United	42	25	10	7	83	51	60
2 Blackpool	42	20	9	13	86	62	49
3 Wolves	42	20	9	13	89	65	49
4 Man City	42	18	10	14	82	69	46
5 Arsenal	42	18	10	14	60	61	46
6 Birmingham	42	18	9	15	75	57	45
7 Burnley	42	18	8	16	64	54	44
8 Bolton	42	18	7	17	71	58	43
9 Sunderland	42	17	9	16	80	95	43
10 Luton	42	17	8	17	66	64	42
11 Newcastle	42	17	7	18	85	70	41
12 Portsmouth	42	16	9	17	78	85	41
13 WBA	42	18	5	19	58	70	41
14 Charlton	42	17	6	19	75	81	40
15 Everton	42	15	10	17	55	69	40
16 Chelsea	42	14	11	17	64	77	39
17 Cardiff	42	15	9	18	55	69	39
18 Tottenham	42	15	7	20	61	71	37
19 Preston	42	14	8	20	73	72	36
20 Aston Villa	42	11	13	18	52	69	35
21 Huddersfield	42	14	7	21	54	83	35
22 Sheff United	42	12	9	21	63	77	33

SECOND DIVISION

	P	W	D	L	F	A	Pts
1 Sheff Wed	42	21	13	8	101	62	55
2 Leeds	42	23	6	13	80	60	52
3 Liverpool	42	21	6	15	85	63	48
4 Blackburn	42	21	6	15	84	65	48
5 Leicester	42	21	6	15	94	78	48
6 Bristol Rovers	42	21	6	15	84	70	48
7 Nottm Forest	42	19	9	14	68	63	47
8 Lincoln	42	18	10	14	79	65	46
9 Fulham	42	20	6	16	89	79	46
10 Swansea	42	20	6	16	83	81	46
11 Bristol City	42	19	7	16	80	64	45
12 Port Vale	42	16	13	13	60	58	45
13 Stoke	42	20	4	18	71	62	44
14 Middlesbrough	42	16	8	18	76	78	40
15 Bury	42	16	8	18	86	90	40
16 West Ham	42	14	11	17	74	69	39
17 Doncaster	42	12	11	19	69	96	35
18 Barnsley	42	11	12	19	47	84	34
19 Rotherham	42	12	9	21	56	75	33
20 Notts County	42	11	9	22	55	82	31
21 Plymouth	42	10	8	24	54	87	28
22 Hull	42	10	6	26	53	97	26

THIRD DIVISION (NORTH)

	P	W	D	L	F	A	Pts
1 Grimsby	46	31	6	9	76	29	68
2 Derby	46	28	7	11	110	55	63
3 Accrington	46	25	9	12	92	57	59
4 Hartlepools	46	26	5	15	81	60	57
5 Southport	46	23	11	12	66	53	57
6 Chesterfield	46	25	4	17	94	66	54
7 Stockport	46	21	9	16	90	61	51
8 Bradford City	46	18	13	15	78	64	49
9 Scunthorpe	46	20	8	18	75	63	48
10 Workington	46	19	9	18	75	63	47
11 York	46	19	9	18	85	72	47
12 Rochdale	46	17	13	16	66	84	47
13 Gateshead	46	17	11	18	77	84	45
14 Wrexham	46	16	10	20	66	73	42
15 Darlington	46	16	9	21	60	73	41
16 Tranmere	46	16	9	21	59	84	41
17 Chester	46	13	14	19	52	82	40
18 Mansfield	46	14	11	21	84	81	39
19 Halifax	46	14	11	21	66	76	39
20 Oldham	46	10	18	18	76	86	38
21 Carlisle	46	15	8	23	71	95	38
22 Barrow	46	12	9	25	61	83	33
23 Bradford PA	46	13	7	26	61	122	33
24 Crewe	46	9	10	27	50	105	28

THIRD DIVISION (SOUTH)

	P	W	D	L	F	A	Pts
1 Leyton Orient	46	29	8	9	106	49	66
2 Brighton	46	29	7	10	112	50	65
3 Ipswich	46	25	14	7	106	60	64
4 Southend	46	21	11	14	88	80	53
5 Torquay	46	20	12	14	86	63	52
6 Brentford	46	19	14	13	69	66	52
7 Norwich	46	19	13	14	86	82	51
8 Coventry	46	20	9	17	73	60	49
9 Bournemouth	46	19	10	17	63	51	48
10 Gillingham	46	19	10	17	69	71	48
11 Northampton	46	20	7	19	67	71	47
12 Colchester	46	18	11	17	76	81	47
13 Shrewsbury	46	17	12	17	69	66	46
14 Southampton	46	18	8	20	91	81	44
15 Aldershot	46	12	16	18	70	90	40
16 Exeter	46	15	10	21	58	77	40
17 Reading	46	15	9	22	70	79	39
18 QPR	46	14	11	21	64	86	39
19 Newport	46	15	9	22	58	79	39
20 Walsall	46	15	8	23	68	84	38
21 Watford	46	13	11	22	52	85	37
22 Millwall	46	15	6	25	83	100	36
23 Crystal Palace	46	12	10	24	54	83	34
24 Swindon	46	8	14	24	34	78	30

1956–57

FIRST DIVISION

	P	W	D	L	F	A	Pts
1 Man United	42	28	8	6	103	54	64
2 Tottenham	42	22	12	8	104	56	56
3 Preston	42	23	10	9	84	56	56
4 Blackpool	42	22	9	11	93	65	53
5 Arsenal	42	21	8	13	85	69	50
6 Wolves	42	20	8	14	94	70	48
7 Burnley	42	18	10	14	56	50	46
8 Leeds	42	15	14	13	72	63	44
9 Bolton	42	16	12	14	65	65	44
10 Aston Villa	42	14	15	13	65	55	43
11 WBA	42	14	14	14	59	61	42
12 Birmingham*	42	15	9	18	69	69	39
13 Chelsea*	42	13	13	16	73	73	39
14 Sheff Wed	42	16	6	20	82	88	38
15 Everton	42	14	10	18	61	79	38
16 Luton	42	14	9	19	58	76	37
17 Newcastle	42	14	8	20	67	87	36
18 Man City	42	13	9	20	78	88	35
19 Portsmouth	42	10	13	19	62	92	33
20 Sunderland	42	12	8	22	67	88	32
21 Cardiff	42	10	9	23	53	88	29
22 Charlton	42	9	4	29	62	120	22

*Equal

SECOND DIVISION

	P	W	D	L	F	A	Pts
1 Leicester	42	25	11	6	109	67	61
2 Nottm Forest	42	22	10	10	94	55	54
3 Liverpool	42	21	11	10	82	54	53
4 Blackburn	42	21	10	11	83	75	52
5 Stoke	42	20	8	14	83	58	48
6 Middlesbrough	42	19	10	13	84	60	48
7 Sheff United	42	19	8	15	87	76	46
8 West Ham	42	19	8	15	59	63	46
9 Bristol Rovers	42	18	9	15	81	67	45
10 Swansea	42	19	7	16	90	90	45
11 Fulham	42	19	4	19	84	76	42
12 Huddersfield	42	18	6	18	68	74	42
13 Bristol City	42	16	9	17	74	79	41
14 Doncaster	42	15	10	17	77	77	40
15 Leyton Orient	42	15	10	17	66	84	40
16 Grimsby	42	17	5	20	61	62	39
17 Rotherham	42	13	11	18	74	75	37
18 Lincoln	42	14	6	22	54	80	34
19 Barnsley	42	12	10	20	59	89	34
20 Notts County	42	9	12	21	58	86	30
21 Bury	42	8	9	25	60	96	25
22 Port Vale	42	8	6	28	57	101	22

THIRD DIVISION (NORTH)

	P	W	D	L	F	A	Pts
1 Derby	46	26	11	9	111	53	63
2 Hartlepools	46	25	9	12	90	63	59
3 Accrington	46	25	8	13	95	64	58
4 Workington	46	24	10	12	93	63	58
5 Stockport	46	23	8	15	91	75	54
6 Chesterfield	46	22	9	15	96	79	53
7 York	46	21	10	15	75	61	52
8 Hull	46	21	10	15	84	69	52
9 Bradford City	46	22	8	16	78	68	52
10 Barrow	46	21	9	16	76	62	51
11 Halifax	46	21	7	18	65	70	49
12 Wrexham	46	19	10	17	97	74	48
13 Rochdale	46	18	12	16	65	65	48
14 Scunthorpe	46	15	15	16	71	69	45
15 Carlisle	46	16	13	17	76	85	45
16 Mansfield	46	17	10	19	91	90	44
17 Gateshead	46	17	10	19	72	90	44
18 Darlington	46	17	8	21	82	95	42
19 Oldham	46	12	15	19	66	74	39
20 Bradford PA	46	16	3	27	66	93	35
21 Chester	46	10	13	23	55	84	33
22 Southport	46	10	12	24	52	94	32
23 Tranmere	46	7	13	26	51	91	27
24 Crewe	46	6	9	31	43	110	21

THIRD DIVISION (SOUTH)

	P	W	D	L	F	A	Pts
1 Ipswich	46	25	9	12	101	54	59
2 Torquay	46	24	11	11	89	64	59
3 Colchester	46	22	14	10	84	56	58
4 Southampton	46	22	10	14	76	52	54
5 Bournemouth	46	19	14	13	88	62	52
6 Brighton	46	19	14	13	86	65	52
7 Southend	46	18	12	16	73	65	48
8 Brentford	46	16	16	14	78	76	48
9 Shrewsbury	46	15	18	13	72	79	48
10 QPR	46	18	11	17	61	60	47
11 Watford	46	18	10	18	72	75	46
12 Newport	46	16	13	17	65	62	45
13 Reading	46	18	9	19	80	81	45
14 Northampton	46	18	9	19	66	73	45
15 Walsall	46	16	12	18	80	74	44
16 Coventry	46	16	12	18	74	84	44
17 Millwall	46	16	12	18	64	84	44
18 Plymouth	46	16	11	19	68	73	43
19 Aldershot	46	15	12	19	79	92	42
20 Crystal Palace	46	11	18	17	62	75	40
21 Exeter	46	12	13	21	61	79	37
22 Gillingham	46	12	13	21	54	85	37
23 Swindon	46	15	6	25	66	96	36
24 Norwich	46	8	15	23	61	94	31

below Leeds United 1969 – League champions for the first time. Back row (l to r): Don Revie (manager), Paul Reaney, Norman Hunter, Rod Belfitt, Eddie Gray. Centre: Mike O'Grady, Jack Charlton, Gary Sprake, David Harvey, Mick Jones, Paul Madeley. Front: Allan Clarke, Terry Cooper, Terry Hibbitt, Billy Bremner, Johnny Giles, Mick Bates.

The best player? The most popular player? These are not questions that record books, films, newspaper reports, panels of judges or passionate saloon bar arguments will ever resolve. But George Best would always be a contender for the title of 'most talented' player – and Bobby Charlton was undoubtedly one of the 'most popular'.

left Defender's view of Bobby Charlton of Manchester United and England. Sir Matt Busby said of Charlton: 'He was idolized from his twentieth year on. There has never been a more popular footballer. He was as near perfection as man and player as it is possible to be.' The defender in the picture is Trevor Hockey of Sheffield United.

right Defender's view of George Best of Manchester United and Northern Ireland. Sir Matt Busby said of Best: 'If ever there was a football genius Best was that player. He had more ways of beating an opponent than any other player I have seen. The number of his gifts was unique and he made people gasp and laugh by his sheer audacity.'

above Happy Valley, 1970. The Valley was the home of Charlton Athletic from 1919 to 1985 before a confusion of problems – financial, safety, planning and personal – forced them to leave and share Selhurst Park with Crystal Palace. But the move did not harm Charlton's spirit on the field: they immediately won promotion to Division One for the first time for 29 years.

left Colchester United of Division Four celebrate the winning of the Watney Cup – the League's first sponsored tournament – in 1971. In the final they beat First Division West Bromwich Albion 4–3 on penalties after a 4–4 draw. The Watney Cup was a pre-season competition competed for by the two top-scoring clubs in each division other than those promoted or in Europe. It was also the first League tournament to use the penalty-kick system for deciding drawn ties. The four winners of the Watney Cup were Derby County, Colchester, Bristol Rovers and Stoke.

LEAGUE TABLES

1957–58

FIRST DIVISION

		P	W	D	L	F	A	Pts
1	Wolves	42	28	8	6	103	47	64
2	Preston	42	26	7	9	100	51	59
3	Tottenham	42	21	9	12	93	77	51
4	WBA	42	18	14	10	92	70	50
5	Man City	42	22	5	15	104	100	49
6	Burnley	42	21	5	16	80	74	47
7	Blackpool	42	19	6	17	80	67	44
8	Luton	42	19	6	17	69	63	44
9	Man United	42	16	11	15	85	75	43
10	Nottm Forest	42	16	10	16	69	63	42
11	Chelsea	42	15	12	15	83	79	42
12	Arsenal	42	16	7	19	73	85	39
13	Birmingham	42	14	11	17	76	89	39
14	Aston Villa	42	16	7	19	73	86	39
15	Bolton	42	14	10	18	65	87	38
16	Everton	42	13	11	18	65	75	37
17	Leeds	42	14	9	19	51	63	37
18	Leicester	42	14	5	23	91	112	33
19	Newcastle	42	12	8	22	73	81	32
20	Portsmouth	42	12	8	22	73	88	32
21	Sunderland	42	10	12	20	54	97	32
22	Sheff Wed	42	12	7	23	69	92	31

SECOND DIVISION

		P	W	D	L	F	A	Pts
1	West Ham	42	23	11	8	101	54	57
2	Blackburn	42	22	12	8	93	57	56
3	Charlton	42	24	7	11	107	69	55
4	Liverpool	42	22	10	10	79	54	54
5	Fulham	42	20	12	10	97	59	52
6	Sheff United	42	21	10	11	75	50	52
7	Middlesbrough	42	19	7	16	83	74	45
8	Ipswich	42	16	12	14	68	69	44
9	Huddersfield	42	14	16	12	63	66	44
10	Bristol Rovers	42	17	8	17	85	80	42
11	Stoke	42	18	6	18	75	73	42
12	Leyton Orient	42	18	5	19	77	79	41
13	Grimsby	42	17	6	19	86	83	40
14	Barnsley	42	14	12	16	70	74	40
15	Cardiff	42	14	9	19	63	77	37
16	Derby	42	14	8	20	60	81	36
17	Bristol City	42	13	9	20	63	88	35
18	Rotherham	42	14	5	23	65	101	33
19	Swansea	42	11	9	22	72	99	31
20	Lincoln	42	11	9	22	55	82	31
21	Notts County	42	12	6	24	44	80	30
22	Doncaster	42	8	11	23	56	88	27

THIRD DIVISION (NORTH)

		P	W	D	L	F	A	Pts
1	Scunthorpe	46	29	8	9	88	50	66
2	Accrington	46	25	9	12	83	61	59
3	Bradford City	46	21	15	10	73	49	57
4	Bury	46	23	10	13	94	62	56
5	Hull	46	19	15	12	78	67	53
6	Mansfield	46	22	8	16	100	92	52
7	Halifax	46	20	11	15	83	69	51
8	Chesterfield	46	18	15	13	71	69	51
9	Stockport	46	18	11	17	74	67	47
10	Rochdale	46	19	8	19	79	67	46
11	Tranmere	46	18	10	18	82	76	46
12	Wrexham	46	17	12	17	61	63	46
13	York	46	17	12	17	68	76	46
14	Gateshead	46	15	15	16	68	76	45
15	Oldham	46	14	17	15	72	84	45
16	Carlisle	46	19	6	21	80	78	44
17	Hartlepools	46	16	12	18	73	76	44
18	Barrow	46	13	15	18	66	74	41
19	Workington	46	14	13	19	72	81	41
20	Darlington	46	17	7	22	78	89	41
21	Chester	46	13	13	20	73	81	39
22	Bradford PA	46	13	11	22	68	95	37
23	Southport	46	11	6	29	52	88	28
24	Crewe	46	8	7	31	47	93	23

THIRD DIVISION (SOUTH)

		P	W	D	L	F	A	Pts
1	Brighton	46	24	12	10	88	64	60
2	Brentford	46	24	10	12	82	56	58
3	Plymouth	46	25	8	13	67	48	58
4	Swindon	46	21	15	10	79	50	57
5	Reading	46	21	13	12	79	51	55
6	Southampton	46	22	10	14	112	72	54
7	Southend	46	21	12	13	90	58	54
8	Norwich	46	19	15	12	75	70	53
9	Bournemouth	46	21	9	16	81	74	51
10	QPR	46	18	14	14	64	65	50
11	Newport	46	17	14	15	73	67	48
12	Colchester	46	17	13	16	77	79	47
13	Northampton	46	19	6	21	87	79	44
14	Crystal Palace	46	15	13	18	70	72	43
15	Port Vale	46	16	10	20	67	58	42
16	Watford	46	13	16	17	59	77	42
17	Shrewsbury	46	15	10	21	49	71	40
18	Aldershot	46	12	16	18	59	89	40
19	Coventry	46	13	13	20	61	81	39
20	Walsall	46	14	9	23	61	75	37
21	Torquay	46	11	13	22	49	74	35
22	Gillingham	46	13	9	24	52	81	35
23	Millwall	46	11	9	26	63	91	31
24	Exeter	46	11	9	26	57	99	31

1958–59

FIRST DIVISION

		P	W	D	L	F	A	Pts
1	Wolves	42	28	5	9	110	49	61
2	Man United	42	24	7	11	103	66	55
3	Arsenal	42	21	8	13	88	68	50
4	Bolton	42	20	10	12	79	66	50
5	WBA	42	18	13	11	88	68	49
6	West Ham	42	21	6	15	85	70	48
7	Burnley	42	19	10	13	81	70	48
8	Blackpool	42	18	11	13	66	49	47
9	Birmingham	42	20	6	16	84	68	46
10	Blackburn	42	17	10	15	76	70	44
11	Newcastle	42	17	7	18	80	80	41
12	Preston	42	17	7	18	70	77	41
13	Nottm Forest	42	17	6	19	71	74	40
14	Chelsea	42	18	4	20	77	98	40
15	Leeds	42	15	9	18	57	74	39
16	Everton	42	17	4	21	71	87	38
17	Luton	42	12	13	17	68	71	37
18	Tottenham	42	13	10	19	85	95	36
19	Leicester	42	11	10	21	67	98	32
20	Man City	42	11	9	22	64	95	31
21	Aston Villa	42	11	8	23	58	87	30
22	Portsmouth	42	6	9	27	64	112	21

SECOND DIVISION

		P	W	D	L	F	A	Pts
1	Sheff Wed	42	28	6	8	106	48	62
2	Fulham	42	27	6	9	96	61	60
3	Sheff United	42	23	7	12	82	48	53
4	Liverpool	42	24	5	13	87	62	53
5	Stoke	42	21	7	14	72	58	49
6	Bristol Rovers	42	18	12	12	80	64	48
7	Derby	42	20	8	14	74	71	48
8	Charlton	42	18	7	17	92	90	43
9	Cardiff	42	18	7	17	65	65	43
10	Bristol City	42	17	7	18	74	70	41
11	Swansea	42	16	9	17	79	81	41
12	Brighton	42	15	11	16	74	90	41
13	Middlesbrough	42	15	10	17	87	71	40
14	Huddersfield	42	16	8	18	62	55	40
15	Sunderland	42	16	8	18	64	75	40
16	Ipswich	42	17	6	19	62	77	40
17	Leyton Orient	42	14	8	20	71	78	36
18	Scunthorpe	42	12	9	21	55	84	33
19	Lincoln	42	11	7	24	63	93	29
20	Rotherham	42	10	9	23	42	82	29
21	Grimsby	42	9	10	23	62	90	28
22	Barnsley	42	10	7	25	55	91	27

THIRD DIVISION

		P	W	D	L	F	A	Pts
1	Plymouth	46	23	16	7	89	59	62
2	Hull	46	26	9	11	90	55	61
3	Brentford	46	21	15	10	76	49	57
4	Norwich	46	22	13	11	89	62	57
5	Colchester	46	21	10	15	71	67	52
6	Reading	46	21	8	17	78	63	50
7	Tranmere	46	21	8	17	82	67	50
8	Southend	46	21	8	17	85	80	50
9	Halifax	46	21	8	17	80	77	50
10	Bury	46	17	14	15	69	58	48
11	Bradford City	46	18	11	17	84	76	47
12	Bournemouth	46	17	12	17	69	69	46
13	QPR	46	19	8	19	74	77	46
14	Southampton	46	17	11	18	88	80	45
15	Swindon	46	16	13	17	59	57	45
16	Chesterfield	46	17	10	19	67	64	44
17	Newport	46	17	9	20	69	68	43
18	Wrexham	46	14	14	18	63	77	42
19	Accrington	46	15	12	19	71	87	42
20	Mansfield	46	14	13	19	73	98	41
21	Stockport	46	13	10	23	65	78	36
22	Doncaster	46	14	5	27	50	90	33
23	Notts County	46	8	13	25	55	96	29
24	Rochdale	46	8	12	26	37	79	28

FOURTH DIVISION

		P	W	D	L	F	A	Pts
1	Port Vale	46	26	12	8	110	58	64
2	Coventry	46	24	12	10	84	47	60
3	York	46	21	18	7	73	52	60
4	Shrewsbury	46	24	10	12	101	63	58
5	Exeter	46	23	11	12	87	61	57
6	Walsall	46	21	10	15	95	64	52
7	Crystal Palace	46	20	12	14	90	71	52
8	Northampton	46	21	9	16	85	78	51
9	Millwall	46	20	10	16	76	69	50
10	Carlisle	46	19	12	15	62	65	50
11	Gillingham	46	20	9	17	82	77	49
12	Torquay	46	16	12	18	78	77	44
13	Chester	46	16	12	18	72	84	44
14	Bradford PA	46	18	7	21	75	77	43
15	Watford	46	16	10	20	81	79	42
16	Darlington	46	13	16	17	66	68	42
17	Workington	46	12	17	17	63	78	41
18	Crewe	46	15	10	21	70	82	40
19	Hartlepools	46	15	10	21	74	88	40
20	Gateshead	46	16	8	22	56	85	40
21	Oldham	46	16	4	26	59	84	36
22	Aldershot	46	14	7	25	63	97	35
23	Barrow	46	9	10	27	51	104	28
24	Southport	46	7	12	27	41	86	26

1959–60

FIRST DIVISION

		P	W	D	L	F	A	Pts
1	Burnley	42	24	7	11	85	61	55
2	Wolves	42	24	6	12	106	67	54
3	Tottenham	42	21	11	10	86	50	53
4	WBA	42	19	11	12	83	57	49
5	Sheff Wed	42	19	11	12	80	59	49
6	Bolton	42	20	8	14	59	51	48
7	Man United	42	19	7	16	102	80	45
8	Newcastle	42	18	8	16	82	78	44
9	Preston	42	16	12	14	79	76	44
10	Fulham	42	17	10	15	73	80	44
11	Blackpool	42	15	10	17	59	71	40
12	Leicester	42	13	13	16	66	75	39
13	Arsenal	42	15	9	18	68	80	39
14	West Ham	42	16	6	20	75	91	38
15	Man City	42	17	3	22	78	84	37
16	Everton	42	13	11	18	73	78	37
17	Blackburn	42	16	5	21	60	70	37
18	Chelsea	42	14	9	19	76	91	37
19	Birmingham	42	13	10	19	63	80	36
20	Nottm Forest	42	13	9	20	50	74	35
21	Leeds	42	12	10	20	65	92	34
22	Luton	42	9	12	21	50	73	30

SECOND DIVISION

		P	W	D	L	F	A	Pts
1	Aston Villa	42	25	9	8	89	43	59
2	Cardiff	42	23	12	7	90	62	58
3	Liverpool	42	20	10	12	90	66	50
4	Sheff United	42	19	12	11	68	51	50
5	Middlesbrough	42	19	10	13	90	64	48
6	Huddersfield	42	19	9	14	73	52	47
7	Charlton	42	17	13	12	90	87	47
8	Rotherham	42	17	13	12	61	60	47
9	Bristol Rovers	42	18	11	13	72	78	47
10	Leyton Orient	42	15	14	13	76	61	44
11	Ipswich	42	19	6	17	78	68	44
12	Swansea	42	15	10	17	82	84	40
13	Lincoln	42	16	7	19	75	78	39
14	Brighton	42	13	12	17	67	76	38
15	Scunthorpe	42	13	10	19	57	71	36
16	Sunderland	42	12	12	18	52	65	36
17	Stoke	42	14	7	21	66	83	35
18	Derby	42	14	7	21	61	77	35
19	Plymouth	42	13	9	20	61	89	35
20	Portsmouth	42	10	12	20	59	77	32
21	Hull	42	10	10	22	48	76	30
22	Bristol City	42	11	5	26	60	97	27

THIRD DIVISION

		P	W	D	L	F	A	Pts
1	Southampton	46	26	9	11	106	75	61
2	Norwich	46	24	11	11	82	54	59
3	Shrewsbury	46	18	16	12	97	75	52
4	Coventry	46	21	10	15	78	63	52
5	Grimsby	46	18	16	12	87	70	52
6	Brentford	46	21	9	16	78	61	51
7	Bury	46	21	9	16	64	51	51
8	QPR	46	18	13	15	73	54	49
9	Colchester	46	18	11	17	83	74	47
10	Bournemouth	46	17	13	16	72	72	47
11	Reading	46	18	10	18	84	77	46
12	Southend	46	19	8	19	76	74	46
13	Newport	46	20	6	20	80	79	46
14	Port Vale	46	19	8	19	80	79	46
15	Halifax	46	18	10	18	70	72	46
16	Swindon	46	19	8	19	69	78	46
17	Barnsley	46	15	14	17	65	66	44
18	Chesterfield	46	18	7	21	71	84	43
19	Bradford City	46	15	12	19	66	74	42
20	Tranmere	46	14	13	19	72	75	41
21	York	46	13	12	21	57	73	38
22	Mansfield	46	15	6	25	81	112	36
23	Wrexham	46	14	8	24	68	101	36
24	Accrington	46	11	5	30	57	123	27

FOURTH DIVISION

		P	W	D	L	F	A	Pts
1	Walsall	46	28	9	9	102	60	65
2	Notts County	46	26	8	12	107	69	60
3	Torquay	46	26	8	12	84	58	60
4	Watford	46	24	9	13	92	67	57
5	Millwall	46	18	17	11	84	61	53
6	Northampton	46	22	9	15	85	63	53
7	Gillingham	46	21	10	15	74	69	52
8	Crystal Palace	46	19	12	15	84	64	50
9	Exeter	46	19	11	16	80	70	49
10	Stockport	46	19	11	16	58	54	49
11	Bradford PA	46	17	15	14	70	68	49
12	Rochdale	46	18	10	18	65	60	46
13	Aldershot	46	18	9	19	77	74	45
14	Crewe	46	18	9	19	79	88	45
15	Darlington	46	17	9	20	63	73	43
16	Workington	46	14	14	18	68	60	42
17	Doncaster	46	16	10	20	69	76	42
18	Barrow	46	15	11	20	77	87	41
19	Carlisle	46	15	11	20	51	66	41
20	Chester	46	14	12	20	59	77	40
21	Southport	46	10	14	22	48	92	34
22	Gateshead	46	12	9	25	58	86	33
23	Oldham	46	8	12	26	41	83	28
24	Hartlepools	46	10	7	29	59	109	27

1960–61

FIRST DIVISION

	P	W	D	L	F	A	Pts
1 Tottenham	42	31	4	7	115	55	66
2 Sheff Wed	42	23	12	7	78	47	58
3 Wolves	42	25	7	10	103	75	57
4 Burnley	42	22	7	13	102	77	51
5 Everton	42	22	6	14	87	69	50
6 Leicester	42	18	9	15	87	70	45
7 Man United	42	18	9	15	88	76	45
8 Blackburn	42	15	13	14	77	76	43
9 Aston Villa	42	17	9	16	78	77	43
10 WBA	42	18	5	19	67	71	41
11 Arsenal	42	15	11	16	77	85	41
12 Chelsea	42	15	7	20	98	100	37
13 Man City	42	13	11	18	79	90	37
14 Nottm Forest	42	14	9	19	62	78	37
15 Cardiff	42	13	11	18	60	85	37
16 West Ham	42	13	10	19	77	88	36
17 Fulham	42	14	8	20	72	95	36
18 Bolton	42	12	11	19	58	73	35
19 Birmingham	42	14	6	22	62	84	34
20 Blackpool	42	12	9	21	68	73	33
21 Newcastle	42	11	10	21	86	109	32
22 Preston	42	10	10	22	43	71	30

SECOND DIVISION

	P	W	D	L	F	A	Pts
1 Ipswich	42	26	7	9	100	55	59
2 Sheff United	42	26	6	10	81	51	58
3 Liverpool	42	21	10	11	87	58	52
4 Norwich	42	20	9	13	70	53	49
5 Middlesbrough	42	18	12	12	83	74	48
6 Sunderland	42	17	13	12	75	60	47
7 Swansea	42	18	11	13	77	73	47
8 Southampton	42	18	8	16	84	81	44
9 Scunthorpe	42	14	15	13	69	64	43
10 Charlton	42	16	11	15	97	91	43
11 Plymouth	42	17	8	17	81	82	42
12 Derby	42	15	10	17	80	80	40
13 Luton	42	15	9	18	71	70	39
14 Leeds	42	14	10	18	75	83	38
15 Rotherham	42	12	13	17	65	64	37
16 Brighton	42	14	9	19	61	75	37
17 Bristol Rovers	42	15	7	20	73	92	37
18 Stoke	42	12	12	18	51	59	36
19 Leyton Orient	42	14	8	20	55	78	36
20 Huddersfield	42	13	9	20	62	71	35
21 Portsmouth	42	11	11	20	64	91	33
22 Lincoln	42	8	8	26	48	95	24

THIRD DIVISION

	P	W	D	L	F	A	Pts
1 Bury	46	30	8	8	108	45	68
2 Walsall	46	28	6	12	98	60	62
3 QPR	46	25	10	11	93	60	60
4 Watford	46	20	12	14	85	72	52
5 Notts County	46	21	9	16	82	77	51
6 Grimsby	46	20	10	16	77	69	50
7 Port Vale	46	17	15	14	96	79	49
8 Barnsley	46	21	7	18	83	80	49
9 Halifax	46	16	17	13	71	78	49
10 Shrewsbury	46	15	16	15	83	75	46
11 Hull	46	17	12	17	73	73	46
12 Torquay	46	14	17	15	75	83	45
13 Newport	46	17	11	18	81	90	45
14 Bristol City	46	17	10	19	70	68	44
15 Coventry	46	16	12	18	80	83	44
16 Swindon	46	14	15	17	62	55	43
17 Brentford	46	13	17	16	56	70	43
18 Reading	46	14	12	20	72	83	40
19 Bournemouth	46	15	10	21	58	76	40
20 Southend	46	14	11	21	60	76	39
21 Tranmere	46	15	8	23	79	115	38
22 Bradford City	46	11	14	21	65	87	36
23 Colchester	46	11	11	24	68	101	33
24 Chesterfield	46	10	12	24	67	87	32

FOURTH DIVISION

	P	W	D	L	F	A	Pts
1 Peterborough	46	28	10	8	134	65	66
2 Crystal Palace	46	29	6	11	110	69	64
3 Northampton	46	25	10	11	90	62	60
4 Bradford PA	46	26	8	12	84	74	60
5 York	46	21	9	16	80	60	51
6 Millwall	46	21	8	17	97	86	50
7 Darlington	46	18	13	15	78	70	49
8 Workington	46	21	7	18	74	76	49
9 Crewe	46	20	9	17	61	67	49
10 Aldershot	46	18	9	19	79	69	45
11 Doncaster	46	19	7	20	76	78	45
12 Oldham	46	19	7	20	79	88	45
13 Stockport	46	18	9	19	57	66	45
14 Southport	46	19	6	21	69	67	44
15 Gillingham	46	15	13	18	64	66	43
16 Wrexham	46	17	8	21	62	56	42
17 Rochdale	46	17	8	21	60	66	42
18 Accrington	46	16	8	22	74	88	40
19 Carlisle	46	13	13	20	61	79	39
20 Mansfield	46	16	6	24	71	78	38
21 Exeter	46	14	10	22	66	94	38
22 Barrow	46	13	11	22	52	79	37
23 Hartlepools	46	12	8	26	71	103	32
24 Chester	46	11	9	26	61	104	31

EIGHT
'66 and all that
1961–1970

'Before the 1966 World Cup I'd always gone with my wife to Romford supermarket. We'd wander round, me pushing the wire trolley, load up and then stop in the cafe there for a cup of tea. But the first visit after the final was pandemonium. We were mobbed. Half the staff came pouring out from behind the counters waving wrapping paper and bags to be autographed; the customers joined in, thrusting soap-packets or bundles of bacon at me to sign. Poor Judith was swept away, still waving her list forlornly, while I was being backed up to the biscuit counter trying to shake a hundred hands at once. Stop for a cup of tea? You must be joking . . . it would have been like trying to have a picnic in Piccadilly.'

Geoff Hurst *of West Ham and England –*
the only man to score a hat-trick in a World Cup final.

These were years that did wonders for the self-respect of the home of football. England won the World Cup, and Manchester United and half a dozen other League clubs won European trophies.

Spurs also completed the League and FA Cup 'double', the first of the century; the League Cup had an awkward birth but grew up to confound its army of critics; and, after a long and fractious squabble, players won the right to bargain over pay and contracts.

The Wembley triumphs of England in 1966 and Manchester United two years later were hugely important achievements in themselves, but history lent them a deeper significance. The winning of the World Cup meant that for the first and only time the English were proven masters of a game they had given to the world nearly a century before; and United's success in the European Cup came ten years after the Munich air disaster – a success that belonged not only to Matt Busby, Bobby Charlton, Bill Foulkes and those who had survived the crash but to Duncan Edwards, Eddie Colman, Roger Byrne and all who had died.

Alf Ramsey, of course, had promised England would win the World Cup; and while a few laughed many accepted him as a man of his word who had already proved his worth as a manager by guiding homely Ipswich Town to the championship of the Second and First Divisions in successive years (1961 and 1962) – a remarkable achievement.

Ramsey had been an outstanding full-back in Tottenham's 'push and run' championship side in 1951 – and Ramsey the player had much in common with Ramsey the manager. He was obstinate, a cunning tactician and single-minded in his pursuit of success; and the side he built to win the Jules Rimet trophy was solid, finely balanced, determined and immensely loyal to their manager.

For a month they were centre-stage. People admired Bobby Moore for his example and icy temperament, knew exactly what Gordon Banks liked for breakfast, loved Nobby Stiles for his toothless grin, roared on George Cohen and the impeccable Ray Wilson when they pushed out of defence, relished the contrast between the Charlton brothers, Bobby and Jack, applauded the subtlety of Martin Peters and the stamina of Alan Ball and chewed over the merits of Geoff Hurst and Roger Hunt in attack.

They were drawn from eight League clubs, each with its own style and character, but together they were a side designed to do a job; and on Saturday, 30 July 1966, with much sweat and an inspired hat-trick by Hurst, they completed their task by beating West Germany by four goals to two. Ramsey, that complex man, barely raised a smile at the moment of victory – but the lift he and his players gave to the pride and confidence of the nation was immeasurable.

Manchester United's triumph mattered in a different way. Celtic, a year before, had become the first British club to win the European Cup but United, when they faced Benfica in the final on Wednesday, 29 May 1968, had more than just a trophy on their minds. They were remembering the Busby Babes. It was a night of fulfilment.

United won the League championship in 1965 and 1967 and Busby's side now

– the third he had put together – was a carefully refined blend of costly signings and young talent. People travelled from all over the country to watch men like Denis Law of Scotland, who joined United for a record £115,000 after a desperately unhappy spell with Torino, George Best of Northern Ireland who had joined the club as a 16-year-old, and, of course, Bobby Charlton himself. Law with his electric pace and limitless energy . . . the audacious Best whom Matt Busby considered the most gifted player he had ever seen . . . and Charlton with his cutting acceleration and elemental shooting. All three were voted European Footballer of the Year – Law in 1964, Charlton 1966, Best 1968.

Cartilage trouble prevented Law from facing Benfica at Wembley but it did not matter. United won 4–1 with Charlton, as captain, scoring twice and Best adding another as only he could, brilliantly, impertinently, impossible until he proved it possible. United took their trophy to the four corners of Wembley but, ten eventful years after Munich, there were also tears and heartache. Matt Busby, who was knighted that same year for services to football, was to be asked many times which of his three great sides he thought the best. Sir Matt's answer was always the same: the pre-Munich side of the 'fifties was *potentially* the best he had ever seen. Some believe, however, that Charlton, Law and Best at their sharpest would give United's team of the 'sixties the edge over any opposition.

No argument about great football sides will end with unanimity – but all such arguments must involve the Tottenham side that completed the first League and FA Cup 'double' of the century in 1961. Bill Nicholson's team rolled over one record after another (eleven straight wins for starters, 31 victories in all, 16 away from home) and then beat Leicester City, with Gordon Banks in goal, by 2–0 in the final. They were a side of many shades and subtleties, a team of individual distinction and collective excellence, always improvising, never wilting. There was a perceptible air of superiority about them and at the heart of their formula were Danny Blanchflower at right-half and Dave Mackay on the left . . . Irish charm and Scottish fire, one thinking the game, the other consuming it. Spurs retained the Cup in 1962 and a year later they became the first English club to win a European trophy – the Cup Winners' Cup.

There will be votes, too, for the Liverpool side that won the League championship in 1964, the Cup in 1965 and the championship again in 1966. It was full of thoroughbreds, Ian St John, Roger Hunt, Ian Callaghan, Peter Thompson and Ronnie Yeats among them, but most of all it had Bill Shankly. 'Shanks', with his cocky strut, crew-cut hair and gravel voice, was all Scot and all Scouse – a manager who turned a game of blood and sweat into a faith. He understood players as few others did; and as a motivator, said one of his players, 'he'd have been great in war, another Winston Churchill.' Shankly was a showman, a spinner of dreams and a master of what he called 'the true joke' – a wicked mixture of exaggeration, whimsy and ego. He was a man of simplicity but never a simple man. 'Me havin' no education,' he once said, 'I had to use my brains.' He was hugely successful and hugely loved.

Leeds United were yet another side which left an indelible print on the 'swinging 'sixties' – a period in which Don Revie transformed a club that was on the brink of relegation into the Third Division into one of the most redoubtable powers in post-war football. To begin with they were hard and unlovable, coldly dedicated to the next point, but the skill of players like Johnny Giles and the combative Billy Bremner slowly blossomed within the system, and they became a side to relish.

Their record at the top over a period of ten years was both astonishing and perplexing. They were League champions in 1969 and 1974 but runners-up in five other seasons. They won the League Cup and the European Fairs Cup in 1968, the Fairs Cup again in 1971 and the FA Cup in 1972 but, home and abroad, they also lost six other finals. They were in at the death for 17 trophies but won only six . . . a team of winners who often finished second. They were only failures, however, by their own remarkable standards.

The League Cup was something new. It was the brainchild of Alan Hardaker, secretary of the Football League for more than 20 years and a man of enormous reputation and influence, and few tournaments have had a more painful or difficult birth. It was a competition just for the 92 clubs of the League, a brand new source of income with a two-legged final on the grounds of the two finalists, but there were many who condemned it as ill-timed, ill-conceived and a burden on an already over-loaded season. Six big clubs even refused to take part.

Aston Villa just pipped Rotherham in the first final and Norwich easily overcame Rochdale of the Fourth Division in the second – some unusual grounds enjoyed the distinction of staging a 'national' event. In 1967, however, the final became a one-shot affair at Wembley with all the trimmings, the winner was promised an automatic place in the European Fairs Cup (later the UEFA Cup) and suddenly attitudes changed. Alan Hardaker was soon able to claim that 'if the FA Cup is football's Ascot then the League Cup is its Derby Day'.

The first League Cup final at Wembley also happened to be rather special. West Bromwich of the First Division met Queen's Park Rangers of the Third in front of a full house – and at half-time Albion were leading 2–0 and looking home and dried. But Rangers, managed with style by Alec Stock and inspired by the delightfully talented Rodney Marsh, came back brilliantly in the second half to score three and help shape a little piece of history. Rangers also won the Third Division championship by a devastating margin of twelve points: a good season.

These were very different times now for players. Their lifestyles and prospects changed dramatically in the early 'sixties with the removal of the maximum wage and the end of the old retain-and-transfer system. The revolution – popularly described as 'the freeing of the slaves' – had been inevitable. A maximum of £20 a week in season and £17 in summer was modest reward for men who gave pleasure to millions; and, led with bravura by chairman Jimmy Hill and with deftness by secretary Cliff Lloyd, the Professional Footballers' Association brought a long and sometimes bitter struggle to a head by threatening to strike. The clubs conceded and the ceiling on wages was removed. And very shortly afterwards Fulham announced that they intended paying £100 a week to Johnny Haynes who was England's captain and a one-club player of surpassing quality and renown.

But that was only half the battle. The old retain-and-transfer system, which enabled a club to keep a player against his will at the end of his contract, was not laid to rest until George Eastham, a skilful inside-forward who played for England, took Newcastle to the High Court in 1963 and Mr Justice Wilberforce ruled that the retention regulation was 'an unreasonable restraint of trade'. Nothing in football can be taken for granted.

SUCCESS OF FOOTBALL LEAGUE CLUBS IN EUROPE

European Cup

1968	Manchester United
1977	Liverpool
1978	Liverpool
1979	Nottingham Forest
1980	Nottingham Forest
1981	Liverpool
1982	Aston Villa
1984	Liverpool

European Cup Winners' Cup

1963	Tottenham
1965	West Ham United
1970	Manchester City
1971	Chelsea
1985	Everton

Inter-cities Fairs Cup/UEFA Cup

1968	Leeds United
1969	Newcastle United
1970	Arsenal
1971	Leeds United
1972	Tottenham
1973	Liverpool
1976	Liverpool
1981	Ipswich Town
1984	Tottenham

DOUBLES – AND NEAR DOUBLES

League Champions and FA Cup Winners

1888–89	Preston North End
1896–97	Aston Villa
1960–61	Tottenham Hotspur
1970–71	Arsenal
1985–86	Liverpool

League Champions and FA Cup Runners-up

1904–05	Newcastle United
1912–13	Sunderland
1956–57	Manchester United
1976–77	Liverpool
1984–85	Everton

League Runners-up and FA Cup Winners

1903–04	Manchester City
1912–13	Aston Villa
1947–48	Manchester United
1953–54	West Bromwich Albion
1959–60	Wolverhampton Wanderers
1971–72	Leeds United
1973–74	Liverpool

Runners-up in both League and FA Cup

1927–28	Huddersfield Town
1931–32	Arsenal
1938–39	Wolverhampton Wanderers
1961–62	Burnley
1964–65	Leeds United
1969–70	Leeds United
1985–86	Everton

League Champions and Winners of League Cup Milk Cup/Littlewoods Cup

1977–78	Nottingham Forest
1981–82	Liverpool
1982–83	Liverpool
1983–84	Liverpool

left Phil Woosnam, a talented and highly articulate inside-forward who played 357 League games for Orient, West Ham and Aston Villa (1954–65) and won 17 caps for Wales – and then joined in the attempt to sell football in the United States. He was a passionate and tireless advocate for the game and eventually became Commissioner of the North American Soccer Association. 'The rules are very simple,' he once told a confused audience. 'Basically, if it moves kick it . . . and if it doesn't move kick it until it does.' But his cause was a losing one. Mistakes were made, fortunes were lost and its demise was slow and painful – although along the way dozens of Football League footballers enjoyed the sun and the money. Americans declined to watch the game; but a new generation is playing it. The goalkeeper foiling Woosnam in the picture is Reg Matthews of Chelsea.

right Tommy Docherty – a manager's dream as a player; and then one of the most travelled and most controversial managers in League history. Docherty was a splendidly consistent and aggressive wing-half who started with Celtic and then played 412 League games for Preston, Arsenal and Chelsea (1949–61) and 25 times for Scotland. His career as a manager, however, was like a bumpy ride on a roller-coaster: he managed Chelsea, Rotherham, Queen's Park Rangers (28 days), Aston Villa, Porto, Hull (assistant manager), Scotland, Manchester United, Derby, Queen's Park Rangers again, Sydney Olympic, Preston and Wolves. His successes included Chelsea in the League Cup (1965) and Manchester United in the FA Cup (1977) – and he could always joke about his failures. 'I promised Rotherham I'd take them out of the Second Divison,' he would say, 'And I did – into the Third Division!' Docherty was unpredictable, headstrong, eccentric, a natural showman and, always, eminently quotable. Fans loved him, the media were grateful to him and there was usually a club somewhere that was willing to give him a new chance. Docherty was one of the game's most colourful characters.

above Peterborough United, record-breaking champions of Division Four in their first season in the League, 1960–1. Peterborough, an ambitious Southern League club with a fine record in the FA Cup and an enviably appointed ground, were elected to the League in 1960 – and many wondered if they would successfully bridge the gap. Their answer was most remarkable. They won the Fourth Division title by scoring 134 goals in 46 games which is still a record for any division. Terry Bly contributed 52 – a record for Divison IV and the only time since World War Two that a player has scored more than 50 League goals in a season. Their average home gate was 14,222. Back row (l to r): Whittaker, Ripley, Walls, Walker, Bly, Rayner. Seated: Hails, Emery, Rigby, Smith, McNamee.

left Jimmy Armfield of Blackpool and England – full-back of pace, aggression and intelligence who was voted the best right-back in the 1962 World Cup in Chile. A one-club man, he played 568 League games for Blackpool (1954–70) and won 43 caps for England, 15 as captain. Armfield led the way in emphasising that full-backs had an important role to play at both ends of the pitch: he had the speed of a winger and could centre like one. He later managed Bolton (Division Three champions 1973) and Leeds (European Cup finalists 1975) . . . and then became a highly respected broadcaster and journalist. Armfield is pictured playing for England against Scotland at Wembley in April 1961 – the famous game which England won 9–3, a record defeat of the Scots that is unlikely to be bettered.

below Peel Park, the home of Accrington Stanley, pictured in August 1961, seven months before heavy debts obliged them to drop out of the League. It was the second time the town had lost a League club for this reason. The first, Accrington FC (a different club) were one of the twelve founder members in 1888, but withdrew in 1893 and disbanded three years later. Accrington Stanley joined the League in 1921 and had some of their most successful years in the mid-1950s when they finished second, third, third and second in successive seasons – at a time when only the winners were promoted. Accrington set a League record in 1955–6 by fielding a side composed entirely of players born in Scotland.

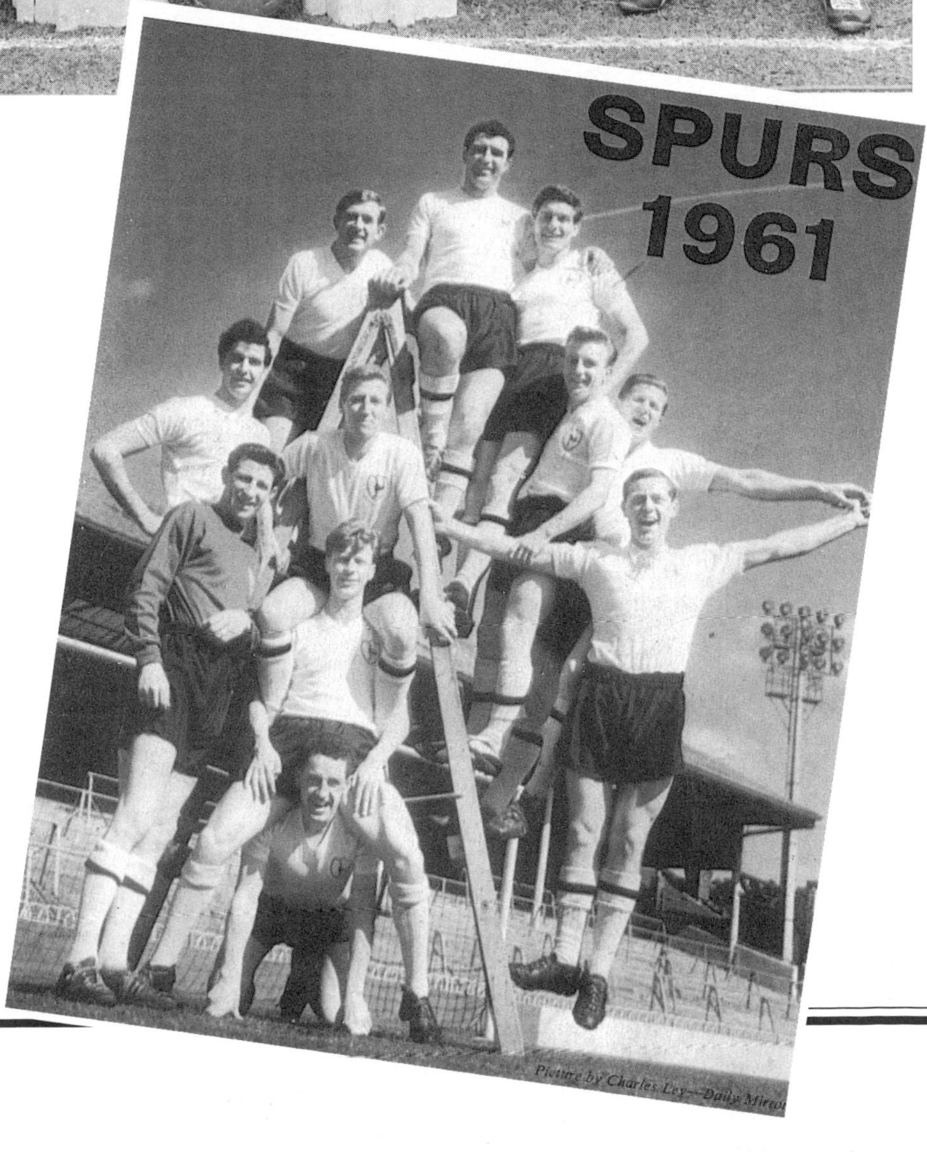

above Tottenham Hotspur's League and FA Cup 'double' side – with trophies, May 1961. Back row (l to r): Bill Brown, Peter Baker, Ron Henry, Bill Nicholson, Danny Blanchflower, Maurice Norman, Dave Mackay. Front: Cliff Jones, John White, Bobby Smith, Les Allen, Terry Dyson. One of the finest sides in the history of English football – but Nicholson, their hugely respected manager, gently criticized their popular description as Super Spurs. 'It is a neat tag but is simply not true,' he said. 'I feel we could so much better.' Spurs retained the FA Cup the following year (1962) and, a season later, won the European Cup Winners' Cup to become the first English club to win a European trophy. White, their brilliant Scottish international inside-forward (front row, second left), was killed by lightning on a London golf course in July 1964. He scored 40 goals in 183 League games during his five years with Spurs – and Nicholson regarded him as 'one of the very best and a player who had so much more to give'.

No-limit soccer wages next season

By PETER LORENZO

SOCCER stars will be able to earn star money next season.

The Football League decided yesterday to scrap the maximum wage at the end of this season—two years earlier than their original proposal.

How much will top players now earn? For some £100 a week is a possibility.

Fulham chairman Tommy Trinder told me two months ago: "I would like to pay Johnny Haynes £100 a week. . . . He's worth it to us."

GREAT CHANCE

Footballers were jubilant with the news last night. Jimmy McIlroy, Burnley's Irish International, said: "Now we have a great chance of matching the Continentals and the rest of the world on their own cash terms."

The wages decision was announced after a meeting of First and Second Division club chairmen in London.

Now the Soccer strike, due to start on Saturday week, is certain to be called off.

above England the poor relation: cartoonist's view of the maximum wage controversy, and *left* the problem resolved, January 1961.

right Johnny Byrne of Crystal Palace, West Ham, Fulham and England – a jewel of a forward who won his first cap for England while still a Third Division player. But soon after he moved from Palace to West Ham and Division One for a British record transfer fee of £65,000 and helped them win the 1964 FA Cup. Ron Greenwood, his manager at Upton Park, described him as 'the Di Stefano of British football' – after the great Argentine who played for Real Madrid during their period of European dominance in the late 1950s. Byrne was small but his talent was enormous, an intuitive player of pace and touch who flickered and darted around like a pin-machine ball. He seemed to need no time to wind up and no space in which to turn; his control was tight, his avoiding actions late and the bigger and tougher his marker the better he played. His impudence was relished by the crowds everywhere. Byrne scored eight goals in his eleven internationals – including a wonderul hat-trick against Portugal in Lisbon in 1964 – and there seemed no limit to what he might achieve. But Byrne, a smart dresser and compulsive talker who was nicknamed 'Budgie', enjoyed life to the full; and in the end, perhaps, he enjoyed it too much. An injury cut short his international career in 1965, and his time at the top after that was desperately short. He scored 160 goals in 395 League games in 13 seasons (1956–69) – and there were many who said he should have done more with his marvellous talent. But Byrne was a happy man; and he left many happy memories. Pictured at Highbury in October 1962. The Arsenal goalkeeper is John McClelland.

below Ipswich Town, winners of the Second Division (1961) and First Division (1962) in successive seasons. Ipswich, managed by Alf Ramsey, were only the fourth club to manage this feat after Liverpool (1905 and 1906), Everton (1931 and 1932) and Tottenham (1950 and 1951). Back row (l to r): Bill Baxter, Larry Carberry, Roy Bailey, John Compton, John Elsworthy. Front row: Roy Stephenson, Doug Moran, Ray Crawford, Andy Nelson, Ted Phillips, Jim Leadbetter. Phillips scored 41 League goals, a club record, in season 1956–7 when Ipswich won the Third Division South: and – another record – Crawford scored 203 goals in 320 League games for the Suffolk club.

above Danny Blanchflower of Barnsley, Aston Villa, Tottenham and Northern Ireland – wing-half of rare intelligence and skill, captain of authority and man of principle. Led Spurs to the first League and FA Cup 'double' of the twentieth century in 1961, to the FA Cup again in 1962 and to the European Cup Winners' Cup in 1963 (the first English success in Europe). Also captained Northern Ireland to the last eight in the 1958 World Cup finals. Played 553 League games (1949–64) and won 56 international caps (1950–63). Twice Footballer of the Year (1958 and 1961).

right George Eastham of Newcastle, Arsenal, Stoke and England – clever and astute inside-forward, son of a celebrated footballer and stubborn centre-figure of the High Court case in 1963 in which the old retain-and-transfer system was ruled 'an unreasonable restraint of trade'. Scored 74 goals in 515 League games (1956–74) and won 19 caps for England (1963–6). Scored Stoke's winning goal against Chelsea (2–1) in 1972 Milk Cup Final – the only major trophy Stoke have ever won. His father, George Eastham senior, played for Blackpool, Swansea, Rochdale and Lincoln.

below Jimmy Greaves of Tottenham and ball in Burnley's billowing net at Turf Moor, March 1962. Brian Miller of Burnley does his best. Final score: 2–2. Two of the teams of the season – Burnley finished runners-up in Division One (to Ipswich) and Tottenham were third. And Spurs retained the FA Cup by beating Burnley 3–1 in the final.

left Peter Bonetti of Chelsea defies the might of Liverpool at Anfield. The old Main Stand, in the background, was replaced in 1973.

below Private moment at Wembley for Billy Bremner. Leeds have been held to a 2–2 draw by Chelsea in the 1970 FA Cup final – and a 2–1 defeat after extra time waits for them in the replay at Old Trafford.

Spot the future England captain and European Footballer of the Year. Scunthorpe United 1970 – and Kevin Keegan is in the second row from the front, second left. The following year Keegan joined Liverpool for a fee of £33,000 and a weekly wage of £50.

above Stoke City with the 1972 League Cup – the first major trophy won by the League's second oldest club (formed 1863). From back (left to right): Mike Bernard, Alan Bloor, Mike Pejic, Jimmy Greenhoff, Gordon Banks, Tony Waddington (manager), George Eastham, John Marsh, John Mahoney, Terry Conroy, Peter Dobing, John Ritchie, Denis Smith.

right Welcome to Turf Moor. Burnley transformed their ground into one of the most modern in the country in the early 1970s – and the new Bob Lord stand (named after their strong and energetic chairman) seemed to be a concrete pointer to continuing success by one of the League's founder members. But the club's fortunes soon declined. They lost their place in the First Division and in 1987 – under a new system – only a dramatic and highly emotional victory in their last Division Four game of the season saved them from automatically losing their League status.

left Bobby Moore of West Ham – England's most capped player. Pictured in his 108th and final international, against Italy at Wembley, November 1973. Left is Peter Shilton who became England's most capped goalkeeper.

below The Air Dome used to protect the Filbert Street pitch from the weather's worst between 1971 and 1982. It covered an area of 90,000 square feet, weighed 24 cwt and was 15 ft high at the centre. It took 15 men two hours to lay out and inflate the cover using four electric fans.

above The White City – aptly named – in January 1963. Referee David Smith (left) and Alec Stock, manager of Queen's Park Rangers, confer briefly before deciding that football is impossible. All records for postponements were broken in a severe spell of snow, ice and sub-zero temperatures that lasted six weeks. More than 400 League and Cup games were called off or abandoned. Queen's Park Rangers left Loftus Road and played at the nearby White City for just a few months in season 1962–3, and hoped to share with another club. But gates fell, form suffered and they returned to Loftus Road. Since their formation in 1885, Rangers have had twelve home grounds – more than any other League club.

Derek Forster who became the youngest player to appear in Division One when he kept goal for Sunderland against Leicester in August 1964 at the age of 15 years 185 days. Forster, an England schoolboy international, played 30 League games in a ten year career with Sunderland, Charlton and Brighton.

Billy Wright, just appointed Arsenal's manager, August 1962, poses alongside the bust of Herbert Chapman in the marbled entrance hall of Highbury. Arsenal's average position during Wright's four years at Highbury was tenth. But he bought well – and, under Bertie Mee, his successor, highly successful years were to follow.

above Bristol City celebrating promotion from Division Three in April 1965 – and at the heart of the Ashton Gate party is a tearful John Atyeo, one of the club's most popular heroes. City pipped Mansfield for promotion by a goal average margin of 0.11, after Atyeo had scored their second goal seven minutes from the end of their final game against Oldham in front of an anxious crowd of 28,000. Atyeo, a powerful and adventurous forward, scored 350 goals in 645 League and Cup games during his 15 seasons with City. And when he won the first of his six caps in 1956 he became the first Bristol City player to represent England since Billy 'Fatty' Wedlock in 1914. A crowd of 16,000 attended Atyeo's testimonial match in 1966, and he retired at the age of 34 – with £4,000 and a gold watch – to become a schoolteacher.

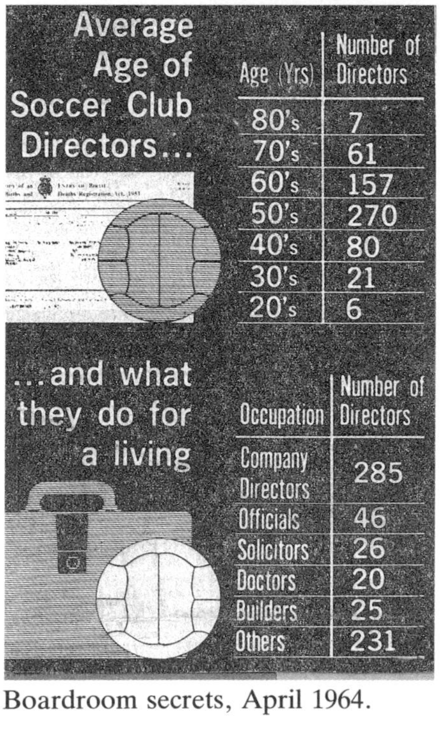

Average Age of Soccer Club Directors...

Age (Yrs)	Number of Directors
80's	7
70's	61
60's	157
50's	270
40's	80
30's	21
20's	6

...and what they do for a living

Occupation	Number of Directors
Company Directors	285
Officials	46
Solicitors	26
Doctors	20
Builders	25
Others	231

Boardroom secrets, April 1964.

Millionaire Spurs

Ground . . . £1,500,000
Players . . . £700,000
Gates . . . £355,100
Profit . . . £131,820

By ROY PESKETT

SPURS are the richest football club on earth. Last year they made a profit of £131,820 and cheerfully paid out income tax of £62,894 – £394 more than Ian Ure cost Arsenal.

Their balance sheet, issued today, shows that their fixed assets are £589,605—most of it, including the ground, at a 1906 valuation.

High finance, September 1963.

above Dave Mackay of Scotland breaks his left leg for the second time in nine months, September 1964. The Tottenham wing-half was making his come-back in a Football Combination game against Shrewsbury reserves at White Hart Lane. The referee beckoning for a stretcher is Peter Songhurst. Alan Mullery of England, one of Mackay's wing-half partners during his ten years with Spurs, said it was 'plain guts' which enabled him to return – and play on for another eight years. Mackay played for Hearts, Tottenham, Derby and Swindon between 1953–72 and won almost every honour available both sides of the border.

left First day cover. Substitutes were allowed for the first time in League football in season 1965–6 – and Bert Murray, Chelsea's first number twelve, wistfully watches his colleagues warm up against Burnley at Stamford Bridge on the opening Saturday of the season. But the man who had the distinction of being the League's first substitute was Keith Peacock of Charlton, playing at Bolton, in Division Two. Substitutes were allowed only for injured players that season; the following year they were permitted for any reason.

above Northampton Town – who moved from Division Four to Division One in five seasons (1960–1 to 1964–5) and then back to Division Four in the next four (1965–6 to 1968–9). Pictured before the start of their only season in Division One, 1965–6: Back row (l to r): Foley, Carr, Everitt, Bates, Kurila, Branston, Walton. Standing: J. Payne (trainer), Lines, Best, Leck, Barron, Linnell, Harvey, Machin, Cockcroft, Kiernan, R. Mills (assistant trainer). Sitting: Walden, Hall, Livesey, Hunt, D. Bowen (manager), Brown, Martin, Etheridge, Robson. Sitting: Howe, Fagar, Price, Bamforth.
right Programme for first home game in Division One.

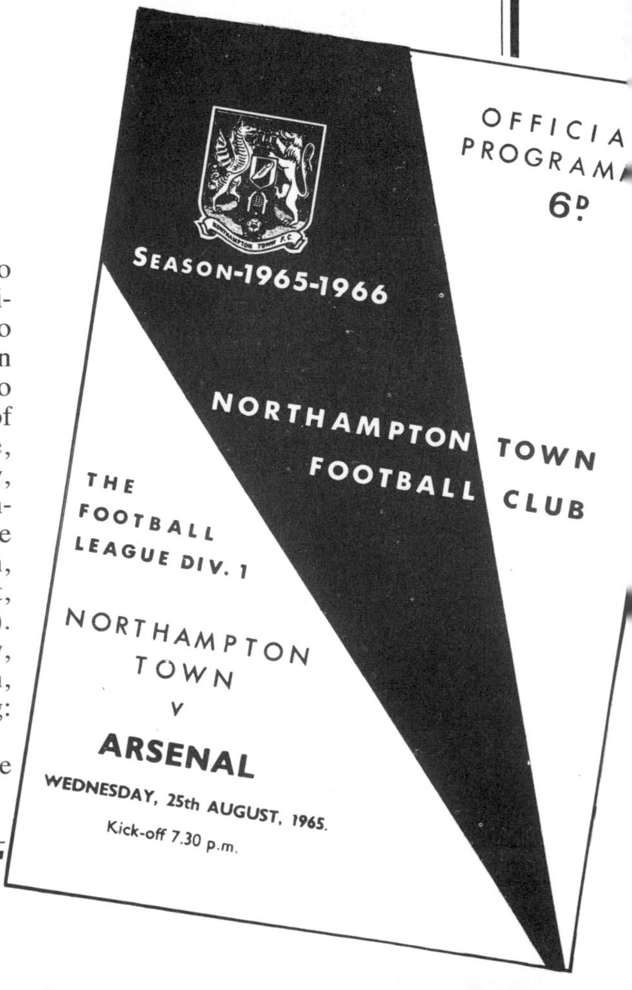

left Bobby Moore of West Ham, Fulham and England: 'The sleep of a labouring man is sweet'. *Ecclesiastes 5:12*. Moore was described by Pele as 'the finest defender in the world', and proved a matchless leader by example when English football's finest hours arrived in the 1966 World Cup Finals. Captain of club and country and a professional who knew his worth, he was a stylist who lent dignity to the simplest chore. He was never hurried or emotional and seemed to work in a dimension of his own choosing. A central defender who was always at his best against the best. He won 108 caps for England (1962–74) and played 668 League games: 544 for West Ham (1958–74) and 124 for Fulham (1974–7). He led West Ham to victory in the FA Cup in 1964 and the European Cup Winners' Cup in 1965 and, when he moved to Fulham, he played a key role in taking them to the 1975 FA Cup Final – against West Ham. Footballer of the Year 1964.

above Bobby Robson of Fulham (right) avoids a challenge from Manchester United's Bobby Charlton, Craven Cottage January 1966. Robson, a constructive and durable inside-forward or wing-half, scored 133 goals in 584 League games (for Fulham and West Bromwich, 1951–67) and won 20 caps for England. And, after a brief and uncertain period in charge at Fulham, Robson became one of the most consistent and stylish managers of his time. He managed Ipswich for 13 years (1969–82), guiding them to success in the FA Cup and UEFA Cup and to a top six place in the First Division on eight occasions (runners-up in 1981 and 1982); and, as national manager, he has since steered England to the quarter-finals of the 1986 World Cup in Mexico.

ZLA

left Roger Hunt of Liverpool, Bolton and England – strong and resourceful striker who helped Liverpool win the League championship twice and the FA Cup, and regular member of England's 1966 World Cup side. Scored 269 goals in 473 League games (1959–71) and won 34 caps for England (1962–9). Holder of two Liverpool records: most League goals – 245 between 1959–69; and most League goals in season – 41 (Second Division) in 1961–2. Confusing things for Hunt in the picture are Jimmy Gabriel (left) and Hugh Fisher of Southampton, 1967.

right Ivor Allchurch of Swansea, Newcastle, Cardiff and Wales – inside-forward of rare elegance and authority and one of the great heroes of Welsh football. He scored 251 goals in 692 League games (1949–1968) and won 68 caps (1951–66). Len Allchurch, Ivor's younger brother by four years, was a quick and elusive winger who played for Swansea, Sheffield United, Stockport County and Wales. Scored 108 goals in 596 League games (1951–70) and won eleven caps (1955–64).

above Martin Peters of West Ham (centre) versus Jimmy Greaves of Tottenham, 1967. They were involved in a straight exchange in 1970: Peters to Spurs, Greaves to West Ham. Peters, one of the England's World Cup winners in 1966, was a midfielder of stealth and high perception who was described by Alf Ramsey as 'a player ten years ahead of his time'. Greaves, dropped by Ramsey after playing in the early games in the 1966 finals, was one of the most prolific strikers in the history of English football, scoring 357 goals in 516 League games for Chelsea, Spurs and West Ham. Peters won 67 caps (1966–74) and Greaves scored 44 goals in 57 internationals (1959–67).

above The Class of '66: left to right – Jack Charlton, Nobby Stiles (with smile), Gordon Banks (half hidden), Alan Ball, Martin Peters, Geoff Hurst, Bobby Moore (with World Cup), Ray Wilson, George Cohen, Bobby Charlton.

right The 1966 World Cup Final has just been won by England – and, at a Government reception, Alf Ramsey, England's manager (left), talks with Denis Howell, Minister for Sport and experienced Football League referee, and Prime Minister Harold Wilson who was always happy to admit that he carried a picture of Huddersfield's famous 1920s side in his wallet. Subject of conversation? An argument, perhaps, about who was *really* responsible for England's victory.

above Dave Mackay (Spurs and Scotland) and Billy Bremner (Leeds and Scotland) in polite conversation on the opening day of the 1966–7 season. Terry Venables of England (left) and referee Norman Burtenshaw show concern for Bremner's health. Spurs finished third in Division One and won the FA Cup. Leeds finished fourth and reached the semi-finals of the Cup. The three players made almost 1,600 League appearances between them, won nearly every medal and honour possible and later became influential managers: Venables with Crystal Palace, Queen's Park Rangers and Barcelona (Spanish championship 1985); Mackay with Swindon and Derby (League championship 1975), and Bremner with Doncaster and Leeds.

above Sir Joseph Richards of Barnsley – president of the Football League 1957–66. Alan Hardaker, who was League secretary during his presidency, wrote of him: 'Joe Richards was a small, dapper man, a tough old bird who learnt the business of life in the Yorkshire coalfields. His only language was honest Yorkshire but he seemed able to make himself understood no matter what country he was in. The impression he left was always lasting and favourable.'

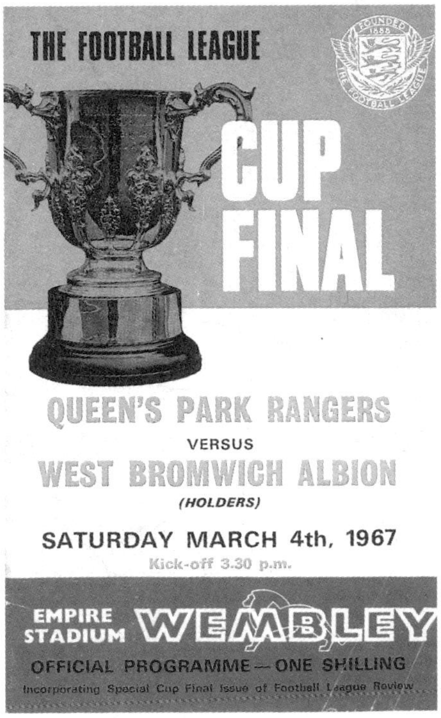
THE FOOTBALL LEAGUE
CUP
FINAL
QUEEN'S PARK RANGERS
VERSUS
WEST BROMWICH ALBION
(HOLDERS)
SATURDAY MARCH 4th, 1967
Kick-off 3.30 p.m.
EMPIRE STADIUM
WEMBLEY
OFFICIAL PROGRAMME—ONE SHILLING
Incorporating Special Cup Final Issue of Football League Review

above March 1967: the first League Cup Final to be held at Wembley.

Queen's Park Rangers of the Third Division score their third and winning goal against West Bromwich Albion in the first League Cup final to be played at Wembley, March 1967. West Bromwich, a Division One side, led by 2–0 at half-time . . . but during the interval Rangers' popular and experienced manager Alec Stock urged his players to 'take the war to them and show everybody what we can do'. The result was goals by Roger Morgan, Rodney Marsh and – wearing the number seven shirt – Mark Lazarus six minutes from the end. Marsh (number 10) is already saluting the Wembley crowd. 'Only in the delirium that followed England's World Cup triumph,' wrote one senior football reporter, 'has Wembley witnessed the kind of wild enthusiasm that climaxed this astonishing triumph by the little team from Loftus Road'. Alan Hardaker, the League secretary who first championed the idea of the tournament, said afterwards: 'My thanks go to Alec Stock and his outstanding team. In 45 minutes they launched the League Cup.' Rangers were the first Third Division club to play in a Wembley final, and they also completed a magnificent 'double' that season by winning the Third Division championship in royal style. They finished twelve points clear and scored 103 goals – 16 more than runners-up Middlesbrough and 42 more than third-placed Watford. Marsh finished as the season's leading scorer with 44 goals (30 League, 11 League Cup, three FA Cup). And the following season Rangers won promotion to Division One for the first time in their history.

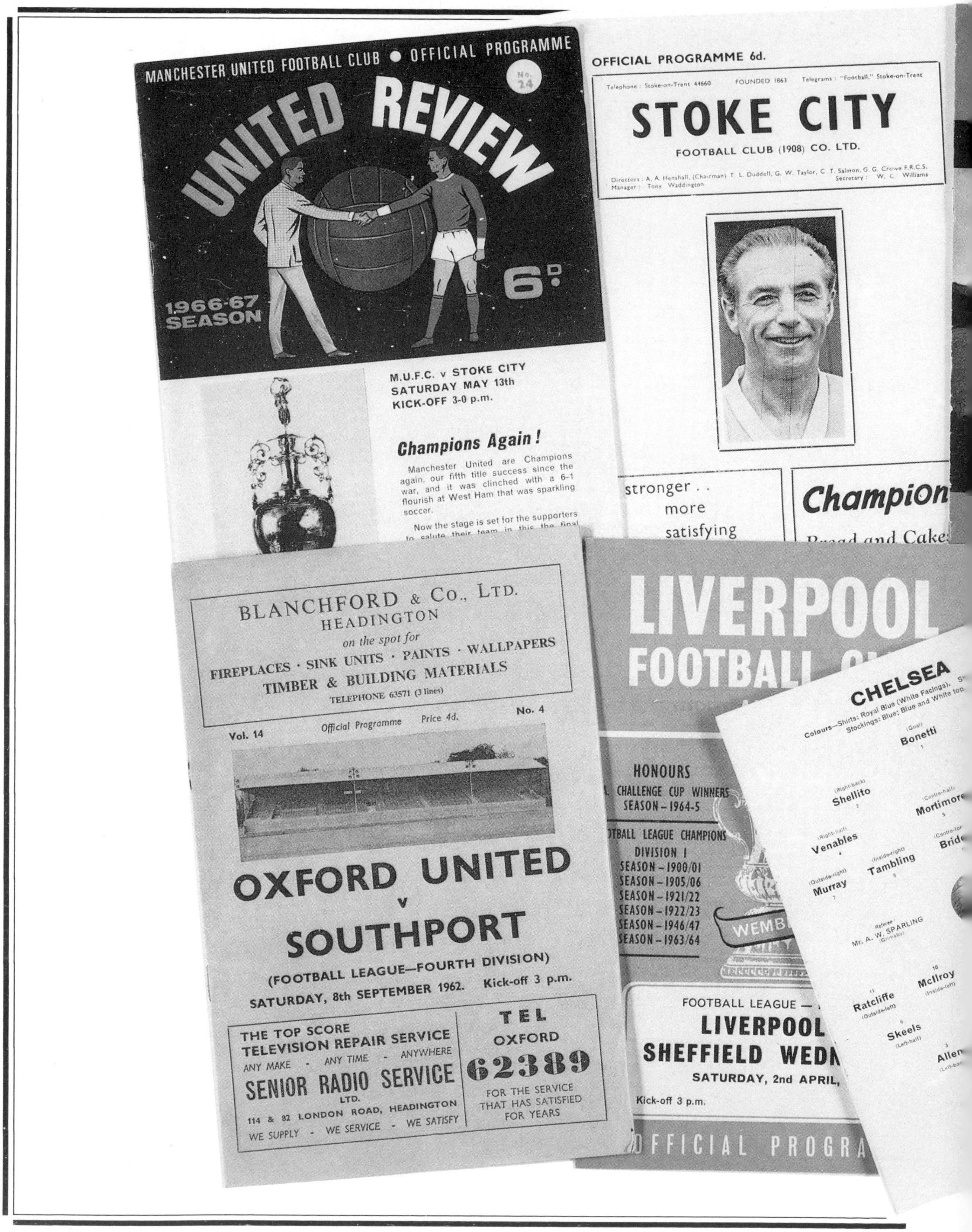
MANCHESTER UNITED FOOTBALL CLUB ● OFFICIAL PROGRAMME
No. 24
UNITED REVIEW
6D.
1966-67 SEASON
M.U.F.C. v STOKE CITY
SATURDAY MAY 13th
KICK-OFF 3-0 p.m.
Champions Again!
Manchester United are Champions again, our fifth title success since the war, and it was clinched with a 6–1 flourish at West Ham that was sparkling soccer.
Now the stage is set for the supporters
OFFICIAL PROGRAMME 6d.
Telephone: Stoke-on-Trent 44660
FOUNDED 1863
Telegrams: "Football," Stoke-on-Trent
STOKE CITY
FOOTBALL CLUB (1908) CO. LTD.
Directors: A. A. Henshall, (Chairman) T. L. Duddell, G. W. Taylor, C. T. Salmon, G. G. Crowe F.R.C.S.
Manager: Tony Waddington
Secretary: W. C. Williams
stronger . .
more
satisfying
BLANCHFORD & Co., LTD.
HEADINGTON
on the spot for
FIREPLACES · SINK UNITS · PAINTS · WALLPAPERS
TIMBER & BUILDING MATERIALS
TELEPHONE 63571 (3 lines)
Vol. 14
Official Programme
Price 4d.
No. 4
OXFORD UNITED
v
SOUTHPORT
(FOOTBALL LEAGUE—FOURTH DIVISION)
SATURDAY, 8th SEPTEMBER 1962.
Kick-off 3 p.m.
THE TOP SCORE
TELEVISION REPAIR SERVICE
ANY MAKE - ANY TIME - ANYWHERE
SENIOR RADIO SERVICE
LTD.
114 & 82 LONDON ROAD, HEADINGTON
WE SUPPLY - WE SERVICE - WE SATISFY
TEL
OXFORD
62389
FOR THE SERVICE THAT HAS SATISFIED FOR YEARS
LIVERPOOL
FOOTBALL
HONOURS
CHALLENGE CUP WINNERS
SEASON – 1964-5
DIVISION I
SEASON – 1900/01
SEASON – 1905/06
SEASON – 1921/22
SEASON – 1922/23
SEASON – 1946/47
SEASON – 1963/64
FOOTBALL LEAGUE —
LIVERPOOL
SHEFFIELD WEDN
SATURDAY, 2nd APRIL,
Kick-off 3 p.m.
CHELSEA
Colours—Shirts: Royal Blue (White Facings),
Stockings: Blue; Blue and White top
Bonetti
Shellito
Mortimore
Venables
Tambling
Murray
Referee:
Mr. A. W. SPARLING
McIlroy
Ratcliffe
Skeels

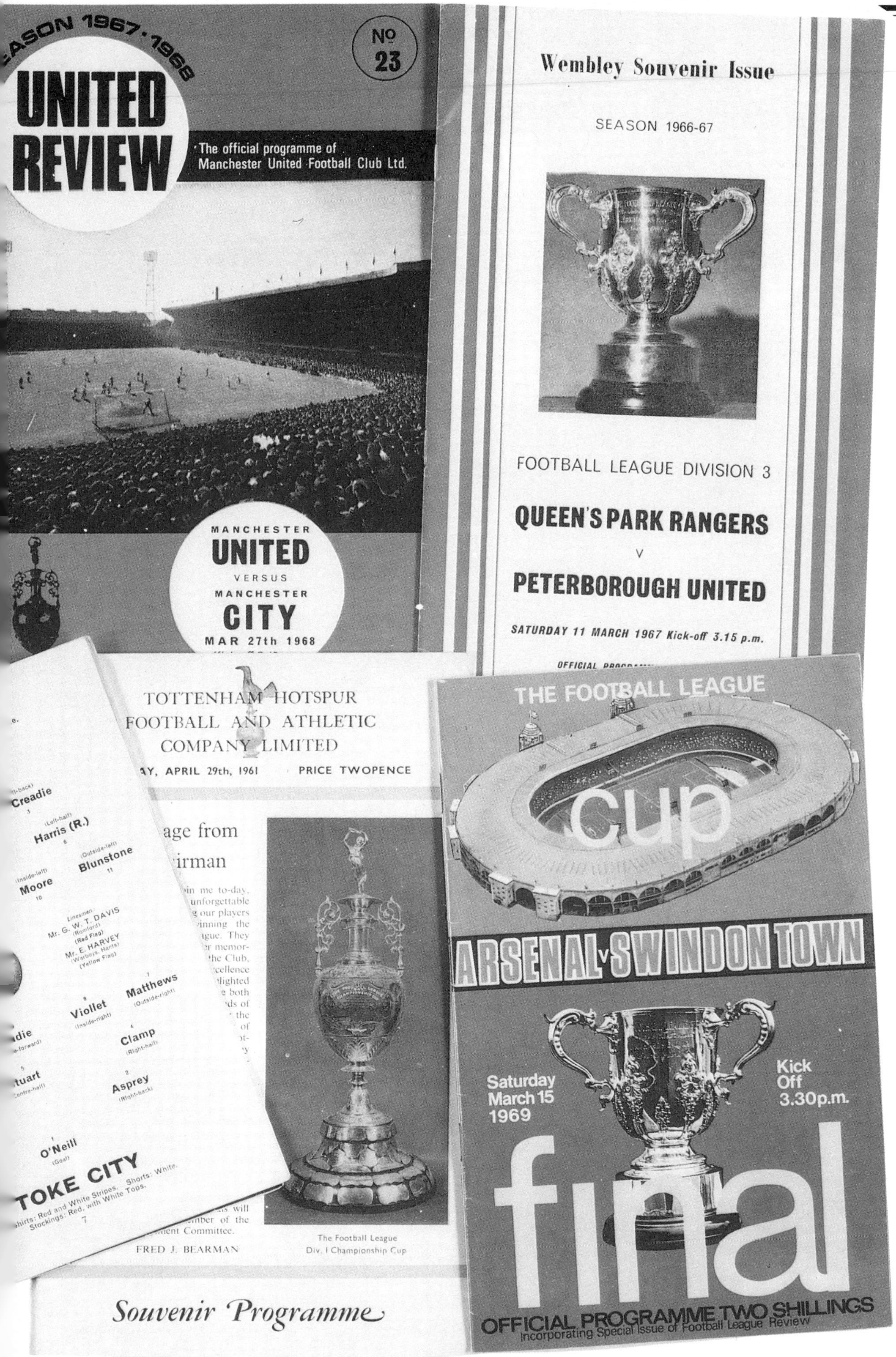
SEASON 1967-1968
No 23
UNITED REVIEW
The official programme of Manchester United Football Club Ltd.
MANCHESTER UNITED VERSUS MANCHESTER CITY
MAR 27th 1968
Wembley Souvenir Issue
SEASON 1966-67
FOOTBALL LEAGUE DIVISION 3
QUEEN'S PARK RANGERS
v
PETERBOROUGH UNITED
SATURDAY 11 MARCH 1967 Kick-off 3.15 p.m.
TOTTENHAM HOTSPUR
FOOTBALL AND ATHLETIC
COMPANY LIMITED
PRICE TWOPENCE
FRED J. BEARMAN
The Football League Div. I Championship Cup
Souvenir Programme
THE FOOTBALL LEAGUE
cup
ARSENAL v SWINDON TOWN
Saturday March 15 1969
Kick Off 3.30p.m.
final
OFFICIAL PROGRAMME TWO SHILLINGS
Incorporating Special Issue of Football League Review

above Denis Law of Huddersfield Town, Manchester City, Torino, Manchester United, Manchester City again and Scotland – known at Old Trafford as 'The King'. Forward of arrestingly distinctive talent and style. Influential, daring, volatile and, according to Bill Shankly, his first manager at Huddersfield, sometimes 'a bloody terror – with ability'. Won two League championship medals (1964–5 and 1966–7) and FA Cup winners' medal (1963) with Manchester United, and was voted European Footballer of the Year in 1964. Scored 217 goals in 452 League games (171 in 305 for United) between 1957–74. Fifty-five caps for Scotland.

below Malcolm Allison (left) and Joe Mercer – a partnership which transformed Manchester City in the 1960s. They came together just before the start of the 1965–6 season: Mercer, a football man of infinite experience, wise, discerning, popular, a distinguished figurehead . . . Allison, a former West Ham player (320 League and Cup games) and manager of Plymouth, a brilliant coach, imaginative, outspoken, sometimes outrageous. The chemistry was perfect. Manchester City immediately won the Second Division championship – and followed with the League championship in 1968 (Manchester United were runners-up), the FA Cup in 1969 and the League Cup and European Cup Winners' Cup in 1970. And City's football was attractive as well as successful. The partnership soured, however, and Mercer left in August 1972. Allison took over but resigned only eight months later. Things were never quite as good again – for City or the two men.

above Graeme Souness in his Middlesbrough days (1973–78). Ahead of him were seven years of success and high acclaim with Liverpool who made him their captain; an enriching spell with Sampdoria in Italy, and the player-managership of Glasgow Rangers who, in his first season (1986–7), won their first Scottish League championship for nine years. Souness, an inventive and resilient midfield player, won more than 50 caps for Scotland.

right Brian Clough (right) and Peter Taylor – one of the most successful partnerships in League history. They led Derby County (1972) and Nottingham Forest (1978) to the League championship; and also managed Forest to two triumphs in the European Cup (1979 and 1980) and two in the League Cup (1978 and 1979).

left Tottenham programmes: penny sheet to colour magazine . . . all part of the changing face of football. Programme collecting is now one of the most popular hobbies in the country with pre-war examples keenly sought. Among the rarest is the programme for the first FA Cup Final at Wembley in 1923 which, in mint condition, can fetch as much as £200. Pre-war League programmes sell for up to £30. Programme fairs are held all over the country but the condition of items is always important: no creases, tears, writing or rusty staples. The price of new League programmes has also risen, from one penny to 60p, 80p and even £1. And the advertising they carry earns important revenue.

right Terry Venables – the first player to appear for a home country at five different levels. He was a school, youth, amateur, under-23 and full international for England. Venables, a wing-half or inside-forward of style and authority, played for Chelsea, Tottenham, Queen's Park Rangers and Crystal Palace (1959–75) and later managed Crystal Palace, Queen's Park Rangers and Barcelona.

below Rochdale play Cambridge in Division Three in front of a crowd of 450 at Spotland, February 1974 – considered to be the lowest gate for a normal League match. The game was played on a Tuesday afternoon because of power cuts.

left 'How are the runner beans coming on?' Joe Mercer and Bill Shankly at Anfield.

below Bob Paisley – 'whose eyes seemed to miss nothing' – the most successful manager in the history of English football. He led the Anfield club to victory in six League championships, three League Cups, three European Cups, one UEFA Cup and five Charity Shields. Left of picture: John Smith, the chairman of Liverpool, a man of vision and authority, and a major figure in the club's success.

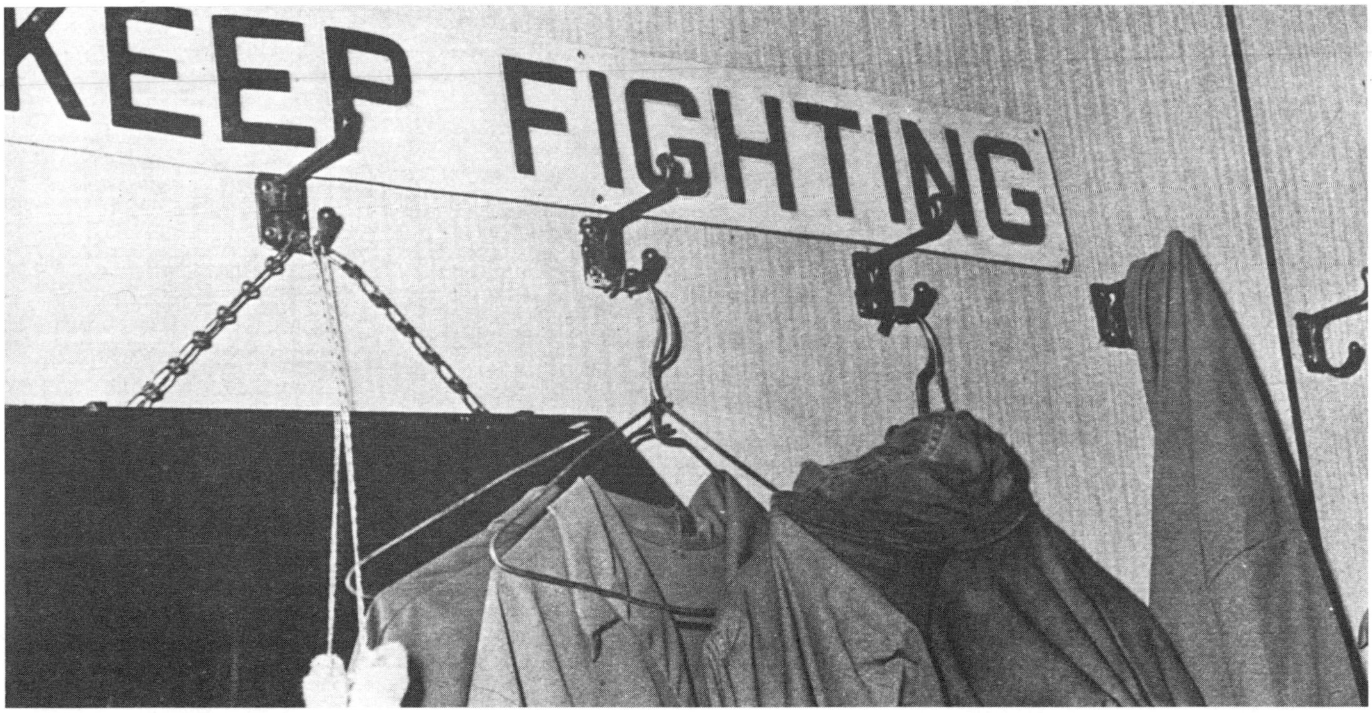

above Sport . . . or war? Leeds dressing room, 1969.

left Archie Gemmill of St Mirren, Preston, Derby, Nottingham Forest, Birmingham and Scotland – defying gravity after scoring for Preston against Leicester, 1969. Gemmill, a small but effervescent midfield player who won two League championship medals with Derby, another with Nottingham Forest and also two European Cup Winners' Cup medals. Forty-three caps for Scotland (1971–81).

overleaf Swindon Town of the Third Division on their way to beating Arsenal 3–1 in the 1969 League Cup final in the mud of Wembley. Centre three (l to r): Stan Harland (Swindon), Bobby Gould (Arsenal) and, on ground, Rod Thomas (Swindon). Between them they played around 1,300 League games for 16 different clubs. Thomas also won 50 caps for Wales.

Faces of loyalty: John Trollope (*below*) who made 770 League appearances for Swindon between 1960–80 – a record number of League appearances for one club; and Roy Sproson (*right*) who played 762 League games for Port Vale between 1950–72. Trollope was a full-back and Sproson played left-half.

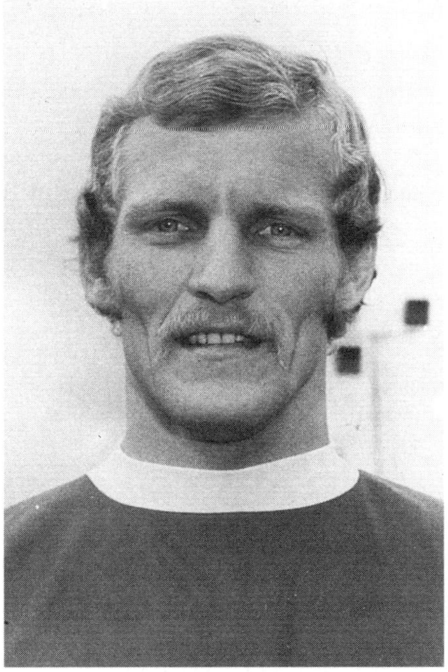

left George Best – who Matt Busby described as 'the most gifted player I have ever seen – and unique in the *number* of his gifts'. Considered by many others to be the most talented British player since World War Two. Best, a winger by trade, was only 17 years and four months old in 1963 when he played his first Division One game for Manchester United, for whom he scored 137 goals in 361 League games. Winners' medals: two League championship, one European Cup. English and European Footballer of the Year in 1968. Thirty-seven caps for Northern Ireland (1964–78).

right George Best again – professional footballer, dedicated playboy and celebrated public figure – enjoying champagne and Majorcan sunshine with actress Susan George in June, 1969. Best was eventually given a free transfer by Manchester United and, throughout his career, provoked every kind of reaction except indifference. He later played for Stockport and Fulham followed by football of a gentler kind in America.

above Dreams can come true, 1969. Huddersfield heard that the dearest wish of 19-year-old David Tagg, who had been bed-ridden for eight years, was to watch them play at Leeds Road. So they sent a removal van to his hospital and transferred David and his bed to a prime spot beside the pitch. Huddersfield beat Blackpool 2–0.

left New star . . . new hope . . . new autograph. January, 1970: Peter Marinello, just signed by Arsenal from Hibernian for £100,000, is given the full Highbury treatment. Marinello, a trendy figure and a Scottish Under-23 winger, was hailed as a new George Best. But he soon moved on to Portsmouth, then Motherwell and Fulham and, altogether, scored eleven goals in 149 League games.

above The closest League grounds, August 1969: centre, the City Ground (Nottingham Forest) and, on the other side of the River Trent, Meadow Lane (Notts County). They are less than 400 yards apart. Notts County (formed 1862) are the League's oldest club; and Forest (1865) are the third oldest. And both previously played at the Trent Bridge cricket ground, bottom left: Forest 1880–2, County 1883–1910.

left David Webb of Orient, Southampton, Chelsea, Queen's Park Rangers, Leicester, Derby, Bournemouth and Torquay – a dreadnought defender who played more than 500 League games for eight clubs, but is best remembered for the goal in extra-time which enabled Chelsea to beat Leeds in the replay of the 1970 FA Cup Final at Old Trafford.

below left Penalty area, circa 1970. Left to right: Dave Webb (Chelsea), Alex Stepney (Manchester United, formerly Chelsea), Francis Burns (United), John Dempsey (Chelsea) and, above, Denis Law (United). Chelsea finished third in Division One in 1969–70 – and won the FA Cup.

right Derek Dougan – 'The Doog' – of Portsmouth, Blackburn, Aston Villa, Peterborough, Leicester, Wolves and Northern Ireland: a centre-foward who knew all the angles, a compound of ability, showmanship and resolution and one of the most acclaimed and controversial players of the 1960s. Pictured playing his 546th and last League game: Molineux, April 1975. Right to the end he skilfully avoided tackles, this one by Terry Yorath of Leeds. Dougan was 6 ft 2 ins tall, a master in the air, a craftsman who was an expert at exploiting weaknesses and the first Irishman to score 200 League goals. He was a complex character: an extrovert, a rebel and even a clown when he was in the mood- . . . but he was also a thinker, an innovator, a worker for charity and an author and broadcaster. He became long-serving chairman of the Professional Footballers' Association – committed to full freedom of contract for players – and in 1982 he was instrumental in saving his old club Wolves from extinction. He found the money and support the ailing club needed to survive (with, literally, only minutes to spare), took over as chairman and chief executive, selected a new back-up team – and Wolves immediately won promotion to Division One (1983). 'I think,' he once said, 'I could put the country right – but then there are 50 million others who think they could do the same.' Dougan won 43 caps for Northern Ireland (1958–73).

LEAGUE TABLES

1961–62

FIRST DIVISION

	P	W	D	L	F	A	Pts
1 Ipswich	42	24	8	10	93	67	56
2 Burnley	42	21	11	10	101	67	53
3 Tottenham	42	21	10	11	88	69	52
4 Everton	42	20	11	11	88	54	51
5 Sheff United	42	19	9	14	61	69	47
6 Sheff Wed	42	20	6	16	72	58	46
7 Aston Villa	42	18	8	16	65	56	44
8 West Ham	42	17	10	15	76	82	44
9 WBA	42	15	13	14	83	67	43
10 Arsenal	42	16	11	15	71	72	43
11 Bolton	42	16	10	16	62	66	42
12 Man City	42	17	7	18	78	81	41
13 Blackpool	42	15	11	16	70	75	41
14 Leicester	42	17	6	19	72	71	40
15 Man United	42	15	9	18	72	75	39
16 Blackburn	42	14	11	17	50	58	39
17 Birmingham	42	14	10	18	65	81	38
18 Wolves	42	13	10	19	73	86	36
19 Nottm Forest	42	13	10	19	63	79	36
20 Fulham	42	13	7	22	66	74	33
21 Cardiff	42	9	14	19	50	81	32
22 Chelsea	42	9	10	23	63	94	28

SECOND DIVISION

	P	W	D	L	F	A	Pts
1 Liverpool	42	27	8	7	99	43	62
2 Leyton Orient	42	22	10	10	69	40	54
3 Sunderland	42	22	9	11	85	50	53
4 Scunthorpe	42	21	7	14	86	71	49
5 Plymouth	42	19	8	15	75	75	46
6 Southampton	42	18	9	15	77	62	45
7 Huddersfield	42	16	12	14	67	59	44
8 Stoke	42	17	8	17	55	57	42
9 Rotherham	42	16	9	17	70	76	41
10 Preston	42	15	10	17	55	57	40
11 Newcastle	42	15	9	18	64	58	39
12 Middlesbrough	42	16	7	19	76	72	39
13 Luton	42	17	5	20	69	71	39
14 Walsall	42	14	11	17	70	75	39
15 Charlton	42	15	9	18	69	75	39
16 Derby	42	14	11	17	68	75	39
17 Norwich	42	14	11	17	61	70	39
18 Bury	42	17	5	20	52	76	39
19 Leeds	42	12	12	18	50	61	36
20 Swansea	42	12	12	18	61	83	36
21 Bristol Rovers	42	13	7	22	53	81	33
22 Brighton	42	10	11	21	42	86	31

THIRD DIVISION

	P	W	D	L	F	A	Pts
1 Portsmouth	46	27	11	8	87	47	65
2 Grimsby	46	28	6	12	80	56	62
3 Bournemouth	46	21	17	8	69	45	59
4 QPR	46	24	11	11	111	73	59
5 Peterborough	46	26	6	14	107	82	58
6 Bristol City	46	23	8	15	94	72	54
7 Reading	46	22	9	15	77	66	53
8 Northampton	46	20	11	15	85	57	51
9 Swindon	46	17	15	14	78	71	49
10 Hull	46	20	8	18	67	54	48
11 Bradford PA	46	20	7	19	80	78	47
12 Port Vale	46	17	11	18	65	58	45
13 Notts County	46	17	9	20	67	74	43
14 Coventry	46	16	11	19	64	71	43
15 Crystal Palace	46	14	14	18	83	80	42
16 Southend	46	13	16	17	57	69	42
17 Watford	46	14	13	19	63	74	41
18 Halifax	46	15	10	21	62	84	40
19 Shrewsbury	46	13	12	21	73	84	38
20 Barnsley	46	13	12	21	71	95	38
21 Torquay	46	15	6	25	76	100	36
22 Lincoln	46	9	17	20	57	87	35
23 Brentford	46	13	8	25	53	93	34
24 Newport	46	7	8	31	46	102	22

FOURTH DIVISION

	P	W	D	L	F	A	Pts
1 Millwall	44	23	10	11	87	62	56
2 Colchester	44	23	9	12	104	71	55
3 Wrexham	44	22	9	13	96	56	53
4 Carlisle	44	22	8	14	64	63	52
5 Bradford City	44	21	9	14	94	86	51
6 York	44	20	10	14	84	53	50
7 Aldershot	44	22	5	17	81	60	49
8 Workington	44	19	11	14	69	70	49
9 Barrow	44	17	14	13	74	58	48
10 Crewe	44	20	6	18	79	70	46
11 Oldham	44	17	12	15	77	70	46
12 Rochdale	44	19	7	18	71	71	45
13 Darlington	44	18	9	17	61	73	45
14 Mansfield	44	19	6	19	77	66	44
15 Tranmere	44	20	4	20	70	81	44
16 Stockport	44	17	9	18	70	69	43
17 Southport	44	17	9	18	61	71	43
18 Exeter	44	13	11	20	62	77	37
19 Chesterfield	44	14	9	21	70	87	37
20 Gillingham	44	13	11	20	73	94	37
21 Doncaster	44	11	7	26	60	85	29
22 Hartlepools	44	8	11	25	52	101	27
23 Chester	44	7	12	25	54	96	26

24 Accrington Stanley resigned from the League

1962–63

FIRST DIVISION

	P	W	D	L	F	A	Pts
1 Everton	42	25	11	6	84	42	61
2 Tottenham	42	23	9	10	111	62	55
3 Burnley	42	22	10	10	78	57	54
4 Leicester	42	20	12	10	79	53	52
5 Wolves	42	20	10	12	93	65	50
6 Sheff Wed	42	19	10	13	77	63	48
7 Arsenal	42	18	10	14	86	77	46
8 Liverpool	42	17	10	15	71	59	44
9 Nottm Forest	42	17	10	15	67	69	44
10 Sheff United	42	16	12	14	58	60	44
11 Blackburn	42	15	12	15	79	71	42
12 West Ham	42	14	12	16	73	69	40
13 Blackpool	42	13	14	15	58	64	40
14 WBA	42	16	7	19	71	79	39
15 Aston Villa	42	15	8	19	62	68	38
16 Fulham	42	14	10	18	50	71	38
17 Ipswich	42	12	11	19	59	78	35
18 Bolton	42	15	5	22	55	75	35
19 Man United	42	12	10	20	67	81	34
20 Birmingham	42	10	13	19	63	90	33
21 Man City	42	10	11	21	58	102	31
22 Leyton Orient	42	6	9	27	37	81	21

SECOND DIVISION

	P	W	D	L	F	A	Pts
1 Stoke	42	20	13	9	73	50	53
2 Chelsea	42	24	4	14	81	42	52
3 Sunderland	42	20	12	10	84	55	52
4 Middlesbrough	42	20	9	13	86	85	49
5 Leeds	42	19	10	13	79	53	48
6 Huddersfield	42	17	14	11	63	50	48
7 Newcastle	42	18	11	13	79	59	47
8 Bury	42	18	11	13	51	47	47
9 Scunthorpe	42	16	12	14	57	59	44
10 Cardiff	42	18	7	17	83	73	43
11 Southampton	42	17	8	17	72	67	42
12 Plymouth	42	15	12	15	76	73	42
13 Norwich	42	17	8	17	80	79	42
14 Rotherham	42	17	6	19	67	74	40
15 Swansea	42	15	9	18	51	72	39
16 Portsmouth	42	13	11	18	63	79	37
17 Preston	42	13	11	18	59	74	37
18 Derby	42	12	12	18	61	72	36
19 Grimsby	42	11	13	18	55	66	35
20 Charlton	42	13	5	24	62	94	31
21 Walsall	42	11	9	22	53	89	31
22 Luton	42	11	7	24	61	84	29

THIRD DIVISION

		P	W	D	L	F	A	Pts
1	Northampton	46	26	10	10	109	60	62
2	Swindon	46	22	14	10	87	56	58
3	Port Vale	46	23	8	15	72	58	54
4	Coventry	46	18	17	11	83	69	53
5	Bournemouth	46	18	16	12	63	46	52
6	Peterborough	46	20	11	15	93	75	51
7	Notts County	46	19	13	14	73	74	51
8	Southend	46	19	12	15	75	77	50
9	Wrexham	46	20	9	17	84	83	49
10	Hull	46	19	10	17	74	69	48
11	Crystal Palace	46	17	13	16	68	58	47
12	Colchester	46	18	11	17	73	93	47
13	QPR	46	17	11	18	85	76	45
14	Bristol City	46	16	13	17	100	92	45
15	Shrewsbury	46	16	12	18	83	81	44
16	Millwall	46	15	13	18	82	87	43
17	Watford	46	17	8	21	82	85	42
18	Barnsley	46	15	11	20	63	74	41
19	Bristol Rovers	46	15	11	20	70	88	41
20	Reading	46	16	8	22	74	78	40
21	Bradford PA	46	14	12	20	79	97	40
22	Brighton	46	12	12	22	58	84	36
23	Carlisle	46	13	9	24	61	89	35
24	Halifax	46	9	12	25	64	106	30

FOURTH DIVISION

		P	W	D	L	F	A	Pts
1	Brentford	46	27	8	11	98	64	62
2	Oldham	46	24	11	11	95	60	59
3	Crewe	46	24	11	11	86	58	59
4	Mansfield	46	24	9	13	108	69	57
5	Gillingham	46	22	13	11	71	49	57
6	Torquay	46	20	16	10	75	56	56
7	Rochdale	46	20	11	15	67	59	51
8	Tranmere	46	20	10	16	81	67	50
9	Barrow	46	19	12	15	82	80	50
10	Workington	46	17	13	16	76	68	47
11	Aldershot	46	15	17	14	73	69	47
12	Darlington	46	19	6	21	72	87	44
13	Southport	46	15	14	17	72	106	44
14	York	46	16	11	19	67	62	43
15	Chesterfield	46	13	16	17	70	64	42
16	Doncaster	46	14	14	18	64	77	42
17	Exeter	46	16	10	20	57	77	42
18	Oxford	46	13	15	18	70	71	41
19	Stockport	46	15	11	20	56	70	41
20	Newport	46	14	11	21	76	90	39
21	Chester	46	15	9	22	51	66	39
22	Lincoln	46	13	9	24	68	89	35
23	Bradford City	46	11	10	25	64	93	32
24	Hartlepools	46	7	11	28	56	104	25

1963–64

FIRST DIVISION

		P	W	D	L	F	A	Pts
1	Liverpool	42	26	5	11	92	45	57
2	Man United	42	23	7	12	90	62	53
3	Everton	42	21	10	11	84	64	52
4	Tottenham	42	22	7	13	97	81	51
5	Chelsea	42	20	10	12	72	56	50
6	Sheff Wed	42	19	11	12	84	67	49
7	Blackburn	42	18	10	14	89	65	46
8	Arsenal	42	17	11	14	90	82	45
9	Burnley	42	17	10	15	71	64	44
10	WBA	42	16	11	15	70	61	43
11	Leicester	42	16	11	15	61	58	43
12	Sheff United	42	16	11	15	61	64	43
13	Nottm Forest	42	16	9	17	64	68	41
14	West Ham	42	14	12	16	69	74	40
15	Fulham	42	13	13	16	58	65	39
16	Wolves	42	12	15	15	70	80	39
17	Stoke	42	14	10	18	77	78	38
18	Blackpool	42	13	9	20	52	73	35
19	Aston Villa	42	11	12	19	62	71	34
20	Birmingham	42	11	7	24	54	92	29
21	Bolton	42	10	8	24	48	80	28
22	Ipswich	42	9	7	26	56	121	25

SECOND DIVISION

		P	W	D	L	F	A	Pts
1	Leeds	42	24	15	3	71	34	63
2	Sunderland	42	25	11	6	81	37	61
3	Preston	42	23	10	9	79	54	56
4	Charlton	42	19	10	13	76	70	48
5	Southampton	42	19	9	14	100	73	47
6	Man City	42	18	10	14	84	66	46
7	Rotherham	42	19	7	16	90	78	45
8	Newcastle	42	20	5	17	74	69	45
9	Portsmouth	42	16	11	15	79	70	43
10	Middlesbrough	42	15	11	16	67	52	41
11	Northampton	42	16	9	17	58	60	41
12	Huddersfield	42	15	10	17	57	64	40
13	Derby	42	14	11	17	56	67	39
14	Swindon	42	14	10	18	57	69	38
15	Cardiff	42	14	10	18	56	81	38
16	Leyton Orient	42	13	10	19	54	72	36
17	Norwich	42	11	13	18	64	80	35
18	Bury	42	13	9	20	57	73	35
19	Swansea	42	12	9	21	63	74	33
20	Plymouth	42	8	16	18	45	67	32
21	Grimsby	42	9	14	19	47	75	32
22	Scunthorpe	42	10	10	22	52	82	30

THIRD DIVISION

		P	W	D	L	F	A	Pts
1	Coventry	46	22	16	8	98	61	60
2	Crystal Palace	46	23	14	9	73	51	60
3	Watford	46	23	12	11	79	59	58
4	Bournemouth	46	24	8	14	79	58	56
5	Bristol City	46	20	15	11	84	64	55
6	Reading	46	21	10	15	79	62	52
7	Mansfield	46	20	11	15	76	62	51
8	Hull	46	16	17	13	73	68	49
9	Oldham	46	20	8	18	73	70	48
10	Peterborough	46	18	11	17	75	70	47
11	Shrewsbury	46	18	11	17	73	80	47
12	Bristol Rovers	46	19	8	19	91	79	46
13	Port Vale	46	16	14	16	53	49	46
14	Southend	46	15	15	16	77	78	45
15	QPR	46	18	9	19	76	78	45
16	Brentford	46	15	14	17	87	80	44
17	Colchester	46	12	19	15	70	68	43
18	Luton	46	16	10	20	64	80	42
19	Walsall	46	13	14	19	59	76	40
20	Barnsley	46	12	15	19	68	94	39
21	Millwall	46	14	10	22	53	67	38
22	Crewe	46	11	12	23	50	77	34
23	Wrexham	46	13	6	27	75	107	32
24	Notts County	46	9	9	28	45	92	27

FOURTH DIVISION

		P	W	D	L	F	A	Pts
1	Gillingham	46	23	14	9	59	30	60
2	Carlisle	46	25	10	11	113	58	60
3	Workington	46	24	11	11	76	52	59
4	Exeter	46	20	18	8	62	37	58
5	Bradford City	46	25	6	15	76	62	56
6	Torquay	46	20	11	15	80	54	51
7	Tranmere	46	20	11	15	85	73	51
8	Brighton	46	19	12	15	71	52	50
9	Aldershot	46	19	10	17	83	78	48
10	Halifax	46	17	14	15	77	77	48
11	Lincoln	46	19	9	18	67	75	47
12	Chester	46	19	8	19	65	60	46
13	Bradford PA	46	18	9	19	75	81	45
14	Doncaster	46	15	12	19	70	75	42
15	Newport	46	17	8	21	64	73	42
16	Chesterfield	46	15	12	19	57	71	42
17	Stockport	46	15	12	19	50	68	42
18	Oxford	46	14	13	19	59	63	41
19	Darlington	46	14	12	20	66	93	40
20	Rochdale	46	12	15	19	56	59	39
21	Southport	46	15	9	22	63	88	39
22	York	46	14	7	25	52	66	35
23	Hartlepools	46	12	9	25	54	93	33
24	Barrow	46	6	18	22	51	93	30

1964–65

FIRST DIVISION

		P	W	D	L	F	A	Pts
1	Man United	42	26	9	7	89	39	61
2	Leeds	42	26	9	7	83	52	61
3	Chelsea	42	24	8	10	89	54	56
4	Everton	42	17	15	10	69	60	49
5	Nottm Forest	42	17	13	12	71	67	47
6	Tottenham	42	19	7	16	87	71	45
7	Liverpool	42	17	10	15	67	73	44
8	Sheff Wed	42	16	11	15	57	55	43
9	West Ham	42	19	4	19	82	71	42
10	Blackburn	42	16	10	16	83	79	42
11	Stoke	42	16	10	16	67	66	42
12	Burnley	42	16	10	16	70	70	42
13	Arsenal	42	17	7	18	69	75	41
14	WBA	42	13	13	16	70	65	39
15	Sunderland	42	14	9	19	64	74	37
16	Aston Villa	42	16	5	21	57	82	37
17	Blackpool	42	12	11	19	67	78	35
18	Leicester	42	11	13	18	69	85	35
19	Sheff United	42	12	11	19	50	64	35
20	Fulham	42	11	12	19	60	78	34
21	Wolves	42	13	4	25	59	89	30
22	Birmingham	42	8	11	23	64	96	27

SECOND DIVISION

		P	W	D	L	F	A	Pts
1	Newcastle	42	24	9	9	81	45	57
2	Northampton	42	20	16	6	66	50	56
3	Bolton	42	20	10	12	80	58	50
4	Southampton	42	17	14	11	83	63	48
5	Ipswich	42	15	17	10	74	67	47
6	Norwich	42	20	7	15	61	57	47
7	Crystal Palace	42	16	13	13	55	51	45
8	Huddersfield	42	17	10	15	53	51	44
9	Derby	42	16	11	15	84	79	43
10	Coventry	42	17	9	16	72	70	43
11	Man City	42	16	9	17	63	62	41
12	Preston	42	14	13	15	76	81	41
13	Cardiff	42	13	14	15	64	57	40
14	Rotherham	42	14	12	16	70	69	40
15	Plymouth	42	16	8	18	63	79	40
16	Bury	42	14	10	18	60	66	38
17	Middlesbrough	42	13	9	20	70	76	35
18	Charlton	42	13	9	20	64	75	35
19	Leyton Orient	42	12	11	19	50	72	35
20	Portsmouth	42	12	10	20	56	77	34
21	Swindon	42	14	5	23	63	81	33
22	Swansea	42	11	10	21	62	84	32

THIRD DIVISION

		P	W	D	L	F	A	Pts
1	Carlisle	46	25	10	11	76	53	60
2	Bristol City	46	24	11	11	92	55	59
3	Mansfield	46	24	11	11	95	61	59
4	Hull	46	23	12	11	91	57	58
5	Brentford	46	24	9	13	83	55	57
6	Bristol Rovers	46	20	15	11	82	58	55
7	Gillingham	46	23	9	14	70	50	55
8	Peterborough	46	22	7	17	85	74	51
9	Watford	46	17	16	13	71	64	50
10	Grimsby	46	16	17	13	68	67	49
11	Bournemouth	46	18	11	17	72	63	47
12	Southend	46	19	8	19	78	71	46
13	Reading	46	16	14	16	70	70	46
14	QPR	46	17	12	17	72	80	46
15	Workington	46	17	12	17	58	69	46
16	Shrewsbury	46	15	12	19	76	84	42
17	Exeter	46	12	17	17	51	52	41
18	Scunthorpe	46	14	12	20	65	72	40
19	Walsall	46	15	7	24	55	80	37
20	Oldham	46	13	10	23	61	83	36
21	Luton	46	11	11	24	51	94	33
22	Port Vale	46	9	14	23	41	76	32
23	Colchester	46	10	10	26	50	89	30
24	Barnsley	46	9	11	26	54	90	29

FOURTH DIVISION

		P	W	D	L	F	A	Pts
1	Brighton	46	26	11	9	102	57	63
2	Millwall	46	23	16	7	78	45	62
3	York	46	28	6	12	91	56	62
4	Oxford	46	23	15	8	87	44	61
5	Tranmere	46	27	6	13	99	56	60
6	Rochdale	46	22	14	10	74	53	58
7	Bradford PA	46	20	17	9	86	62	57
8	Chester	46	25	6	15	119	81	56
9	Doncaster	46	20	11	15	84	72	51
10	Crewe	46	18	13	15	90	81	49
11	Torquay	46	21	7	18	70	70	49
12	Chesterfield	46	20	8	18	58	70	48
13	Notts County	46	15	14	17	61	73	44
14	Wrexham	46	17	9	20	84	92	43
15	Hartlepools	46	15	13	18	61	85	43
16	Newport	46	17	8	21	85	81	42
17	Darlington	46	18	6	22	84	87	42
18	Aldershot	46	15	7	24	64	84	37
19	Bradford City	46	12	8	26	70	88	32
20	Southport	46	8	16	22	58	89	32
21	Barrow	46	12	6	28	59	105	30
22	Lincoln	46	11	6	29	58	99	28
23	Halifax	46	11	6	29	54	103	28
24	Stockport	46	10	7	29	44	87	27

1965–66

FIRST DIVISION

		P	W	D	L	F	A	Pts
1	Liverpool	42	26	9	7	79	34	61
2	Leeds	42	23	9	10	79	38	55
3	Burnley	42	24	7	11	79	47	55
4	Man United	42	18	15	9	84	59	51
5	Chelsea	42	22	7	13	65	53	51
6	WBA	42	19	12	11	91	69	50
7	Leicester	42	21	7	14	80	65	49
8	Tottenham	42	16	12	14	75	66	44
9	Sheff United	42	16	11	15	56	59	43
10	Stoke	42	15	12	15	65	64	42
11	Everton	42	15	11	16	56	62	41
12	West Ham	42	15	9	18	70	83	39
13	Blackpool	42	14	9	19	55	65	37
14	Arsenal	42	12	13	17	62	75	37
15	Newcastle	42	14	9	19	50	63	37
16	Aston Villa	42	15	6	21	69	80	36
17	Sheff Wed	42	14	8	20	56	66	36
18	Nottm Forest	42	14	8	20	56	72	36
19	Sunderland	42	14	8	20	51	72	36
20	Fulham	42	14	7	21	67	85	35
21	Northampton	42	10	13	19	55	92	33
22	Blackburn	42	8	4	30	57	88	20

SECOND DIVISION

		P	W	D	L	F	A	Pts
1	Man City	42	22	15	5	76	44	59
2	Southampton	42	22	10	10	85	56	54
3	Coventry	42	20	13	9	73	53	53
4	Huddersfield	42	19	13	10	62	36	51
5	Bristol City	42	17	17	8	63	48	51
6	Wolves	42	20	10	12	87	61	50
7	Rotherham	42	16	14	12	75	74	46
8	Derby	42	16	11	15	71	68	43
9	Bolton	42	16	9	17	62	59	41
10	Birmingham	42	16	9	17	70	75	41
11	Crystal Palace	42	14	13	15	47	52	41
12	Portsmouth	42	16	8	18	74	78	40
13	Norwich	42	12	15	15	52	52	39
14	Carlisle	42	17	5	20	60	63	39
15	Ipswich	42	15	9	18	58	66	39
16	Charlton	42	12	14	16	61	70	38
17	Preston	42	11	15	16	62	70	37
18	Plymouth	42	12	13	17	54	63	37
19	Bury	42	14	7	21	62	76	35
20	Cardiff	42	12	10	20	71	91	34
21	Middlesbrough	42	10	13	19	58	86	33
22	Leyton Orient	42	5	13	24	38	80	23

THIRD DIVISION

	P	W	D	L	F	A	Pts
1 Hull	46	31	7	8	109	62	69
2 Millwall	46	27	11	8	76	43	65
3 QPR	46	24	9	13	95	65	57
4 Scunthorpe	46	21	11	14	80	67	53
5 Workington	46	19	14	13	67	57	52
6 Gillingham	46	22	8	16	62	54	52
7 Swindon	46	19	13	14	74	48	51
8 Reading	46	19	13	14	70	63	51
9 Walsall	46	20	10	16	77	64	50
10 Shrewsbury	46	19	11	16	73	64	49
11 Grimsby	46	17	13	16	68	62	47
12 Watford	46	17	13	16	55	51	47
13 Peterborough	46	17	12	17	80	66	46
14 Oxford	46	19	8	19	70	74	46
15 Brighton	46	16	11	19	67	65	43
16 Bristol Rovers	46	14	14	18	64	64	42
17 Swansea	46	15	11	20	81	96	41
18 Bournemouth	46	13	12	21	38	56	38
19 Mansfield	46	15	8	23	59	89	38
20 Oldham	46	12	13	21	55	81	37
21 Southend	46	16	4	26	54	83	36
22 Exeter	46	12	11	23	53	79	35
23 Brentford	46	10	12	24	48	69	32
24 York	46	9	9	28	53	106	27

FOURTH DIVISION

	P	W	D	L	F	A	Pts
1 Doncaster	46	24	11	11	85	54	59
2 Darlington	46	25	9	12	72	53	59
3 Torquay	46	24	10	12	72	49	58
4 Colchester	46	23	10	13	70	47	56
5 Tranmere	46	24	8	14	93	66	56
6 Luton	46	24	8	14	90	70	56
7 Chester	46	20	12	14	79	70	52
8 Notts County	46	19	12	15	61	53	50
9 Newport	46	18	12	16	75	75	48
10 Southport	46	18	12	16	68	69	48
11 Bradford PA	46	21	5	20	102	92	47
12 Barrow	46	16	15	15	72	76	47
13 Stockport	46	18	6	22	71	70	42
14 Crewe	46	16	9	21	61	63	41
15 Halifax	46	15	11	20	67	75	41
16 Barnsley	46	15	10	21	74	78	40
17 Aldershot	46	15	10	21	75	84	40
18 Hartlepools	46	16	8	22	63	75	40
19 Port Vale	46	15	9	22	48	59	39
20 Chesterfield	46	13	13	20	62	78	39
21 Rochdale	46	16	5	25	71	87	37
22 Lincoln	46	13	11	22	57	82	37
23 Bradford City	46	12	13	21	63	94	37
24 Wrexham	46	13	9	24	72	104	35

1966–67

FIRST DIVISION

	P	W	D	L	F	A	Pts
1 Man United	42	24	12	6	84	45	60
2 Nottm Forest	42	23	10	9	64	41	56
3 Tottenham	42	24	8	10	71	48	56
4 Leeds	42	22	11	9	62	42	55
5 Liverpool	42	19	13	10	64	47	51
6 Everton	42	19	10	13	65	46	48
7 Arsenal	42	16	14	12	58	47	46
8 Leicester	42	18	8	16	78	71	44
9 Chelsea	42	15	14	13	67	62	44
10 Sheff United	42	16	10	16	52	59	42
11 Sheff Wed	42	14	13	15	56	47	41
12 Stoke	42	17	7	18	63	58	41
13 WBA	42	16	7	19	77	73	39
14 Burnley	42	15	9	18	66	76	39
15 Man City	42	12	15	15	43	52	39
16 West Ham	42	14	8	20	80	84	36
17 Sunderland	42	14	8	20	58	72	36
18 Fulham	42	11	12	19	71	83	34
19 Southampton	42	14	6	22	74	92	34
20 Newcastle	42	12	9	21	39	81	33
21 Aston Villa	42	11	7	24	54	85	29
22 Blackpool	42	6	9	27	41	76	21

SECOND DIVISION

	P	W	D	L	F	A	Pts
1 Coventry	42	23	13	6	74	43	59
2 Wolves	42	25	8	9	88	48	58
3 Carlisle	42	23	6	13	71	54	52
4 Blackburn	42	19	13	10	56	46	51
5 Ipswich	42	17	16	9	70	54	50
6 Huddersfield	42	20	9	13	58	46	49
7 Crystal Palace	42	19	10	13	61	55	48
8 Millwall	42	18	9	15	49	58	45
9 Bolton	42	14	14	14	64	58	42
10 Birmingham	42	16	8	18	70	66	40
11 Norwich	42	13	14	15	49	55	40
12 Hull	42	16	7	19	77	72	39
13 Preston	42	16	7	19	65	67	39
14 Portsmouth	42	13	13	16	59	70	39
15 Bristol City	42	12	14	16	56	62	38
16 Plymouth	42	14	9	19	59	58	37
17 Derby	42	12	12	18	68	72	36
18 Rotherham	42	13	10	19	61	70	36
19 Charlton	42	13	9	20	49	53	35
20 Cardiff	42	12	9	21	61	87	33
21 Northampton	42	12	6	24	47	84	30
22 Bury	42	11	6	25	49	83	28

THIRD DIVISION

	P	W	D	L	F	A	Pts
1 QPR	46	26	15	5	103	38	67
2 Middlesbrough	46	23	9	14	87	64	55
3 Watford	46	20	14	12	61	46	54
4 Reading	46	22	9	15	76	57	53
5 Bristol Rovers	46	20	13	13	76	67	53
6 Shrewsbury	46	20	12	14	77	62	52
7 Torquay	46	21	9	16	73	54	51
8 Swindon	46	20	10	16	81	59	50
9 Mansfield	46	20	9	17	84	79	49
10 Oldham	46	19	10	17	80	63	48
11 Gillingham	46	15	16	15	58	62	46
12 Walsall	46	18	10	18	65	72	46
13 Colchester	46	17	10	19	76	73	44
14 Leyton Orient	46	13	18	15	58	68	44
15 Peterborough	46	14	15	17	66	71	43
16 Oxford	46	15	13	18	61	66	43
17 Grimsby	46	17	9	20	61	68	43
18 Scunthorpe	46	17	8	21	58	73	42
19 Brighton	46	13	15	18	61	71	41
20 Bournemouth	46	12	17	17	39	57	41
21 Swansea	46	12	15	19	85	89	39
22 Darlington	46	13	11	22	47	81	37
23 Doncaster	46	12	8	26	58	117	32
24 Workington	46	12	7	27	55	89	31

FOURTH DIVISION

	P	W	D	L	F	A	Pts
1 Stockport	46	26	12	8	69	42	64
2 Southport	46	23	13	10	69	42	59
3 Barrow	46	24	11	11	76	54	59
4 Tranmere	46	22	14	10	66	43	58
5 Crewe	46	21	12	13	70	55	54
6 Southend	46	22	9	15	70	49	53
7 Wrexham	46	16	20	10	76	62	52
8 Hartlepools	46	22	7	17	66	64	51
9 Brentford	46	18	13	15	58	56	49
10 Aldershot	46	18	12	16	72	57	48
11 Bradford City	46	19	10	17	74	62	48
12 Halifax	46	15	14	17	59	68	44
13 Port Vale	46	14	15	17	55	58	43
14 Exeter	46	14	15	17	50	60	43
15 Chesterfield	46	17	8	21	60	63	42
16 Barnsley	46	13	15	18	60	64	41
17 Luton	46	16	9	21	59	73	41
18 Newport	46	12	16	18	56	63	40
19 Chester	46	15	10	21	54	78	40
20 Notts County	46	13	11	22	53	72	37
21 Rochdale	46	13	11	22	53	75	37
22 York	46	12	11	23	65	79	35
23 Bradford PA	46	11	13	22	52	79	35
24 Lincoln	46	9	13	24	58	82	31

1967–68

FIRST DIVISION

		P	W	D	L	F	A	Pts
1	Man City	42	26	6	10	86	43	58
2	Man United	42	24	8	10	89	55	56
3	Liverpool	42	22	11	9	71	40	55
4	Leeds	42	22	9	11	71	41	53
5	Everton	42	23	6	13	67	40	52
6	Chelsea	42	18	12	12	62	68	48
7	Tottenham	42	19	9	14	70	59	47
8	WBA	42	17	12	13	75	62	46
9	Arsenal	42	17	10	15	60	56	44
10	Newcastle	42	13	15	14	54	67	41
11	Nottm Forest	42	14	11	17	52	64	39
12	West Ham	42	14	10	18	73	69	38
13	Leicester	42	13	12	17	64	69	38
14	Burnley	42	14	10	18	64	71	38
15	Sunderland	42	13	11	18	51	61	37
16	Southampton	42	13	11	18	66	83	37
17	Wolves	42	14	8	20	66	75	36
18	Stoke	42	14	7	21	50	73	35
19	Sheff Wed	42	11	12	19	51	63	34
20	Coventry	42	9	15	18	51	71	33
21	Sheff United	42	11	10	21	49	70	32
22	Fulham	42	10	7	25	56	98	27

SECOND DIVISION

		P	W	D	L	F	A	Pts
1	Ipswich	42	22	15	5	79	44	59
2	QPR	42	25	8	9	67	36	58
3	Blackpool	42	24	10	8	71	43	58
4	Birmingham	42	19	14	9	83	51	52
5	Portsmouth	42	18	13	11	68	55	49
6	Middlesbrough	42	17	12	13	60	54	46
7	Millwall	42	14	17	11	62	50	45
8	Blackburn	42	16	11	15	56	49	43
9	Norwich	42	16	11	15	60	65	43
10	Carlisle	42	14	13	15	58	52	41
11	Crystal Palace	42	14	11	17	56	56	39
12	Bolton	42	13	13	16	60	63	39
13	Cardiff	42	13	12	17	60	66	38
14	Huddersfield	42	13	12	17	46	61	38
15	Charlton	42	12	13	17	63	68	37
16	Aston Villa	42	15	7	20	54	64	37
17	Hull	42	12	13	17	58	73	37
18	Derby	42	13	10	19	71	78	36
19	Bristol City	42	13	10	19	48	62	36
20	Preston	42	12	11	19	43	65	35
21	Rotherham	42	10	11	21	42	76	31
22	Plymouth	42	9	9	24	38	72	27

THIRD DIVISION

		P	W	D	L	F	A	Pts
1	Oxford	46	22	13	11	69	47	57
2	Bury	46	24	8	14	91	66	56
3	Shrewsbury	46	20	15	11	61	49	55
4	Torquay	46	21	11	14	60	56	53
5	Reading	46	21	9	16	70	60	51
6	Watford	46	21	8	17	74	50	50
7	Walsall	46	19	12	15	74	61	50
8	Barrow	46	21	8	17	65	54	50
9	Swindon	46	16	17	13	74	51	49
10	Brighton	46	16	16	14	57	55	48
11	Gillingham	46	18	12	16	59	63	48
12	Bournemouth	46	16	15	15	56	51	47
13	Stockport	46	19	9	18	70	75	47
14	Southport	46	17	12	17	65	65	46
15	Bristol Rovers	46	17	9	20	72	78	43
16	Oldham	46	18	7	21	60	65	43
17	Northampton	46	14	13	19	58	72	41
18	Leyton Orient	46	12	17	17	46	62	41
19	Tranmere	46	14	12	20	62	74	40
20	Mansfield	46	12	13	21	51	67	37
21	Grimsby	46	14	9	23	52	69	37
22	Colchester	46	9	15	22	50	87	33
23	Scunthorpe	46	10	12	24	56	87	32
24	Peterborough	46	20	10	16	79	67	31†

†Peterborough had 19 points deducted for offering irregular bonuses to their players. They were automatically demoted to the Fourth Division.

FOURTH DIVISION

		P	W	D	L	F	A	Pts
1	Luton	46	27	12	7	87	44	66
2	Barnsley	46	24	13	9	68	46	61
3	Hartlepools	46	25	10	11	60	46	60
4	Crewe	46	20	18	8	74	49	58
5	Bradford City	46	23	11	12	72	51	57
6	Southend	46	20	14	12	77	58	54
7	Chesterfield	46	21	11	14	71	50	53
8	Wrexham	46	20	13	13	72	53	53
9	Aldershot	46	18	17	11	70	55	53
10	Doncaster	46	18	15	13	66	56	51
11	Halifax	46	15	16	15	52	49	46
12	Newport	46	16	13	17	58	63	45
13	Lincoln	46	17	9	20	71	68	43
14	Brentford	46	18	7	21	61	64	43
15	Swansea	46	16	10	20	63	77	42
16	Darlington	46	12	17	17	47	53	41
17	Notts County	46	15	11	20	53	79	41
18	Port Vale	46	12	15	19	61	72	39†
19	Rochdale	46	12	14	20	51	72	38
20	Exeter	46	11	16	19	45	65	38
21	York	46	11	14	21	65	68	36
22	Chester	46	9	14	23	57	78	32
23	Workington	46	10	11	25	54	87	31
24	Bradford PA	46	4	15	27	30	82	23

†Port Vale were expelled from the League at the end of the season for making unauthorised payments. They were re-elected immediately.

1968–69

FIRST DIVISION

		P	W	D	L	F	A	Pts
1	Leeds	42	27	13	2	66	26	67
2	Liverpool	42	25	11	6	63	24	61
3	Everton	42	21	15	6	77	36	57
4	Arsenal	42	22	12	8	56	27	56
5	Chelsea	42	20	10	12	73	53	50
6	Tottenham	42	14	17	11	61	51	45
7	Southampton	42	16	13	13	57	48	45
8	West Ham	42	13	18	11	66	50	44
9	Newcastle	42	15	14	13	61	55	44
10	WBA	42	16	11	15	64	67	43
11	Man United	42	15	12	15	57	53	42
12	Ipswich	42	15	11	16	59	60	41
13	Man City	42	15	10	17	64	55	40
14	Burnley	42	15	9	18	55	82	39
15	Sheff Wed	42	10	16	16	41	54	36
16	Wolves	42	10	15	17	41	58	35
17	Sunderland	42	11	12	19	43	67	34
18	Nottm Forest	42	10	13	19	45	57	33
19	Stoke	42	9	15	18	40	63	33
20	Coventry	42	10	11	21	46	64	31
21	Leicester	42	9	12	21	39	68	30
22	QPR	42	4	10	28	39	95	18

SECOND DIVISION

		P	W	D	L	F	A	Pts
1	Derby	42	26	11	5	65	32	63
2	Crystal Palace	42	22	12	8	70	47	56
3	Charlton	42	18	14	10	61	52	50
4	Middlesbrough	42	19	11	12	58	49	49
5	Cardiff	42	20	7	15	67	54	47
6	Huddersfield	42	17	12	13	53	46	46
7	Birmingham	42	18	8	16	73	59	44
8	Blackpool	42	14	15	13	51	41	43
9	Sheff United	42	16	11	15	61	50	43
10	Millwall	42	17	9	16	57	49	43
11	Hull	42	13	16	13	59	52	42
12	Carlisle	42	16	10	16	46	49	42
13	Norwich	42	15	10	17	53	56	40
14	Preston	42	12	15	15	38	44	39
15	Portsmouth	42	12	14	16	58	58	38
16	Bristol City	42	11	16	15	46	53	38
17	Bolton	42	12	14	16	55	67	38
18	Aston Villa	42	12	14	16	37	48	38
19	Blackburn	42	13	11	18	52	63	37
20	Oxford	42	12	9	21	34	55	33
21	Bury	42	11	8	23	51	80	30
22	Fulham	42	7	11	24	40	81	25

THIRD DIVISION

	P	W	D	L	F	A	Pts
1 Watford	46	27	10	9	74	34	64
2 Swindon	46	27	10	9	71	35	64
3 Luton	46	25	11	10	74	38	61
4 Bournemouth	46	21	9	16	60	45	51
5 Plymouth	46	17	15	14	53	49	49
6 Torquay	46	18	12	16	54	46	48
7 Tranmere	46	19	10	17	70	68	48
8 Southport	46	17	13	16	71	64	47
9 Stockport	46	16	14	16	67	68	46
10 Barnsley	46	16	14	16	58	63	46
11 Rotherham	46	16	13	17	56	50	45
12 Brighton	46	16	13	17	72	65	45
13 Walsall	46	14	16	16	50	49	44
14 Reading	46	15	13	18	67	66	43
15 Mansfield	46	16	11	19	58	62	43
16 Bristol Rovers	46	16	11	19	63	71	43
17 Shrewsbury	46	16	11	19	51	67	43
18 Orient	46	14	14	18	51	58	42
19 Barrow	46	17	8	21	56	75	42
20 Gillingham	46	13	15	18	54	63	41
21 Northampton	46	14	12	20	54	61	40
22 Hartlepool	46	10	19	17	40	70	39
23 Crewe	46	13	9	24	52	76	35
24 Oldham	46	13	9	24	50	83	35

FOURTH DIVISION

	P	W	D	L	F	A	Pts
1 Doncaster	46	21	17	8	65	38	59
2 Halifax	46	20	17	9	53	37	57
3 Rochdale	46	18	20	8	68	35	56
4 Bradford City	46	18	20	8	65	46	56
5 Darlington	46	17	18	11	62	45	52
6 Colchester	46	20	12	14	57	53	52
7 Southend	46	19	13	14	78	61	51
8 Lincoln	46	17	17	12	54	52	51
9 Wrexham	46	18	14	14	61	52	50
10 Swansea	46	19	11	16	58	54	49
11 Brentford	46	18	12	16	64	65	48
12 Workington	46	15	17	14	40	43	47
13 Port Vale	46	16	14	16	46	46	46
14 Chester	46	16	13	17	76	66	45
15 Aldershot	46	19	7	20	66	66	45
16 Scunthorpe	46	18	8	20	61	60	44
17 Exeter	46	16	11	19	66	65	43
18 Peterborough	46	13	16	17	60	57	42
19 Notts County	46	12	18	16	48	57	42
20 Chesterfield	46	13	15	18	43	50	41
21 York	46	14	11	21	53	75	39
22 Newport	46	11	14	21	49	74	36
23 Grimsby	46	9	15	22	47	69	33
24 Bradford PA	46	5	10	31	32	106	20

1969–70

FIRST DIVISION

	P	W	D	L	F	A	Pts
1 Everton	42	29	8	5	72	34	66
2 Leeds	42	21	15	6	84	49	57
3 Chelsea	42	21	13	8	70	50	55
4 Derby	42	22	9	11	64	37	53
5 Liverpool	42	20	11	11	65	42	51
6 Coventry	42	19	11	12	58	48	49
7 Newcastle	42	17	13	12	57	35	47
8 Man United	42	14	17	11	66	61	45
9 Stoke	42	15	15	12	56	52	45
10 Man City	42	16	11	15	55	48	43
11 Tottenham	42	17	9	16	54	55	43
12 Arsenal	42	12	18	12	51	49	42
13 Wolves	42	12	16	14	55	57	40
14 Burnley	42	12	15	15	56	61	39
15 Nottm Forest	42	10	18	14	50	71	38
16 WBA	42	14	9	19	58	66	37
17 West Ham	42	12	12	18	51	60	36
18 Ipswich	42	10	11	21	40	63	31
19 Southampton	42	6	17	19	46	67	29
20 Crystal Palace	42	6	15	21	34	68	27
21 Sunderland	42	6	14	22	30	68	26
22 Sheff Wed	42	8	9	25	40	71	25

SECOND DIVISION

	P	W	D	L	F	A	Pts
1 Huddersfield	42	24	12	6	68	37	60
2 Blackpool	42	20	13	9	56	45	53
3 Leicester	42	19	13	10	64	50	51
4 Middlesbrough	42	20	10	12	55	45	50
5 Swindon	42	17	16	9	57	47	50
6 Sheff United	42	22	5	15	73	38	49
7 Cardiff	42	18	13	11	61	41	49
8 Blackburn	42	20	7	15	54	50	47
9 QPR	42	17	11	14	66	57	45
10 Millwall	42	15	14	13	56	56	44
11 Norwich	42	16	11	15	49	46	43
12 Carlisle	42	14	13	15	58	56	41
13 Hull	42	15	11	16	72	70	41
14 Bristol City	42	13	13	16	54	50	39
15 Oxford	42	12	15	15	35	42	39
16 Bolton	42	12	12	18	54	61	36
17 Portsmouth	42	13	9	20	66	80	35
18 Birmingham	42	11	11	20	51	78	33
19 Watford	42	9	13	20	44	57	31
20 Charlton	42	7	17	18	35	76	31
21 Aston Villa	42	8	13	21	36	62	29
22 Preston	42	8	12	22	43	63	28

THIRD DIVISION

	P	W	D	L	F	A	Pts
1 Orient	46	25	12	9	67	36	62
2 Luton	46	23	14	9	77	43	60
3 Bristol Rovers	46	20	16	10	80	59	56
4 Fulham	46	20	15	11	81	55	55
5 Brighton	46	23	9	14	57	43	55
6 Mansfield	46	21	11	14	70	49	53
7 Barnsley	46	19	15	12	68	59	53
8 Reading	46	21	11	14	87	77	53
9 Rochdale	46	18	10	18	69	60	46
10 Bradford City	46	17	12	17	57	50	46
11 Doncaster	46	17	12	17	52	54	46
12 Walsall	46	17	12	17	54	67	46
13 Torquay	46	14	17	15	62	59	45
14 Rotherham	46	15	14	17	62	54	44
15 Shrewsbury	46	13	18	15	62	63	44
16 Tranmere	46	14	16	16	56	72	44
17 Plymouth	46	16	11	19	56	64	43
18 Halifax	46	14	15	17	47	63	43
19 Bury	46	15	11	20	75	80	41
20 Gillingham	46	13	13	20	52	64	39
21 Bournemouth	46	12	15	19	48	71	39
22 Southport	46	14	10	22	48	66	38
23 Barrow	46	8	14	24	46	81	30
24 Stockport	46	6	11	29	27	71	23

FOURTH DIVISION

	P	W	D	L	F	A	Pts
1 Chesterfield	46	27	10	9	77	32	64
2 Wrexham	46	26	9	11	84	49	61
3 Swansea	46	21	18	7	66	45	60
4 Port Vale	46	20	19	7	61	33	59
5 Brentford	46	20	16	10	58	39	56
6 Aldershot	46	20	13	13	78	65	53
7 Notts County	46	22	8	16	73	62	52
8 Lincoln	46	17	16	13	66	52	50
9 Peterborough	46	17	14	15	77	69	48
10 Colchester	46	17	14	15	64	63	48
11 Chester	46	21	6	19	58	66	48
12 Scunthorpe	46	18	10	18	67	65	46
13 York	46	16	14	16	55	62	46
14 Northampton	46	16	12	18	64	55	44
15 Crewe	46	16	12	18	51	51	44
16 Grimsby	46	14	15	17	54	58	43
17 Southend	46	15	10	21	59	85	40
18 Exeter	46	14	11	21	57	59	39
19 Oldham	46	13	13	20	60	65	39
20 Workington	46	12	14	20	46	64	38
21 Newport	46	13	11	22	53	74	37
22 Darlington	46	13	10	23	53	73	36
23 Hartlepool	46	10	10	26	42	82	30
24 Bradford P A	46	6	11	29	41	96	23

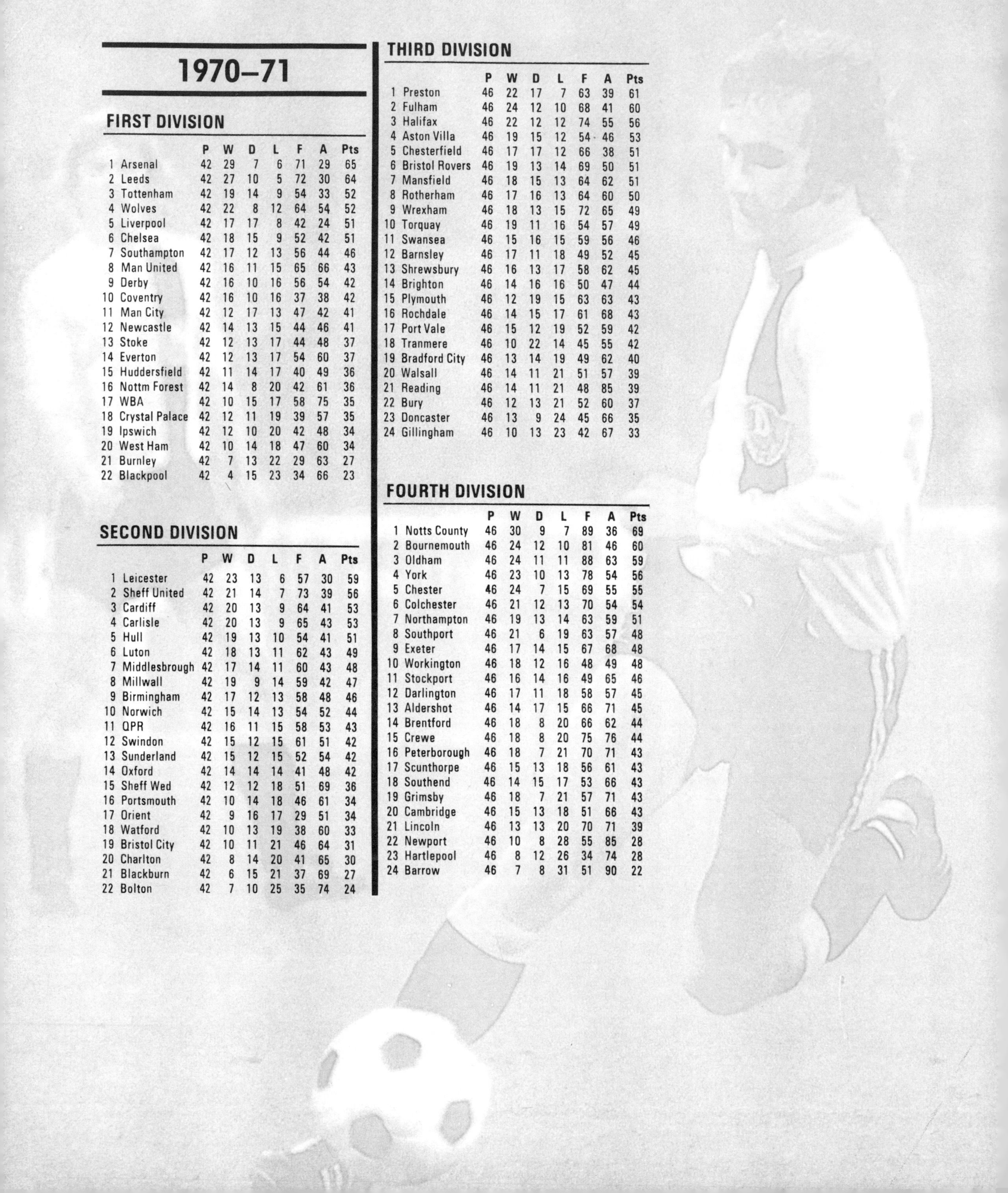

1970–71

FIRST DIVISION

		P	W	D	L	F	A	Pts
1	Arsenal	42	29	7	6	71	29	65
2	Leeds	42	27	10	5	72	30	64
3	Tottenham	42	19	14	9	54	33	52
4	Wolves	42	22	8	12	64	54	52
5	Liverpool	42	17	17	8	42	24	51
6	Chelsea	42	18	15	9	52	42	51
7	Southampton	42	17	12	13	56	44	46
8	Man United	42	16	11	15	65	66	43
9	Derby	42	16	10	16	56	54	42
10	Coventry	42	16	10	16	37	38	42
11	Man City	42	12	17	13	47	42	41
12	Newcastle	42	14	13	15	44	46	41
13	Stoke	42	12	13	17	44	48	37
14	Everton	42	12	13	17	54	60	37
15	Huddersfield	42	11	14	17	40	49	36
16	Nottm Forest	42	14	8	20	42	61	36
17	WBA	42	10	15	17	58	75	35
18	Crystal Palace	42	12	11	19	39	57	35
19	Ipswich	42	12	10	20	42	48	34
20	West Ham	42	10	14	18	47	60	34
21	Burnley	42	7	13	22	29	63	27
22	Blackpool	42	4	15	23	34	66	23

SECOND DIVISION

		P	W	D	L	F	A	Pts
1	Leicester	42	23	13	6	57	30	59
2	Sheff United	42	21	14	7	73	39	56
3	Cardiff	42	20	13	9	64	41	53
4	Carlisle	42	20	13	9	65	43	53
5	Hull	42	19	13	10	54	41	51
6	Luton	42	18	13	11	62	43	49
7	Middlesbrough	42	17	14	11	60	43	48
8	Millwall	42	19	9	14	59	42	47
9	Birmingham	42	17	12	13	58	48	46
10	Norwich	42	15	14	13	54	52	44
11	QPR	42	16	11	15	58	53	43
12	Swindon	42	15	12	15	61	51	42
13	Sunderland	42	15	12	15	52	54	42
14	Oxford	42	14	14	14	41	48	42
15	Sheff Wed	42	12	12	18	51	69	36
16	Portsmouth	42	10	14	18	46	61	34
17	Orient	42	9	16	17	29	51	34
18	Watford	42	10	13	19	38	60	33
19	Bristol City	42	10	11	21	46	64	31
20	Charlton	42	8	14	20	41	65	30
21	Blackburn	42	6	15	21	37	69	27
22	Bolton	42	7	10	25	35	74	24

THIRD DIVISION

		P	W	D	L	F	A	Pts
1	Preston	46	22	17	7	63	39	61
2	Fulham	46	24	12	10	68	41	60
3	Halifax	46	22	12	12	74	55	56
4	Aston Villa	46	19	15	12	54	46	53
5	Chesterfield	46	17	17	12	66	38	51
6	Bristol Rovers	46	19	13	14	69	50	51
7	Mansfield	46	18	15	13	64	62	51
8	Rotherham	46	17	16	13	64	60	50
9	Wrexham	46	18	13	15	72	65	49
10	Torquay	46	19	11	16	54	57	49
11	Swansea	46	15	16	15	59	56	46
12	Barnsley	46	17	11	18	49	52	45
13	Shrewsbury	46	16	13	17	58	62	45
14	Brighton	46	14	16	16	50	47	44
15	Plymouth	46	12	19	15	63	63	43
16	Rochdale	46	14	15	17	61	68	43
17	Port Vale	46	15	12	19	52	59	42
18	Tranmere	46	10	22	14	45	55	42
19	Bradford City	46	13	14	19	49	62	40
20	Walsall	46	14	11	21	51	57	39
21	Reading	46	14	11	21	48	85	39
22	Bury	46	12	13	21	52	60	37
23	Doncaster	46	13	9	24	45	66	35
24	Gillingham	46	10	13	23	42	67	33

FOURTH DIVISION

		P	W	D	L	F	A	Pts
1	Notts County	46	30	9	7	89	36	69
2	Bournemouth	46	24	12	10	81	46	60
3	Oldham	46	24	11	11	88	63	59
4	York	46	23	10	13	78	54	56
5	Chester	46	24	7	15	69	55	55
6	Colchester	46	21	12	13	70	54	54
7	Northampton	46	19	13	14	63	59	51
8	Southport	46	21	6	19	63	57	48
9	Exeter	46	17	14	15	67	68	48
10	Workington	46	18	12	16	48	49	48
11	Stockport	46	16	14	16	49	65	46
12	Darlington	46	17	11	18	58	57	45
13	Aldershot	46	14	17	15	66	71	45
14	Brentford	46	18	8	20	66	62	44
15	Crewe	46	18	8	20	75	76	44
16	Peterborough	46	18	7	21	70	71	43
17	Scunthorpe	46	15	13	18	56	61	43
18	Southend	46	14	15	17	53	66	43
19	Grimsby	46	18	7	21	57	71	43
20	Cambridge	46	15	13	18	51	66	43
21	Lincoln	46	13	13	20	70	71	39
22	Newport	46	10	8	28	55	85	28
23	Hartlepool	46	8	12	26	34	74	28
24	Barrow	46	7	8	31	51	90	22

BP
4

overleaf Kevin Keegan of Scunthorpe, Liverpool, Hamburg, Southampton, Newcastle and England – the only British player to be twice named European Footballer of the Year (1978 and 1979). Keegan (in blue) in action for Hamburg. Only five other players have won the award twice: Alfredo di Stefano (Real Madrid), Johan Cruyff (Ajax and Barcelona), Franz Beckenbauer (Bayern Munich), Karl-Heinz Rummenigge (Bayern Munich) and Michel Platini (Juventus).

right Trevor Francis heading Nottingham Forest's winning goal against Malmo of Sweden in the 1979 European Cup Final in Munich – only three months after joining Forest from Birmingham for the first British transfer fee of one million pounds. It was his first European competitive club game.

left Tommy Docherty – League football's most travelled manager: Chelsea, Rotherham, Queen's Park Rangers, Aston Villa, Porto, Hull (assistant manager), Scotland, Manchester United, Derby, Queen's Park Rangers again, Sydney Olympic, Preston and Wolves. 'I've had more clubs,' he claimed, 'than Jack Nicklaus'.

below The first League goal on an artificial pitch: scored by Andy King of Queen's Park Rangers against Luton of Loftus Road, September 1981. The Luton goalkeeper is Jake Findlay. Result: QPR 1 Luton 2.

above The 100th Manchester League derby: United 1 (Mickey Thomas) City 0, 22 March 1980. Old Trafford crowd: 56,384. The record (1894–1980): Played 100, United 37 wins, City 30 wins, 33 draws, United 140 goals, City 140.

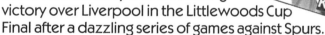

NINE
The Reds
1971–1980

'The first priority of everybody in professional football should be to attract as many paying customers as possible, and we are kidding ourselves if we believe otherwise. Spectators are what professional football is all about. Without them it has no point, no status and no future. I know professionals who see the game as their own property and the fans as people whose part in the ritual is a kind of privilege. The positions should be reversed.'

Alan Hardaker, *secretary of the Football League (1957–1977).*

A period of growing problems – worst of all the blight of hooliganism – but also a period of imposing teams and lustrous achievement. Arsenal became the fourth club to complete the League and FA Cup 'double', Brian Clough inspired both Derby County and Nottingham Forest to their first championship and Liverpool began a matchless period of sovereignty.

Arsenal followed Preston and Aston Villa of the Victorian era and Bill Nicholson's Tottenham to the 'double' and, at the end of season 1970–1, the club's chairman Denis Hill-Wood proudly declared 'this is the greatest team Arsenal have ever had'. There was still a smile, however, on the face of the bust of Herbert Chapman in the Highbury entrance hall.

One thing is certain: no club has grafted harder or longer than Arsenal did during that remarkable season. They were seven points behind Leeds at one stage and eventually needed to win their forty-second and last game – at Tottenham of all places – to be sure of the title. Arsenal made it with a late goal by Ray Kennedy with nearly 52,000 people inside the ground and nearly as many locked out – and in the jubilant chaos which followed manager Bertie Mee lost his tie and cufflinks. In the FA Cup they were not given the comfort of a single home draw; and in the final, after being a goal down to Bill Shankly's Liverpool, Charlie George thumped in Arsenal's winner in the second period of extra time.

Frank McLintock, Arsenal's captain, a defender of wit and indomitable will, was voted Footballer of the Year and Bertie Mee was named Manager of the Year. Mee was an unusual man and a rare kind of manager. He had been the club's physiotherapist, a softly-spoken, intelligent man who agreed to become manager only after a lot of thought; but, the nettle once grasped, he proved himself a perceptive judge of talent and character. 'I am not important,' he would say. 'Only the players are important.'

Another manager was moving to the front of the grid at around this time – a younger, rather different sort of chap. Brian Clough had been an arrogantly exciting goalscorer (251 in 274 League games for Middlesbrough and Sunderland) before injury ended his playing days; and then he showed immediate promise as a manager with Hartlepools United (later just Hartlepool) in the Fourth Division. He even drove the team's bus and worked without wages for a couple of months.

Clough and his first mate Peter Taylor joined Derby County in 1967 and together they ruffled establishment feathers, actively whipped up controversy and pronounced like High Priests on everything from politics to pease pudding. Clough, most of all, was a tilter at windmills, a natural reformer, a socialist 'of the heart' and a champion of honest old Britain – with fish-and-chips high among his priorities.

Clough and Taylor also built very good football teams. In five years they took Derby from the muddy end of the Second Division to the semi-finals of the European Cup. The night – and the way – they won the title in 1972 has no parallel. Leeds, needing only a point to complete the 'double', lost at Wolverhampton; Liverpool, who could have taken the title with a good win, drew at Arsenal, and, away in Majorca where they were on holiday, Derby's players raised their glasses to the club's first championship. Derby finished with 58 points, Leeds, Liverpool and Manchester City all with 57.

The town, as well as the club, seemed to belong to Clough and Taylor. But their relationship with some of Derby's directors soured into open hostility and, despite protests from players and public, they resigned in late 1973. They moved to Brighton together and then – an extraordinary appointment – Clough moved on alone to a club he had often fiercely criticized, Leeds United. His comments were remembered, the mood in the dressing room was rebellious, the directors had second thoughts and Clough was dismissed after just 44 days.

Nottingham Forest had the vision – and courage – to bring Clough and Taylor together again and the pair's unique style of leadership transformed a conservative, middle-order Second Division club. Forest had been more noted for selling good players than buying them; but that soon changed. John McGovern, John O'Hare and later Archie Gemmill, familiar faces from Derby's champion side, were among the players bought – and as Forest's fortune rose so did the investment in talent.

A record fee for a goalkeeper of £275,000 was paid for the magnificent Peter Shilton of Stoke and England and then, in February 1979, they brushed aside all other British transfer records by paying the first million pound fee – £1,150,000 including VAT and a few bits and pieces – for Trevor Francis of Birmingham. Francis, slim and boyish-looking, was a forward of whippet pace and, at his best, as hard to nail as a puppy off the leash. He was good enough to turn any match – a point he proved by scoring Forest's winning goal against Malmo of Sweden in the 1979 European Cup Final in Munich.

Clough's way always defied precise analysis but it was unquestionably a winning way. Forest won promotion in 1977, the First Division championship and League Cup in 1978, the European Cup and League Cup again in 1979 and the European Cup once more in 1980. Clough takes his place alongside Herbert Chapman as the only managers to guide two clubs to the championship.

Liverpool, however, stand above all. No club has equalled their dreadnought consistency during the 'seventies and onwards. Liverpool's 1973 championship, their last under Bill Shankly who retired the following year, was their eighth title and equalled the record set by Arsenal in their 'double' season. By 1986 Liverpool had 16 championships to their credit. The sight of the Anfield club at the top became one of the familiar signs of spring – like blossom on trees or the sound of the cuckoo. They stopped making news by *winning* the title: portents of decline were considered much more interesting.

When Shankly stepped aside, surprisingly, there were many who assumed – and even hoped – that Liverpool would lose their momentum. 'Shanks' had been the club's life-force. He was irreplaceable. But Bob Paisley simply shifted from one chair to another and launched Liverpool into the finest period in their history. The continuity was perfect.

Paisley was on nodding terms with every nut, bolt and blade of grass at Anfield. He had served his time there as player, trainer and assistant manager, and understood 'the Liverpool way' better than anyone. Paisley was not another Shankly: he was a round and homely Durham man with eyes that seemed to miss nothing and an engaging way of rarely finishing a sentence. He would be seen in his office wearing a cardigan and slippers. Yet Paisley was to prove himself even tougher than his predecessor. Shankly was more aggressive: Paisley, unquestionably, more ruthless. Paisley bought shrewdly, and expensively if need be, but no player was allowed to feel secure and no team was so good it could not be improved.

One outstanding side merged into another, player replaced player without a break in step. Kevin Keegan, for example, symbolized Liverpool during his six wonderfully successful years with the club. Shankly bought him for £33,000 from Scunthorpe in 1971, a little chap with unusual potential who developed into a complete modern all-round footballer, dynamic, consistent, influential. 'Kevin Keegan, Superstar' roared the Anfield Kop in huge, booming harmony. The gap he left when he joined Hamburg in 1977 seemed unfillable. But before the start of the next season Paisley's Liverpool had bought Kenny Dalglish from Celtic for £440,000 – and before long new banners were being unfurled: 'Kenny's from Heaven' they read. Dalglish, like Keegan, was a model professional but his talent, courage, perception and ability to score accomplished goals, the sort of goals which reduce crowds to a moment's awed silence before they find their voice, set him apart from his contemporaries. He was not a simple replacement for Keegan: Dalglish was an original. Liverpool had solved another problem – and they kept on winning.

Yet the 'seventies did not belong exclusively to the likes of Shankly, Paisley, Clough and Mee. Stoke City, one of the League's original twelve, won their first major trophy – the League Cup in 1972. Sunderland (1973), Southampton (1976) and West Ham (1980) emphasized the quality and spirit of the Second Division by winning the FA Cup. Middlesbrough won the Second Division championship in 1974 by a record margin of 15 points – and this in days when only two points were awarded for a win. Three points for a win did not come until 1981. The 'seventies, however, did see the first change in the system of promotion and relegation for the two top divisions for nearly 80 years. Three up and three down, instead of two, came into force for the 1973–4 season – a change designed to stimulate interest by spreading more hope and fear around at the end of every season.

Crowds fell – from 29,600,972 in 1969–70 to 24,623,975 in 1979–80 – but this was not surprising. The post-war boom belonged to a period of austerity and escape while attendances in the 'seventies reflected a different kind of society, a more affluent society with cars, television and many more affordable options to fill its leisure hours. It is a wonder football held onto so many spectators as long as it did.

Yet society itself provided one major reason for the decline in gates. Football did not create the hooligan; it merely provided a convenient platform for his wretched behaviour. Clubs put a lot of money and thought into containing the problem and most grounds remained acceptably safe places on a Saturday afternoon. But trouble persisted, no one could predict where or when, and many thousands decided the risk was too great. Football did its best, but the problem was going to get worse.

MASTER MANAGER

Bob Paisley's record during his nine seasons as manager of Liverpool – a record without equal.

1974–75	Division One runners-up
1975–76	League Champions, UEFA Cup winners
1976–77	League Champions, European Cup winners, FA Cup runners-up, Charity Shield winners
1977–78	European Cup winners, League Cup runners-up, European Super Cup winners, Charity Shield shared winners, Division One runners-up
1978–79	League Champions, FA Cup semi-finalists
1979–80	League Champions, FA Cup semi-finalists, League Cup semi-finalists, Charity Shield winners
1980–81	European Cup winners, League Cup winners, Charity Shield winners
1981–82	League Champions, League Cup winners
1982–83	League Champions, Charity Shield winners, Milk Cup winners

PLAYER – MANAGERS

Only eight men have played in and managed League championship teams.

Ted Drake	Player – Arsenal 1934, 1935, 1938 Manager – Chelsea 1955
Bill Nicholson	Player – Tottenham 1951 Manager – Tottenham 1961
Alf Ramsey	Player – Tottenham 1951 Manager – Ipswich 1962
Joe Mercer	Player – Everton 1939, Arsenal 1948, 1953 Manager – Manchester City 1968
Dave Mackay	Player – Tottenham 1961 Manager – Derby County 1975
Bob Paisley	Player – Liverpool 1947 Manager – Liverpool 1976, 1977, 1979, 1980, 1982, 1983
Howard Kendall	Player – Everton 1970 Manager – Everton 1985
Kenny Dalglish	Player – Liverpool 1979, 1980, 1982, 1983, 1984 Player-manager – Liverpool 1986

CITY

overleaf Charlie George (in hair raising form) of Arsenal, Derby, Southampton and Nottingham Forest. An exciting, often controversial striker remembered above all for his spectacular 25-yard extra-time winner for Arsenal against Liverpool in the 1971 FA Cup Final – Arsenal's League and FA Cup 'double' year. One cap for England (1977). Pictured in action against John Sjoberg of Leicester in March 1971.

below Sweet smiles of success: Arsenal have completed the League and FA Cup 'double' by beating Liverpool 2–1 at Wembley with extra-time goals from Eddie Kelly and Charlie George, May 1971. Left to right: Bob McNab, George Armstrong, Eddie Kelly, Peter Storey, Bob Wilson, Charlie George, Frank McLintock (with Cup), Pat Rice and Peter Simpson. *right* Bertie Mee, Arsenal's manager, with the two trophies.

right Referee Tommy Dawes of Blofield, Norwich, inquiring about the health of Steve Kember of Crystal Palace in a Division One match, August 1971.

below West Ham's only score on an April afternoon in 1972 at Upton Park. Bonzo 1 Liverpool 2. Ray Clemence, Liverpool's goalkeeper, watches a little hitch in a matchless career of more than 1,100 first class matches with Scunthorpe, Liverpool and Tottenham – a goalkeeping record. Clemence won 61 caps for England (1973–84) and a remarkable collection of winners medals: five League championship, two FA Cup, three European Cup, two UEFA Cup and one League Cup. Bob Paisley described Clemence as the greatest goalkeeper he had seen.

left Terry Paine of Southampton, Hereford and England – unchallenged holder of the record for most League appearances. In a 20-year playing career (1957–77) he played in 824 League games, 713 for Southampton, 111 for Hereford. Paine, a winger of pace and cunning, also scored 168 goals and played a major role in helping Southampton into the First Division for the first time in 1966. Won 19 caps for England.

right Trevor Brooking of West Ham and England – midfield player of style, invention and impeccable character, one of the most popular players to wear the claret-and-blue of Upton Park. Made 528 League appearances (88 goals) between 1967–84 and won 47 caps for England (1974–82). Helped West Ham win two FA Cup Finals – 1975 (v Fulham) and 1980 (heading only goal of match to beat Arsenal).

right Fred Davies, Shrewsbury Town's official ball retriever for more than a quarter of a century. Gay Meadow, the club's home since 1910, is on the banks of the River Severn – and when the ball was lofted into the water (on average once a game but occasionally as many as four times) Fred and coracle fetched it back at 25p a round trip.

above The FA Cup tournament is a hundred years old – and Bertie Mee of Arsenal and Don Revie of Leeds United lead their sides into the Wembley sunshine at the start of the Centenary final, May 1972. Arsenal were the holders – having completed the League and FA Cup 'double' the season before – but Leeds won with a second-half goal by Allan Clarke. And Leeds finished runners-up in Division One, just a point behind Derby County.

right Don Revie, manager of Leeds United from 1962 to 1974: he transformed a club that was on the brink of relegation to the Third Division into one of the most eminent powers in post-war football. Revie was a complex figure who was hugely professional but highly superstitious, a man of broad vision who was obsessed by detail, generous in many ways but coldly single-minded. He became England's manager in 1974 but struggled with the challenges and frustrations of the job and, three years later, he suddenly resigned and took a handsomely paid job in the United Arab Emirates. Revie was suspended from domestic football for ten years by the FA for 'bringing the game into disrepute', but later he successfully challenged the ban in the High Court.

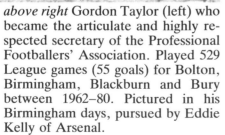

above right Gordon Taylor (left) who became the articulate and highly respected secretary of the Professional Footballers' Association. Played 529 League games (55 goals) for Bolton, Birmingham, Blackburn and Bury between 1962–80. Pictured in his Birmingham days, pursued by Eddie Kelly of Arsenal.

28 April 1973 was an important day for the celebrated Charlton brothers. Bobby played his last game for Manchester United at Stamford Bridge . . . and Jack retired on the same day. It was Bobby's 606th League game (198 goals) for United – 44,000 people turning out to make it a memorable occasion – and Jack's last game, at Southampton, was his 629th for Leeds. Bobby won 106 caps for England (scoring a record 49 goals) with Jack winning the first of his 35 caps against Scotland in 1965 on the day that Bobby, three years younger, won his 57th. It was the first time since the turn of the century that two brothers had played in a full international for England – and, of course, they were still together when England won the World Cup. They were English football's most distinguished brothers.

left Bobby Charlton – making his last farewell in a United shirt at Chelsea – was one of the small handful of professionals who gave more to the game than sweat and ability. He elevated his profession; he represented an ideal. He played the game and he graced the game. He was modest, honest, unaffected and, in action, he mutely accepted physical abuse and respected his fellow professionals. But he was also a player whose whiplash speed and thunderous shooting, a natural fusion of power and grace, illuminated games like lightning in the night sky. Bobby began his career as an inside-forward, switched to the left-wing as United rebuilt after the Munich air-crash and returned to the middle of the field as England moved towards her finest hours in 1966 and Manchester United towards their European Cup two years later. Bobby went on to manage Preston (and play 38 more games) after leaving Old Trafford – and was later elected to the Manchester United board.

right Jack Charlton became manager of Middlesbrough immediately after retiring as a player: he collected track suits, remembered all the hard lessons he had learned at Leeds and guided the Ayresome Park club to the 1974 Second Division championship by a record margin of 15 points. He was named as the Bell's Scotch Whisky Manager of the Year – and later managed Sheffield Wednesday, Newcastle and the Republic of Ireland. Jack was a very different sort of player – and man – to brother Bobby. He was tall and guardsman straight, a natural destroyer whose long legs scythed into tackles with biting effect and whose long neck seemed to stretch to reach everything in the air. He was a daunting competitor and an obvious threat when he moved forward for corners and free-kicks; he scored 70 League goals for Leeds – a rare total for a centre-half. Jack Charlton was independent, outspoken, no respecter of authority and, always, his own man.

left Pat Jennings of Watford, Tottenham, Arsenal and Northern Ireland – the most capped player in the history of international football and the first British player to complete 1,000 first class appearances. Won his 119th cap on his forty-first birthday against Brazil during the 1986 World Cup Finals in Mexico; and then he retired. Played his first League game in May 1963 (for Watford) and his 1,000th senior game in February 1983 (for Arsenal). Grand total: 1,097 – 757 League, 119 full internationals, 84 FA Cup, 72 League/Milk Cup, 55 European club matches, two Charity Shield, two other internationals, one Under-23 international, two Texaco Cup, two Anglo-Italian and one Super Cup. A goalkeeper whose hands were considered the biggest in football and who scored a goal for Tottenham against Manchester United in the 1967 Charity Shield match with a wind-assisted 100 yard clearance that sent the ball, first bounce, into the net. Footballer of the Year 1973.

The sensible chairman of a Crazy Gang

RICHARD YALLOP talks to Pat Jennings, "possibly the world's best goalkeeper, but still learning to live with his blunders"

right Jimmy Hill – man of many parts and talents – in a new role during the game between Arsenal and Liverpool at Highbury, September 1972. One of the linesmen, Dennis Drewitt, tore a leg muscle and Hill, a qualified referee, foresook his job as television commentator to take over. Hill handled the emergency expertly – just as he did as a player, chairman of the Professional Footballers' Association, coach, manager, television presenter and summariser and hard-pressed committee-man, trouble-shooter and consultant.

above Bryan Robson, sold by West Bromwich Albion to Manchester United in October 1981 for £1,500,000.

right Cigarette cards were once a unique source of information and an open encouragement to smoke. Now they are highly collectable.

below 'Help', 1982.

above Low profile. Cops on the Kop Shop at Wrexham, May 1982.

right Norman Whiteside of Manchester United and Northern Ireland, who became the youngest British international and the youngest player to appear in the final stages of a World Cup when he played against France in Spain in 1982 at the age of 17 years 42 days. Pictured in action against France, 1982. He is also the youngest player to score in a major Wembley final – for Manchester United against Liverpool in the 1983 Milk Cup Final at the age of 17 years 324 days.

above The start of regular 'live' League football on television: Tottenham 2 Nottingham Forest 1, October 1983. The ITV commentator on the White Hart Lane gantry is Brian Moore, and the expert summarizer is Ian St John, the former Liverpool and Scotland forward.

below Thanksgiving at the Manor Ground. Oxford United have won the Second Division championship – and chairman Robert Maxwell savours the triumph with the fans, May 1985. Oxford had just beaten Barnsley 4–0 and completed their rise from Third Division to First in successive seasons.

above Jason Dozzell of Ipswich – youngest scorer of a goal in Division One. He was 16 years 57 days and still a schoolboy when he scored against Coventry at Portman Road in February 1984.

MILLWALL
FULHAM
FOOTBALL LEAGUE DIVISION TWO
SUNDAY 20 JANUARY 1974 KICK OFF 11.30 AM
Admission will be afforded free to anyone who has purchased this official Programme which will only be available at the Turnstiles

above The first League match on a Sunday – 20 January 1974. Millwall 1 Fulham 0. Attendance: 15,143 – more than 5,000 higher than Millwall's average home attendance for that season. The switch was made during a power crisis and railway go-slow.

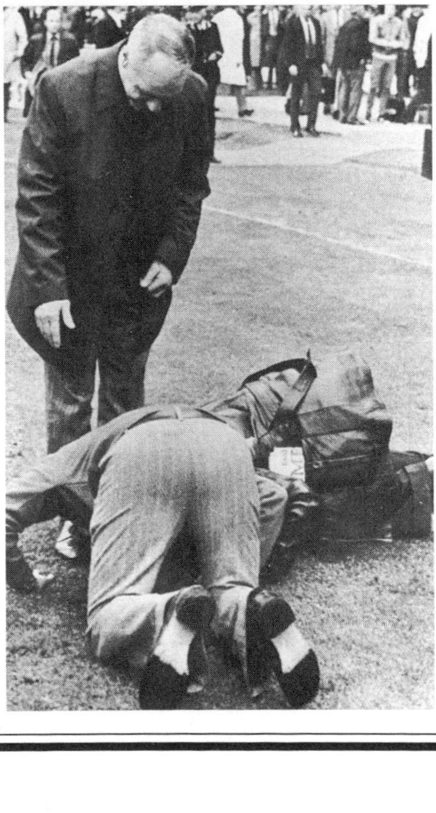

right Bill Shankly – and two of his grateful 'Red Army'. Wembley 1974: Liverpool 3 Newcastle 0.

below Jack Wheeler who did not miss a single game in 26 years (1957–83) as Notts County's trainer. He kept himself fit by keeping County's players fit for nearly 1,400 games. For two spells (one of 14 months) he ran the playing side of the club single-handed – manager, coach, trainer and scout – and often worked 18-hour days. Wheeler, a goalkeeper in his playing days, was Harry Hibbs' understudy with Birmingham City before the war and made his League debut in 1938. He moved to Huddersfield in 1948 and was a member of a celebrated defence – Wheeler; Staniforth, Kelly; McGarry, McEvoy and Quested – which remained unchanged throughout season 1952–3 when they won promotion to Division One . . . a record never remotely challenged. Jack says he learnt to keep fit in his early days when most clubs had 40 and more professionals – 'Competition was so keen that there was always a fight for places, every week, every position. We had to look after ourselves.' He retired in 1983 at the age of 64.

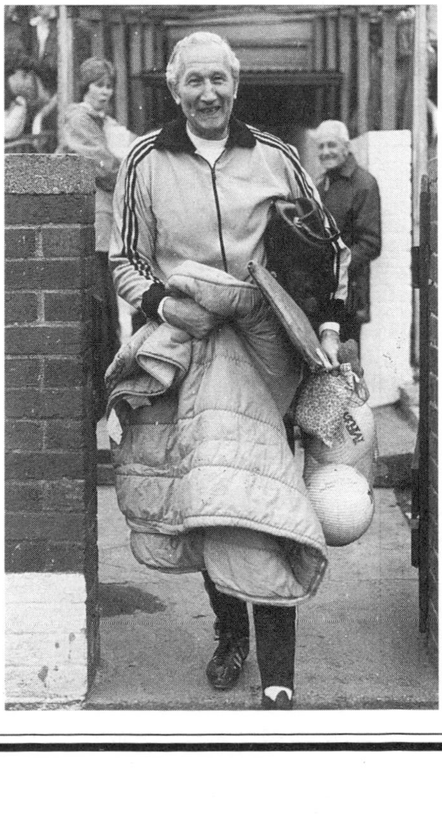

overleaf Old Trafford – the home of Manchester United since 1910 and variously described as 'a tabernacle of worship,' 'a theatre of dreams,' 'a cathedral of football' and 'a sound trap of red and white aggression'. Record League crowd: 70,504 (receipts £4,824) for a First Division game against Aston Villa on Boxing Day 1920. Present capacity: 57,000.

right Denis Law just after scoring the goal for Manchester City that doomed Manchester United – his old club – to relegation, 27 April 1974. Old Trafford fans invaded the pitch after 82 minutes, play was stopped, a scarf was wrapped around Law's neck – and referee David Smith took the players off the field before abandoning the match. City led 1–0; and six days later the League confirmed the result would stand. United became a Second Division club for the first time since 1938. It was Law's last League game and he admitted later: 'I didn't want to play in the match but as a professional I had to. After eleven years with United most of the people there were my friends, and I certainly didn't want to put the nail in their coffin. I have seldom felt so depressed as I did that weekend.'

right Ron Saunders, manager of Aston Villa, receiving the Bell's Scotch Whisky Manager of the Year award in 1975 from a celebrity who wished to remain anonymous. Centre: Raymond Miquel, chairman of Bells. Aston Villa had won promotion from Division Two and the League Cup. Saunders, who was to become Manager of the Year again in 1981 when Villa won the League championship, played for Everton, Gillingham, Portsmouth, Watford and Charlton and then managed Oxford, Norwich, Manchester City, Aston Villa, Birmingham and West Bromwich. Managers of the Year: 1966 & 1967 Jock Stein (Celtic), 1968 Matt Busby (Manchester United), 1969 & 1970 Don Revie (Leeds), 1971 Bertie Mee (Arsenal), 1972 Don Revie, 1973 Bill Shankly (Liverpool), 1974 Jack Charlton (Middlesbrough), 1975 Ron Saunders (Aston Villa), 1976 & 1977 Bob Paisley (Liverpool), 1978 Brian Clough (Nottingham Forest), 1979 & 1980 Bob Paisley, 1981 Ron Saunders, 1982 & 1983 Bob Paisley, 1984 Joe Fagan (Liverpool), 1985 Howard Kendall (Everton), 1986 Kenny Dalglish (Liverpool), 1987 Howard Kendall.

left The celebrity unmasked: Eric Morecambe, much loved comedian and director of Luton Town from 1976–83.

overleaf Double indemnity. Peter Shilton (left) and Gordon Banks – both described, in their time, as the best goalkeeper in the world. Banks played 510 League games for Chesterfield, Leicester and Stoke (1958–72), won 73 caps for England and was one of Alf Ramsey's World Cup winners in 1966 . . . Shilton played for Leicester, Stoke, Nottingham Forest, Southampton and Derby in nearly 800 League games, and won more than 90 caps for England. Ron Greenwood, the former England manager, has said of them: 'Banks was the supreme all-rounder – and Shilton has been very much in the same mould, which is not surprising because in his early, formative days he was Banks's understudy at Leicester. They made it look so easy.'

below Hereford United's first season in the League, 1972–3.

below The start of the rise of Watford, 1977–8.

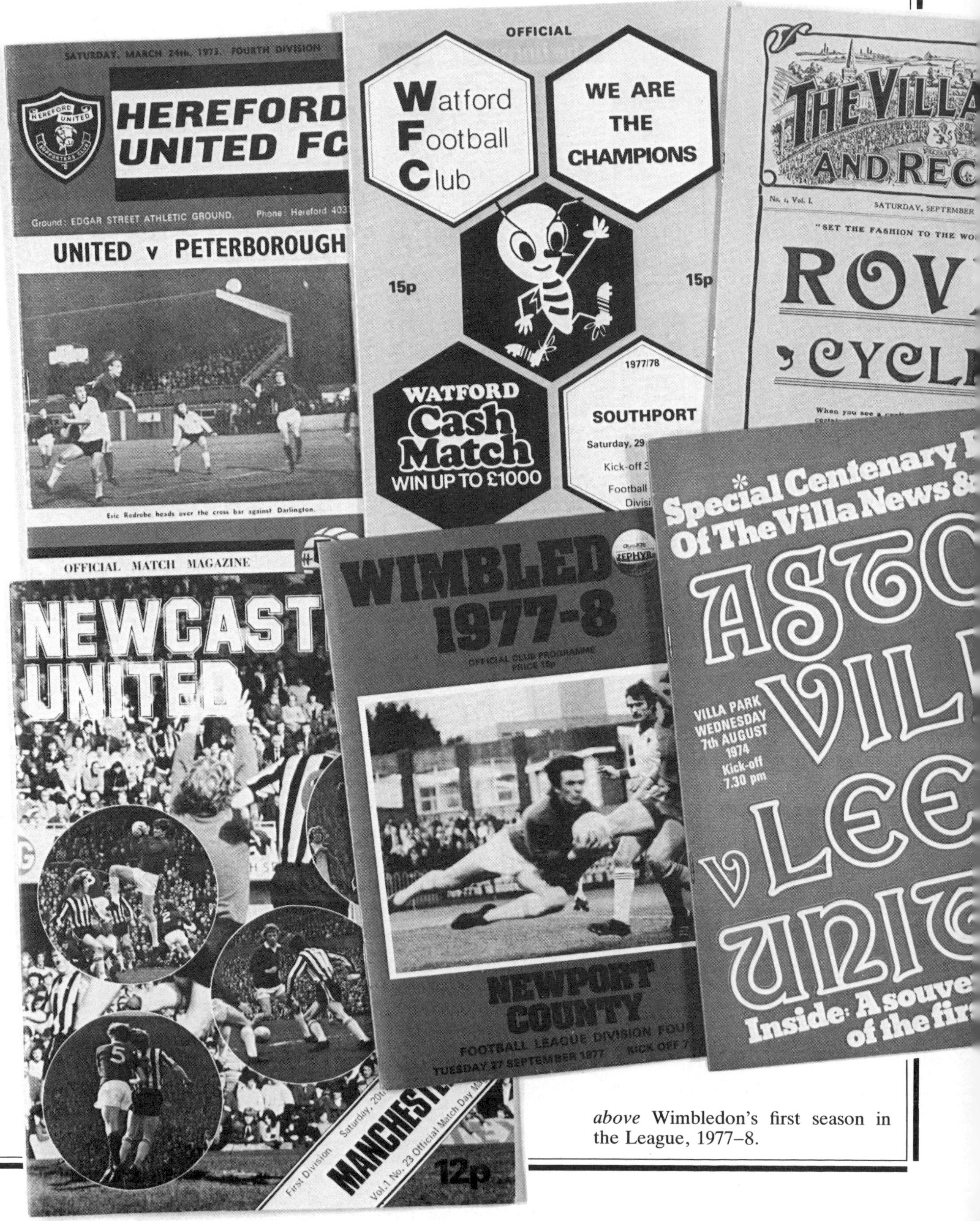

above Wimbledon's first season in the League, 1977–8.

below Luton are back in Division One, May 1974.

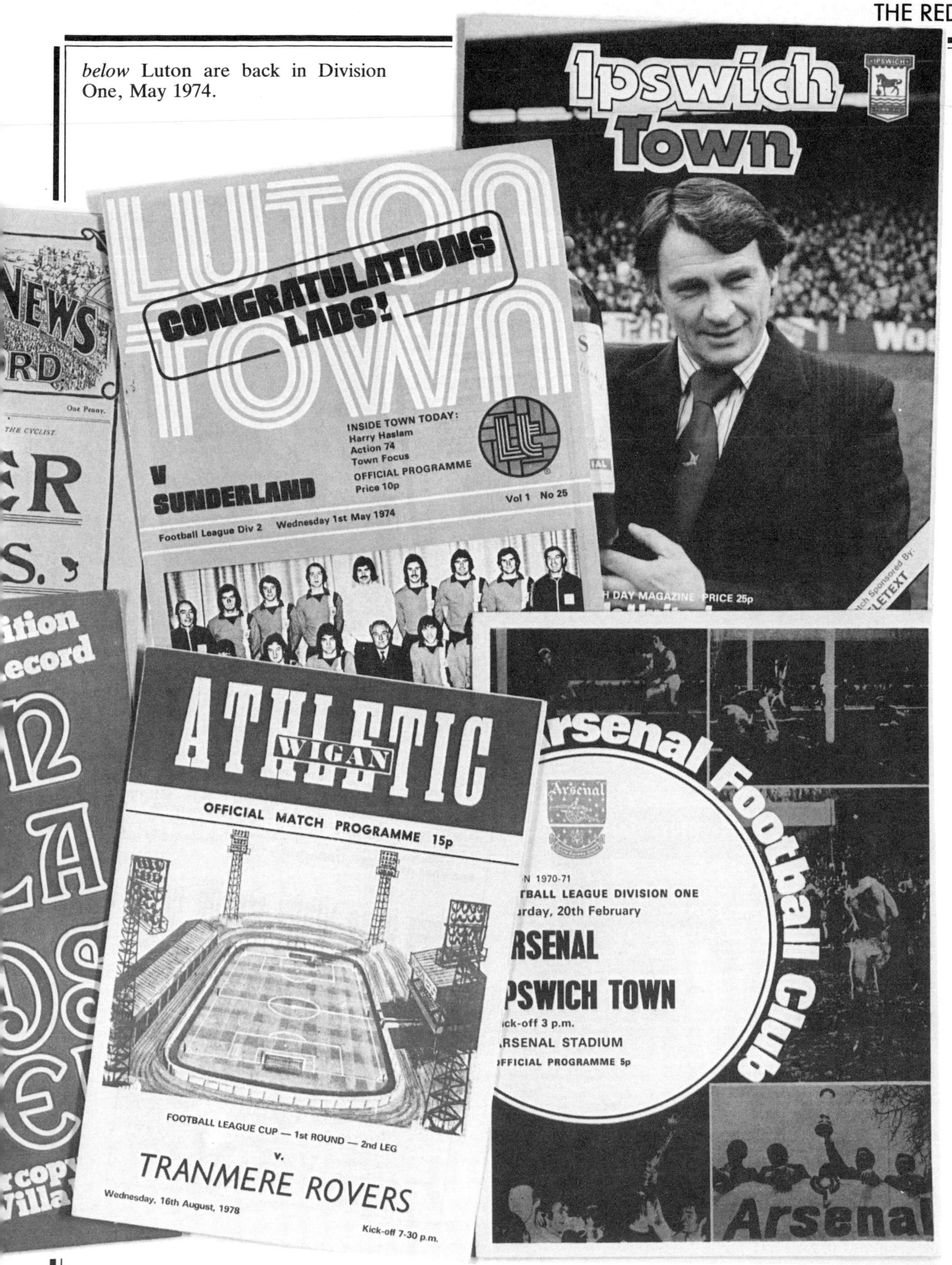

above Wigan Athletic's first game as a League club, Wednesday 16 August 1978.

above Arsenal are on their way to the League and FA Cup 'double', 1971.

above Frank Worthington of Huddersfield, Leicester, Bolton, Birmingham, Leeds, Sunderland, Southampton, Brighton, Tranmere (player-manager), Preston and England – goalscorer, entertainer, traveller, rebel and all-round swashbuckler. Ten clubs in a career of more than 20 years and 700 League games. Eight caps for England (1974–75).

above Alan Hardaker, secretary of the Football League 1957–1979. One of the most respected, influential and controversial figures in the history of the League. Lord Westwood of Newcastle United (League president 1974–81) once said of him: 'I doubt if there is any football administrator who is better known or held in higher esteem.' Hardaker was variously known as 'St Alan of St Annes,' 'the great dictator,' 'football's Godfather,' 'Cagney of the League' and 'the League's most celebrated enforcer'.

right The good old days at Molineux – an early episode in the melodramatic decline of the once mighty Midlands club.

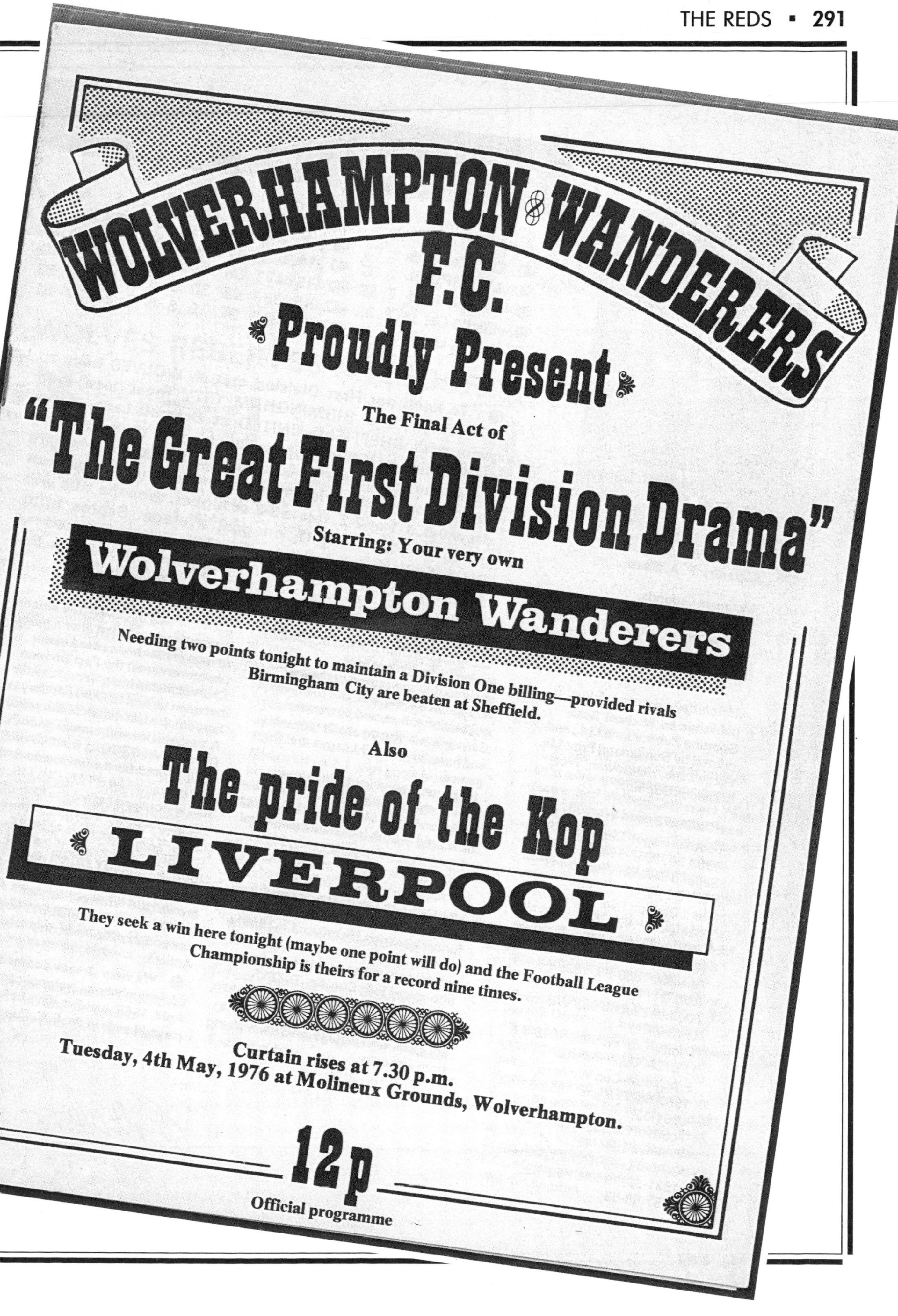
WOLVERHAMPTON WANDERERS F.C.
Proudly Present
The Final Act of
"The Great First Division Drama"
Starring: Your very own
Wolverhampton Wanderers
Needing two points tonight to maintain a Division One billing—provided rivals Birmingham City are beaten at Sheffield.
Also
The pride of the Kop
LIVERPOOL
They seek a win here tonight (maybe one point will do) and the Football League Championship is theirs for a record nine times.
Curtain rises at 7.30 p.m.
Tuesday, 4th May, 1976 at Molineux Grounds, Wolverhampton.
12p
Official programme

WHETHER YOU ARE
OUT OF FORM
OR IN FORM
OR LEFT OUTSIDE
GROUND FULL
OUTSIDE LEFT
Where's the Ball?
INSIDE RIGHT OR INSIDE NOT SO RIGHT
CENTRE FORWARD OR CENTRE TOO FORWARD
PUTTING IN A CORNER
OR JUST PUT IN A CORNER
D
FOUL! OFFSIDE!
GOING TO HEAD
OR GOING TO ANOTHER "HEAD"
BE A FOOTBALLER, NOT A FOOTBAWLER!
REMEMBER, IT'S HOW YOU PLAY THE GAME THAT COUNTS!
Roy ULLYETT.

above Jimmy Case (left) and Phil Neal of Liverpool kiss the European Cup after helping beat Borussia Moenchengladbach 3–1 in the 1977 final in Rome. It was the start of something big. Football League clubs went on to win the trophy – the most important in European club football – seven times in eight years (Liverpool four times, Nottingham Forest twice and Aston Villa once).

right Brian Clough – 'tilter at windmills, natural reformer and socialist "of the heart"'. Only Herbert Chapman has matched Clough's achievement of managing two clubs to the League championship – Derby County (1972) and Nottingham Forest (1978).

right Bradford Park Avenue. Members of the Football League 1908–1970. RIP. The wasteland of Park Avenue nearly ten years after Bradford PA dropped out of the League in 1970 after finishing bottom of the Fourth Division three years in succession. Bradford PA won promotion to Division One just before World War One; and, as respected members of Division Two during the late 1920s and 1930s, attracted a record gate of 34,429 (1931) for a match with Leeds. But a place, when the picture was taken, of memories, bushes, twisted metal – and impressive gables.

below Brighton's proud programme for their first match in Division One, August 1979. Managed with style by Alan Mullery, the former Fulham, Tottenham and England wing-half, Brighton had gained promotion from Third to First Division in three seasons (1977–79). But their start in Division One was painful: a crowd of 28,604 saw Arsenal win 4–0.

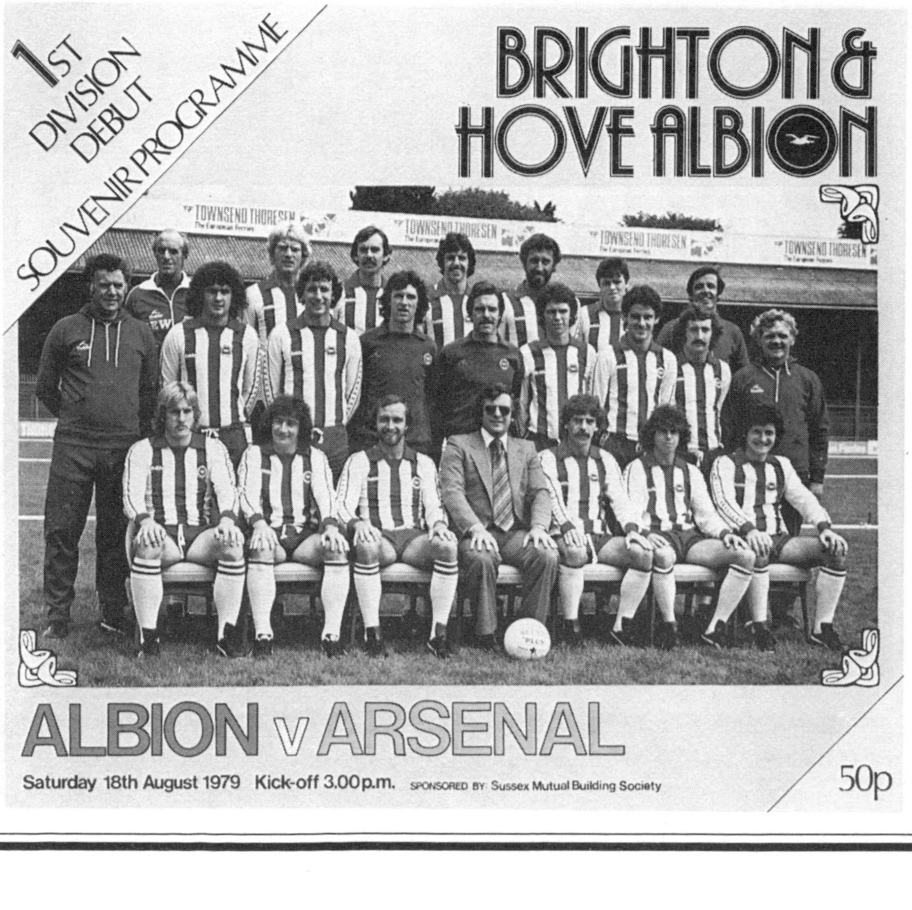

right Trevor Francis – elegant subject of the first British transfer fee of a million pounds when he moved from Birmingham to Nottingham Forest in February 1979. Three months later he scored Forest's winning goal against Malmo of Sweden in the European Cup Final in Munich. In September 1981 he was again sold for more than a million pounds – to Manchester City – and just ten months later he moved to Sampdoria in Italy for £900,000. Began as a 16-year-old sensation with Birmingham with whom he stayed for nine years (118 goals in 278 League games). Won 52 caps for England (1977–86) and would have won many more but for proneness to injury.

nr
Phonola

LEAGUE TABLES

1971–72

FIRST DIVISION

	P	W	D	L	F	A	Pts
1 Derby	42	24	10	8	69	33	58
2 Leeds	42	24	9	9	73	31	57
3 Liverpool	42	24	9	9	64	30	57
4 Man City	42	23	11	8	77	45	57
5 Arsenal	42	22	8	12	58	40	52
6 Tottenham	42	19	13	10	63	42	51
7 Chelsea	42	18	12	12	58	49	48
8 Man United	42	19	10	13	69	61	48
9 Wolves	42	18	11	13	65	57	47
10 Sheff United	42	17	12	13	61	60	46
11 Newcastle	42	15	11	16	49	52	41
12 Leicester	42	13	13	16	41	46	39
13 Ipswich	42	11	16	15	39	53	38
14 West Ham	42	12	12	18	47	51	36
15 Everton	42	9	18	15	37	48	36
16 WBA	42	12	11	19	42	54	35
17 Stoke	42	10	15	17	39	56	35
18 Coventry	42	9	15	18	44	67	33
19 Southampton	42	12	7	23	52	80	31
20 Crystal Palace	42	8	13	21	39	65	29
21 Nottm Forest	42	8	9	25	47	81	25
22 Huddersfield	42	6	13	23	27	59	25

SECOND DIVISION

	P	W	D	L	F	A	Pts
1 Norwich	42	21	15	6	60	36	57
2 Birmingham	42	19	18	5	60	31	56
3 Millwall	42	19	17	6	64	46	55
4 QPR	42	20	14	8	57	28	54
5 Sunderland	42	17	16	9	67	57	50
6 Blackpool	42	20	7	15	70	50	47
7 Burnley	42	20	6	16	70	55	46
8 Bristol City	42	18	10	14	61	49	46
9 Middlesbrough	42	19	8	15	50	48	46
10 Carlisle	42	17	9	16	61	57	43
11 Swindon	42	15	12	15	47	47	42
12 Hull	42	14	10	18	49	53	38
13 Luton	42	10	18	14	43	48	38
14 Sheff Wed	42	13	12	17	51	58	38
15 Oxford	42	12	14	16	43	55	38
16 Portsmouth	42	12	13	17	59	68	37
17 Orient	42	14	9	19	50	61	37
18 Preston	42	12	12	18	52	58	36
19 Cardiff	42	10	14	18	56	69	34
20 Fulham	42	12	10	20	45	68	34
21 Charlton	42	12	9	21	55	77	33
22 Watford	42	5	9	28	24	75	19

THIRD DIVISION

	P	W	D	L	F	A	Pts
1 Aston Villa	46	32	6	8	85	32	70
2 Brighton	46	27	11	8	82	47	65
3 Bournemouth	46	23	16	7	73	37	62
4 Notts County	46	25	12	9	74	44	62
5 Rotherham	46	20	15	11	69	52	55
6 Bristol Rovers	46	21	12	13	75	56	54
7 Bolton	46	17	16	13	51	41	50
8 Plymouth	46	20	10	16	74	64	50
9 Walsall	46	15	18	13	62	57	48
10 Blackburn	46	19	9	18	54	57	47
11 Oldham	46	17	11	18	59	63	45
12 Shrewsbury	46	17	10	19	73	65	44
13 Chesterfield	46	18	8	20	57	57	44
14 Swansea	46	17	10	19	46	59	44
15 Port Vale	46	13	15	18	43	59	41
16 Wrexham	46	16	8	22	59	63	40
17 Halifax	46	13	12	21	48	61	38
18 Rochdale	46	12	13	21	57	83	37
19 York	46	12	12	22	57	66	36
20 Tranmere	46	10	16	20	50	71	36
21 Mansfield	46	8	20	18	41	63	36
22 Barnsley	46	9	18	19	32	64	36
23 Torquay	46	10	12	24	41	69	32
24 Bradford City	46	11	10	25	45	77	32

FOURTH DIVISION

	P	W	D	L	F	A	Pts
1 Grimsby	46	28	7	11	88	56	63
2 Southend	46	24	12	10	81	55	60
3 Brentford	46	24	11	11	76	44	59
4 Scunthorpe	46	22	13	11	56	37	57
5 Lincoln	46	21	14	11	77	59	56
6 Workington	46	16	19	11	50	34	51
7 Southport	46	18	14	14	66	46	50
8 Peterborough	46	17	16	13	82	64	50
9 Bury	46	19	12	15	73	59	50
10 Cambridge	46	17	14	15	62	60	48
11 Colchester	46	19	10	17	70	69	48
12 Doncaster	46	16	14	16	56	63	46
13 Gillingham	46	16	13	17	61	67	45
14 Newport	46	18	8	20	60	72	44
15 Exeter	46	16	11	19	61	68	43
16 Reading	46	17	8	21	56	76	42
17 Aldershot	46	9	22	15	48	54	40
18 Hartlepool	46	17	6	23	58	69	40
19 Darlington	46	14	11	21	64	82	39
20 Chester	46	10	18	18	47	56	38
21 Northampton	46	12	13	21	66	79	37
22 Barrow	46	13	11	22	40	71	37
23 Stockport	46	9	14	23	55	87	32
24 Crewe	46	10	9	27	43	69	29

1972–73

FIRST DIVISION

	P	W	D	L	F	A	Pts
1 Liverpool	42	25	10	6	72	42	60
2 Arsenal	42	23	11	8	57	43	57
3 Leeds	42	21	11	10	77	45	53
4 Ipswich	42	17	14	11	55	45	48
5 Wolves	42	18	11	13	66	54	47
6 West Ham	42	17	12	13	67	53	46
7 Derby	42	19	8	15	56	54	46
8 Tottenham	42	16	13	13	58	48	45
9 Newcastle	42	16	13	13	60	51	45
10 Birmingham	42	15	12	15	53	54	42
11 Man City	42	15	11	16	57	60	41
12 Chelsea	42	13	14	15	49	51	40
13 Southampton	42	11	18	13	47	52	40
14 Sheff United	42	15	10	17	51	59	40
15 Stoke	42	14	10	18	61	56	38
16 Leicester	42	10	17	15	40	46	37
17 Everton	42	13	11	18	41	49	37
18 Man United	42	12	13	17	44	60	37
19 Coventry	42	13	9	20	40	55	35
20 Norwich	42	11	10	21	36	63	32
21 Crystal Palace	42	9	12	21	41	58	30
22 WBA	42	9	10	23	38	62	28

SECOND DIVISION

	P	W	D	L	F	A	Pts
1 Burnley	42	24	14	4	72	35	62
2 QPR	42	24	13	5	81	37	61
3 Aston Villa	42	18	14	10	51	47	50
4 Middlesbrough	42	17	13	12	46	43	47
5 Bristol City	42	17	12	13	63	51	46
6 Sunderland	42	17	12	13	59	49	46
7 Blackpool	42	18	10	14	56	51	46
8 Oxford	42	19	7	16	52	43	45
9 Fulham	42	16	12	14	58	49	44
10 Sheff Wed	42	17	10	15	59	55	44
11 Millwall	42	16	10	16	55	47	42
12 Luton	42	15	11	16	44	53	41
13 Hull	42	14	12	16	64	59	40
14 Nottm Forest	42	14	12	16	47	52	40
15 Orient	42	12	12	18	49	53	36
16 Swindon	42	10	16	16	46	60	36
17 Portsmouth	42	12	11	19	42	59	35
18 Carlisle	42	11	12	19	50	52	34
19 Preston	42	11	12	19	37	64	34
20 Cardiff	42	11	11	20	43	58	33
21 Huddersfield	42	8	17	17	36	56	33
22 Brighton	42	8	13	21	46	83	29

above Snow? What snow? The artificial pitch at Luton Town's Kenilworth Road was laid in 1985.

left Something worth celebrating. Reading supporters mark the club's Third Division championship, 1985–6. Reading won their first 13 games – the best start to a season by any club in the history of the League. *Below*: philatelic cover commemorating their record.

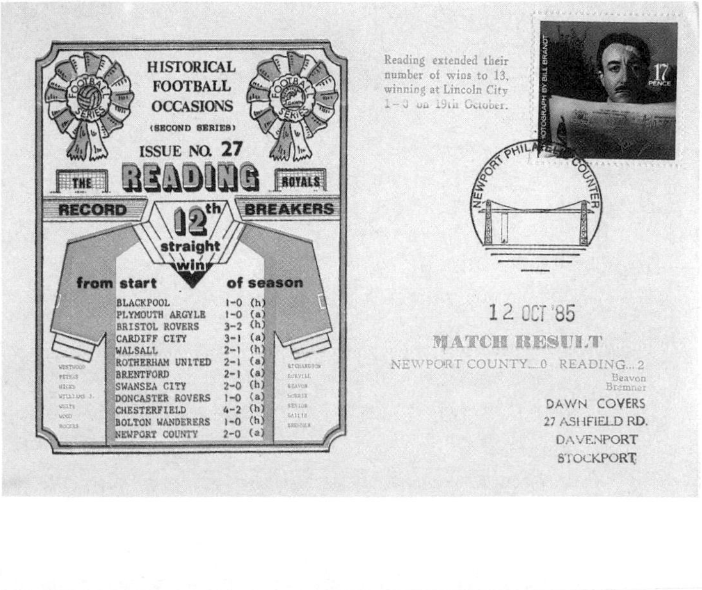

above Kenny Dalgish – 'King Kenny' – celebrates his championship-clinching goal for Liverpool against Chelsea at Stamford Bridge, May 1986 – the first player-manager to guide his side to the title. A week later Liverpool beat Everton 3–1 at Wembley to become only the fifth club in a hundred years to complete the League and FA Cup 'double'. He won his 100th cap for Scotland in the same season.

right Ian Rush leading Liverpool towards their League and FA Cup 'double' in the first all-Merseyside final – Liverpool 3 (Rush 2) Everton 1, Wembley, May 1986. Rush scored 139 goals in 224 League games for Liverpool (1980–1987) and then became the most expensive British player of all by joining Juventus of Turin for a transfer fee of £3.2 million.

Candy

above Gary Lineker of Everton (who was soon to join Barcelona for £2.75 million) on his way to becoming the leading scorer with six goals in the 1986 World Cup Finals in Mexico. Lineker, his injured left wrist heavily strapped, scored all three of England's goals against Poland. Lineker was the League's leading scorer with 30 First Division goals in season 1985–6 and was also voted Footballer of the Year.

right Aston Villa's North Stand – with 'A' and 'V' floodlights.

THIRD DIVISION

		P	W	D	L	F	A	Pts
1	Bolton	46	25	11	10	73	39	61
2	Notts County	46	23	11	12	67	47	57
3	Blackburn	46	20	15	11	57	47	55
4	Oldham	46	19	16	11	72	54	54
5	Bristol Rovers	46	20	13	13	77	56	53
6	Port Vale	46	21	11	14	56	69	53
7	Bournemouth	46	17	16	13	66	44	50
8	Plymouth	46	20	10	16	74	66	50
9	Grimsby	46	20	8	18	67	61	48
10	Tranmere	46	15	16	15	56	52	46
11	Charlton	46	17	11	18	69	67	45
12	Wrexham	46	14	17	15	55	54	45
13	Rochdale	46	14	17	15	48	54	45
14	Southend	46	17	10	19	61	54	44
15	Shrewsbury	46	15	14	17	46	54	44
16	Chesterfield	46	17	9	20	57	61	43
17	Walsall	46	18	7	21	56	66	43
18	York	46	13	15	18	42	46	41
19	Watford	46	12	17	17	43	48	41
20	Halifax	46	13	15	18	43	53	41
21	Rotherham	46	17	7	22	51	65	41
22	Brentford	46	15	7	24	51	69	37
23	Swansea	46	14	9	23	51	73	37
24	Scunthorpe	46	10	10	26	33	72	30

FOURTH DIVISION

		P	W	D	L	F	A	Pts
1	Southport	46	36	10	10	71	48	62
2	Hereford	46	23	12	11	56	38	58
3	Cambridge	46	20	17	9	67	57	57
4	Aldershot	46	22	12	12	60	38	56
5	Newport	46	22	12	12	64	44	56
6	Mansfield	46	20	14	12	78	51	54
7	Reading	46	17	18	11	51	38	52
8	Exeter	46	18	14	14	57	51	50
9	Gillingham	46	19	11	16	63	58	49
10	Lincoln	46	16	16	14	64	57	48
11	Stockport	46	18	12	16	53	53	48
12	Bury	46	14	18	14	58	51	46
13	Workington	46	17	12	17	59	61	46
14	Barnsley	46	14	16	16	58	60	44
15	Chester	46	14	15	17	61	52	43
16	Bradford	46	16	11	19	61	65	43
17	Doncaster	46	15	12	19	49	58	42
18	Torquay	46	12	17	17	44	47	41
19	Peterborough	46	14	13	19	71	76	41
20	Hartlepool	46	12	17	17	34	49	41
21	Crewe	46	9	18	19	38	61	36
22	Colchester	46	10	11	25	48	76	31
23	Northampton	46	10	11	25	40	73	31
24	Darlington	46	7	15	24	42	85	29

1973–74

FIRST DIVISION

		P	W	D	L	F	A	Pts
1	Leeds	42	24	14	4	66	31	62
2	Liverpool	42	22	13	7	52	31	57
3	Derby	42	17	14	11	52	42	48
4	Ipswich	42	18	11	13	67	58	47
5	Stoke	42	15	16	11	54	42	46
6	Burnley	42	16	14	12	56	53	46
7	Everton	42	16	12	14	50	48	44
8	QPR	42	13	17	12	56	52	43
9	Leicester	42	13	16	13	51	41	42
10	Arsenal	42	14	14	14	49	51	42
11	Tottenham	42	14	14	14	45	50	42
12	Wolves	42	13	15	14	49	49	41
13	Sheff United	42	14	12	16	44	49	40
14	Man City	42	14	12	16	39	46	40
15	Newcastle	42	13	12	17	49	48	38
16	Coventry	42	14	10	18	43	54	38
17	Chelsea	42	12	13	17	56	60	37
18	West Ham	42	11	15	16	55	60	37
19	Birmingham	42	12	13	17	52	64	37
20	Southampton*	42	11	14	17	47	68	36
21	Man United*	42	10	12	20	38	48	32
22	Norwich*	42	7	15	20	37	62	29

*Three clubs relegated.

SECOND DIVISION

		P	W	D	L	F	A	Pts
1	Middlesbrough*	42	27	11	4	77	30	65
2	Luton*	42	19	12	11	64	51	50
3	Carlisle*	42	20	9	13	61	48	49
4	Orient	42	15	18	9	55	42	48
5	Blackpool	42	17	13	12	57	40	47
6	Sunderland	42	19	9	14	58	44	47
7	Nottm Forest	42	15	15	12	57	43	45
8	WBA	42	14	16	12	48	45	44
9	Hull	42	13	17	12	46	47	43
10	Notts County	42	15	13	14	55	60	43
11	Bolton	42	15	12	15	44	40	42
12	Millwall	42	14	14	14	51	51	42
13	Fulham	42	16	10	16	39	43	42
14	Aston Villa	42	13	15	14	48	45	41
15	Portsmouth	42	14	12	16	45	62	40
16	Bristol City	42	14	10	18	47	54	38
17	Cardiff	42	10	16	16	49	62	36
18	Oxford	42	10	16	16	35	46	36
19	Sheff Wed	42	12	11	19	51	63	35
20	Crystal Palace‡	42	11	12	19	43	56	34
21	Preston‡§	42	9	14	19	40	62	31
22	Swindon‡	42	7	11	24	36	72	25

* Three clubs promoted.
‡ Three clubs relegated.
§ Preston had one point deducted for fielding an ineligible player.

THIRD DIVISION

		P	W	D	L	F	A	Pts
1	Oldham‡	46	25	12	9	83	47	62
2	Bristol Rovers‡	46	22	17	7	65	33	61
3	York‡	46	21	19	6	67	38	61
4	Wrexham	46	22	12	12	63	43	56
5	Chesterfield	46	21	14	11	55	42	56
6	Grimsby	46	18	15	13	67	50	51
7	Watford	46	19	12	15	64	56	50
8	Aldershot	46	19	11	16	65	52	49
9	Halifax	46	14	21	11	48	51	49
10	Huddersfield	46	17	13	16	56	55	47
11	Bournemouth	46	16	15	15	54	58	47
12	Southend	46	16	14	16	62	62	46
13	Blackburn	46	18	10	18	62	64	46
14	Charlton	46	19	8	19	66	73	46
15	Walsall	46	16	13	17	57	48	45
16	Tranmere	46	15	15	16	50	44	45
17	Plymouth	46	17	10	19	59	54	44
18	Hereford	46	14	15	17	53	57	43
19	Brighton	46	16	11	19	52	58	43
20	Port Vale	46	14	14	18	52	58	42
21	Cambridge*	46	13	9	24	48	81	35
22	Shrewsbury*	46	10	11	25	41	62	31
23	Southport*	46	6	16	24	35	82	28
24	Rochdale*	46	2	17	27	38	94	21

‡ Three clubs promoted.
* Four clubs relegated.

FOURTH DIVISION

		P	W	D	L	F	A	Pts
1	Peterborough*	46	27	11	8	75	38	65
2	Gillingham*	46	25	12	9	90	49	62
3	Colchester*	46	24	12	10	73	36	60
4	Bury*	46	24	11	11	81	49	59
5	Northampton	46	20	13	13	63	48	53
6	Reading	46	16	19	11	58	37	51
7	Chester	46	17	15	14	54	55	49
8	Bradford	46	17	14	15	58	52	48
9	Newport‡	46	16	14	16	56	65	45
10	Exeter†	45	18	8	19	58	55	44
11	Hartlepool	46	16	12	18	48	47	44
12	Lincoln	46	16	12	18	63	67	44
13	Barnsley	46	17	10	19	58	64	44
14	Swansea	46	16	11	19	45	46	43
15	Rotherham	46	15	13	18	56	58	43
16	Torquay	46	13	17	16	52	57	43
17	Mansfield	46	13	17	16	62	69	43
18	Scunthorpe†	45	14	12	19	47	64	42
19	Brentford	46	12	16	18	48	50	40
20	Darlington	46	13	13	20	40	62	39
21	Crewe	46	14	10	22	43	71	38
22	Doncaster	46	12	11	23	47	80	35
23	Workington	46	11	13	22	43	74	35
24	Stockport	46	7	20	19	44	69	34

† Exeter failed to turn up for their fixture at Scunthorpe and the latter were awarded both points.
‡ Newport had one point deducted for fielding an ineligible player.
* Four clubs promoted.

1974–75

FIRST DIVISION

		P	W	D	L	F	A	Pts
1	Derby	42	21	11	10	67	49	53
2	Liverpool	42	20	11	11	60	39	51
3	Ipswich	42	23	5	14	66	44	51
4	Everton	42	16	18	8	56	42	50
5	Stoke	42	17	15	10	64	48	49
6	Sheff United	42	18	13	11	58	51	49
7	Middlesbrough	42	18	12	12	54	40	48
8	Man City	42	18	10	14	54	54	46
9	Leeds	42	16	13	13	57	49	45
10	Burnley	42	17	11	14	68	67	45
11	QPR	42	16	10	16	54	54	42
12	Wolverhampton	42	14	11	17	57	54	39
13	West Ham	42	13	13	16	58	59	39
14	Coventry	42	12	15	15	51	62	39
15	Newcastle	42	15	9	18	59	72	39
16	Arsenal	42	13	11	18	47	49	37
17	Birmingham	42	14	9	19	53	61	37
18	Leicester	42	12	12	18	46	60	36
19	Tottenham	42	13	8	21	52	63	34
20	Luton	42	11	11	20	47	65	33
21	Chelsea	42	9	15	18	42	72	33
22	Carlisle	42	12	5	25	43	59	29

SECOND DIVISION

		P	W	D	L	F	A	Pts
1	Man United	42	26	9	7	66	30	61
2	Aston Villa	42	25	8	9	69	32	58
3	Norwich	42	20	13	9	58	37	53
4	Sunderland	42	19	13	10	65	35	51
5	Bristol City	42	21	8	13	47	33	50
6	WBA	42	18	9	15	54	42	45
7	Blackpool	42	14	17	11	38	33	45
8	Hull	42	15	14	13	40	53	44
9	Fulham	42	13	16	13	44	39	42
10	Bolton	42	15	12	15	45	41	42
11	Oxford	42	15	12	15	41	51	42
12	Orient	42	11	20	11	28	39	42
13	Southampton	42	15	11	16	53	54	41
14	Notts County	42	12	16	14	49	59	40
15	York	42	14	10	18	51	55	38
16	Nottm Forest	42	12	14	16	43	55	38
17	Portsmouth	42	12	13	17	44	54	37
18	Oldham	42	10	15	17	40	48	35
19	Bristol Rovers	42	12	11	19	42	64	35
20	Millwall	42	10	12	20	44	56	32
21	Cardiff	42	9	14	19	36	62	32
22	Sheff Wed	42	5	11	26	29	64	21

THIRD DIVISION

		P	W	D	L	F	A	Pts
1	Blackburn	46	22	16	8	68	45	60
2	Plymouth	46	24	11	11	79	58	59
3	Charlton Ath	46	22	11	13	76	61	55
4	Swindon	46	21	11	14	64	58	53
5	Crystal Palace	46	18	15	13	66	57	51
6	Port Vale	46	18	15	13	61	54	51
7	Peterborough	46	19	12	15	47	53	50
8	Walsall	46	18	13	15	67	52	49
9	Preston NE	46	19	11	16	63	56	49
10	Gillingham	46	17	14	15	65	60	48
11	Colchester	46	17	13	16	70	63	47
12	Hereford	46	16	14	16	64	66	46
13	Wrexham	46	15	15	16	65	55	45
14	Bury	46	16	12	18	53	50	44
15	Chesterfield	46	16	12	18	62	66	44
16	Grimsby	46	15	13	18	55	64	43
17	Halifax	46	13	17	16	49	65	43
18	Southend	46	13	16	17	46	51	42
19	Brighton	46	16	10	20	56	64	42
20	Aldershot	46	14	11	21	53	63	38*
21	Bournemouth	46	13	12	21	44	58	38
22	Tranmere	46	14	9	23	55	57	37
23	Watford	46	10	17	19	52	75	37
24	Huddersfield	46	11	10	25	47	76	32

*One point deducted for playing unregistered player.

FOURTH DIVISION

		P	W	D	L	F	A	Pts
1	Mansfield	46	28	12	6	90	40	68
2	Shrewsbury	46	26	10	10	80	43	62
3	Rotherham	46	22	15	9	71	41	59
4	Chester	46	23	11	12	64	38	57
5	Lincoln	46	21	15	10	79	48	57
6	Cambridge	46	20	14	12	62	44	54
7	Reading	46	21	10	15	63	47	52
8	Brentford	46	18	13	15	53	45	49
9	Exeter	46	19	11	16	60	63	49
10	Bradford	46	17	13	16	56	51	47
11	Southport	46	15	17	14	56	56	47
12	Newport	46	19	9	18	68	75	47
13	Hartlepool	46	16	11	19	52	62	43
14	Torquay	46	14	14	18	46	61	42
15	Barnsley	46	15	11	20	62	65	41
16	Northampton	46	15	11	20	67	73	41
17	Doncaster	46	14	12	20	65	79	40
18	Crewe	46	11	18	17	34	47	40
19	Rochdale	46	13	13	20	59	75	39
20	Stockport	46	12	14	20	43	70	38
21	Darlington	46	13	10	23	54	67	36
22	Swansea	46	15	6	25	46	73	36
23	Workington	46	10	11	25	36	66	31
24	Scunthorpe	46	7	15	24	41	78	29

1975–76

FIRST DIVISION

		P	W	D	L	F	A	Pts
1	Liverpool	42	23	14	5	66	31	60
2	QPR	42	24	11	7	67	33	59
3	Man United	42	23	10	10	68	42	56
4	Derby	42	21	11	10	75	58	53
5	Leeds	42	21	9	12	65	46	51
6	Ipswich	42	16	14	12	54	48	46
7	Leicester	42	13	19	10	48	51	45
8	Man City	42	16	12	15	64	46	43
9	Tottenham	42	14	15	13	63	63	43
10	Norwich	42	16	10	16	58	58	42
11	Everton	42	15	12	15	60	66	42
12	Stoke	42	15	11	16	48	50	41
13	Middlesbrough	42	15	10	17	46	45	40
14	Coventry	42	13	14	15	47	57	40
15	Newcastle	42	15	9	18	71	62	39
16	Aston Villa	42	11	17	14	51	59	39
17	Arsenal	42	13	10	19	47	53	36
18	West Ham	42	13	10	19	48	71	36
19	Birmingham	42	13	7	22	57	75	33
20	Wolverhampton	42	10	10	22	51	68	30
21	Burnley	42	9	10	23	43	66	28
22	Sheff United	42	6	10	26	33	82	22

SECOND DIVISION

		P	W	D	L	F	A	Pts
1	Sunderland	42	24	8	10	67	36	56
2	Bristol City	42	19	15	8	59	35	53
3	WBA	42	20	13	9	50	33	53
4	Bolton	42	20	12	10	64	38	52
5	Notts County	42	19	11	12	60	41	49
6	Southampton	42	21	7	14	66	50	49
7	Luton	42	19	10	13	61	51	48
8	Nottm Forest	42	17	12	13	55	40	46
9	Charlton	42	15	12	15	61	72	42
10	Blackpool	42	14	14	14	40	49	42
11	Chelsea	42	12	16	14	53	54	40
12	Fulham	42	13	14	15	45	47	40
13	Orient	42	13	14	15	37	39	40
14	Hull	42	14	11	17	45	49	39
15	Blackburn	42	12	14	16	45	50	38
16	Plymouth	42	13	12	17	48	54	38
17	Oldham	42	13	12	17	57	68	38
18	Bristol Rovers	42	11	16	15	38	50	38
19	Carlisle	42	12	13	17	45	59	37
20	Oxford	42	11	11	20	39	59	33
21	York	42	10	8	24	39	71	28
22	Portsmouth	42	9	7	26	32	61	25

THIRD DIVISION

	P	W	D	L	F	A	Pts
1 Hereford	46	26	11	9	86	55	63
2 Cardiff	46	22	13	11	69	48	57
3 Millwall	46	20	16	10	54	43	56
4 Brighton	46	22	9	15	78	53	53
5 Crystal Palace	46	18	17	11	61	46	53
6 Wrexham	46	20	12	14	66	55	52
7 Walsall	46	18	14	14	74	61	50
8 Preston	46	19	10	17	62	57	48
9 Shrewsbury	46	19	10	17	61	59	48
10 Peterborough	46	15	18	13	63	63	48
11 Mansfield	46	16	15	15	58	52	47
12 Port Vale	46	15	16	15	55	54	46
13 Bury	46	14	16	16	51	46	44
14 Chesterfield	46	17	9	20	69	69	43
15 Gillingham	46	12	19	15	58	68	43
16 Rotherham	46	15	12	19	54	65	42
17 Chester	46	15	12	19	53	62	42
18 Grimsby	46	15	10	21	62	74	40
19 Swindon	46	16	8	22	62	75	40
20 Sheff Wed	46	12	16	18	48	59	40
21 Aldershot	46	13	13	20	59	75	39
22 Colchester	46	12	14	20	41	65	38
23 Southend	46	12	13	21	65	75	37
24 Halifax	46	11	13	22	41	61	35

FOURTH DIVISION

	P	W	D	L	F	A	Pts
1 Lincoln	46	32	10	4	111	39	74
2 Northampton	46	29	10	7	87	40	68
3 Reading	46	24	12	10	70	51	60
4 Tranmere	46	24	10	12	89	55	58
5 Huddersfield	46	21	14	11	55	41	56
6 Bournemouth	46	20	12	14	57	48	52
7 Exeter	46	18	14	14	56	47	50
8 Watford	46	22	6	18	62	62	50
9 Torquay	46	18	14	14	55	63	50
10 Doncaster	46	19	11	16	75	69	49
11 Swansea	46	16	15	15	66	57	47
12 Barnsley	46	14	16	16	52	48	44
13 Cambridge	46	14	15	17	58	62	43
14 Hartlepool	46	16	10	20	62	78	42
15 Rochdale	46	12	18	16	40	54	42
16 Crewe	46	13	15	18	58	57	41
17 Bradford	46	12	17	17	63	65	41
18 Brentford	46	14	13	19	56	60	41
19 Scunthorpe	46	14	10	22	50	59	38
20 Darlington	46	14	10	22	48	57	38
21 Stockport	46	13	12	21	43	76	38
22 Newport	46	13	9	24	57	90	35
23 Southport	46	8	10	28	41	57	26
24 Workington	46	7	7	32	30	87	27

1976–77

FIRST DIVISION

	P	W	D	L	F	A	Pts
1 Liverpool	42	23	11	8	62	33	57
2 Man City	42	21	14	7	60	34	56
3 Ipswich	42	22	8	12	66	39	56
4 Aston Villa	42	22	7	13	76	50	51
5 Newcastle	42	18	13	11	64	49	49
6 Man United	42	18	11	13	71	62	47
7 WBA	42	16	13	13	62	56	45
8 Arsenal	42	16	11	15	64	59	43
9 Everton	42	14	14	14	62	64	42
10 Leeds	42	15	12	15	48	51	42
11 Leicester	42	12	18	12	47	60	42
12 Middlesbrough	42	14	13	15	40	45	41
13 Birmingham	42	13	12	17	63	61	38
14 QPR	42	13	12	17	47	52	38
15 Derby	42	9	19	14	50	55	37
16 Norwich	42	14	9	19	47	64	37
17 West Ham	42	11	14	17	46	65	36
18 Bristol City	42	11	13	18	38	48	35
19 Coventry	42	10	15	17	48	59	35
20 Sunderland	42	11	12	19	46	54	34
21 Stoke	42	10	14	18	28	51	34
22 Tottenham	42	12	9	21	48	72	33

SECOND DIVISION

	P	W	D	L	F	A	Pts
1 Wolves	42	22	13	7	84	45	57
2 Chelsea	42	21	13	8	73	53	55
3 Nottm Forest	42	21	10	11	77	43	52
4 Bolton	42	10	11	11	74	54	51
5 Blackpool	42	17	17	8	58	42	51
6 Luton	42	23	6	15	67	48	48
7 Charlton	42	16	16	10	71	58	48
8 Notts County	42	19	10	13	65	60	48
9 Southampton	42	17	10	15	72	67	44
10 Millwall	42	17	13	14	57	53	43
11 Sheff United	42	14	12	16	54	63	40
12 Blackburn	42	15	9	18	42	54	39
13 Oldham	42	14	10	18	52	64	38
14 Hull	42	10	17	15	45	53	37
15 Bristol Rovers	42	12	13	17	53	68	37
16 Burnley	42	11	14	17	46	64	36
17 Fulham	42	11	13	18	44	61	35
18 Cardiff	42	12	10	20	56	67	34
19 Orient	42	9	16	17	37	55	34
20 Carlisle	42	11	12	19	49	75	34
21 Plymouth	42	8	16	18	46	65	32
22 Hereford	42	8	15	19	57	78	31

THIRD DIVISION

	P	W	D	L	F	A	Pts
1 Mansfield	46	28	8	10	78	33	64
2 Brighton	46	25	11	10	83	39	61
3 Crystal Palace	46	23	13	10	68	40	59
4 Rotherham	46	22	15	9	69	44	59
5 Wrexham	46	24	10	12	80	54	58
6 Preston	46	21	12	13	64	43	54
7 Bury	46	23	8	15	64	59	54
8 Sheff Wed	46	22	9	15	65	55	53
9 Lincoln	46	25	14	13	77	70	52
10 Shrewsbury	46	18	11	17	65	59	47
11 Swindon	46	15	15	16	68	75	45
12 Gillingham	46	14	12	18	55	64	44
13 Chester	46	18	8	20	48	58	44
14 Tranmere	46	13	17	16	51	53	43
15 Walsall	46	13	15	18	57	65	41
16 Peterborough	46	13	15	18	55	65	41
17 Oxford	46	12	15	19	55	65	39
18 Chesterfield	46	14	10	22	56	64	38
19 Port Vale	46	11	16	19	47	71	38
20 Portsmouth	46	11	14	21	43	70	35
21 Reading	46	13	9	24	49	73	35
22 Northampton	46	13	8	25	60	75	34
23 Grimsby	46	12	9	25	45	69	33
24 York	46	10	12	24	50	89	32

FOURTH DIVISION

	P	W	D	L	F	A	Pts
1 Cambridge	46	26	13	7	87	40	65
2 Exeter	46	25	12	9	70	46	62
3 Colchester	46	25	9	12	77	43	59
4 Bradford	46	23	13	10	71	51	59
5 Swansea	46	25	8	13	82	68	58
6 Barnsley	46	23	9	14	62	39	55
7 Watford	46	18	15	13	67	55	51
8 Doncaster	46	21	9	16	61	65	51
9 Huddersfield	46	19	12	15	60	49	50
10 Southend	46	15	19	12	52	45	49
11 Darlington	46	18	13	15	59	64	49
12 Crewe	46	19	11	16	47	60	49
13 Bournemouth	46	15	18	13	55	44	48
14 Stockport	46	13	19	14	53	57	45
15 Brentford	46	18	7	21	77	76	43
16 Torquay	46	17	9	20	59	67	43
17 Aldershot	46	16	11	19	45	59	43
18 Rochdale	46	13	12	21	50	59	38
19 Newport	46	14	10	22	42	58	38
20 Scunthorpe	46	13	11	22	49	73	37
21 Halifax	46	11	14	21	47	58	36
22 Hartlepool	46	10	12	24	77	73	32
23 Southport	46	3	19	24	53	77	25
24 Workington	46	4	11	31	41	102	19

1977–78

FIRST DIVISION

		P	W	D	L	F	A	Pts
1	Nottm Forest	42	25	14	3	69	24	64
2	Liverpool	42	24	9	9	65	34	57
3	Everton	42	22	11	9	76	45	55
4	Man City	42	20	12	10	74	51	52
5	Arsenal	42	21	10	11	60	37	52
6	WBA	42	18	14	10	62	53	50
7	Coventry	42	18	12	12	75	62	48
8	Aston Villa	42	18	10	14	57	42	46
9	Leeds	42	18	10	14	63	53	46
10	Man United	42	16	10	16	67	63	42
11	Birmingham	42	16	9	17	55	60	41
12	Derby	42	14	13	15	54	59	41
13	Norwich	42	11	18	13	52	66	40
14	Middlesbrough	42	12	15	15	42	54	39
15	Wolves	42	12	12	18	51	64	36
16	Chelsea	42	11	14	17	46	69	36
17	Bristol City	42	11	13	18	49	53	35
18	Ipswich	42	11	13	18	47	61	35
19	QPR	42	9	15	18	47	64	33
20	West Ham	42	12	8	22	52	69	32
21	Newcastle	42	6	10	26	42	78	22
22	Leicester	42	5	12	25	26	70	22

SECOND DIVISION

		P	W	D	L	F	A	Pts
1	Bolton	42	24	10	8	63	33	58
2	Southampton	42	22	13	7	70	39	57
3	Tottenham	42	20	16	6	83	49	56
4	Brighton	42	22	12	8	63	38	56
5	Blackburn	42	16	13	13	56	60	45
6	Sunderland	42	14	16	12	67	59	44
7	Stoke	42	16	10	16	53	49	42
8	Oldham	42	13	16	13	54	58	42
9	Crystal Palace	42	13	15	14	50	47	41
10	Fulham	42	14	13	15	49	49	41
11	Burnley	42	15	10	17	56	64	40
12	Sheff United	42	16	8	18	62	73	40
13	Luton	42	14	10	18	54	52	38
14	Orient	42	10	18	14	43	49	38
15	Notts County	42	11	16	15	54	62	38
16	Millwall	42	12	14	16	49	57	38
17	Charlton	42	13	12	17	55	68	38
18	Bristol Rovers	42	13	12	17	61	77	38
19	Cardiff	42	13	12	17	51	71	38
20	Blackpool	42	12	13	17	59	60	37
21	Mansfield	42	10	11	21	49	69	31
22	Hull	42	8	12	22	34	52	28

THIRD DIVISION

		P	W	D	L	F	A	Pts
1	Wrexham	46	23	15	8	78	45	61
2	Cambridge	46	23	12	11	72	51	58
3	Preston	46	20	16	10	63	38	56
4	Peterborough	46	20	16	10	47	33	56
5	Chester	46	16	22	8	59	56	54
6	Walsall	46	18	17	11	61	50	53
7	Gillingham	46	15	20	11	67	60	50
8	Colchester	46	15	18	13	55	44	48
9	Chesterfield	46	17	14	15	58	49	48
10	Swindon	46	16	16	14	67	60	48
11	Shrewsbury	46	16	15	15	63	57	47
12	Tranmere	46	16	15	15	57	52	47
13	Carlisle	46	14	19	13	59	59	47
14	Sheff Wed	46	15	16	15	50	52	46
15	Bury	46	13	19	14	62	56	45
16	Lincoln	46	15	15	16	53	61	45
17	Exeter	46	15	14	17	49	59	44
18	Oxford	46	13	14	19	64	67	40
19	Plymouth	46	11	17	18	61	68	39
20	Rotherham	46	13	13	20	51	68	39
21	Port Vale	46	8	20	18	46	67	36
22	Bradford	46	12	10	24	56	86	34
23	Hereford	46	9	14	23	34	60	32
24	Portsmouth	46	7	17	22	31	75	31

FOURTH DIVISION

		P	W	D	L	F	A	Pts
1	Watford	46	30	11	5	85	38	71
2	Southend	46	25	10	11	66	39	60
3	Swansea	46	23	10	13	87	47	56
4	Brentford	46	21	14	11	86	54	56
5	Aldershot	46	19	16	11	67	47	54
6	Grimsby	46	21	11	14	57	51	53
7	Barnsley	46	18	14	14	61	49	50
8	Reading	46	18	14	14	55	52	50
9	Torquay	46	16	15	15	57	56	47
10	Northampton	46	17	13	16	63	68	47
11	Huddersfield	46	15	15	16	63	55	45
12	Doncaster	46	14	17	15	52	65	45
13	Wimbledon	46	14	16	16	66	67	44
14	Scunthorpe	46	14	16	16	50	55	44
15	Crewe	46	15	14	17	50	69	44
16	Newport	46	16	11	19	65	73	43
17	Bournemouth	46	14	15	17	41	51	43
18	Stockport	46	16	10	20	56	56	42
19	Darlington	46	14	13	19	52	59	41
20	Halifax	46	10	21	15	52	62	41
21	Hartlepool	46	15	7	24	51	84	37
22	York	46	12	12	22	50	69	36
23	Southport	46	6	19	21	52	76	31
24	Rochdale	46	8	8	30	43	85	24

1978–79

FIRST DIVISION

		P	W	D	L	F	A	Pts
1	Liverpool	42	30	8	4	85	16	68
2	Nottm Forest	42	21	18	3	61	26	60
3	WBA	42	24	11	7	72	35	59
4	Everton	42	17	17	8	52	40	51
5	Leeds	42	18	14	10	70	52	50
6	Ipswich	42	20	9	13	63	49	49
7	Arsenal	42	17	14	11	61	48	48
8	Aston Villa	42	15	16	11	59	49	46
9	Man United	42	15	15	12	60	63	45
10	Coventry	42	14	16	12	58	68	44
11	Tottenham	42	13	15	14	48	61	41
12	Middlesbrough	42	15	10	17	57	50	40
13	Bristol City	42	15	10	17	47	51	40
14	Southampton	42	12	16	14	47	53	40
15	Man City	42	13	13	16	58	56	39
16	Norwich	42	7	23	12	51	57	37
17	Bolton	42	12	11	19	54	75	35
18	Wolves	42	13	8	21	44	68	34
19	Derby	42	10	11	21	44	71	31
20	QPR	42	6	13	23	45	73	25
21	Birmingham	42	6	10	26	37	64	22
22	Chelsea	42	5	10	27	44	92	20

SECOND DIVISION

		P	W	D	L	F	A	Pts
1	Crystal Palace	42	19	19	4	51	24	57
2	Brighton	42	23	10	9	72	39	56
3	Stoke	42	20	16	6	58	31	56
4	Sunderland	42	22	11	9	70	44	55
5	West Ham	42	18	14	10	70	39	50
6	Notts County	42	14	16	12	48	60	44
7	Preston	42	12	18	12	59	57	42
8	Newcastle	42	17	8	17	51	55	42
9	Cardiff	42	16	10	16	56	70	42
10	Fulham	42	13	15	14	50	47	41
11	Orient	42	15	10	17	51	51	40
12	Cambridge	42	12	16	14	44	52	40
13	Burnley	42	14	12	16	51	62	40
14	Oldham	42	13	13	16	52	61	39
15	Wrexham	42	12	14	16	45	42	38
16	Bristol Rovers	42	14	10	18	48	60	38
17	Leicester	42	10	17	15	43	52	37
18	Luton	42	13	10	19	60	57	36
19	Charlton	42	11	13	18	60	69	35
20	Sheff United	42	11	12	19	52	69	34
21	Millwall	42	11	10	21	42	61	32
22	Blackburn	42	10	10	22	41	72	30

THIRD DIVISION

		P	W	D	L	F	A	Pts
1	Shrewsbury	46	21	19	6	61	41	61
2	Watford	46	24	12	10	83	52	60
3	Swansea	46	24	12	10	83	61	60
4	Gillingham	46	21	17	8	65	42	59
5	Swindon	46	25	7	14	74	52	57
6	Carlisle	46	15	22	9	53	42	52
7	Colchester	46	17	17	12	60	55	51
8	Hull	46	19	11	16	66	61	49
9	Exeter	46	17	15	14	61	56	49
10	Brentford	46	19	9	18	53	49	47
11	Oxford	46	14	18	14	44	50	46
12	Blackpool	46	18	9	19	61	59	45
13	Southend	46	15	15	16	51	49	45
14	Sheff Wed	46	13	19	14	53	53	45
15	Plymouth	46	15	14	17	67	68	44
16	Chester	46	14	16	16	57	61	44
17	Rotherham	46	17	10	19	49	55	44
18	Mansfield	46	12	19	15	51	52	43
19	Bury	46	11	20	15	59	65	42
20	Chesterfield	46	13	14	19	51	65	40
21	Peterborough	46	11	14	21	44	63	36
22	Walsall	46	10	12	24	56	71	32
23	Tranmere	46	6	16	24	45	78	28
24	Lincoln	46	7	11	28	41	88	25

FOURTH DIVISION

		P	W	D	L	F	A	Pts
1	Reading	46	26	13	7	76	35	65
2	Grimsby	46	26	9	11	82	49	61
3	Wimbledon	46	25	11	10	78	46	61
4	Barnsley	46	24	13	9	73	42	61
5	Aldershot	46	20	17	9	63	47	57
6	Wigan	46	21	13	12	63	48	55
7	Portsmouth	46	20	12	14	62	48	52
8	Newport	46	21	10	15	66	55	52
9	Huddersfield	46	18	11	17	57	53	47
10	York	46	18	11	17	51	55	47
11	Torquay	46	19	8	19	58	65	46
12	Scunthorpe	46	17	11	18	54	60	45
13	Hartlepool	46	13	18	15	57	66	44
14	Hereford	46	15	13	18	53	53	43
15	Bradford C.	46	17	9	20	62	68	43
16	Port Vale	46	14	14	18	57	70	42
17	Stockport	46	14	12	20	58	60	40
18	Bournemouth	46	14	11	21	47	48	39
19	Northampton	46	15	9	22	64	76	39
20	Rochdale	46	15	9	22	47	64	39
21	Darlington	46	11	15	20	49	66	37
22	Doncaster	46	13	11	22	50	73	37
23	Halifax	46	9	8	29	39	72	26
24	Crewe	46	6	14	26	43	90	26

1979–80

FIRST DIVISION

		P	W	D	L	F	A	Pts
1	Liverpool	42	25	10	7	81	30	60
2	Man United	42	24	10	8	65	35	58
3	Ipswich	42	22	9	11	68	39	53
4	Arsenal	42	18	16	8	52	36	52
5	Nottm Forest	42	20	8	14	63	43	48
6	Wolves	42	19	9	14	58	47	47
7	Aston Villa	42	16	14	12	51	50	46
8	Southampton	42	18	9	15	65	53	45
9	Middlesbrough	42	16	12	14	50	44	44
10	WBA	42	11	19	12	54	50	41
11	Leeds	42	13	14	15	46	50	40
12	Norwich	42	13	14	15	58	66	40
13	Crystal Palace	42	12	16	14	41	50	40
14	Tottenham	42	15	10	17	52	62	40
15	Coventry	42	16	7	19	56	66	39
16	Brighton	42	11	15	16	47	57	37
17	Man City	42	12	13	17	43	66	37
18	Stoke	42	13	10	19	44	58	36
19	Everton	42	9	17	16	43	51	35
20	Bristol City	42	9	13	20	37	66	31
21	Derby	42	11	8	23	47	67	30
22	Bolton	42	5	15	22	38	73	25

SECOND DIVISION

		P	W	D	L	F	A	Pts
1	Leicester	42	21	13	8	58	38	55
2	Sunderland	42	21	12	9	69	42	54
3	Birmingham	42	21	11	10	58	38	53
4	Chelsea	42	23	7	12	66	52	53
5	QPR	42	18	13	11	75	53	49
6	Luton	42	16	17	9	66	45	49
7	West Ham	42	20	7	15	54	43	47
8	Cambridge	42	14	16	12	61	53	44
9	Newcastle	42	15	14	13	53	49	44
10	Preston	42	12	19	11	56	52	43
11	Oldham	42	16	11	15	49	53	43
12	Swansea	42	17	9	16	48	53	43
13	Shrewsbury	42	18	5	19	60	53	41
14	Orient	42	12	17	13	48	54	41
15	Cardiff	42	16	8	18	41	48	40
16	Wrexham	42	16	6	20	40	49	38
17	Notts County	42	11	15	16	51	52	37
18	Watford	42	12	13	17	39	46	37
19	Bristol Rovers	42	11	13	18	50	64	35
20	Fulham	42	11	7	24	42	74	29
21	Burnley	42	6	15	21	39	73	27
22	Charlton	42	6	10	26	39	78	22

THIRD DIVISION

		P	W	D	L	F	A	Pts
1	Grimsby	46	26	10	10	73	42	62
2	Blackburn	46	25	9	12	58	36	59
3	Sheff Wed	46	21	16	9	81	47	58
4	Chesterfield	46	23	11	12	71	46	57
5	Colchester	46	20	12	14	64	56	52
6	Carlisle	46	18	12	16	66	56	48
7	Reading	46	16	16	14	66	65	48
8	Exeter	46	19	10	17	60	68	48
9	Chester	46	17	13	16	49	57	47
10	Swindon	46	19	8	19	71	63	46
11	Barnsley	46	16	14	16	53	56	46
12	Sheff United	46	18	10	18	60	66	46
13	Rotherham	46	18	10	18	58	66	46
14	Millwall	46	16	13	17	65	59	45
15	Plymouth	46	16	12	18	59	55	44
16	Gillingham	46	14	14	18	49	51	42
17	Oxford	46	14	13	19	57	62	41
18	Blackpool	46	15	11	20	62	74	41
19	Brentford	46	15	11	20	59	73	41
20	Hull	46	12	16	18	51	69	40
21	Bury	46	16	7	23	45	59	39
22	Southend	46	14	10	22	47	58	38
23	Mansfield	46	10	16	20	47	58	36
24	Wimbledon	46	10	14	22	52	81	34

FOURTH DIVISION

		P	W	D	L	F	A	Pts
1	Huddersfield	46	27	12	7	101	48	66
2	Walsall	46	23	18	5	75	47	64
3	Newport	46	27	7	12	83	50	61
4	Portsmouth	46	24	12	10	91	49	60
5	Bradford	46	24	12	10	77	50	60
6	Wigan	46	21	13	12	76	61	55
7	Lincoln	46	18	17	11	64	42	53
8	Peterborough	46	21	10	15	58	47	52
9	Torquay	46	15	17	14	70	69	47
10	Aldershot	46	16	13	17	62	53	45
11	Bournemouth	46	13	18	15	52	51	44
12	Doncaster	46	15	14	17	62	63	44
13	Northampton	46	16	12	18	51	66	44
14	Scunthorpe	46	14	15	17	58	75	43
15	Tranmere	46	14	13	19	50	56	41
16	Stockport	46	14	12	20	48	72	40
17	York	46	14	11	21	65	82	39
18	Halifax	46	13	13	20	46	72	39
19	Hartlepool	46	14	10	22	59	64	38
20	Port Vale	46	12	12	22	56	70	36
21	Hereford	46	11	14	21	38	52	36
22	Darlington	46	9	17	20	50	74	35
23	Crewe	46	11	13	22	35	68	35
24	Rochdale	46	7	13	26	33	79	27

1980–81

FIRST DIVISION

		P	W	D	L	F	A	Pts
1	Aston Villa	42	26	8	8	72	40	60
2	Ipswich	42	23	10	9	77	43	56
3	Arsenal	42	19	15	8	61	45	53
4	WBA	42	20	12	10	60	42	52
5	Liverpool	42	17	17	8	62	46	51
6	Southampton	42	20	10	12	76	56	50
7	Nottm Forest	42	19	12	11	62	45	50
8	Man United	42	15	18	9	51	36	48
9	Leeds	42	17	10	15	39	47	44
10	Tottenham	42	14	15	13	70	68	43
11	Stoke	42	12	18	12	51	60	42
12	Man City	42	14	11	17	56	59	39
13	Birmingham	42	13	12	17	50	61	38
14	Middlesbrough	42	16	5	21	53	51	37
15	Everton	42	13	10	19	55	58	36
16	Coventry	42	13	10	19	48	68	36
17	Sunderland	42	14	7	21	58	53	35
18	Wolves	42	13	9	20	47	55	35
19	Brighton	42	14	7	21	54	67	35
20	Norwich	42	13	7	22	49	73	33
21	Leicester	42	13	6	23	40	67	32
22	Crystal Palace	42	6	7	29	47	83	19

SECOND DIVISION

		P	W	D	L	F	A	Pts
1	West Ham	42	28	10	4	79	29	66
2	Notts County	42	18	17	7	49	38	53
3	Swansea	42	18	14	10	64	44	50
4	Blackburn	42	16	18	8	42	29	50
5	Luton	42	18	12	12	61	46	48
6	Derby	42	15	15	12	57	52	45
7	Grimsby	42	15	15	12	44	42	45
8	QPR	42	15	13	14	56	46	43
9	Watford	42	16	11	15	50	45	43
10	Sheff Wed	42	17	8	17	53	51	42
11	Newcastle	42	14	14	14	30	45	42
12	Chelsea	42	14	12	16	46	41	40
13	Cambridge	42	17	6	17	53	65	40
14	Shrewsbury	42	11	17	14	46	47	39
15	Oldham	42	12	15	15	39	48	39
16	Wrexham	42	12	14	16	43	45	38
17	Orient	42	13	12	17	52	56	38
18	Bolton	42	14	10	18	61	66	38
19	Cardiff	42	12	12	18	44	60	36
20	Preston	42	11	14	17	41	62	36
21	Bristol City	42	7	16	19	29	51	30
22	Bristol Rovers	42	5	13	24	34	65	23

THIRD DIVISION

		P	W	D	L	F	A	Pts
1	Rotherham	46	24	13	9	62	32	61
2	Barnsley	46	21	17	8	72	45	59
3	Charlton	46	25	9	12	63	44	59
4	Huddersfield	46	21	14	11	71	40	56
5	Chesterfield	46	23	10	13	72	48	56
6	Portsmouth	46	22	9	15	55	47	53
7	Plymouth	46	19	14	13	56	44	52
8	Burnley	46	18	14	14	60	48	50
9	Brentford	46	14	19	13	52	49	47
10	Reading	46	18	10	18	62	62	46
11	Exeter	46	16	13	17	62	66	45
12	Newport	46	15	13	18	64	61	43
13	Fulham	46	15	13	18	57	64	43
14	Oxford	46	13	17	16	39	47	43
15	Gillingham	46	12	18	16	48	58	42
16	Millwall	46	14	14	18	43	60	42
17	Swindon	46	13	15	18	51	56	41
18	Chester	46	15	11	20	41	48	41
19	Carlisle	46	14	13	19	57	70	41
20	Walsall	46	13	15	18	59	74	41
21	Sheff United	46	14	13	19	65	62	40
22	Colchester	46	14	11	21	45	65	39
23	Blackpool	46	9	14	23	45	75	32
24	Hull	46	8	16	22	40	71	32

FOURTH DIVISION

		P	W	D	L	F	A	Pts
1	Southend	46	30	7	9	79	31	67
2	Lincoln	46	25	15	6	66	25	65
3	Doncaster	46	22	12	12	59	49	56
4	Wimbledon	46	23	9	14	64	46	55
5	Peterborough	46	17	18	11	68	54	52
6	Aldershot	46	18	14	14	43	41	50
7	Mansfield	46	20	9	17	58	44	49
8	Darlington	46	19	11	16	65	59	49
9	Hartlepool	46	20	9	17	64	61	49
10	Northampton	46	18	13	15	65	67	49
11	Wigan	46	18	11	17	51	55	47
12	Bury	46	17	11	18	70	62	45
13	Bournemouth	46	16	13	17	47	48	45
14	Bradford	46	14	16	16	53	60	44
15	Rochdale	46	14	15	17	60	70	43
16	Scunthorpe	46	11	20	15	60	69	42
17	Torquay	46	18	5	23	55	63	41
18	Crewe	46	13	14	19	48	61	40
19	Port Vale	46	12	15	19	57	68	39
20	Stockport	46	16	7	23	44	57	39
21	Tranmere	46	13	10	23	59	73	36
22	Hereford	46	11	13	22	38	62	35
23	Halifax	46	11	12	23	44	71	34
24	York	46	12	9	25	47	66	33

TEN
Time for Change
1981 –

'There is no mystery or mystique about football. There is nothing about the game that can't be easily grasped by the chap on the terrace. Its techniques and patterns can all be described in plain, honest words. As in everything there are degrees of knowledge and experience; some learn much from little, others little from much. But the joy of the game is its dramatic simplicity.'

Ron Greenwood, *member of Chelsea's League championship side in 1954–55 and later a much respected manager of West Ham and England.*

What would William McGregor, the father of the Football League, have made of million pound transfers, artificial pitches, floodlights, hooliganism, sponsorship, Sunday football and television beaming 'live' matches into the nation's homes? And what would he have thought of Preston – the 'Old Invincibles' – finishing ninety-first out of 92 in 1986 and needing, cap in hand, to apply for re-election?

Professional football is a mirror of its time, reflecting society and sometimes, like theatre, exaggerating it; and in a period of chronic economic uncertainty, affluence but also unemployment, changing leisure patterns, protest and dissent, increasing violence and new technology the Football League is now faced by more problems than at any time in a hundred years.

The heartbeat of this simple game, though, is still strong. There are more players and clubs at both professional and amateur level than ever before and, despite a serious decline in League gates, more people continue to watch football than any other spectator sport. Televised games command huge audiences and newspapers devote more space to the game than any other subject. It is still the game of the people.

There has been remarkably little change in the character of the Football League during its century of drama and expansion, but who would care to predict its shape and standing in a hundred years from now. We can only suppose, on the evidence of the second half of the twentieth century, that Liverpool FC will still be there – and still winning.

Liverpool were awesomely successful in the 1970s – and then they stepped up the pace. Bob Paisley became the most successful manager in the history of League football before he stepped aside in 1983: in a decade he led the Anfield club to victory in six championships, three League 'Milk' Cups, three European Cups, one UEFA Cup and five Charity Shields. He did not, however, manage to win three major trophies in one season or to complete the League and FA Cup 'double'. He left that to the men who succeeded him.

First there was Joe Fagan, another insider from the famous Anfield 'boot-room' – the hideaway where Paisley and his closest staff had discussed players, opponents and general strategy. Fagan captained Manchester City during his playing days but Liverpool was his own town and he joined the Anfield club as assistant trainer in 1958. He was a step behind Paisley all the way and succeeded him so smoothly that his first season, 1983–4, was the most successful that Liverpool or any other League club had ever enjoyed. They not only won three major honours, the League title, the European Cup and the Milk Cup, but the championship was Liverpool's third in succession – equalling the old record, of course, of Huddersfield and Arsenal. The Milk Cup (previously the League Cup) was also theirs for the fourth year running. Just another record.

As one opposing manager wearily put it: 'How can they fail? They've got the League's best footballer, the best brain, the best goal-scorer and the best athlete.' He was referring, in turn, to Kenny Dalglish, Graeme Souness, Ian Rush and Mark Lawrenson. Dalglish was the master; Souness, who had come from Middlesbrough in 1978, was the conductor, hard, beautifully composed and full of ideas; Rush, from Chester, was the hit-man, a natural predator; and

Lawrenson, a record buy from Brighton for £900,000, was the all-action, all-purpose prop in defence or midfield. Liverpool were studied and analysed and repeatedly asked for their 'secret'. The theories were many: experience and harmony at all levels, continuity, common sense, lack of sentiment, the ingrained quality of their passing game, the passion of their supporters – and, never to be overlooked, good players. The real answer, Paisley would say, is simplicity – which only seemed to confirm that the art of simplicity is very complicated.

Fagan was succeeded after two years by yet another insider, Dalglish himself who had been with Liverpool eight years and now became that rarest of animals, a First Division player-manager. Odd doubts were voiced about his appointment but Dalglish – who would soon win his hundredth cap for Scotland – was battle-hardened, ambitious and confident. And in his first season, 1985–6, Liverpool completed the League and FA Cup 'double', the fifth club to manage it in all, the third of the twentieth century.

Liverpool's achievements on the field, however, stood for nothing against the tragedy which took place on the terraces of the Heysel Stadium in Brussels on 29 May 1985. Liverpool were there to play Juventus in the final of the European Cup but, more than an hour before the kick-off, a force of Liverpool supporters invaded a section holding Italian fans. A containing wall collapsed, panic followed, police action was inadequate or too late and the place became a battleground. Thirty-nine people (31 Italian) were trampled or crushed to death and nearly 450 injured. Retribution followed swiftly. English clubs were banned from competing in Europe for an indefinite period and, later, the organizers, police and the inadequacy of the stadium were all severely criticized. Norwich, winners of the Milk Cup and looking forward to their first season in Europe, were hit hardest of all by the ban; but, whoever was really to blame, the 'English disease' of hooliganism made wounding headlines all around the world.

Yet, unbearably, this was the second major tragedy of that terrible month of May in 1985. Eighteen days before the Brussels disaster Bradford City played Lincoln City at Valley Parade – their last match of the season and a day of joy because the Yorkshire club were Third Division champions. Sometime during the first half, though, a carelessly discarded cigarette set light to piles of old paper which had been allowed to collect under loose fitting floorboards in the main stand. The fire spread quickly, going sideways because of the construction of the stand, and in less than five minutes the building was a wall of flame. A day of celebration turned into one of horror in front of television cameras. Fifty-six people were burnt to death and more than 200 injured.

In the days of shock and inquiry which followed there was talk of ignored warnings, locked exits and narrow passageways; and, of course, there were stringent and wide-ranging reforms. Life eventually returned to something like normal. A new stand rose out of the ashes of the old. But the people of Bradford share a grief they will never forget.

The tragedies of Bradford and Brussels cast a shadow over everything – but Everton, by then, had illuminated all that is good in the game. The Goodison Park club had been eclipsed by Liverpool for 15 years but now, with great style and rich spirit, they won the 1985 League championship by an uncompromising margin of 13 points and completed a rare 'double' by beating Rapid Vienna 3–1 in the final of the European Cup Winners' Cup in Rotterdam. It was a night on which 20,000 Merseyside fans were a credit to their club and country – and no one knew, as Everton celebrated their first success in Europe, that it would also be the last before the continent turned its back on the English game.

Just one other club broke Liverpool's monopoly of the championship in the early 1980s. Aston Villa won the title in 1981 – their first for 71 years – with a side of such strength and durability that in the course of the season they used only 14 players; seven played in every game. Their success was popular as well as overdue because Villa, like Everton, are one of the game's originals, one of the traditional seats of power. Villa followed up hard by winning the European Cup in 1982 – a success all the more notable for a sudden, mid-season change of manager. Ron Saunders, bluff and uncompromising, resigned and his place was taken by the quiet and likeable Tony Barton – but not once did Villa falter.

Aston Villa's triumph over Bayern Munich in Rotterdam in 1982 contributed to a towering run of success in Europe by League clubs – a run which re-established the First Division as the most powerful in Europe. The Italian League, with its many brilliant imports, the Spanish League and the West German Bundesliga are all strong and influential; but if European competition is any sort of yardstick then the First Division of the League made an impressive case for itself over a long period.

The European Cup, competed for only by champions, was in an English trophy case for seven of the eight seasons between 1977 and 1984, a sequence almost matched (seven in nine) by League clubs in the UEFA Cup between 1968 and 1976. Success in the World Cup has proved elusive – but English clubs, shaping talent from all over the British Isles into competitive and disciplined units, were undoubtedly the pace-setters in Europe until the Heysel disaster.

It was a period, too, of other remarkable success stories. Swansea climbed from Fourth Division to First in four seasons (1978–81); Watford made the same jump in five seasons (1978–82) and finished as runners-up in their first season in Division One; Oxford United, a club in danger of liquidation in 1982, won the championships of the Third and Second Divisions in successive seasons to reach Division One for the first time in their history, and then triumphed in the 1986 Milk Cup just for good measure; and Wimbledon, astonishingly, made the long jump from non-League football to the First Division in just nine seasons (1977–86). All had the good fortune to have men at the top of vision, courage and substance.

But as the League celebrates its centenary it is obvious that the professional game faces grave problems and new challenges. Attendances have fallen critically, many clubs cannot balance income and expenditure, hooliganism damagingly persists and too many outstanding players are leasing their talents to wealthy clubs on the continent. Artificial pitches and membership schemes for supporters are among many areas of dispute; and, for the first time in a hundred years, the number of clubs in the First Division has been pruned.

The foundations, however, are still solid. The appeal of the game endures. The Football League has good reason to look forward as well as back.

LEAGUE CUP/MILK CUP/LITTLEWOODS CUP FINALS

League Cup

1960–61	Rotherham United 2 Aston Villa 0/Aston Villa 3 Rotherham 0 aet (Aston Villa won 3–2 on aggregate)
1961–62	Rochdale 0 Norwich City 3/Norwich 1 Rochdale 0 (Norwich won 4–0 on aggregate)
1962–63	Birmingham City 3 Aston Villa 1/Aston Villa 0 Birmingham 0 (Birmingham won 3–1 on aggregate)
1963–64	Stoke City 1 Leicester City 1/Leicester 3 Stoke 2 (Leicester won 4–3 on aggregate)
1964–65	Chelsea 3 Leicester City 2/Leicester 0 Chelsea 0 (Chelsea won 3–2 on aggregate)
1965–66	West Ham United 2 West Bromwich Albion 1/West Bromwich Albion 4 West Ham 1 (W.B.A. won 5–3 on aggregate)

(At Wembley)

1966–67	Queen's Park Rangers 3 West Bromwich Albion 2
1967–68	Leeds United 1 Arsenal 0
1968–69	Swindon Town 3 Arsenal 1 aet
1969–70	Manchester City 2 West Bromwich Albion 1 aet
1970–71	Tottenham Hotspur 2 Aston Villa 0
1971–72	Stoke City 2 Chelsea 1
1972–73	Tottenham Hotspur 1 Norwich City 0
1973–74	Wolverhampton Wanderers 2 Manchester City 1
1974–75	Aston Villa 1 Norwich City 0
1975–76	Manchester City 2 Newcastle United 1
1976–77	Aston Villa 3 Everton 2 aet (at Old Trafford) (after 0–0 and 1–1 aet draws – first replay at Hillsborough)
1977–78	Nottingham Forest 1 Liverpool 0 (at Old Trafford) (after 0–0 aet draw)
1978–79	Nottingham Forest 3 Southampton 2
1979–80	Wolverhampton Wanderers 1 Nottingham Forest 0
1980–81	Liverpool 2 West Ham United 1 (at Villa Park) (after 1–1 aet draw)
1981–82	Liverpool 3 Tottenham Hotspur 1 aet

Milk Cup

1982–83	Liverpool 2 Manchester United 1 aet
1983–84	Liverpool 1 Everton 0 (at Maine Road) (after 0–0 draw aet)
1984–85	Norwich City 1 Sunderland 0
1985–86	Oxford 3 Queen's Park Rangers 0

Littlewoods Cup

1986–87	Arsenal 2 Liverpool 1

below Dick Pym of Bolton, Exeter and England who, as the League entered its centenary year, was believed to be the oldest living former League footballer. The picture was taken at Topsham, near Exeter, in 1963 when Pym was 70. He gave up salmon fishing when he was 81 and attended the 100th FA Cup Final at Wembley in 1981 when he was 88. *right* Pym was Bolton's goalkeeper in three FA Cup Finals (1923 – the first at Wembley, 1926 and 1929) – Bolton won all three and Pym did not let a goal in. Pym won three caps for England (1925–6) and broke his collarbone, ribs, an arm and several fingers during his career. 'Not bad,' he would say, 'considering what used to happen to goalkeepers then.'

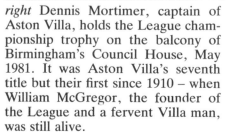

right Dennis Mortimer, captain of Aston Villa, holds the League championship trophy on the balcony of Birmingham's Council House, May 1981. It was Aston Villa's seventh title but their first since 1910 – when William McGregor, the founder of the League and a fervent Villa man, was still alive.

ARGOS CATALOGUE SHOWROOMS
SERVIS
FUJI FILM
DAF

above And things were never the same again. John Toshack, manager of Swansea City, watches his team lose at Coventry and, at the same time, lose their leadership of the First Division, October 1981. Swansea had enjoyed four years of breathtaking success: Fourth Division to First in four seasons (1978–81) and then, with seven wins and a draw in their first ten games in their first season in Division One, they found themselves at the top of the League. They finished sixth (1981–2) but were relegated the following season – and kept on falling. By 1986 they were back in Division Four. Toshack had brought knowledge and players to the Vetch Field from Liverpool where he had been a great favourite with the crowd and an ideal goal-scoring partner for Kevin Keegan. Forty caps for Wales (1969–80).

left The first League game to be played on synthetic turf: Queen's Park Rangers v Luton at Loftus Road, September 1981. Rangers' decision to lay an artificial pitch at a cost of £350,000 was one of the most controversial in the history of League football; and the arguments still go on. A handful of other clubs followed with improved surfaces – including Luton. But further installation of synthetic pitches was halted in season 1986–7 to give manufacturers time to develop a surface with bounce and pace nearer to that of grass. Rangers lost their first game on 'plastic' by 2–1.

below Kevin Keegan (on backside) and Alan Ball battle for Southampton in mid-winter English mud 1982 – two of the outstanding figures lured to the Dell by Lawrie McMenemy (*right*) during his twelve eventful years as manager of Southampton. Ball, one of England's World Cup winners in 1966, also played for Blackpool, Everton, Arsenal and Bristol Rovers before becoming manager of Portsmouth in 1984, and leading them to promotion in Division One in 1987. McMenemy, who led Southampton to FA Cup victory in 1976 when they were in the Second Division, moved to Sunderland in 1985 – and left, mission unfulfilled, in April 1987. A month later, after failing in the play-offs, Sunderland were relegated to Division Three for the first time in their history.

above Pat Jennings of Watford, Tottenham, Arsenal and Northern Ireland – the most capped international in football history. He won his 119th and last cap on his 41st birthday against Brazil during the 1986 World Cup Finals in Mexico. He also became the first British player to complete 1,000 first class appearances in February 1983. His final total in a 24-season career was 1,098.

above Everton congregation. The Church of St Luke the Evangelist – Goodison's famous landmark – is behind. Everton once attempted to pay for its removal.

below Everton's championship for the second time in three seasons, May 1987. Philip Carter – President of the League and Chairman of Everton – presents the trophy to Kevin Ratcliffe, Everton's captain, at Goodison Park. Everton finished nine points ahead of Liverpool; and it was their ninth title.

above The tide turns and Coventry head for the first major trophy in their 104-year history – the 1987 FA Cup. A dramatic header by Keith Houchen (left) beats Ray Clemence, Tottenham's goalkeeper, for Coventry's second equaliser in the final at Wembley. Coventry won 3–2 with the help of an 'own goal' by Gary Mabbutt in extra-time.

above right Mud – 'the great leveller' – at Orient's Brisbane Road.

right Stained glass windows at Sheffield United's Bramall Lane – an elegant reminder that once the ground was also one of the homes of Yorkshire cricket. The 4 ft by 2 ft windows used to adorn a staircase in the old cricket pavilion but are now in the Directors' Suite in the new South Stand. The last county cricket match at Bramall Lane was in August 1973.

above Craven Cottage, the Thames-side home of Fulham football since 1896. Property developers with plans for filling these green and expensive acres with luxury housing nearly got their way in 1987. But the protests of local councillors, MPs and supporters prevailed, several buildings at the ground were protectively listed and a consortium headed by Jimmy Hill bought the club's name and players' contracts. The role of Craven Cottage as a football ground was assured for 'the foreseeable future'.

below The old North Stand at Stamford Bridge – one of football's architectural curiosities. It was built in 1939 with stilts, glass screens at either end, a roof that looked about to fall in and seats for around 1,000. It was demolished after the rise of Chelsea's massive new East Stand in the early 1970s.

below To the future . . .

A poignant reminder, August 1982.

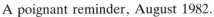

above Nottingham Forest supporters amuse themselves at the City Ground mid-way through a League match against Birmingham in January 1982 – and mid-way through one of the severest winters since World War Two. Snow and ice prevented a full Saturday programme for eight weeks. And again there were impassioned demands for a mid-winter break.

left Ossie Ardiles who helped Argentina win the World Cup in 1978 and then joined Tottenham to become one of the most popular and successful of all the many foreign stars who have played League football. Ardiles, a small, quick and highly perceptive midfield player, a master craftsman, was a member of Tottenham's FA Cup-winning side in 1981 – and here, centre stage, he expertly helps them reach Wembley again the following season by beating Leicester in a Villa Park semi-final. The date of the semi-final: 3 April 1982 – and Ardiles knew that 24 hours earlier Argentina had invaded the Falklands. He did not play in the final.

above Kevin Keegan scores the winning goal in his first game for Newcastle (v Queen's Park Rangers) at St James's Park, August 1982 – a stunning start to the fifth phase of an illustrious career. He bowed out at the end of the 1983 season with a goal in his last and 500th League game (v Brighton) to help Newcastle clinch promotion from Division Two. It ensured his place as one of the celebrated heroes of Tyneside. Keegan – described as 'the most modern of modern footballers' – played for Scunthorpe (124 League games), Liverpool (230), Hamburg (90), Southampton (68) and Newcastle (78). He won three Championship medals, three European medals and an FA Cup Winners' medal with Liverpool, and was twice voted European Footballer of the Year (1978 and 1979) during his influential period with Hamburg in the Bundesliga. English Footballer of the Year 1976. Captain of England: 63 caps (1973–82). One of the most remarkable – and marketable – footballers of the post-war period.

above Watford celebrate finishing as runners-up in their first season in Division One, May 1983. They had just beaten Liverpool 2–1 in their final game of the season, at Vicarage Road, to finish a point ahead of Manchester United who lost 2–3 at Notts County. Standing (l to r): Steve Sherwood, Steve Sims, Kenny Jackett, Paul Franklin, Luther Blissett, John Barnes, Nigel Callaghan, Worrell Sterling, Wilf Rostron, Pat Rice. Front row: Jan Lohman, Martin Patching, Elton John, Graham Taylor, John Ward. Taylor left to become Aston Villa's manager in May 1987 saying: 'After ten years I want to put my reputation on the line again. I want a fresh challenge, a different experience.' Villa had just been relegated to Division Two.

right English football chairman 1981. Elton John, chairman of Watford and pop super-star, at Heathrow Airport – complete with Watford holdall. Watford were a mid-table Fourth Division club when John became chairman in May 1976 – and he soon completed his 'top' team with Graham Taylor (manager), Eddie Plumley (chief executive and secretary) and Bertie Mee (assistant manager and later director) after his distinguished career with Arsenal. Watford were promoted in 1978 and moved from Fourth Division to First in just five seasons.

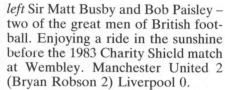

left Sir Matt Busby and Bob Paisley – two of the great men of British football. Enjoying a ride in the sunshine before the 1983 Charity Shield match at Wembley. Manchester United 2 (Bryan Robson 2) Liverpool 0.

above Bob Paisley of Liverpool – the most successful club manager in the history of League football – walks down the Anfield tunnel with the championship trophy just before his last home match in charge, May 1983. Liverpool 1 Aston Villa 1.

Bryan Robson of West Bromwich, Manchester United and England – centre of the first transfer of £1,500,000 involving two British clubs: West Bromwich to Manchester United in October 1981. Dynamic, goal-scoring midfield player and captain of club and country. *left* scores his second goal for England v France in opening match of 1982 World Cup Finals in Spain. His first goal came 27 seconds after kick-off – the fastest goal in any World Cup Finals. *right* the stress of routine League combat v Leicester at Old Trafford, March 1984. Robson is sandwiched by Andy Peake and Andy Feeley.

HARP
IND COOPE

right Howard Kendall and friend. Before his departure to Athletic Bilbao in 1987, manager Kendall inspired Everton, one of the League's founder members, to the most successful period in their history – with season 1984–5 the highpoint. Everton won the League championship by a margin of 13 points, stylishly won the club's first European trophy, the Cup Winners' Cup, and reached the final of the FA Cup (beaten 1–0 by Manchester United). In 1964, with Preston he became the youngest player to appear in an FA Cup Final (Preston 2 West Ham 3) and completed a renowned midfield with Alan Ball and Colin Harvey in Everton's outstanding championship side of 1970. Was player-manager of Blackburn when they won promotion from Division Three in 1980 and joined Everton in May 1981.

left The unacceptable face of football. Leeds fans riot at St Andrew's on the final Saturday of the 1984–5 season. A boy died after being injured by a collapsing wall and police were among many hurt. The second half started 30 minutes late. Birmingham won 1–0 and finished runners-up in Division Two. It happened on the same day as the Bradford fire disaster.

above Seats of power: Anfield (right) and Goodison Park – separated by the famous Stanley Park. The picture was taken in 1985 when Everton were League champions and Liverpool runners-up. In 1986 Liverpool won the title for a record sixteenth time and Everton were runners-up; and in 1987 the position was again reversed, Everton winning the championship for the ninth time. Everton played at Anfield for eight years (1884–92) but, after a heated rent dispute with their landlord, they bought a plot on the other side of the park and Goodison, the first major football stadium in England, opened in August 1892. And Liverpool – instantly formed – took over Anfield. Goodison's record attendance: 78,299 v Liverpool, Division One, September 1948. Anfield: 61,905 v Wolves, FA Cup fourth round, 1952.

left The inferno of Bradford at its height: Valley Parade, Saturday 11 May 1985. Fifty-five people died, more than 200 were injured.

SPECTATORS ARE KINDLY REQUESTED
TO - REFRAIN FROM BRINGING
BOTTLES OF ANY KIND INTO THE
STADIUM -

HAFNIA
EFC

left The Heysel Stadium disaster before the European Cup Final between Liverpool and Juventus in Brussels, 29 May 1985. No stretchers are available: victims are carried away. Fences have been flattened. Crumpled banners carpet the terraces. The electric notice-board gives the time (7.54 pm) and requests spectators not to throw objects. Thirty-nine people die, nearly 450 are injured. Five days later English clubs are banned from European tournaments for an indefinite period.

right Reflective Press Conference 1985: Jack Dunnett, President of the League (1981–6) and chairman of Notts County, listens with approval as Graham Kelly, only the fifth secretary of the League (from 1979) in a hundred years, explains with confidence.

The two faces of Ken Bates – chairman of Chelsea and of the Football League Centenary Committee.

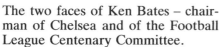

left Everton, winners of the 1985 Canon League championship. Back row (l to r): Kevin Richardson, Ian Atkins, Derek Mountfield, Andy Gray, Neville Southall, Paul Bracewell, Gary Stevens, Pat Van Den Hauwe. Front row: Peter Reid, Kevin Sheedy, Graeme Sharp, Kevin Ratcliffe, Trevor Steven.

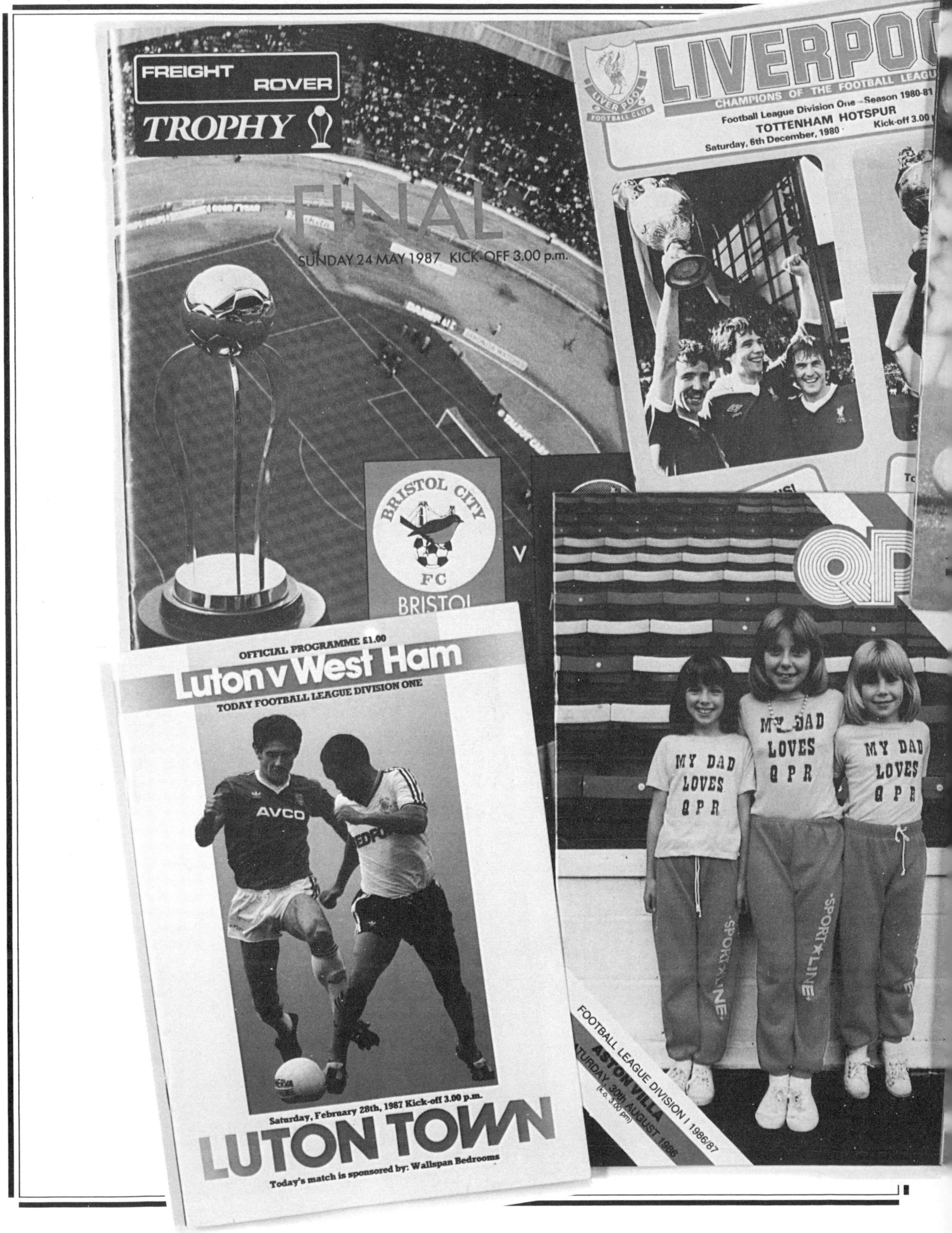
FREIGHT ROVER TROPHY
FINAL
SUNDAY 24 MAY 1987 KICK-OFF 3.00 p.m.
BRISTOL CITY FC
BRISTOL
LIVERPOOL FOOTBALL CLUB
LIVERPOO
CHAMPIONS OF THE FOOTBALL LEAGU
Football League Division One – Season 1980-81
TOTTENHAM HOTSPUR
Saturday, 6th December, 1980 · Kick-off 3.00
OFFICIAL PROGRAMME £1.00
Luton v West Ham
TODAY FOOTBALL LEAGUE DIVISION ONE
AVCO
Saturday, February 28th, 1987 Kick-off 3.00 p.m.
LUTON TOWN
Today's match is sponsored by: Wallspan Bedrooms
QP
MY DAD LOVES QPR
MY DAD LOVES QPR
MY DAD LOVES QPR
FOOTBALL LEAGUE DIVISION I 1986/87
ASTON VILLA
SATURDAY 30th AUGUST 1986
(k.o. 3.00 pm)

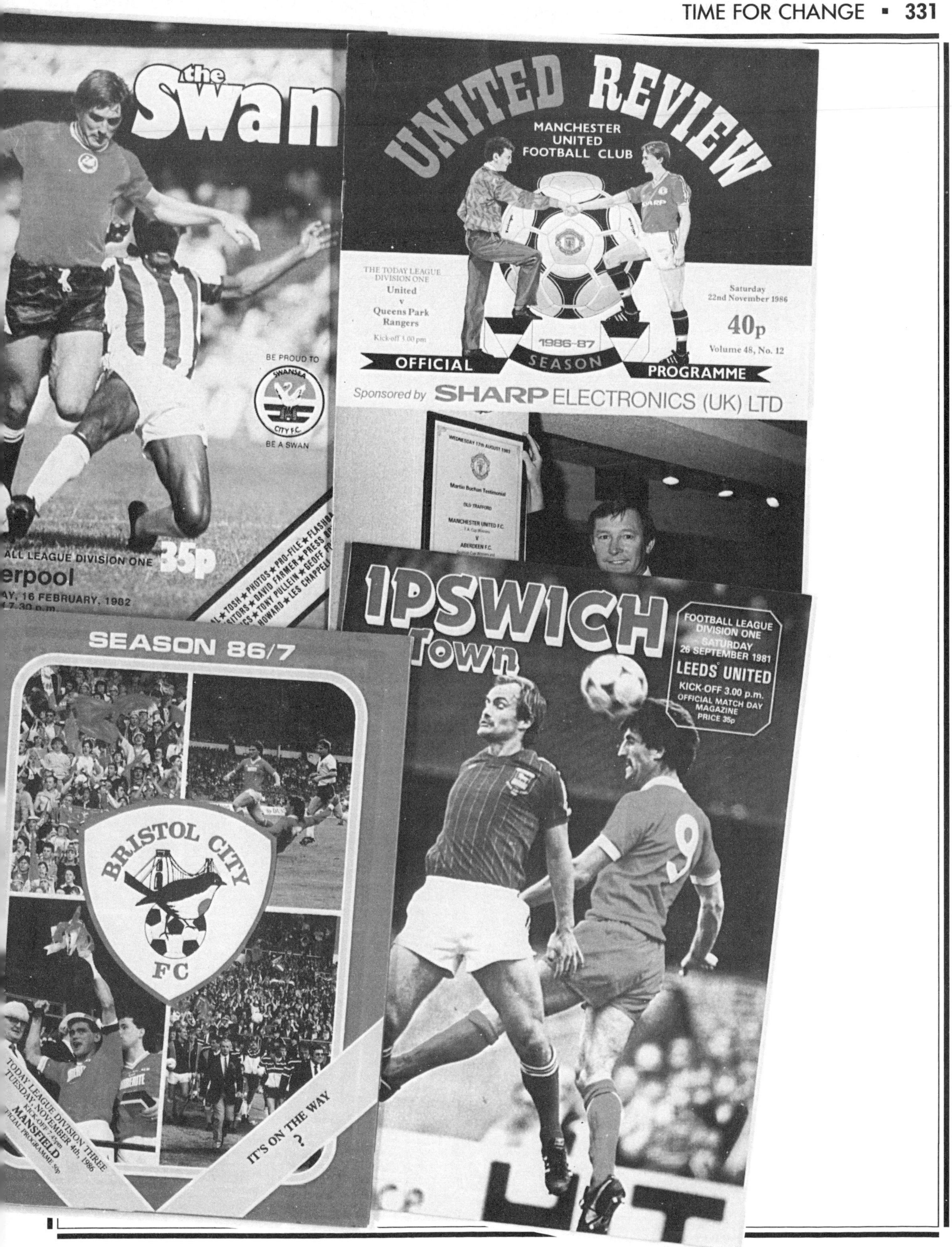
the Swan
BE PROUD TO
SWANSEA CITY F.C.
BE A SWAN
ALL LEAGUE DIVISION ONE 35p
erpool
AY, 16 FEBRUARY, 1982
UNITED REVIEW
MANCHESTER UNITED FOOTBALL CLUB
THE TODAY LEAGUE DIVISION ONE
United v Queens Park Rangers
Kick-off 3.00 pm
Saturday 22nd November 1986
40p
Volume 48, No. 12
1986-87
OFFICIAL SEASON PROGRAMME
Sponsored by SHARP ELECTRONICS (UK) LTD
WEDNESDAY 17th AUGUST 1983
Martin Buchan Testimonial
OLD TRAFFORD
MANCHESTER UNITED F.C.
V
ABERDEEN F.C.
IPSWICH Town
FOOTBALL LEAGUE DIVISION ONE
SATURDAY 26 SEPTEMBER 1981
LEEDS UNITED
KICK-OFF 3.00 p.m.
OFFICIAL MATCH DAY MAGAZINE
PRICE 35p
SEASON 86/7
BRISTOL CITY FC
TODAY LEAGUE DIVISION THREE
TUESDAY, NOVEMBER 4th, 1986
MANSFIELD
IT'S ON THE WAY
?

above Last day at the Valley. Charlton supporters cut pieces of turf as souvenirs after the club's last game at the Valley in September 1985. The ground, situated in old Woolwich just south of the point where the Thames straightens out through the busiest part of London's dockland and heads for the sea, had been Charlton's home since 1919. Charlton found themselves obliged to share Selhurst Park with Crystal Palace – and won immediate promotion to Division One in 1985–6.

right Members only at Luton Town, 1986. Admission to Kenilworth Road was restricted to holders of a £1-a-year membership card – and only home fans were allowed to join. The scheme was strongly criticized and Luton were not allowed to take part in the Littlewoods Cup (the League Cup) after refusing admission to Cardiff supporters. Luton insisted their scheme prevented crowd trouble – and local fans, police, councillors and shopkeepers all backed them.

left Happiness is a goal. Frank McAvennie (left) and Tony Cottee of West Ham celebrate McAvennie's second goal against Everton at Upton Park, November 1985. West Ham 2 Everton 1. Everton finished season 1985–6 as runners-up, West Ham in third place (their highest ever position in Division One). McAvennie joined West Ham from St Mirren for about £340,000 in June 1985 and scored 26 League goals in his first season of English football; Cottee, a former West Ham apprentice, finished with 20. Both were to become internationals – McAvennie for Scotland, Cottee for England.

WANG
WANG
WANG

Broad smiles, bright Wembley sunshine and a silver trophy illuminate Oxford United's remarkable success story, April 1986. Oxford have just won the Milk Cup by beating Queen's Park Rangers 3–0 – their first major trophy in their first season in Division One. Oxford reached the First Division by winning the Third and Second Division championships in successive seasons (1983–4 and 1984–5) – and all this after being near to liquidation in 1982. Robert Maxwell, financial emperor and local resident, then took over; and a modest club knew that life would never be the same again. 'I helped the club because I felt I had an obligation,' said Maxwell, 'and I will remain as long as I can do anything useful.' Maxwell left Oxford in May 1987 to become chairman of Derby County, newly-promoted to Division One, and his son Kevin took the Chair at the Manor Ground. Pictured left to right: back row – Ray Graydon (coach), Ray Houghton, John Aldridge, Trevor Hebberd, Andy Thomas, Alan Judge, Gary Briggs. Front row: Kevin Brock, Les Phillips, John Trewick, Malcolm Shotton, David Langan, Jeremy Charles.

Wimbledon FC: Southern League to First Division in ten seasons (1977–86). Programme for their first home game in Division One shows manager Dave Bassett (top, white sweater) and players on 3 May 1986 – the day they clinched promotion from Division Two. Bassett had been with Wimbledon, as player and manager, since their non-League days; and his personality and dedication were central to the club's remarkable climb. He left to join Watford in May 1987.

above Wimbledon even hit the top in their first month in Division One – and this goal by Welsh international Glyn Hodges (left) against Watford at Vicarage Road confirmed their pole position. *right* Wimbledon still flying high. John Fashanu (left) celebrates after scoring against Southampton at Plough Lane. Carlton Fairweather is next on the runway. Wimbledon finished in sixth position.

TRUMAN
BISWE

Arsenal win the League Cup under the new sponsorship of the Littlewoods Organisation, Wembley April 1987. Liverpool took the lead in a memorable final through Ian Rush of Wales but two goals by Charlie Nicholas of Scotland gave Arsenal victory by 2–1.

above Nicholas (left of post) squeezes the ball past Liverpool's goalkeeper Bruce Grobbelaar for his first goal. *left* celebration by Nicholas who joined Arsenal from Celtic for £750,000 in 1983. It was Liverpool's 19th appearance at Wembley in 14 seasons (six League Cup, three FA Cup, one European Cup and nine Charity Chields) . . . but it was the first time Arsenal had won the League Cup and their first major success for eight years. The handsome Littlewoods Cup is one of the oldest football trophies in the world – cast, modelled and engraved by a leading Victorian silversmith in 1895. It was originally competed for by ship-builders in the north-east and was later discovered – tarnished and forgotten – in a locked cupboard.

Gillingham
v
Swindon Town
AT CRYSTAL PALACE F.C.
SELHURST PARK
FOOTBALL LEAGUE
SWINDON TOWN F.C.
CHAMPIONS
SECOND DIVISION
PLAY-OFF FINAL TIE
FRIDAY 29th MAY 1987
KICK-OFF 8.00 p.m.
Official Programme
Price 60p

left Swindon and Gillingham needed a third match to settle their play-off final for promotion to Division Two in late May 1987. It was the 51st Third Division match (46 scheduled, five play-offs) of the season for both of them – a League record. Swindon won 2–0 on the neutral pitch of Selhurst Park.

MERSEY BATTLE ROYAL GIVES LIVERPOOL A TITLE CHANCE

Rush the songster in land of Dixie

By COLIN MALAM

Liverpool 3, Everton 1

LIVERPOOL gave Everton due warning yesterday in a searing Merseyside derby that they will fight to the bitter end to stop them taking the First Division title away from Anfield and back down the road to Goodison Park.

This tumultuous and courageous victory for the Reds cut the Blues lead at the top to three points — or a single win. And even though Everton have a game in hand, they know now they cannot afford another slip in the few weeks of the season that remain.

Not that this defeat could be called a slip. Everton often looked ... equal-

the ninth minute, the leggy full-back squared the ball to Rush. He touched it on across the field, and McMahon strode forward to thump a breathtaking shot past Southall's straining leap and into the top corner from 25 yards.

When Ablett's adventurousness provided Spackman with a shot that Southall had to dive ... save, it looked brie...

to have climbed on Clarke's back 25 yards out to the right of goal, the free kick was entrusted as usual to Sheedy's mighty left foot. Liverpool formed a wall, but need not have bothered since the Irishman sent the ball hurtling into the top corner like a guided missile.

But as the first half went into ... caused by an ... looded ...

his chance to head past Southall from close range.

As Everton pressed harder for equaltiy, Whelan had to head out a shot by Sheedy, while Hooper barely managed to scramble away a header by Steven.

Rush, however, made them pay heavily for their commitment to attack. Denied a goal by Southall's brilliant save after 75 minutes, the deadly Welshman destroyed Everton's hopes and equalled Dixie Dean's record of 19 goals in these matches by prodding an Ablett centre into the net off Southall's ... left.

...nison,

below The pools panel, 17 January 1987 – just before settling down to guess the results of nearly 50 games called off because of snow and ice. A panel was first called together during the devastatingly bad winter of 1962–3 when so many Saturday fixtures were postponed that coupons were declared void week after week and the Pools Promoters Association faced huge losses in revenue. Left to right: Stan Mortensen, Ronnie Simpson, Lord Bath (chairman), Tony Green, Arthur Ellis and Roger Hunt.

above Headline after Ian Rush of Liverpool had scored twice against Everton at Anfield, April 1987, to equal the 19 goals scored by Dixie Dean in Merseyside 'derby' matches.

Scarboro' F.
FIRSTDIVISION CHAMPIONS
FINAL
F.A

above Lincoln City's last home game before they were automatically relegated from the Football League in May 1987.

Scarborough celebrate

above Scarborough became the first club to win automatic promotion to the Football League when they won the GM Vauxhall Conference in 1987. Neil Warnock, Scarborough's manager, said the only other thing he had won in his playing career with eight League clubs was Hartlepool's 'Player of the Year' award in 1972. Scarborough replaced the bottom club in Division Four – Lincoln City.

left Modest promise. Supporters of Scarborough, new members of the Football League after winning the GM Vauxhall Conference, at the 1987 FA Cup final.

LEAGUE TABLES

1981–82

FIRST DIVISION

	P	W	D	L	F	A	Pts
1 Liverpool	42	26	9	7	80	32	87
2 Ipswich	42	26	5	11	75	53	83
3 Man United	42	22	12	8	59	29	78
4 Tottenham	42	20	11	11	67	48	71
5 Arsenal	42	20	11	11	48	37	71
6 Swansea	42	21	6	15	58	51	69
7 Southampton	42	19	9	14	72	67	66
8 Everton	42	17	13	12	56	50	64
9 West Ham	42	14	16	12	66	57	58
10 Man City	42	15	13	14	49	50	58
11 Aston Villa	42	15	12	15	55	53	57
12 Nottm Forest	42	15	12	15	42	48	57
13 Brighton	42	13	13	16	43	52	52
14 Coventry	42	13	11	18	56	62	50
15 Notts County	42	13	8	21	45	69	47
16 Birmingham	42	10	14	18	53	61	44
17 WBA	42	11	11	20	46	57	44
18 Stoke	42	12	8	22	44	63	44
19 Sunderland	42	11	11	20	38	58	44
20 Leeds	42	10	12	20	39	61	42
21 Wolves	42	10	10	22	32	63	40
22 Middlesbrough	42	8	15	19	34	52	39

SECOND DIVISION

	P	W	D	L	F	A	Pts
1 Luton	42	25	13	4	86	46	88
2 Watford	42	23	11	8	76	42	80
3 Norwich	42	22	5	15	64	50	71
4 Sheff Wed	42	20	10	12	55	51	70
5 QPR	42	21	6	15	65	43	69
6 Barnsley	42	19	10	13	59	41	67
7 Rotherham	42	20	7	15	66	54	67
8 Leicester	42	18	12	12	56	48	66
9 Newcastle	42	18	8	16	52	50	62
10 Blackburn	42	16	11	15	47	43	59
11 Oldham	42	15	14	13	50	51	59
12 Chelsea	42	15	12	15	60	60	57
13 Charlton	42	13	12	17	50	65	51
14 Cambridge	42	13	9	20	48	53	48
15 Crystal Palace	42	13	9	20	34	45	48
16 Derby	42	12	12	18	53	68	48
17 Grimsby	42	11	13	18	53	65	46
18 Shrewsbury	42	11	3	18	37	57	46
19 Bolton	42	13	7	22	39	61	46
20 Cardiff	42	12	8	22	45	61	44
21 Wrexham	42	11	11	20	40	56	44
22 Orient	42	10	9	23	39	61	39

THIRD DIVISION

	P	W	D	L	F	A	Pts
1 Burnley	46	21	17	8	66	49	80
2 Carlisle	46	23	11	12	65	50	80
3 Fulham	46	21	15	10	77	51	78
4 Lincoln	46	21	14	11	66	40	77
5 Oxford	46	19	14	13	63	49	71
6 Gillingham	46	20	11	15	64	56	71
7 Southend	46	18	15	13	63	51	69
8 Brentford	46	19	11	16	56	47	68
9 Millwall	46	18	13	15	62	62	67
10 Plymouth	46	18	11	17	64	56	65
11 Chesterfield	46	18	10	18	67	58	64
12 Reading	46	17	11	18	67	75	62
13 Portsmouth	46	14	19	13	56	51	61
14 Preston	46	16	13	17	50	56	61
15 Bristol Rovers*	46	18	9	19	58	65	61
16 Newport	46	14	16	16	54	54	58
17 Huddersfield	46	15	12	19	64	59	57
18 Exeter	46	16	9	21	71	84	57
19 Doncaster	46	13	17	16	55	68	56
20 Walsall	46	13	14	19	51	55	53
21 Wimbledon	46	14	11	21	61	75	53
22 Swindon	46	13	13	20	55	71	52
23 Bristol City	46	11	13	22	40	65	46
24 Chester	46	7	11	28	36	78	32

* Two points deducted by League.

FOURTH DIVISION

	P	W	D	L	F	A	Pts
1 Sheff United	46	27	15	4	94	41	96
2 Bradford	46	26	13	7	88	45	91
3 Wigan	46	26	13	7	80	46	91
4 Bournemouth	46	23	19	4	62	30	88
5 Peterborough	46	24	10	12	71	57	82
6 Colchester	46	20	12	14	82	57	72
7 Port Vale	46	18	16	12	56	49	70
8 Hull	46	19	12	15	70	61	69
9 Bury	46	17	17	12	80	59	68
10 Hereford	46	16	19	11	64	58	67
11 Tranmere	46	14	18	14	51	56	60
12 Blackpool	46	15	13	18	66	60	58
13 Darlington	46	15	13	18	61	62	58
14 Hartlepool	46	13	16	17	73	84	55
15 Torquay	46	14	13	19	47	59	55
16 Aldershot	46	13	15	18	57	68	54
17 York	46	14	8	24	69	91	50
18 Stockport	46	12	13	21	48	67	49
19 Halifax	46	9	22	15	51	72	49
20 Mansfield*	46	13	10	23	63	81	47
21 Rochdale	46	10	16	20	50	62	46
22 Northampton	46	11	9	26	57	84	42
23 Scunthorpe	46	9	15	22	43	79	42
24 Crewe	46	6	9	31	29	84	27

* Two points deducted by League.

1982–83

FIRST DIVISION

	P	W	D	L	F	A	Pts
1 Liverpool	42	24	10	8	87	37	82
2 Watford	42	22	5	15	74	57	71
3 Man United	42	19	13	8	56	38	70
4 Tottenham	42	20	9	13	65	50	69
5 Nottm Forest	42	20	9	13	62	50	69
6 Aston Villa	42	21	5	16	62	50	68
7 Everton	42	18	10	14	66	48	64
8 West Ham	42	20	4	18	68	62	64
9 Ipswich	42	15	13	14	64	50	58
10 Arsenal	42	16	10	16	58	56	58
11 WBA	42	15	12	15	51	49	57
12 Southampton	42	15	12	15	54	58	57
13 Stoke	42	16	9	17	53	64	57
14 Norwich	42	14	12	16	52	58	54
15 Notts County	42	15	7	21	55	71	52
16 Sunderland	42	12	14	16	48	61	50
17 Birmingham	42	12	15	16	40	55	50
18 Luton	42	12	13	17	65	84	49
19 Coventry	42	13	9	20	48	59	48
20 Man City	42	13	8	21	47	70	47
21 Swansea	42	10	11	21	51	69	41
22 Brighton	42	9	13	20	38	67	40

SECOND DIVISION

	P	W	D	L	F	A	Pts
1 QPR	42	26	7	9	77	36	85
2 Wolves	42	20	15	7	68	44	75
3 Leicester	42	20	10	12	72	44	70
4 Fulham	42	20	9	13	64	47	69*
5 Newcastle	42	18	13	11	75	53	67
6 Sheff Wed	42	16	15	11	60	47	63
7 Oldham	42	14	19	9	64	47	61
8 Leeds	42	13	21	8	51	46	60
9 Shrewsbury	42	15	14	13	48	48	59
10 Barnsley	42	14	15	13	57	55	57
11 Blackburn	42	15	12	15	58	58	57
12 Cambridge	42	13	12	17	42	60	51
13 Derby	42	10	19	13	49	58	49*
14 Carlisle	42	12	12	18	68	70	48
15 Crystal Palace	42	12	12	18	43	52	48
16 Middlesbrough	42	11	15	16	46	67	48
17 Charlton	42	13	9	20	63	86	48
18 Chelsea	42	11	14	17	51	61	47
19 Grimsby	42	12	11	19	45	70	47
20 Rotherham	42	10	15	17	45	68	45
21 Burnley	42	12	8	22	56	66	44
22 Bolton	42	11	11	20	42	61	44

*Game between Derby and Fulham abandoned after 88 minutes but result allowed to stand at 1-0.

THIRD DIVISION

		P	W	D	L	F	A	Pts
1	Portsmouth	46	27	10	9	74	41	91
2	Cardiff	46	25	11	10	76	50	86
3	Huddersfield	46	23	13	10	84	49	82
4	Newport	46	23	9	14	76	54	78
5	Oxford	46	22	12	12	71	53	78
6	Lincoln	46	23	7	16	77	51	76
8	Bristol Rovers	46	22	9	15	84	57	75
8	Plymouth	46	19	8	19	61	66	65
9	Brentford	46	18	10	18	88	77	64
10	Walsall	46	17	13	16	64	63	64
11	Sheff United	46	19	7	20	62	64	64
12	Bradford City	46	16	13	17	68	69	61
13	Gillingham	46	16	13	17	58	59	61
14	Bournemouth	46	16	13	17	59	68	61
15	Southend	46	15	14	17	66	65	59
16	Preston	46	15	13	18	60	69	58
17	Millwall	46	14	13	19	64	78	55
18	Wigan	46	15	9	22	60	72	54
19	Exeter	46	14	12	20	81	104	54
20	Orient	46	15	9	22	64	88	54
21	Reading	46	12	17	17	63	80	53
22	Wrexham	46	12	15	19	57	76	51
23	Doncaster	46	9	11	26	57	97	38
24	Chesterfield	46	8	13	25	44	68	37

FOURTH DIVISION

		P	W	D	L	F	A	Pts
1	Wimbledon	46	29	11	6	96	45	98
2	Hull	46	25	15	6	75	34	90
3	Port Vale	46	26	10	10	67	34	88
4	Scunthorpe	46	23	14	9	71	42	83
5	Bury	46	24	12	11	76	44	81
6	Colchester	46	24	9	13	75	55	81
7	York	46	22	13	11	88	58	79
8	Swindon	46	19	11	16	61	54	68
9	Peterborough	46	17	13	16	58	52	64
10	Mansfield	46	16	13	17	61	70	61
11	Halifax	46	16	12	18	59	66	60
12	Torquay	46	17	7	22	56	65	58
13	Chester	46	15	11	20	55	60	56
14	Bristol City	46	13	17	16	59	70	56
15	Northampton	46	14	12	20	67	75	54
16	Stockport	46	14	12	20	60	79	54
17	Darlington	46	13	13	20	61	71	52
18	Aldershot	46	12	15	19	61	82	51
19	Tranmere	46	13	11	22	49	71	50
20	Rochdale	46	11	16	19	55	73	49
21	Blackpool	46	13	12	21	55	74	49
22	Hartlepool	46	13	9	24	46	76	48
23	Crewe	46	11	8	27	53	71	41
24	Hereford	46	11	8	27	43	79	41

1983–84

FIRST DIVISION

		P	W	D	L	F	A	Pts
1	Liverpool	42	22	14	6	73	32	80
2	Southampton	42	22	11	9	66	38	77
3	Nottm Forest	42	22	8	12	76	45	74
4	Man United	42	20	14	8	71	41	74
5	QPR	42	22	7	13	67	37	73
6	Arsenal	42	19	9	15	74	60	63
7	Everton	42	16	14	12	44	42	62
8	Tottenham	42	17	10	15	64	65	61
9	West Ham	42	17	9	16	60	55	60
10	Aston Villa	42	17	9	16	59	61	60
11	Watford	42	16	9	17	68	77	57
12	Ipswich	42	15	8	19	55	57	53
13	Sunderland	42	13	13	16	42	53	52
14	Norwich	42	12	15	15	48	49	51
15	Leicester	42	13	12	17	65	68	51
16	Luton	42	14	9	19	53	66	51
17	WBA	42	14	9	19	48	62	51
18	Stoke	42	13	11	18	44	63	50
19	Coventry	42	13	11	18	57	77	50
20	Birmingham	42	12	12	18	39	50	48
21	Notts County	42	10	11	21	50	72	41
22	Wolves	42	6	11	25	27	80	29

SECOND DIVISION

		P	W	D	L	F	A	Pts
1	Chelsea	42	25	13	4	90	40	89
2	Sheff Wed	42	26	10	6	72	34	89
3	Newcastle	42	24	8	10	85	53	80
4	Man City	42	20	10	12	66	48	70
5	Grimsby	42	19	13	10	60	47	70
6	Blackburn	42	17	16	9	57	46	67
7	Carlisle	42	16	16	10	48	41	64
8	Shrewsbury	42	17	10	15	49	53	61
9	Brighton	42	17	9	16	69	60	60
10	Leeds	42	16	12	14	55	56	60
11	Fulham	42	15	12	15	60	53	57
12	Huddersfield	42	14	15	13	56	49	57
13	Charlton	42	16	9	17	53	64	57
14	Barnsley	42	15	7	20	57	53	52
15	Cardiff	42	15	6	21	53	66	51
16	Portsmouth	42	14	7	21	73	64	49
17	Middlesbrough	42	12	13	17	41	47	49
18	Crystal Palace	42	12	11	19	42	52	47
19	Oldham	42	13	8	21	47	73	47
20	Derby	42	11	9	22	36	72	42
21	Swansea	42	7	8	27	36	85	29
22	Cambridge	42	4	12	26	28	77	24

THIRD DIVISION

		P	W	D	L	F	A	Pts
1	Oxford	46	28	11	7	91	50	95
2	Wimbledon	46	26	9	11	97	76	87
3	Sheff United	46	24	11	11	86	53	83
4	Hull	46	23	14	9	71	38	83
5	Bristol Rovers	46	22	13	11	68	54	79
6	Walsall	46	22	9	15	68	61	75
7	Bradford	46	20	11	15	73	65	71
8	Gillingham	46	20	10	16	74	69	70
9	Millwall	46	18	13	15	71	65	67
10	Bolton	46	18	10	18	56	60	64
11	Orient	46	18	9	19	71	81	63
12	Burnley	46	16	14	16	76	61	62
13	Newport	46	16	14	16	58	75	62
14	Lincoln	46	17	10	19	59	62	61
15	Wigan	46	16	13	17	46	56	61
16	Preston	46	15	11	20	66	66	56
17	Bournemouth	46	16	7	23	63	73	55
18	Rotherham	46	15	9	22	57	64	54
19	Plymouth	46	13	12	21	56	62	51
20	Brentford	46	11	16	19	69	79	49
21	Scunthorpe	46	9	19	18	54	73	46
22	Southend	46	10	14	22	55	76	44
23	Port Vale	46	11	10	25	51	83	43
24	Exeter	46	6	15	25	50	84	33

FOURTH DIVISION

		P	W	D	L	F	A	Pts
1	York	46	31	8	7	96	39	101
2	Doncaster	46	24	13	9	82	54	85
3	Reading	46	22	16	8	84	56	82
4	Bristol City	46	24	10	12	70	44	82
5	Aldershot	46	22	9	15	76	69	75
6	Blackpool	46	21	9	16	70	52	72
7	Peterborough	46	18	14	14	72	48	68
8	Colchester	46	17	16	13	69	53	67
9	Torquay	46	18	13	15	59	64	67
10	Tranmere	46	17	15	14	53	53	66
11	Hereford	46	16	15	15	54	53	63
12	Stockport	46	17	11	18	60	64	62
13	Chesterfield	46	15	15	16	59	61	60
14	Darlington	46	17	8	21	49	50	59
15	Bury	46	15	14	17	61	64	59
16	Crewe	46	16	11	19	56	57	59
17	Swindon	46	15	13	18	58	56	58
18	Northampton	46	13	14	19	53	78	53
19	Mansfield	46	13	13	20	66	70	52
20	Wrexham	46	11	15	20	59	74	48
21	Halifax	46	12	12	22	55	89	48
22	Rochdale	46	11	13	22	52	80	46
23	Hartlepool	46	10	10	26	47	85	40
24	Chester	46	7	13	26	45	82	34

1984–85

FIRST DIVISION

		P	W	D	L	F	A	Pts
1	Everton	42	28	6	8	88	43	90
2	Liverpool	42	22	11	9	78	35	77
3	Tottenham	42	23	8	11	78	51	77
4	Man United	42	22	10	10	77	47	76
5	Southampton	42	19	11	12	56	47	68
6	Chelsea	42	18	12	12	63	48	66
7	Arsenal	42	19	9	14	61	49	66
8	Sheffield Wed	42	17	14	11	58	45	65
9	Nottm Forest	42	19	7	16	56	48	64
10	Aston Villa	42	15	11	16	60	60	56
11	Watford	42	14	13	15	81	71	55
12	West Brom	42	16	7	19	58	62	55
13	Luton	42	15	9	18	57	61	54
14	Newcastle	42	13	13	16	55	70	52
15	Leicester	42	15	6	21	65	73	51
16	West Ham	42	13	12	17	51	68	51
17	Ipswich	42	13	11	18	46	57	50
18	Coventry	42	15	5	22	47	64	50
19	QPR	42	13	11	18	53	72	50
20	Norwich	42	13	10	19	46	64	49
21	Sunderland	42	10	10	22	40	62	40
22	Stoke	42	3	8	31	24	91	17

SECOND DIVISION

		P	W	D	L	F	A	Pts
1	Oxford	42	25	9	8	84	36	84
2	Birmingham	42	25	7	10	59	33	82
3	Man City	42	21	11	10	66	40	74
4	Portsmouth	42	20	14	8	69	50	74
5	Blackburn	42	21	10	11	66	41	73
6	Brighton	42	20	12	10	58	34	72
7	Leeds	42	19	12	11	66	43	69
8	Shrewsbury	42	18	11	13	66	53	65
9	Fulham	42	19	8	15	68	64	65
10	Grimsby	42	18	8	16	72	64	62
11	Barnsley	42	14	16	12	42	42	58
12	Wimbledon	42	16	10	16	71	75	58
13	Huddersfield	42	15	10	17	52	64	55
14	Oldham Ath	42	15	8	19	49	67	53
15	Crystal Palace	42	12	12	18	46	65	48
16	Carlisle	42	13	8	21	50	67	47
17	Charlton	42	11	12	19	51	63	45
18	Sheffield Utd	42	10	14	18	54	66	44
19	Middlesborough	42	10	10	22	41	57	40
20	Notts Co	42	10	7	25	45	73	37
21	Cardiff	42	9	8	25	47	79	35
22	Wolves	42	8	9	25	37	79	33

THIRD DIVISION

		P	W	D	L	F	A	Pts
1	Bradford	46	28	10	8	77	45	94
2	Millwall	46	26	12	8	83	42	90
3	Hull City	46	25	12	9	88	49	87
4	Gillingham	46	25	8	13	80	62	83
5	Bristol City	46	24	9	13	74	47	81
6	Bristol Rovers	46	21	12	13	66	48	75
7	Derby	46	19	13	14	65	54	70
8	York	46	20	9	17	70	57	69
9	Reading	46	19	12	15	68	62	69
10	Bournemouth	46	19	11	16	57	46	68
11	Walsall	46	18	13	15	58	52	67
12	Rotherham	46	18	11	17	55	55	65
13	Brentford	46	16	14	16	62	64	62
14	Doncaster	46	17	8	21	72	74	59
15	Plymouth	46	15	14	17	62	65	59
16	Wigan	46	15	14	17	60	64	59
17	Bolton	46	16	6	24	69	75	54
18	Newport	46	13	13	20	55	67	52
19	Lincoln	46	11	18	17	50	51	51
20	Swansea	46	12	11	23	53	80	47
21	Burnley	46	11	13	22	60	73	46
22	Orient	46	11	13	22	51	76	46
23	Preston	46	13	7	26	51	100	46
24	Cambridge	46	4	9	33	37	95	21

FOURTH DIVISION

		P	W	D	L	F	A	Pts
1	Chesterfield	46	26	13	7	64	35	91
2	Blackpool	46	24	14	8	73	39	86
3	Darlington	46	24	13	9	66	49	85
4	Bury	46	24	12	10	76	50	84
5	Hereford	46	22	11	13	65	47	77
6	Tranmere	46	24	3	19	83	66	75
7	Colchester	46	20	14	12	87	65	74
8	Swindon	46	21	9	16	62	58	72
9	Scunthorpe	46	19	14	13	83	62	71
10	Crewe	46	18	12	16	65	69	66
11	Peterborough	46	16	14	16	54	53	62
12	Port Vale	46	14	18	14	61	59	60
13	Aldershot	46	17	8	21	56	63	59
14	Mansfield	46	13	18	15	41	38	57
15	Wrexham	46	15	9	22	67	70	54
16	Chester	46	15	9	22	60	72	54
17	Rochdale	46	13	14	19	55	69	53
18	Exeter	46	13	14	19	57	79	53
19	Hartlepool	46	14	10	22	54	67	52
20	Southend	46	13	11	22	58	83	50
21	Halifax	46	14	5	26	42	69	50
22	Stockport	46	13	8	25	58	79	47
23	Northampton	46	14	5	27	53	74	47
24	Torquay	46	9	14	23	38	63	41

1985–86

FIRST DIVISION

		P	W	D	L	F	A	Pts
1	Liverpool	42	26	10	6	89	37	88
2	Everton	42	26	8	8	87	41	86
3	West Ham	42	26	6	10	74	40	84
4	Man United	42	22	10	10	70	36	76
5	Sheffield Wed	42	21	10	11	63	54	73
6	Chelsea	42	20	11	11	57	56	71
7	Arsenal	42	20	9	13	49	47	69
8	Nottm Forest	42	19	11	12	69	53	68
9	Luton	42	18	12	12	61	44	66
10	Tottenham	42	19	8	15	74	52	65
11	Newcastle	42	17	12	13	67	72	63
12	Watford	42	16	11	15	69	62	59
13	QPR	42	15	7	20	53	64	52
14	Southampton	42	12	10	20	51	62	46
15	Man City	42	11	12	19	43	57	45
16	Aston Villa	42	10	14	18	51	67	44
17	Coventry	42	11	10	21	48	71	43
18	Oxford	42	10	12	20	62	80	42
19	Leicester	42	10	12	20	54	76	42
20	Ipswich	42	11	8	23	32	55	41
21	Birmingham	42	8	5	29	30	73	29
22	West Brom	42	4	12	26	35	89	24

SECOND DIVISION

		P	W	D	L	F	A	Pts
1	Norwich	42	25	9	8	84	39	84
2	Charlton	42	22	11	9	78	45	77
3	Wimbledon	42	21	13	8	58	37	76
4	Portsmouth	42	22	7	13	69	41	73
5	Crystal Palace	42	19	9	14	57	52	66
6	Hull	42	17	13	12	65	55	64
7	Sheffield United	42	17	11	14	64	63	62
8	Oldham	42	17	9	16	62	61	60
9	Millwall	42	17	8	17	64	65	59
10	Stoke	42	14	15	13	48	50	57
11	Brighton	42	16	8	18	64	64	56
12	Barnsley	42	14	14	14	47	50	56
13	Bradford	42	16	6	20	51	63	54
14	Leeds	42	15	8	19	56	72	53
15	Grimsby	42	14	10	18	58	62	52
16	Huddersfield	42	14	10	18	51	67	52
17	Shrewsbury	42	14	9	19	52	64	51
18	Sunderland	42	13	11	18	47	61	50
19	Blackburn	42	12	13	17	53	62	49
20	Carlisle	42	13	7	22	47	71	46
21	Middlesborough	42	12	9	21	44	53	45
22	Fulham	42	10	6	26	45	69	36

THIRD DIVISION

		P	W	D	L	F	A	Pts
1	Reading	46	29	7	10	67	50	94
2	Plymouth	46	26	9	11	88	53	87
3	Derby	46	23	15	8	80	41	84
4	Wigan	46	23	14	9	82	48	83
5	Gillingham	46	22	13	11	81	54	79
6	Waisall	46	22	9	15	90	64	75
7	York	46	20	11	15	77	58	71
8	Notts County	46	19	14	13	71	60	71
9	Bristol City	46	18	14	14	69	60	68
10	Brentford	46	18	12	16	58	61	66
11	Doncaster	46	16	16	14	45	52	64
12	Blackpool	46	17	12	17	66	55	63
13	Darlington	46	15	13	18	61	78	58
14	Rotherham	46	15	12	19	61	59	57
15	Bournemouth	46	15	9	22	65	72	54
16	Bristol Rovers	46	14	12	20	51	75	54
17	Chesterfield	46	13	14	19	61	64	53
18	Bolton	46	15	8	23	54	68	53
19	Newport	46	11	18	17	52	65	51
20	Bury	46	12	13	21	63	65	49
21	Lincoln	46	10	16	20	55	77	46
22	Cardiff	46	12	9	25	53	83	45
23	Wolves	46	11	10	25	57	98	43
24	Swansea	46	11	10	25	43	87	43

FOURTH DIVISION

		P	W	D	L	F	A	Pts
1	Swindon	46	32	6	8	82	43	102
2	Chester	46	23	15	8	83	50	84
3	Mansfield	46	23	12	11	74	47	81
4	Port Vale	46	21	16	9	67	37	79
5	Orient	46	20	12	14	79	64	72
6	Colchester	46	19	13	14	88	63	70
7	Hartlepool	46	20	10	16	68	67	70
8	Northampton	46	18	10	18	79	58	64
9	Southend	46	18	10	18	69	67	64
10	Hereford	46	18	10	18	74	73	64
11	Stockport	46	17	13	16	63	71	64
12	Crewe	46	18	9	19	54	61	63
13	Wrexham	46	17	9	20	68	80	60
14	Burnley	46	16	11	19	60	65	59
15	Scunthorpe	46	15	14	19	50	55	59
16	Aldershot	46	17	7	22	66	74	58
17	Peterborough	46	13	17	16	52	64	56
18	Rochdale	46	14	13	19	57	77	55
19	Tranmere	46	15	9	22	74	73	54
20	Halifax	46	14	12	20	60	71	54
21	Exeter	46	13	15	18	47	59	54
22	Cambridge	46	15	9	22	65	80	54
23	Preston	46	11	10	25	54	89	43
24	Torquay	46	9	10	27	43	88	37

1986–87

FIRST DIVISION

		P	W	D	L	F	A	Pts
1	Everton	42	26	8	8	76	31	86
2	Liverpool	42	23	8	11	72	42	77
3	Tottenham	42	21	8	13	68	43	71
4	Arsenal	42	20	10	12	58	35	70
5	Norwich	42	17	17	8	53	51	68
6	Wimbledon	42	19	9	14	57	50	66
7	Luton	42	18	12	12	47	45	66
8	Nottm Forest	42	18	11	13	64	51	65
9	Watford	42	18	9	15	67	54	63
10	Coventry	42	17	12	13	50	45	63
11	Man United	42	14	14	14	52	45	56
12	Southampton	42	14	10	18	69	68	52
13	Sheffield Wed	42	13	13	16	58	59	52
14	Chelsea	42	13	13	16	53	64	52
15	West Ham	42	14	10	18	52	67	52
16	QPR	42	13	11	18	48	64	50
17	Newcastle	42	12	11	19	47	65	47
18	Oxford	42	11	13	18	44	69	46
19	Charlton	42	11	11	20	45	55	44
20	Leicester	42	11	9	22	54	76	42
21	Man City	42	8	15	19	36	57	39
22	Aston Villa	42	8	12	22	45	79	36

SECOND DIVISION

		P	W	D	L	F	A	Pts
1	Derby Co	42	25	9	8	64	38	84
2	Portsmouth	42	23	9	10	53	28	78
3	Oldham	42	22	9	11	65	44	75
4	Leeds	42	19	11	12	58	44	68
5	Ipswich	42	17	13	12	59	43	64
6	Crystal Palace	42	19	5	18	51	53	62
7	Plymouth	42	16	13	13	62	57	61
8	Stoke	42	16	10	16	63	53	58
9	Sheffield Utd	42	15	13	14	50	49	58
10	Bradford	42	15	10	17	62	62	55
11	Barnsley	42	14	13	15	49	52	55
12	Blackburn	42	15	10	17	45	55	55
13	Reading	42	14	11	17	52	59	53
14	Hull	42	13	14	15	41	55	53
15	West Brom	42	13	12	17	51	49	51
16	Millwall	42	14	9	19	39	45	51
17	Huddersfield	42	13	12	17	54	61	51
18	Shrewsbury	42	15	6	21	41	53	51
19	Birmingham	42	11	17	14	47	59	50
20	Sunderland	42	12	12	18	49	59	48
21	Grimsby	42	10	14	18	39	59	44
22	Brighton	42	9	12	21	37	54	39

THIRD DIVISION

		P	W	D	L	F	A	Pts
1	Bournemouth	46	29	10	7	76	40	97
2	Middlesborough	46	28	10	8	67	30	94
3	Swindon	46	25	12	9	77	47	87
4	Wigan	46	25	10	11	83	60	85
5	Gillingham	46	23	9	14	65	48	78
6	Bristol City	46	21	14	11	63	36	77
7	Notts County	46	21	13	12	77	56	76
8	Walsall	46	22	9	15	80	67	75
9	Blackpool	46	16	16	14	74	59	64
10	Mansfield	46	15	16	15	52	55	61
11	Brentford	46	15	15	16	64	66	60
12	Port Vale	46	15	12	19	76	70	57
13	Doncaster	46	14	15	17	56	62	57
14	Rotherham	46	15	12	19	48	57	57
15	Chester	46	13	17	16	61	59	56
16	Bury	46	14	13	19	54	60	55
17	Chesterfield	46	13	15	18	56	69	54
18	Fulham	46	12	17	17	59	77	53
19	Bristol Rovers	46	13	12	21	49	75	51
20	York	46	12	13	21	55	79	49
21	Bolton	46	10	15	21	46	58	45
22	Carlisle	46	10	8	28	39	78	38
23	Darlington	46	7	16	23	45	77	37
24	Newport	46	8	13	25	49	86	37

FOURTH DIVISION

		P	W	D	L	F	A	Pts
1	Northampton	46	30	9	7	103	53	99
2	Preston	46	26	12	8	72	47	90
3	Southend	46	25	5	16	68	55	80
4	Wolves	46	24	7	15	69	50	79
5	Colchester	46	21	7	18	64	56	70
6	Aldershot	46	20	10	16	64	57	70
7	Orient	46	20	9	17	64	61	69
8	Scunthorpe	46	18	12	16	73	57	66
9	Wrexham	46	15	20	11	70	51	65
10	Peterborough	46	17	14	15	57	50	65
11	Cambridge	46	17	11	18	60	62	62
12	Swansea	46	17	11	18	56	61	62
13	Cardiff	46	15	16	15	48	50	61
14	Exeter	46	11	23	12	53	49	56
15	Halifax	46	15	10	21	59	74	55
16	Hereford	46	14	11	21	60	61	53
17	Crewe	46	13	14	19	70	72	53
18	Hartlepool	46	11	18	17	44	65	51
19	Stockport	46	13	12	21	40	69	51
20	Tranmere	46	11	17	18	54	72	50
21	Rochdale	46	11	17	18	54	73	50
22	Burnley	46	12	13	21	53	74	49
23	Torquay	46	10	18	18	56	72	48
24	Lincoln	46	12	12	22	45	65	48

PLAY-OFFS

Promotion and relegation play-offs were introduced in 1986/7 involving all four divisions. They were used, in part, to reduce the First Division to 20 clubs over two seasons.

Leeds	1	Oldham	0	
Oldham	2	Leeds	1	(aet)
Ipswich	0	Charlton	0	
Charlton	2	Ipswich	1	
Charlton	1	Leeds	0	
Leeds	1	Charlton	0	
Charlton	2	Leeds	1	(aet)

(*at St Andrews*)

Charlton remain in First Division

Gillingham	3	Sunderland	2	
Sunderland	4	Gillingham	3	(aet)
Wigan	2	Swindon	3	
Swindon	0	Wigan	0	
Gillingham	1	Swindon	0	
Swindon	2	Gillingham	1	(aet)
Swindon	2	Gillingham	0	

(*at Selhurst Park*)

Swindon promoted to Second Division;
Sunderland relegated to Third Division

Aldershot	1	Bolton	0	
Bolton	2	Aldershot	2	(aet)
Colchester	0	Wolves	2	
Wolves	0	Colchester	0	
Aldershot	2	Wolves	0	
Wolves	0	Aldershot	1	

Aldershot promoted to Third Division;
Bolton Wanderers relegated to Fourth Division

Index